GL

# CONTEMPORARY STUDIES IN DESCRIPTIVE LINGUISTICS

VOL. 31

Edited by

DR GRAEME DAVIS & KARL A. BERNHARDT

**PETER LANG**
Oxford · Bern · Berlin · Bruxelles · Frankfurt am Main · New York · Wien

Ahmad Al-Issa and Laila S. Dahan (eds)

# GLOBAL ENGLISH AND ARABIC

## ISSUES OF LANGUAGE, CULTURE, AND IDENTITY

PETER LANG
Oxford • Bern • Berlin • Bruxelles • Frankfurt am Main • New York • Wien

**Bibliographic information published by Die Deutsche Nationalbibliothek**
Die Deutsche Nationalbibliothek lists this publication in the Deutsche National-
bibliografie; detailed bibliographic data is available on the Internet at
http://dnb.d-nb.de.

A catalogue record for this book is available from the British Library.

Library of Congress Cataloging-in-Publication Data:

Global English and Arabic : issues of language, culture and identity /
Ahmad Al-Issa and Laila S. Dahan (eds).
    p. cm.
  Includes bibliographical references and index.
  1. Arabic language–Foreign elements–English 2. Arabic
language–Foreign words and phrases–English. 3. English
language–Influence on Arabic. 4. English language–Foreign countries.
I. Al-Issa, Ahmad, 1965- II. Dahan, Laila S. (Laila Suleiman), 1962-
  PJ6582.E5G56 2011
  306.440917'5927–dc22
                                    2011004821


ISSN 1660-9301
ISBN 978-3-0343-0293-7


© Peter Lang AG, International Academic Publishers, Bern 2011
Hochfeldstrasse 32, CH-3012 Bern, Switzerland
info@peterlang.com, www.peterlang.com, www.peterlang.net

All rights reserved.
All parts of this publication are protected by copyright.
Any utilisation outside the strict limits of the copyright law, without
the permission of the publisher, is forbidden and liable to prosecution.
This applies in particular to reproductions, translations, microfilming,
and storage and processing in electronic retrieval systems.

Printed in Germany

# Contents

Introduction     vii

AHMAD AL-ISSA AND LAILA S. DAHAN

1    Global English and Endangered Arabic in the United Arab Emirates     1

SALAH TROUDI AND ADEL JENDLI

2    Emirati Students' Experiences of English as a Medium of Instruction     23

LYNNE RONESI

3    Who Am I as an Arab English Speaker? Perspectives from Female University Students in the United Arab Emirates     49

FATIMA BADRY

4    Appropriating English: Languages in Identity Construction in the United Arab Emirates     81

HASSAN R. ABDEL-JAWAD AND ADEL S. ABU RADWAN

5    The Status of English in Institutions of Higher Education in Oman: Sultan Qaboos University as a Model     123

SILVIA PESSOA AND MOHANALAKSHMI RAJAKUMAR

6    The Impact of English-medium Higher Education: The Case of Qatar     153

FATMA FAISAL SAAD SAID

7   "*Ahyaanan* I text in English '*ashaan* it's *ashal*": Language Crisis or Linguistic Development? The Case of How Gulf Arabs Perceive the Future of their Language, Culture, and Identity    179

ELIZABETH S. BUCKNER

8   The Growth of English Language Learning in Morocco: Culture, Class, and Status Competition    213

RAGHDA EL ESSAWI

9   Arabic in Latin Script in Egypt: Who Uses It and Why?    253

ANISSA DAOUDI

10  Computer-mediated Communication: The Emergence of e-Arabic in the Arab World    285

JOHN ANDREW MORROW AND BARBARA CASTLETON

11  The Impact of Global English on the Arabic Language: The Loss of the Allah Lexicon    307

NADINE SINNO

12  Navigating Linguistic Imperialism, Cultural Hybridity, and Language Pedagogy    335

Notes on Contributors    355

Index    363

Acknowledgements    367

AHMAD AL-ISSA AND LAILA S. DAHAN

# Introduction

In a world rapidly changing through the efforts of globalization and its accompanying lingua franca, English, it is important to view how today's global English is affecting other languages, cultures, and even identities. The Arab world is an understudied region of the world when it comes to this subject. Its importance, however, cannot be overlooked. Because much of the Arab world today is moving towards accepting and using English as a second language, it is essential to be aware of how this is affecting the role of Arabic. Today, even some Arab countries which used to rely on French as their second language are beginning to move towards adding English to the mix.

The effects of global English are not always nefarious and have not, as yet, caused an obvious major decline in Arabic usage. However, the studies in this volume all point to a concern on the part of most authors that Arabic is losing its position in a variety of ways, subtly at the moment, but there seem to be some flickers of unease over where Arabic is headed when the role of English is continually brought out as the language of modernity, education, and the future. With the continual focus on English as the new and trendy, youth in the Arab world are tending to use the lingua franca more than their own Arabic. Additionally, with Modern Standard Arabic (MSA) used only in certain educational contexts, media newscasts, and religion, its usage is in decline and many academics are finding that Arabic-speaking students are facing difficulties in writing MSA, as most Arabs use dialects in order to carry out daily communication. This issue of diglossia is another reason for worries about the maintenance of Arabic. Since children study MSA in school, but use dialects at home or outside of school, there are few opportunities for them to develop a strong grounding in MSA.

The first seven chapters of this volume focus on the Arabian Gulf region. As a region which has experienced dramatic changes, both economically and socially, the Gulf has been a magnet for incoming expatriate populations whose expertise in all fields is highly valued and essential. With the continuous influx of migrant populations, there is a requirement for a language in which the many nationalities can communicate. Furthermore, those who move to the Arabian Gulf region need educational facilities for their children, which has also led to more rationales for a lingua franca. As English is the language of today's globalizing world, it has taken a central role in the Gulf and for some, has eclipsed the role of Arabic as a language of communication. It is for this reason that the current volume is heavy on chapters that reveal the concerns of academics, both those residing in the region and beyond, on the role of English in the Arabian Gulf.

The overall message from most of the chapters in this book is that there is a greater need for a move towards bilingualism, rather than the continuing focus on English. Many of the participants in the various studies carried out for this volume voiced concerns with their own facility with their native language of Arabic and the difficulties found in studying it (see chapters by Said and Sinno in this volume). Many would like the opportunity to use their Arabic in similar situations in which they use English. However, at this point there is a gap between when and where English is used, usually for education, business, and intellectual pursuits and Arabic is used for more personal interactions and traditional forums.

In order for a language to be maintained, it must be used by children and youth. In the case of Arabic, due to the diglossic situation, it is even more important that MSA be used throughout the educational experience, in order for students to be allowed to gain full mastery and develop facility and fluency with their own language. Unfortunately, as evidenced by the research carried out for this volume, many Arab countries are lessening the amount of MSA in schools, while increasing English language opportunities.

This edited collection has given us new empirical evidence and understanding about the role of global English in the Arab world. We entered the writing of this collection being extremely concerned about the place of Arabic in the Arab world. However, after reading the many submissions received we have had some of our immediate concerns allayed regarding

# Introduction

the role of Arabic and its immediate future. But long term, there are still many questions that must be addressed and policies overhauled if Arabic is to remain strong and viable.

We did not plan or expect that this volume would give full coverage of this topic. Instead we hoped it would be a start towards helping educators and policy makers look into the role English has taken on in many of the Arab countries. We anticipate through this effort that the place of Arabic can be reconsidered and its essential status as a representative of the Arab world will remain strong. Furthermore, we hope that the important up-to-date information found in this book will encourage and promote more research in the field and more dialogue among educators, policy makers, and language learners in the Arab world.

This volume brings together mainly empirical research from a broad variety of individuals. Most of our writers currently reside in the Arab world, but some live in the West and have done research in the region and they too have their own concerns about the status of Arabic vis-à-vis English.

In Chapter 1, we discuss the role of global English in the United Arab Emirates (UAE). We endeavour to bring forth the many ways English is being used in place of Arabic in both education and business contexts, in addition to its mass appeal through pop culture. Our concerns are viewed within the context of how Arabic has lost ground and continues to do so in other Arabic-speaking nations and the UAE.

The second chapter, by Troudi and Jendli, looks closely at how university students are experiencing and working within the confines of English as a medium of instruction (EMI) in the UAE. The authors carried out exploratory research in order to understand the students' experiences with EMI. Their findings reveal that students associated their Arabic language with heritage and traditional activities, while English has become the language of education.

Ronesi's chapter examines how female university students, who are native speakers of Arabic, understand their identity as Arabs while being immersed in English. Through written responses to the prompt "Who am I as a writer in English?" the author was able to draw out the students' linguistic attitudes and determine how they manage their use of both languages, and how they feel about each.

Chapter 4, by Badry, looks at how global English affects the cultural identity of young people in the UAE. Using survey data, she finds that despite an increasing acceptance of western cultural behaviours, they still use their Arabic for traditional activities. English however is preferred for intellectual or modern domains.

In Chapter 5, a case study of Sultan Qaboos University in Oman is presented. Abdel-Jawad and Abu Radwan find that English has taken on a considerable role as the dominant language of interaction among faculty, staff, and even some students at the university. They reveal that English is promoted and given more resources and usage than Arabic.

Pessoa and Rajakumar, in Chapter 6, carried out similar studies at two institutions in Qatar. They look at undergraduate students' perspectives on the impact of English as a medium of instruction on the language, culture, and identity of Arab Muslims. Their findings indicate that Arabic as an academic or professional language may lose ground in the future, but will remain as the language of the home and a link to students' culture.

Chapter 7 looks at Gulf Arabs from a more general perspective and is based on information obtained through discussion groups, blogs, and interviews. Said acquires first-hand accounts of how Arabs regard the loss of their language, culture, and identity.

Morocco's acceptance and expanding use of English is the subject of Buckner's chapter. She argues that since English does not have a colonial legacy in Morocco, people are more open to learning it. After carrying out intensive fieldwork, Buckner found that those who study English are less likely to consider Arabic important for their futures or as a favourite language, when compared with English or French.

In Chapter 9, El Essawi brings to light the results of her study on why Egyptian bilinguals (Arabic–English) utilize Latin script to write any number of message types. Her chapter discusses the effect of computer-mediated communication (CMC) and communication technology in tandem with global English on producing these hybrid texts.

In another look at computer-mediated communication, Daoudi uses Chapter 10 to highlight the emergence of what she terms e-Arabic as a new variety of language. This chapter attempts to show the relationship between language and politics in the Arab world. Data for this was collected using an internet-based corpus, semi-structured interviews, and observation in the Arab world. Her findings reveal that the main source of borrowing into Arabic – both Modern Standard Arabic and vernaculars – is English and this phenomenon is now spreading to former francophone North African countries.

Morrow and Castleton discuss their research on the Allah Lexicon in Chapter 11. This unique linguistic phenomenon in the Arabic language is an important part of culture among Arab Muslims. However, their research finds that this feature is beginning to erode in the face of global English.

The final chapter is a narrative written by Sinno, who grew up in Lebanon speaking and learning both Arabic and English. Her personal story reveals the difficulties she faced when studying Arabic and how the teaching methods used between Arabic and English made all the difference in how she gravitated towards English and away from Arabic.

These chapters are all important for revealing that there is a growing problem between the spread of global English and the tendency of Arabic to lessen in prominence. In nations from Morocco to the Arabian Gulf, studies show that students still find Arabic useful for their encounters with family and for cultural and religious issues; however, English is taking precedence in terms of technology, education, and business. It is even encroaching on their social interactions, especially in written form, but also verbally.

Our own beliefs that Arabic is weakening are supported by the findings in this volume. No one is espousing the immediate death of Arabic, but the warning signs of a possible future loss of MSA continue to grow and these signs are backed up by the research found here. Educators, parents, and policy makers in the Arab world must be more cognizant of the role global English currently exerts on Arabic-speaking youth. They can no longer ignore the signs that English, along with popular culture, are a dangerous pairing that long term can lead young people away from their native Arabic. It is our hope that these concerns can and will be addressed and that those who can stop this movement away from Arabic will see fit to endeavour that bilingualism take precedence over the continual promotion of one language, English, over the other, Arabic.

AHMAD AL-ISSA AND LAILA S. DAHAN

# 1 Global English and Endangered Arabic in the United Arab Emirates

## ABSTRACT

Global English in tandem with the phenomenon of globalization is marching across the globe. In many instances the new lingua franca makes life easier through allowing communication across borders and boundaries through one common language. However, despite the positive factors that come with English, there are concerns about its effect on the languages and cultures of nations around the world. This particular chapter looks at the spread of global English, globalization, and endangered Arabic in the UAE. With consistent incoming migrant populations, the UAE requires a lingua franca and English carries out that role. However, over time, English seems to be moving beyond a foreign language and into the place of a second language. This chapter looks at the concerns this has for the Arabic language in the UAE.

## Introduction

In today's world, which is driven by globalization, technology, and the rapid exchange of goods, services, and ideas, one language stands out: English. More precisely, it is often referred to as *global English*. English today is not just a language to be learned for furthering education or job prospects; it has gone beyond that to stand out as the sole lingua franca of our rapidly globalizing world. For better or for worse, it is English that has taken centre stage in the quest for a language that can unite the world's multilingual people in order to meet the need for a common communication tool.

## Globalization

Prior to focusing on global English, it is relevant to briefly discuss the phenomenon of globalization. There are a myriad of definitions of globalization found in the literature. The initial meaning that focused on the economic side of globalization has expanded over the years to include discussions of politics, society, and culture.

In today's world globalization is not viewed only as the spread of a global economy, but it is further seen as a cultural occurrence. As Jay (2001) notes, cultural forms such as cinema, television, literary narrative, and more are now commodities. These various types of cultural products are able to travel across borders worldwide and their ease of mobility is in large part due to global English. Mignolo (2000) notes that globalization's progress today is not new, but it is the "*way* in which it is taking place that is without precedent" (p. 236, emphasis is ours). Furthermore, when we view globalization, we have to look at it as a "comprehensive phenomenon" (Abed, 2007, p. 3), which incorporates economics, politics, social structures, and culture. Another definition of globalization comes from Waters (1995) who indicates that it is a "social process in which the constraints of geography on social and cultural arrangements recede and in which people become increasingly aware that they are receding" (p. 3).

When we look at a country like the UAE we observe that it is constructed based on the shared origins of its people, or a shared culture, which includes religion, language, and history. This notion is one that has been stressed by the ruler of the emirate of Sharjah, Sheikh Dr Sultan Al Qassimi, who consistently reminds the people of Sharjah that it is their duty to preserve their heritage and language. However, globalization, according to its critics, is challenging national states and the enormous adjustments caused by globalization are in many ways "undermining the stability" of nation states and their formations (Ozkirimli, 2005, p. 126). Therefore, despite the encouragement of leaders to maintain language and heritage, globalization is often too strong to resist.

## 1  Global English and Endangered Arabic in the United Arab Emirates

Globalization and global English are both usually discussed in a positive manner and with great optimism by most. Those living in wealthy nations assume that globalization and the English that goes with it affect everyone equally. However, this is not always the case, and as this chapter reveals, the unchecked spread of global English, through globalization, has had some negative effects on languages in general, but specifically on Arabic in the United Arab Emirates.

Despite the positives that go along with having a global language, such as more easily understood international encounters, air and sea traffic guidance, and more, there are negatives. In fact, there are serious detriments to other languages in the world due to the phenomenon of global English; Arabic is one of those languages at risk. The growth of global English in the Arab world, and the Arabian Gulf region specifically, has begun to take on a dangerous precedent. There is an obvious trend in the region to adopt English as both a status and academic language (Harrison, Kamphuis, & Barnes, 2007). People increasingly learn English not only to enjoy the access it grants speakers to its power and prestige, but also because it is needed today to help carry out and move forward "structures of an increasingly postnational system" (Wright, 2003, p. 172). What we must acknowledge in today's global world is the fact that mother tongues are deeply tied to identity building, while learned languages (especially English) are a stronger factor in terms of innovation and state-building (Ennaji & Sadiqi, 2008).

The nefarious role that English seems to play appears designed to eventually remove Arabic from a place of prestige and power on the local scene, both educationally and socially. In fact, in the UAE today English has gone beyond the status of a foreign language and has become a second language (Al Mansoori, 2001, cited in Troudi, 2007, p. 4). As the UAE continues to advance in the fields of business, technology, and education, in addition to its role as a major tourism destination in the Middle East, it requires English more than other countries in the region. While the UAE continues to gain prestige in the Gulf, the wider Arab world, and the globe, it utilizes English because this is the language that can propel it forward in terms of modernization and innovation. Unfortunately, this is being done at the expense of Arabic. The country expects most of the expatriates it hires to speak and utilize English for interpersonal and professional communication. Therefore, it is mainly the demographics of the country which are the driving force behind the continual need for English. As we have discussed at length (Al-Issa & Dahan, 2007) it is the volatile mixture of globalization and global English that is the main factor threatening languages today generally and Arabic in the United Arab Emirates.

This chapter has carefully considered the importance of the role of Arabic in the cultural and religious life of Arabs in the region. Unfortunately, no matter how important the Arabic language appears to be, the way in which it is utilized reveals that its power is not and will not be sufficient to persist in its duel with global English. In fact, Arabic in the UAE is facing the very real possibility of becoming very limited in use within the next two or three generations. Not only will the potential loss of Arabic have a negative effect on the people of the UAE, but it is possible that any gradual loss of Arabic could lead to a lessening of unity among Arab neighbours in the region. According to Barakat (1993) one of the "building blocks of unity [in the Arab world] includes the Arabic language and shared culture" (p. 4). If the UAE continues to assign Arabic to a lower rank than global English, then one of the keystones of Arab harmony may be at risk.

Discussion about global English's power, its colonial past, current imperialism, and its ability to endanger languages is not a new concept and has been carefully analysed and discussed at length by many scholars in the field (Canagarajah, 1999; Nelson, 1992; Pennycook, 1994, 1998; Phillipson, 1992, 1998, 1999, 2001; Skutnabb-Kangas, 1994, 1998, 2001; Skutnabb-Kangas & Phillipson, 1998; Tupas, 2001). Concerns about the negative impact of global English seem to be spreading rather than abating. The argument, as viewed by many in the fields of language, English language teaching, and linguistics all revolve around the notion that global English has been offered a position of power that local languages are hard-pressed to deny. Writers in these fields see global English possessing a role that is not equivalent to other languages in terms of power, prestige, and attitude (Al-Issa, 2006; Pennycook, 1998; Phillipson, 1998; Sridhar, 1996). In fact, there is even concern that the loss of languages can be viewed as genocide according to the 1948 United Nations International Convention on the Prevention and Punishment of the Crime of Genocide (Skutnabb-Kangas

& Phillipson, 1998), which states that genocide is related to language and that "prohibiting the use of the language of the group in daily intercourse or in schools, or the printing and circulation of publications in the language of the groups" could be perceived as language genocide (p. 32). The rationale for the continued focus on English is that countries believe that in order for their citizens to progress and keep up with the modern world and the spread of globalization, global English is a must. Those researching in this field accept the notion that English is important. However, the positive method to enable the use of global English to work for all is to encourage bilingualism. In other words, it is fine to push global English, even in the educational system; however, it should and must be confined to the place of a second language initially. It should not, which is what it is currently doing in the UAE, be used in a subtractive way (Skutnabb-Kangas, 2000) that sees Arabic relegated to second class status in an Arab country.

## The case of English and Arabic in the UAE

It is regrettable that in the UAE the desire to ensure proficiency in English seems to outweigh the desire to maintain the study of Arabic in all subject areas. English is introduced in both public and private schools as early as kindergarten and continues through the university level. According to Troudi (2007), "English is the first and only foreign language students are learning in both elementary and secondary schools" (p. 3) in the UAE. Public schools do teach content areas in Arabic; however, many parents prefer that their children study at English medium international schools in order to obtain better fluency in English. Although no research has been carried out that we are aware of, the lack of parental concern about the focus on English might indicate that parents in the UAE are satisfied with this arrangement. Local parents and native speakers of Arabic are consistently observed, by the researchers, speaking English to their children as they drop them off at their English medium schools. The parents' continual veneration of English is another threat to Arabic in the UAE (Al-Issa & Dahan, 2007). For further discussion regarding parental attitudes toward English see Troudi and Jendli in this volume.

English has already become the official language of instruction in most higher education institutions in the UAE (Troudi, 2007). In 2009 some of the universities in the UAE, which had maintained Arabic as the language of instruction switched to English. These include the community colleges, where mostly locals study and had been taught all their content in Arabic up until 2009. This is an adverse move as it again gives the impression that Arabic is not as useful or even important as a means of education. In an Arab country, it further sends implications to parents and students that English is better for them and will give them better opportunities for future employment. English then becomes prestigious, while Arabic is sent back to primary and secondary school, but even there it is not at the forefront. Nearly all private schools in the UAE utilize English as the language of instruction; a few use French. Arabic is used solely for Arabic language, Islamic studies, and sometimes social studies. Students are asked to learn mathematics, science, and even history in a foreign language. By pursuing this method students may come to view Arabic as a language that is not scientific and the language will then become relegated to a "language of literature, theology, social and emotional communication" (Troudi, 2007, p. 6). This is detrimental to them as learners as there is strong evidence to show that children learn better and absorb more if they are taught in their native language (Brock-Utne, 2001). Therefore English should be taught and remain as a second language in the UAE. Unfortunately English seems to be the main language children are encouraged to study in the Emirates and this is interfering with their ability to learn as fully as they could. In fact, most linguists concur that the best basis for learning a foreign language is to first have an excellent command of one's own language, which means using a native language up to a high level of schooling (Brock-Utne, 2001).

The latest instance of English and its perennial role occurred in the fall school term of 2010. The Abu Dhabi Education Council (Adec), in Abu Dhabi, brought in nearly 1,000 native speakers of English to work in the capital. The role of these "teachers" is to take a place in each classroom in the emirate alongside the children's regular Arabic-speaking teacher. The rationale behind the recent move is that children must have English as part of their daily instruction from primary school. According to Hamilton, a writer for *The National*, this recruitment drive is part of a multimillion-dirham initiative aimed at transforming education with the New School Model teaching strategy. Under the system, being phased in over the next six years; pupils will be taught by both a native English speaker and an Arabic speaker (22 September 2010).

As mentioned, not just any speaker of English is acceptable, but only those who are native speakers. This is an old debate, but one which continues to be overlooked in the Arab world. The idea that a native speaker is in anyway better at teaching his/her own language or has skills that are not available to non native speakers is a notion that has been discarded by most scholars (see Canagarajah, 1999; Kachru, 1992; Kramsch, 1993; McKay 2002, 2003; Strevens, 1992).

This new approach to curriculum design in Abu Dhabi gives us pause on several grounds. First and foremost, there have been no studies or any research carried out in the UAE that prove that imbedding a native speaker in the classroom will foster second language learning any better than traditional methods. Secondly, there was no coverage among all the newspaper articles which described this new system that ever discussed the qualifications of these teachers. This is extremely worrisome, because in the UAE and the Arab world generally, a native speaker is often given carte blanche to a teaching job just by virtue of their native fluency in English. Very often a background in education is not required nor asked about. As long as the person is a native speaker then he/she is given the right to step in front of a classroom full of children and "teach". This new batch of 1,000 has never been lauded in the news, for anything other than their native language, no one has praised or mentioned the degrees they hold or their years of teaching experience, if any, they have with young children.

There have been some voices of dissatisfaction with this new plan in Abu Dhabi, and these may grow over time. The concerns, in line with our own, centre around what qualifications these people hold and how they will fit in to an Emirati classroom. They will, of course, bring with them their own cultural and traditional values and some UAE nationals have voiced negative feelings towards having these types of people with their children on a daily basis, when their actual role is supposed to be teaching English. There are fears that the consistent input from these new teachers will have effects on their children. The permanent location of these teachers in the classroom with a native speaker of Arabic is seen as unnecessary and a bit disturbing in terms of what they can and might bring to their students. There is little doubt that very few if any of these new teachers have ever studied the Arabic language, or very much about Arab and Muslim culture. Unfortunately, it is these types of continual new policies that constantly inject English into the curriculum of the UAE students and leave little time or opportunity for them to truly develop and learn to love and express themselves in their native Arabic.

There are several reasons why there is real concern that Arabic could be lost in the UAE. First of all, the language itself is notoriously difficult to learn and has quite a complex grammar. Students need to study Arabic and use it in written form throughout their secondary years if they are ever to truly master it. Arabic requires practice and that insinuates that it must be used for all course work through the final year in high school. If students don't develop a facility with their native language during the formative years and high school there can be no assurance that the language and its grammar will remain with them. Learning Modern Standard Arabic (MSA), or *foos'ha*, "can only be done through lengthy and sustained schooling" (Holt, 1996, p. 21). Reading as a skill must also be practiced and therefore is needed by Arabic speaking students in order to ensure complete comprehension and the attainment of a vocabulary level that is useful and acceptable for a high school graduate.

A cogent example of an Arab nation that fought and continues to fight what appears to be a losing battle on the language front is Morocco. Before French colonization an "Islamic traditional system of education was prevalent" (Ennaji, 2002, p. 74). During the French colonization period the French language was imposed as the language of education, and after independence, according to Ennaji, MSA was declared the official language of Morocco while French became the second language. However, since 1957 the government of Morocco has attempted, without much success, to improve the educational system by "revitalizing" MSA. Although the initial purpose was to preserve Arabic and "Moroccan cultural identity" it has continually faced roadblocks (Ennaji, p. 74). In the late 1970s there was an attempt to "Arabize" the universities, but it was not possible and French remains the language of instruction. The reason for this failure, Ennaji notes, is that all textbooks are in English or French and there is a serious lack of university professionals who have the capability to lecture in Arabic. In 2002 a study was carried out in Morocco using high school graduates and teachers in order to review their attitudes towards Arabization. The results of that study further support our concerns for Arabic in the UAE. The outcome of the study revealed that the majority of students and teachers indicated that their competence in French was good or very good; whereas, their assessment of their abilities in MSA was mostly average to poor. The summation of this data shows that the majority of students and teachers had no favourable attitudes toward Arabization. And their unfortunate lack of competence in MSA "reinforces their perception of Arabization as an unsuccessful project" (Ennaji, p. 83). The importance of this study in Morocco cannot be overlooked in terms of the possibility of a similar situation occurring in the UAE. Just as the Moroccans have little access to Arabic in their high school or university years, many UAE students are in the same predicament. Their interest in Arabic as a language for "serious" study has been taken away due to an excessive focus on global English, much in the same way that French has been paramount in Morocco. For current information on the role of Arabic in Morocco, see Buckner's chapter in this book.

Despite the many who proclaim concern over the loss of Arabic, there are a number of scholars and lay people who consistently raise their voices in support of the strength of Arabic in the face of global English. Their support is based mainly on the role of Islam (Karmani, 1995; Zughoul, 2002). Arabic is the language of Islam, and the Quran, the Muslim holy book, was originally written in Arabic and all Muslims pray in Arabic. Unfortunately the reality becomes that millions of non-Arabic speaking people are Muslims. They have never needed to learn the Arabic language in order to pray, because they memorize the verses needed for prayer. They have never been required to learn to read Arabic because the Quran has been translated into hundreds of language. These are the examples that must be acknowledged by those who claim Arabic is untouchable by virtue of Islam. Their justification is not necessarily holding up under scrutiny. In fact, Indonesia has the largest population of Muslims anywhere in the world, including the entire Arabic speaking world; however, all Indonesians do not speak Arabic nor do they find it a necessity to be fluent in Arabic in order to be practicing Muslims. Therefore the possibility of Arabic being endangered remains, despite its ties to Islam (see Morrow and Castleton in this volume for more on this specific issue).

Furthermore, with students learning very little Arabic throughout their high school years in the UAE private school system, other than being able to recite verses from the Quran by virtue of rote memorization, they will most likely find the beauty of the classical Arabic style of the Quran difficult to follow when reading it. This factor is already becoming apparent among students in the UAE, many of whom claim that reading in Arabic is difficult. In fact, through studies we have conducted at our university in the UAE (see for example, Al-Issa, 2006; Al-Issa & Dahan, 2008; Dahan, 2007) we have noted that students have slowly begun voicing concerns about the role Arabic plays in their lives. Some students are quite concerned with how their native language seems to be losing ground despite Arabic being the language of Islam and of the UAE.

Another reason for the possible loss of Arabic is the nature of the language itself. Arabic does not have one dialect that everyone uses on a daily basis. Modern Standard Arabic, which is also known as classical Arabic or *foos'ha*, is used solely for the written word, news broadcasts, and religious issues. People in their daily lives certainly do not communicate in MSA. In many ways speaking in *foos'ha* would be tantamount to speaking Shakespearian English in contemporary society. There is no common Arabic dialect and every region of the Arab world from Morocco in the West to Iraq in the East and Yemen to the South has a different vernacular. More often than not, dialects from very distant geographic regions are unintelligible to others. Even within each Arabic speaking country there are a variety of dialects, which is the case with most nations of the world. However, since the Arabic-speaking region, geographically, is so large these dialects are often unintelligible to one another.

There currently is not and there probably will never be a successful movement to use any of the Arabic dialects in written form. According to Suleiman (2003, 2004) historically there has been a battle to maintain the purity of *foos'ha*. The defenders of the classical language remain adamant that the dialects should never be allowed in written form and that *foos'ha* must remain unsullied. Some of these concerns go back to the seventh century; wherein, the Prophet of Islam was reported to have likened using a dialect while reading the Quran to deviating from the true path of the religion (Suleiman, 2004).

However, when one combines the lack of a common language with the many dialects available, it becomes obvious that the possibility of losing MSA, as a mode for spoken encounters, can be a possibility. As an example, at present when Arabs from various regions encounter one another, they may find it very difficult to communicate in their different dialects and therefore any meaningful interaction is all but impossible. Instead of turning to MSA to get them through their conversation, they will often turn to English: the trusty language of the twenty-first century, the language that guarantees communication. English is easy, because it is written and spoken by everyone the same way. People may have their dialects, but the general English-speaking population of the world speaks English as it is written and taught in books and taught in school. There is no "classical" English; all English is similar and perhaps an egalitarian language for the new world.

There is no doubt that the many dialects of Arabic will probably remain, at least in the short term, especially in the smaller towns and villages of the Arab world. These are places where people have avoided continual exposure to global English. And these dialects can survive quite well as long as there are people who use them to communicate. But the beauty of MSA may soon be relegated to a minor part of the population, especially in the UAE, solely from lack of use. As children grow up with an ease in global English, but suffering through Arabic, they will tend to choose what is easier to learn and then speak it with their friends (see Sinno's chapter in this volume regarding the difficulties associated with learning Arabic). Already in the UAE there is a prestige associated with English use. Even parents admit to speaking English with their children in the hopes that they will grow up and be successful. Unfortunately this view of the parents eventually transfers to their children, who begin to believe that global English is the language required for their future, at the expense of their mother tongue.

## Language and identity

As global English continues to spread and take hold around the world, there are some concerns over the issue of identity. This is so because numerous scholars see language and identity as being inseparable (see Giles & Johnson, 1981, 1987; Goldstein, 1995; Gumperz, 1982; Heller, 1988). If we view language and identity as having an attachment, then the continued duality of global English and globalization can have a negative impact on the identity of UAE nationals.

Identity however is not a singular unit and any discussion of it must include how a person defines him/herself in terms of gender, religion, nationality, and so on. And furthermore, one's identity includes a social identity, which would include those groups the person associates with and any ethnic group one is a part of. Personal identity is what makes an individual unique, distinct, and special. And therefore according to Khashan (2000) identity "forms the raison d'être of human earthly beings" (p. 18). It is this unique quality, intertwined with cultural diversity that gives humans their quality of life.

In today's rapidly changing world, many scholars have now begun challenging the idea that identity and culture are static and ever-lasting. In fact, identity is seen by many as something dynamic, shifting, and not constrained by culture or physical space (see Joseph, 2004; Khashan, 2000; Suleiman, 2006; Wright, 2003). It is the consistent fluidity found in both globalization as a phenomenon and identity as an entity that can lead people to either endeavour to maintain their current identities or begin evolving and changing them.

However, despite the fluidity inherent in identity, a native language does continue to play an important role in defining people, and this is especially true in the Arabic-speaking world. A person's identity, both individual and social, is reconciled through language (May, 2001). Languages do, in fact, transmit values from one generation to another (Suleiman, 2003) along with "cultural heritage, assumptions, values, and beliefs" (Ennaji & Sadiqi, 2008, p. 44). Therefore, the lack of focus and concern regarding Arabic in the UAE is a cause for unease. In order for the Emirati identity

*1 Global English and Endangered Arabic in the United Arab Emirates*

to remain strong, the Arabic language must also remain firmly grounded in a place of prestige. Despite identity's fluidity, we must not allow our acceptance of a fluid identity to transform entire segments of what makes people who they are.

One can say that in the UAE the shifting of identity starts with the younger citizens. There is evidence found in studies conducted in the UAE revealing that Emirati nationals holding university degrees and under the age of twenty-five are "significantly more secular and individualistic than their older siblings or parents" (Mourtada-Sabbah, Al-Mutawa, Fox, & Walters, 2008, p. 128). The world around them has opened up wider possibilities; therefore, they are culturally quite different from the older generations. And although identity can be considered fluid, it is the rapidity at which the young generation is able to obtain and assimilate outside cultural sources, mostly western and English-based, that leads to consternation. In the past, there was, of course, cultural borrowing and expanding of identities. But those contacts were not consistent and did not lead to immediate changes. However, today's world of global English and globalization allows everything new and foreign or culturally "different" to be made available almost immediately in the UAE. It is the speed at which the continual input arrives that is making the difference today and is causing disquiet within the country.

## Young people and global English in the UAE

Since English is paramount in the very early years of children's education in the UAE, they develop more of a rapport and facility with utilizing this language in terms of reading and literacy than they do with Arabic. When asked, many university-level UAE students, who attended private English medium schools will either complain about the difficulties they faced with Arabic in school or claim that they really see no major use for Arabic anymore as everyone who is anybody speaks English. As our own research has shown, due to the limited interaction with Arabic in an educational setting, students lose the bond with their native language (see Al-Issa, 2006).

As a general rule, youth in any culture are rarely concerned about the maintenance of culture, traditions, or language. Those details in life are not at the forefront of what young people think of or are interested in. For them whatever is new or modern or what their peers are involved in are the things they take to heart. In our globalized world most things young people are interested in are related to pop culture brought through the medium of English. With this being the case, they need their English to understand the lyrics to the trendiest music, the words to all the western films they watch, for the articles in entertainment magazines they may read, and to chat on-line and on Facebook. Their world needs global English. Their young worlds are not concerned with the endangerment of their native Arabic, because they have not given it much thought. Students are learning and using English because they believe it is in their best interest and they are not concerned about its negative effects on their language and culture (Harrison et al., 2007; Zughoul, 2003). They are not anxious about their culture or traditions because those are 'old-fashioned' worries that parents and grandparents are concerned with. They are certainly not the things that young, hip people care about in their college years.

The unfortunate part is that when they grow into adulthood their fascination and use of global English will eventually pave the way to raising a family that may speak only English at home. Or even if the UAE dialect does exist in the home, these parents will be eager to push global English on their children ensuring their success in the globalized world. Where might this lead? It can very well lead to a new generation counting on English as their constant language of schooling, entertainment, and communication with their peers. It could lead to Arabic being viewed as something old-fashioned which does not merit their attention because, after all, what they are taught and continually reminded of, by everything and everyone surrounding them, is that English is the global language. English is the language of technology, business, medicine, and education – therefore, it must be more important than Arabic because it does so much more for them than Arabic ever has the opportunity to.

With the continual focus on English and its prestigious role in every day life in the UAE, there is concern that Arabic could become at risk, or even endangered. Granted, Arabic is still spoken by many in various dialects; however, MSA is losing its place of power and prestige.

## Endangered languages

Today languages are becoming endangered at a very rapid rate, much faster than in the past. This is happening for several reasons including: globalization, economic markets, urbanization, and governmental language policies. When the planet loses a language, more than words are lost; ideas, traditions, identities, and cultural diversity also vanish.

The fact remains that languages can become endangered and, in fact, "language death is real" (Crystal, 2002, p. ix). Part of the problem is that most of the educated public does not realize that the "world is facing a linguistic crisis of unprecedented scale" (Crystal, p. viii). There is a need for people to obtain knowledge about language loss (Fishman, 2006), but currently the entire issue of language endangerment is confusing. There might be some awareness that languages are dying around the world, but most people have no idea at what rate these deaths are occurring (Crystal, 2002).

If we look at languages throughout history we find that most have changed over time rather than remained static (Maffi, 2002). However, concerns about the disappearance of minority languages began to arise in the 1990s when linguists began noticing minority languages disappearing exceptionally fast and being replaced by lingua francas (Grenoble & Whaley, 2006; Maffi, 2002). To remain strong a language needs a large number of speakers (Yamamoto, Brenzinger, & Villalon, 2008), and furthermore it will only survive and flourish if it has speakers who are part of a community (Nettle & Romaine, 2000; Yamamoto et al., 2008). It also needs parents who pass the language on to their children (Nettle & Romaine, 2000).

There are many factors which lead to the phenomenon of language death and the issue will always be complex (Crystal, 2002; Yamamoto, et al., 2008). The simplest rationale is that they die when they are no longer spoken and are not passed on to the next generation (Crystal, 2002; Grenoble, 2008; Maffi, 2002; Ostler, 2008; Patrick, 2004). When parents no longer pass the language on to their children, either voluntarily or for political reasons, the language will be lost. For the language to remain healthy, children must speak it (Grenoble, 2008). Unfortunately, in the UAE many children are not realizing the importance of Arabic and not using it on a daily basis. This continual lack of consistent use will weaken the language.

Languages also decline when their speakers have a poor attitude about their language, or it becomes marginalized in their nation and is seen as inferior (Crystal, 2002; Harrison, 2007; May, 2004; Ostler, 2008; Skutnabb-Kangas, 2000). In the UAE, some of the youth are seeing Arabic as being unable to help them get ahead in a world full of technology and modernization, and they turn instead to English. It is unfortunate that people start to view their own language as unimportant or inferior, but it does happen. As long as governmental policies promote global English in the classroom at the expense of MSA, these speakers will have negative feelings towards their native language.

Many people believe that they can attain socio-economic improvement if they learn to use the dominant language in their region (Dalby, 2003; Grenoble, 2008). This is certainly the case in the UAE, the local language gets abandoned by speakers as they start to favour the more prestigious or well-known tongue (Harrison, 2007; Patrick, 2004), currently global English. As long as those in power and those who write language and education policies revere a lingua franca over the indigenous languages within their own countries, languages will be lost.

When we lose a language, we are not just losing words. Languages once lost are irreplaceable. The extent of language loss is infinitely deeper and more disconcerting than just losing something which we can write off as unnecessary or readily substituted. When a language disappears not only words are lost, but ideas, ways of knowing, and cultural diversity also vanish (Dalby, 2003; Fishman, 1991, 2001; Hale, 1992; Harrison, 2007; Nettle & Romaine, 2000; Skutnabb-Kangas, 2001; Wurm, 1999). Entire worldviews of accumulated wisdom including religious beliefs and observations about life will disappear in the absence of languages (Harrison, 2007; Nettle & Romaine, 2000).

In the view of Skutnabb-Kangas (2001) "linguistic genocide" is occurring on an immense scale brought on by the media and formal education as the major "culprits" (p. 207). She views as genocidal any formal education which is subtractive. This refers to education that teaches children about the dominant language while ignoring or overlooking their first language.

This problem is occurring in the UAE. Government policies towards education in the UAE and Gulf region allow schools to focus on English and import it into the classroom at the primary level. If this is done in order to achieve fluency in a second language, this method is fine. However, English is taking over and children are being taught many of their subjects in the second language. Long term this is leading to a decline in their native language skills, because English becomes the language of education. Furthermore, due to easy access to media, most children are inundated with television shows that are in English, and that which is entertaining is what they choose to emulate.

## Conclusion

The purpose of this chapter is to reveal the potential danger that Arabic confronts in the UAE in the face of global English. Students feel the need to master English because they view it as the language of knowledge in addition to the prestige it brings the user. The objective of this work is the hope that educational policy makers in the UAE and the Gulf region generally will realize the significance of maintaining a role of importance for the Arabic language. It is certainly acceptable and indeed a necessity for students to learn English in our globalized world. However, the goal must be bilingualism and the schools and universities must be equipped to teach and nurture bilingualism and not assume that students learning in English will be able to maintain their Arabic. History has revealed that bilinguals are able to negotiate their way through two languages and cultures and improve their lifestyles by virtue of their ability to cross not only linguistic barriers but cultural ones as well. This is what is required for students in the UAE. There is no need for them to lose any of their Modern Standard Arabic through neglect or lack of use; it is their right to have their own language in addition to English or whatever other language they choose to study and speak. The point is that they should and must maintain their Arabic as it carries with it their heritage and culture.

There is an obvious need to raise awareness among Arabs generally, but in the UAE specifically, that they must use their language for all types of communication, not just speaking with their friends or families. Modern Standard Arabic must be read and studied by students throughout their high school years if it is to be strong enough to fight the possibility of disappearing as a language that is understood by many.

The UAE government has recently made a declaration about the importance of Arabic in the country and the fact that Arabic is the official language of the nation (see Youssef, 2008). It is interesting to note this factor because it reveals that perhaps the government has observed the negative effects of global English. Therefore, the UAE government now requires employees in certain governmental sectors to speak and work in Arabic. The many foreigners who come to the UAE to work, do so based on the knowledge that when they work here the language they will use will be English. Very few, if any, take the time to learn the language of the country: Arabic.

The remaining chapters in this book carry the same message found here. There is concern that global English does pose a threat to Arabic, especially Modern Standard Arabic, and contributors to this volume all reveal the many ways and instances global English is encroaching upon the Arabic language throughout the Arab world.

# References

Abed, S. (2007). *Arabic language and culture amid the demands of globalization*. Abu Dhabi, UAE: The Emirates Centre for Strategic Studies and Research.
Al-Issa, A. (2006). The culture cost: Has globalization led Arab students to focus on Western topics and neglect their own heritage? *English Language Gazette*, 321.
Al-Issa, A., & Dahan, L.S. (2007). Globalization, English language, and Muslim students in the United Arab Emirates. *Educational Awakening: Journal of the Educational Sciences*, 4(2), 147–163.

Al-Issa, A., & Dahan, L.S. (2008). Prior knowledge and writing in the college EFL composition classroom. In C. Coombe, A. Jendli, & P. Davidson (eds), *Teaching writing skills in EFL: Theory, research and pedagogy* (pp. 17–26). Dubai: TESOL Arabia Publications.

Barakat, H. (1993). *The Arab world: Society, culture, and state.* Berkeley and Los Angeles: University of California Press.

Brock-Utne, B. (2001). Education for all – in whose language? *Oxford Review of Education*, 27 (1), 115–134.

Canagarajah, A.S. (1999). *Resisting linguistic imperialism in English teaching.* Oxford: Oxford University Press.

Crystal, D. (2002). *Language death.* Cambridge: Cambridge University Press.

Dahan, L.S. (2007). English as an international language in the Arabian Gulf: Student and teacher views on the role of culture. In S. Midraj, A. Jendli, & A. Sellami (eds), *Research in ELT contexts* (pp. 158–172). Dubai: TESOL Arabia Publications.

Dalby, A. (2003). *Language in danger.* New York: Columbia University Press.

Ennaji, M. (2002). Language contact, Arabization policy and education in Morocco. In A. Rouchdy (ed.), *Language contact and language conflict in Arabic: Variations on a sociolinguistic theme* (pp. 70–88). London: Routledge Curzon.

Ennaji, M., & Sadiqi, F. (2008). Morocco: Language, nationalism, and gender. In A. Simpson (ed.), *Language and national identity in Africa* (pp. 44–60). Oxford: Oxford University Press.

Fishman, J.A. (1991). *Reversing language shift.* Clevedon: Multilingual Matters Ltd.

Fishman, J.A. (ed.) (2001). *Can threatened languages be saved?* Clevedon: Multilingual Matters Ltd.

Fishman, J.A. (2006). *Do not leave your language alone.* Mahwah, NJ: Lawrence Erlbaum Associates.

Giles, H., & Johnson, P. (1981). The role of language in ethnic group formation. In J. Turner & H. Giles (eds), *Intergroup behavior* (pp. 199–243). Oxford, UK: Basil Blackwell.

Giles, H., & Johnson, P. (1987). Ethnolinguistic identity theory: A social psychological approach to language maintenance. *International Journal of Sociology of Language, 68*, 69–99.

Goldstein, T. (1995). Nobody is talking bad. In K. Hall & M. Bucholtz (eds), *Gender articulated: Language and the socially constructed self* (pp. 375–400). New York: Routledge.

Grenoble, L. (2008). Endangered languages. In P.K. Austin (ed.), *One thousand languages* (pp. 214–235). Berkeley: University of California Press.

Grenoble, L.A., & Whaley, L.J. (2006). *Saving languages: An introduction to language revitalization.* Cambridge: Cambridge University Press.

Gumperz, J.J. (1982). *Discourse strategies*. Cambridge: Cambridge University Press.

Hale, K. (1992). Language endangerment and the human value of linguistic diversity. *Language, 68*(1), 35–41.

Hamilton, C. (2010, September 20). Teachers complain of visa chaos as 1,000 arrive to start work at once. *The National*. Retrieved January 11, 2011 from <http://www.thenational.ae/news/uae-news/education/teachers-complain-of-visa-chaos-as-1-000-arrive-to-start-work-at-once>

Harrison, D., Kamphuis, D., & Barnes, M. (2007). Linguistic imperialism in 21st century Arabia. In A. Jendli, S. Troudi, & C. Coombe (eds), *The power of language: Perspectives from Arabia* (pp. 20–34). Dubai: TESOL Arabia.

Harrison, K.D. (2007). *When languages die*. Oxford: Oxford University Press.

Heller, M. (1988). *Codeswitching: Anthropological and sociolinguistic perspectives*. New York: Mouton de Gruyter.

Holt, M. (1996). Divided loyalties: Language and ethnic identity in the Arab world. In Y. Suleiman (ed.), *Language and identity in the Middle East and North Africa* (pp. 11–24). Surrey, UK: Curzon.

Jay, P. (2001). Beyond discipline? Globalization and the future of English. *PMLA, 116*(1), 32–47.

Joseph, J.E. (2004). *Language and identity: National, ethnic, religious*. New York: Palgrave Macmillan.

Kachru, B. (1992). Teaching world Englishes. In B. Kachru (ed.), *The other tongue: English across cultures* (2nd edn, pp. 355–365). Urbana: University of Illinois Press.

Karmani, S. (1995). Islam, politics, and English language teaching. *Muslim Education Quarterly, 13*(1), 12–32.

Khashan, H. (2000). *Arabs at the crossroads: Political identity and nationalism*. Gainesville, FL: University Press of Florida.

Kramsch, C. (1993). *Context and culture in language teaching*. Oxford: Oxford University Press.

Maffi, L. (2002). Endangered languages, endangered knowledge. *International Social Science Journal, 54*(173), 385–393.

McKay, S.L. (2002). *Teaching English as an international language: Rethinking goals and approaches*. Oxford: Oxford University Press.

McKay, S.L. (2003). Toward an appropriate EIL pedagogy: Re-examining common ELT assumptions. *International Journal of Applied Linguistics, 13*(1), 1–22.

May, S. (2001). *Language and minority rights: Ethnicity, nationalism and the politics of language*. Essex, UK: Pearson Education Ltd.

May, S. (2004). Rethinking linguistic human rights: Answering questions of identity, essentialism and mobility. In J. Freeland & D. Patrick (eds), *Language rights and language survival* (pp. 35–53). Manchester, UK: St Jerome Publishing.

Mignolo, W. (2000). *Local histories/global designs: Coloniality, subaltern knowledges, and border thinking*. Princeton, NJ: Princeton University Press.

Mourtada-Sabbah, N., al-Mutawa, M., Fox, J., & Walters, T. (2008). Media as social matrix in the United Arab Emirates. In A. Alsharekh & R. Springborg (eds), *Popular culture and political identity in the Arab Gulf States* (pp. 121–142). London: Saqi.

Nelson, C. (1992). My language, your culture: Whose communicative competence? In B. Kachru (ed.), *The other tongue: English across cultures* (2nd edn, pp. 327–339). Urbana: University of Illinois Press.

Nettle, D., & Romaine, S. (2000). *Vanishing voices: The extinction of the world's languages*. New York: Oxford University Press.

Ostler, N. (2008). Extinct languages. In P.K. Austin (ed.), *One thousand languages* (pp. 236–255). Berkeley: University of California Press.

Ozkirimli, U. (2005). *Contemporary debates on nationalism: A critical engagement*. Houndsmill Basingstoke, UK: Palgrave Macmillan.

Patrick, D. (2004). The politics of language rights in the eastern Canadian Arctic. In J. Freeland & D. Patrick (eds), *Language rights and language survival* (pp. 171–190). Manchester, UK: St Jerome Publishing.

Pennycook, A. (1994). *The cultural politics of English as an international language*. Essex, UK: Longman Group Ltd.

Pennycook, A. (1998). *English and the discourse of colonialism*. New York: Routledge.

Phillipson, R. (1992). *Linguistic imperialism*. Oxford: Oxford University Press.

Phillipson, R. (1998). Globalizing English: Are linguistic human rights an alternative to linguistic imperialism? *Language Sciences, 20*(1), 101–112.

Phillipson, R. (1999). Political science. In J. Fishman (ed.), *Handbook of language and ethnic identity* (pp. 94–108). New York: New York University Press.

Phillipson, R. (2001). English for globalisation or for the world's people? *International Review of Education, 47*(3/4), 185–200.

Skutnabb-Kangas, T. (1994). *Linguistic human rights: Overcoming linguistic discrimination*. Berlin: Mouton de Gruyter.

Skutnabb-Kangas, T. (1998). Human rights and language wrongs – A future for diversity? *Language Sciences, 20*(1), 5–27.

Skutnabb-Kangas, T. (2000). *Linguistic genocide in education – or worldwide diversity and human rights?* London: Lawrence Erlbaum Associates.

Skutnabb-Kangas, T. (2001). The globalization of (educational) language rights. *International Review of Education, 47*(3/4), 201–219.

Skutnabb-Kangas, T., & Phillipson, R. (1998). Language in human rights. *Gazette, 60*(1), 27–46.

Sridhar, K. (1996). Societal multilingualism. In S. McKay & N. Hornberger (eds), *Sociolinguistics and language teaching* (pp. 47–70). Cambridge: Cambridge University Press.

Strevens, P. (1992). English as an international language: Directions in the 1990s. In B. Kachru (ed.), *The other tongue: English across cultures* (2nd edn, pp. 340–352). Urbana: University of Illinois Press.

Suleiman, Y. (2003). *The Arabic language and national identity: A study in ideology*. Washington, DC: Georgetown University Press.

Suleiman, Y. (2004). *A war of words: Language and conflict in the Middle East*. Cambridge: Cambridge University Press.

Suleiman, Y. (2006). Constructing languages, constructing national identities. In T. Omoniyi & G. White (eds), *Sociolinguistics of identity* (pp. 50–71). London and New York: Continuum.

Troudi, S. (2007). The effects of English as a medium of instruction. In A. Jendli, S. Troudi, & C. Coombe (eds), *The power of language: Perspectives from Arabia* (pp. 3–19). Dubai: TESOL Arabia.

Tupas, T. (2001). Global politics and the Englishes of the world. In J. Cotterill & A. Ife (eds), *Language across boundaries* (pp. 81–98). London: British Association for Applied Linguistics.

Waters, M. (1995). *Globalization*. New York: Routledge.

Wright, S. (2003). *Language policy and language planning: From nationalism to globalisation*. Houndsmill Basingstoke, UK: Palgrave Macmillan.

Wurm, S.A. (1999). Endangered languages, multilingualism and linguistics. *Diogenes*, *47*(185), 56–66.

Yamamoto, A., Brenzinger, M., & Villalon, M.E. (2008). A place for all languages: On language vitality and revitalization. *Museum International (UNESCO)*, *60*(3), 60–70.

Youssef, M. (2008, March 11). Use of Arabic will preserve our cultural identity – intellectuals. *Gulf News*, p. 8.

Zughoul, M.R. (2002). The power of language and the language of power in higher education in the Arab world: Conflict, dominance and shift. *College of Islamic and Arabic Studies Journal*, *23*. Retrieved June 1, 2005, from <www.tesolislamia.org/articles/html>

Zughoul, M.R. (2003). Globalization and EFL/ESL pedagogy in the Arab world. *Journal of Language and Learning*, *1*(2), 106–142.

SALAH TROUDI AND ADEL JENDLI

# 2 Emirati Students' Experiences of English as a Medium of Instruction

## ABSTRACT

The English language has become the medium of instruction (EMI) in higher educational institutions in the United Arab Emirates (UAE). The main purpose of this project is to explore and investigate what Emirati university students think of EMI. In particular we investigated the effects EMI has on their educational achievement and learning experiences. The study also revealed students' views about the status of Arabic as a language of instruction at the tertiary level and the possibility of a dual language education. An exploratory research strategy with qualitative data obtained through semi-structured interviews revealed that students' experiences with EMI at the university level were shaped by a number of educational and sociocultural factors. The nature of the primary and secondary school experience and the students' overall competence in English has to a large extent formed their views of EMI. Students who attended private English-medium schools were much more prepared to face the academic demands of EMI than their colleagues who learned English as a foreign language and a subject among others in the curriculum of the government primary and secondary schools. Family background and parental attitudes towards English have also played a role in students' acceptance of EMI and in many cases a tendency to prefer English to Arabic. However, the data did reveal that Emirati students were also interested in Arabic as a medium of instruction for a number of university subjects. Thinking of employability and market forces, the students had a realistic if not a pragmatic attitude towards Arabic. They also, as expected, associated Arabic with discourses of identity, linguistic, and cultural heritage. One major implication of this study is the inadequacy of the old binary division between Arabic and English as languages of instruction. The study challenges established discourses that have been reinforcing English as a language of science and academia while relegating Arabic to a language of heritage and religion. Arabic and English can mutually co-exist in a model of dual language instruction for university students.

## Introduction

The role of English in the United Arab Emirates (UAE) has in the last 20 years surpassed its initial status of a foreign language learned for the sake of communicating with the rest of the world. Being very much aware of its increasingly global status and its central place in preparing a technologically and scientifically competent workforce, the educational authorities of the country have embarked on major infrastructural, educational, and financial efforts to put in place a tertiary educational system with English as the primary language of instruction (Osman, 2009; Troudi, 2009b). This has now become an established policy in the wider region as other countries such as Qatar, Kuwait, and Bahrain have also opted for the same approach. The current research project aims to study how Emirati students at the tertiary level have reacted to the policy of English as a medium of instruction and what their views are about their educational experiences under such a policy.

## Perspectives on EMI and the UAE context

This chapter is situated within the wide areas of English language teaching (ELT) and language policy, and more specifically the field of language of instruction policy, also known as medium of instruction policies (Tollefson & Tsui, 2004). We start from the premise that a language of instruction policy is not ideologically free and is often politically and economically motivated. Taking on board the main tenets of critical language policy research such as power, struggle, hegemony, ideology, and resistance, our study will look into how practices of English-medium instruction in the (UAE) have come to be seen as acceptable and legitimate (Tollefson, 2007). The debate over the place of English as a medium of instruction (EMI) in a context such as the UAE needs to be seen in light of opposing views and schools of thought on the increasingly powerful role English plays around the world. It is perhaps necessary to state that because of the complexity of language in society and education there cannot be an overarching theory to account for all aspects and areas of language policy (Ricento, 2006). For instance, in the areas of language ecology and linguistic human rights, Phillipson's theory (1992) of linguistic imperialism was proposed to account for the hegemonic influences of English on indigenous languages and its effects on pedagogy in the area of English language teaching around the world.

While "linguistic imperialism" has had considerable effect on the study and debate over the global spread of English, it has been challenged by other theorists like Pennycook (2003), who while challenging the analytical neutrality of the predominant spread of English paradigms, also rejects the structural determinism of some of the critical views on English in the world. Accepting that ELT professionals are intimately involved with the diffusion of English, he states "we should be acutely aware of the implications of this spread for the production and reproduction of global inequalities" (p. 87). The spread of English is not a neutral phenomenon as it serves major economic interests of certain inner circle countries and it can contribute to the marginalization of indigenous cultures and languages.

Another critical but less radical view is Canagarajah's model which sets the conditions for pedagogy of appropriating discourses. This model recognizes that language learning is ideological and that learners face a number of challenges but the solution is "to negotiate with the agencies of power for personal and collective empowerment" (1999, p. 173). The solution therefore is not to reject English but to appropriate it to one's needs. Canagarajah advocates a third way that "avoids the traditional extremes of rejecting English outright for its linguistic imperialism or accepting it wholesale for its benefits" (Canagarajah, 1999, p. 173.). This "third way" strikes a balance between an uneasy awareness of the potential effects English can have on local cultures, languages, and learners' identities on one side, and a need for English for social status and economic progress on the other.

Jenkins' (2007) construct of English as a lingua franca (ELF) does, to a large extent, describe the ways many residents of different linguistic backgrounds use English in the UAE for social communication. In this model Jenkins argues that it is "NNSs [*non-native speakers*] rather than NS [*native speakers*] who are at the forefront of innovation and change in lingua franca English" (2007, p. 4; emphasis is ours). It is beyond the scope of this chapter to see if linguistic and discoursal features of ELF have been accepted in academic contexts in the UAE. However, based on our experience teaching in two academic institutions in the UAE, we can suggest that the situation is typical of English in international contexts where the native speaker model is the norm or "the point of reference" as described by Brutt-Griffler (2002, p. 179).

In the UAE, and the Gulf in general, proponents of the diffusion of the English paradigm employ discourses of social progress, economic and technological advancement, global communication, and trade as forces behind an inevitable EMI policy at the tertiary level, especially for scientific and a large number of academic subjects. Within this school of thought, government officials and academics make ideological and practical associations between the learning of English and through English and economic viability, competitive national workforce, and an active role in this era of globalization. Accepting that English plays a major role in the world economy, the UAE "has no choice other than to prepare its workforce to function in this economy through a good command of English" (Troudi, 2009b, p. 203).

There are also wider socio-cultural, political, and educational factors that helped lay the foundation for an EMI policy in most tertiary institutions in the UAE. English represents power and success, modernism, liberalism, freedom, and equality. It also represents a departure from old-fashioned and inefficient educational systems and didactic teacher-centered approaches where the focus is on knowledge transmission rather than construction.

To enact an EMI policy at the tertiary level, a number of conditions needed to be met. At the tertiary institution structural, administrative, technological, and academic facilities were put in place to provide the necessary conditions for teaching to be conducted in English. A substantially intensive English programme was put in place to help students progress to their academic departments where instruction is in English. At the start of the programme students are classified into different levels of English according to their achievement on initial English placement tests (Guefrachi & Troudi, 2000). This kind of support is available across the country in all tertiary institutions. It should be mentioned in this context that all these institutions have put in place English admission requirements demonstrated via international standardized tests such as the TOEFL and IELTS.

English as foreign or second language professionals are contractually recruited to teach in these intensive programmes and to help students reach the required level of English proficiency to be admitted into their prospective academic disciplines. The trend is to recruit mostly, and in some institutions exclusively, native speaker teachers from inner circle countries (Karmani, 2005).

In the last 10 years very few studies informed by two mainly opposing paradigms, the diffusion of English and the critical stance, have explored how English is used as a medium of instruction in the UAE's educational system. We hope that this study will fill this gap by shedding some light on the issue of EMI and students' learning experiences at the tertiary level.

On the protagonist side of EMI, perhaps even triumphalist, Jongsma and Jongsma (2006) report encouraging results of a small scale pilot study to introduce the teaching of sciences and mathematics in English to first and second grade pupils in the Abu Dhabi educational zone. Participating teachers grew in confidence in their ability to teach scientific subjects through English. The authors also reported pedagogical gains for teachers who embraced collaborative teaching and team work. Pupils were also reported to be using more English both in the classroom and at home. There were also challenges as some teachers still focused on the whole class with little attention to students with special needs and materials were not always used meaningfully. What the authors should have added in their analysis is that the teachers' challenge to teach sciences in the English language is a major problem. These teachers, who were hired from Arab countries to teach in the primary sector, had no prior training in English and neither were they expected to teach through English. Therefore, the decision to switch the medium of instruction to English will have caused them major anxiety and even fear of job loss. These teachers have now had to undergo language training in order to achieve a certain score on IELTs if they wish to keep their jobs. This is one of the professional and human consequences of an EMI policy at the primary and secondary levels. To our knowledge, no research has been conducted in this area to explore the aftermath of such a policy on the lives and morale of the teachers.

Furthermore, within the predominant EMI paradigm, Bielenberg (2004) argues that mathematics and information technology teachers at the UAE University, where this study was conducted, had to make a number of pedagogical and linguistic devices to help their students understand the content. The "special English" they used featured the use of a slow speed and a focus on selected vocabulary. The students' learning experience was characterized by major challenges they encountered at the level of "the linguistic structures in academic textbooks and the 'normal' academic language of a content area classroom" (p. 109). Bielenberg's study is one of the very few that delineate in some detail the nature of academic complexities encountered by university students in the UAE. These students mostly come from the same primary and secondary school system as those of our study, except for those who went to private schools where English is the medium of instruction. Bielenberg stops short of questioning or challenging EMI and accepts it as a legitimate educational policy.

Related to one of the main aims of this study, Findlow's (2006) qualitative research investigated the role of English language teaching in the UAE and how it is implicated in the configuring of collective identities especially in higher education. She argues that with all academic, economic, and political discourses acknowledging the role of English as the language of globalization, native languages such as Arabic have become "symbolic of nostalgia and authenticity" (Findlow, 2006, p. 2).

Participants in Findlow's study argued for the necessity of a dual language system in education. Linguistic dualism fits a fluid and dialogic view of the language-culture relationship where culture is not static but continually re-defined in a changing world. Students have to learn and adjust to new modes of communication to be able to adapt to changing circumstances and purposes. This linguistic dualism, though not equal with English as the dominant language, is a feature of the current educational system in the UAE. Findlow suggests that it enables "two identities and cultures to be claimed at once, [which] can thus be claimed as inevitable, even essential, for societies undergoing processes of acute global-local transition"

(Findlow, 2006, p. 22). While linguistic dualism as an educational approach is not officially stated in language policy documents (Clarke, 2006) it has become common practice in all sectors of the educational systems of most Gulf states, albeit an unbalanced kind of dualism.

Troudi (2009a, 2009b) problematized and questioned EMI in the UAE and the Arab world on the premise that students are more likely to do well in academic subjects when these are taught in the language most familiar to them. A second major argument was the effect of EMI on Arabic as a language of science and academia, a topic still widely ignored by educationalists and ELT professionals in the Arab world, except for some efforts by Arabic scholars (Al Askari, 2002; Al-Dhubaib, 2006; Mohamed, 2007). Troudi's work however, did not delve into the experiences of the students under EMI and its effect on the quality of their educational experience. The current study is an attempt at filling this gap. Overall, we do not espouse an essentialist view about the position of English nor an anti-English position, but we position our work within a critical and postmodern perspective on the pedagogical hegemony of English and its effect on Arabic as a language of academia.

## The study

The following are the main preliminary research questions:

1. What are students' attitudes towards English as medium of instruction at Zayed University?
2. What is the nature of the challenges students face when studying through EMI?
3. How do students cope with these challenges?

## Methodology

The nature of the above research questions and our theoretical positions necessitate an exploratory methodology, which seeks to understand how individuals in a given social and educational context make meaning, draw conclusions and make suggestions about their own learning and the language policy being investigated (Perry, 2005; Richie & Lewis, 2003). Because the study does not seek to make predictions or generalizations the focus will be on understanding the views of the participants and the reasons they provide for their choices and actions. This focus naturally justifies the centrality of qualitative data in this research project. The study can also be methodologically placed around the middle of the "basic/applied continuum" (Perry, 2005, p. 72). On the theoretical side the study deals with some abstract concepts such as identity, sense of belonging, and heritage. The study also has an applied dimension as some of the findings and implications can be directly related to areas such as language policy, curriculum development, materials selection, and classroom pedagogy. The overall design of the study is a sequential exploratory design as we used "the quantitative data and results to assist in the interpretation of qualitative findings" (Creswell, 2009, p. 211).

## The participants

In total, 110 female Zayed university students ranging in age between 18 and 22 years took part in this study by answering a five-point Likert-scale survey to measure general trends about the constructs of the research questions. Survey participants represented a wide array of academic disciplines such as business, communication and media, education, and information technology where more than 90% of instruction is done in English. For this research report the focus is on the 10 participants who took part in the semi-structured interviews.

We received the consent of the 10 students to be interviewed once the aims of the study were explained to them. They were assured of confidentiality and total anonymity. Pseudonyms were used to protect their identities.

They were also guaranteed the right to withdraw from the study and to change their minds about what they said in the interview at the respondent validation stage (Ritchie & Lewis, 2003). The transcribed manuscripts were shared with the participants for confirmation, addition, or deletion of any item of their choice. The purpose of this validation is to provide, as accurately as possible, a real representation of the students' opinions. In addition to these ethical procedures, an ethical research form was completed and sent to the ethics committee to ensure that the research project was conducted according to the University of Exeter ethical regulations. The ten participants are all juniors or seniors pursuing bachelor's degrees in a number of disciplines. The participants, all Emiratis, come from both public and private schools. The secondary school background proved to be an important factor in shaping students' views of EMI at tertiary level.

Semi-structured interviews averaging one hour in length were conducted with the 10 participants in a space of four weeks. Keeping with the tradition of naturalistic research, the semi-structured format allowed us to be both structured and flexible at the same time. This kind of interview has the advantage of keeping the researcher on the agenda of the study while being open-minded to account for spontaneous and emerging themes that respondents are willing to share with the interviewer (Kvale, 2009; Radnor, 2001). To Kvale (2007) the interview is "a uniquely sensitive and powerful method for capturing the experiences and lived meanings of the subjects' everyday world" (p. 11). The main items of the interview were developed from the major constructs in mainstream and critical literature on EMI and learners' experiences. A number of prompts were used to elicit data (see appendix). The nature of the interview allowed for emerging questions to be asked.

*Data analysis*

The interview transcripts were analysed for general content. We followed an exploratory approach using the main aims of the study as a guide for topic ordering and construction of categories, which form the "heart of qualitative data analysis" (Creswell, 1998, p. 144). This thematic organization and subsequent interpretation (Radnor, 2001) were done with a "strategic and technical detachment" approach to the whole process of data analysis (Holliday, 2001, p. 178). Qualitative data analysis was conducted in stages of describing, classifying, and interpreting. The last stage was initially based on textural "the what" and structural descriptions "the how." The essence of the participants' experiences were constructed through "seeking all possible meanings and divergent perspectives, varying the frames of reference about the phenomenon, and constructing a description of how the phenomenon was experienced" (Creswell, 1998, p. 149).

## Results

### EMI and school background

The analysis revealed that the students' primary and secondary school backgrounds and experiences played a significant role in shaping their attitudes towards English in general and using it as a medium of instruction for university subjects. Students who went to private schools where instruction was in English talked of their comfort in studying through English and how it was the normal thing to do as stated by Fatma, "actually I am more comfortable studying these courses in English rather than Arabic. I studied in English my whole life so if I studied these courses in Arabic that will be somehow a challenge." This was echoed by Khadija who explains that "studying in English made more sense to me since I talk in English even at home. It's a benefit for us to study in English because if we want to continue our masters or get a job, most of the places require using the English language." Here a reference is made to the use of English for communication at home, which is increasingly gaining status as a common linguistic and cultural feature in the daily life of a number of Emirati families. Students described how in many families' domestic helpers and child carers hired from some Asian countries speak to Emirati children in English and in many cases r reduce the children's exposure to

Arabic. This was well captured by Maryam who mentions how "there is something that really affect kids. For example kids have nannies, and my nanny talks to me in English since I was a baby, because she didn't know how to talk in Arabic but through living here and living with us she did learn eventually Arabic."

Some parents also play a significant role in creating an Anglophone environment for their children from a very early age. In many cases parents with an awareness of the global role of English and its potential for opening educational and economic horizons for their children, or simply because of cultural trends in modern media and associations between speaking English and discourses of modernity and development encourage English. Arabic, even at home, loses its major role as the mother tongue and the language of one's heritage. While this should not be interpreted as a conscious or a deliberate attempt at marginalizing Arabic, in fact, many parents are aware of the effect of English on their children's Arabic, the obvious result is that these children will grow up thinking English is the natural language to use for both communication and education. Against such a sociocultural background English has gained a major status before children are even introduced to it at school. Arabic on the other hand, is increasingly introduced as a minor subject relegated to the areas of social studies and religion. The following excerpt from Maryam shows how parents' linguistic decisions have affected a child's ability to speak what is naturally supposed to be her first language, "My cousin has a small daughter she talks to her in English all the time so now it's a problem cause her daughter doesn't understand Arabic. But now she started to talk to her in Arabic and she's progressing."

Prior to their transition to university many of the participants were informed by school advisors, and through visits to higher colleges and universities, about the system of education and the language of instruction at the tertiary level. One participant explains her reason for choosing Zayed University: "Well it [English] was one of the reasons that we chose ZU actually. I mean I had the choice of going to either United Arab Emirates University, Zayed University, or Higher Colleges of Technology, and I knew that some of the courses in UAEU are taught in Arabic. Because we've been in private schools we started our education in English and we wanted to continue in the same American system." In the case of these students there was full awareness of the system ahead of them and the kind of linguistic environment they were going to join.

According to one participant from the College of Communication and Media Sciences, in a typical class of 30 students only one third would be from private school background, which implies that the majority of the students experienced a total shift in the medium of instruction at the time of their transition to tertiary education. To address the linguistic and academic needs of students with low English proficiency, a language preparation programme was established with a focus on the major language skills. The aim of such an academic and linguistic provision is to prepare students to join their academic departments where subjects are mostly taught in English. Such programmes are a common feature of tertiary education in the UAE and large numbers of EFL specialists are employed to cater for the students' linguistic needs and provide academic support. The majority of the students in these intensive English programmes come from public school backgrounds, where content subjects were taught in Arabic.

Among the interviewed participants there was a general acceptance and recognition of the international status of English and its role in development, economy, and global communication. Many participants provided realistic and pragmatic reasons for the necessity of EMI as described by Leila in the following excerpt:

> Well in university at this level it's not about just the fact that it's easier for us, and it's more flexible for us to be taught in English because we can express ourselves better. But it is also the fact that at this point you need to know these terms in English because you are going to go to the workforce. The majority of them are not locals. Whether we are in an Arabic country or not. So you need to interact with people who are going to be speaking in English.

Leila's views on the position of English can be seen in light of the English as a lingua franca (ELF) framework which postulates that the changing role of English "seems to be an entirely logical and natural development arising out of new language contact situations in an expanding circle context" (Jenkins, 2007, p. 5). However, this seemingly neutral view of English needs to be balanced against an opposite view that challenges the neutrality of ELF. Working within a broader paradigm of linguistic imperialism and the hegemonic spread of English, Phillipson (2009) prefers to use the term *lingua academica* to refer to the international use of English in higher education. In fact, English is now spreading to primary and secondary schools in a number of countries both in the private and public sectors, as in the case of the UAE. Phillipson challenges the discourse of neutrality and objectivity of ELF and argues that its advocates "falsely assume that the language is neutral, free of all cultural ties and serves all equally well" (p. 338). While questioning and challenging the role English plays in tertiary education, especially in a context like the UAE, is necessary for a balanced analysis of any language of instruction policy, the forces of economic reality and issues of employability remain too strong to ignore. Students are thinking of their careers and self-interest and are well aware of the competitive edge of EMI and the advantage their ability to speak English fluently offers them in the job market.

*Arabic as a medium of instruction*

Views on the possibility and necessity of Arabic as a medium of instruction at the university level varied. Some participants saw no scope for using Arabic to teach content classes in their academic departments and were very clear in their positions vis-a-vis English and Arabic. For them the issue is settled and is not open for reconsideration. Arabic cannot be used because they are more familiar with English and more comfortable with its associated approaches and methodologies. Salwa, one of the participants from a private school background, expressed her realistic and functional view on the issue, "honestly we are against Arabic taught in the university, so I don't know if that's going to help with anything ... because we are used to English, it's much easier to write in English than writing in Arabic ... because we got used to it ... Because we were in private schools, and English is taught in most of our subjects."

Given this kind of educational background of students like Salwa, who come from an English medium private school background, Arabic does not seem to have a role to play at the tertiary level. It will simply hinder the quality of their educational experience and cause too many unwanted challenges. However, this view was not shared by all the participants of the study. In spite of a consensus on the importance of English as a medium of instruction some students lamented the situation of Arabic at the tertiary level and in the wider social environment in general. For some students like Khadija, in addition to being her first language Arabic serves a utilitarian purpose. Thinking of employability in an increasingly competitive job market, Arabic would provide an added edge. She explains this in the following excerpt:

> I think it's a good thing that we are studying in English but again I think that they are doing that on the expense of our own language. I might be more comfortable with English but I still think that we should take courses in Arabic because when we'll graduate we are going to work in the UAE and not all companies use the English language. For instance the government companies use Arabic language, so how am I supposed to work in Arabic if I didn't study in Arabic. I suggest that they add maybe more courses in Arabic instead of just the writing courses in which there is only the Arabic Professional Writing course and the Arabic lab course; those are the only courses taught in Arabic and then there are the three courses in the colloquy and the rest are all in English.

It is obvious that according to Khadija the current curriculum at Zayed University does not provide enough content courses in Arabic. The current provision of Arabic courses is to help the students with their writing and oral skills. It needs to be mentioned that these Arabic courses are a part of the curriculum of the College of Communication and Media Sciences as a response to a need identified by future employers. Available courses are media storytelling in Arabic 1 and 2 for intermediate and advanced, public speaking in Arabic, and media translation workshop. However, such provisions for Arabic courses in other colleges such as Education or Business and Information Technology are nominal and limited to one credit lab courses where the focus is to provide students with equivalent Arabic terminology to the subjects taught in English. Khadija's views were echoed by other participants with similar utilitarian and realistic views. Many have come to the realization that in the job context of the UAE English proficiency is now the norm and Emirati citizens are expected to be proficient in Arabic as well as in English if they are to compete for jobs. Fatma, who is aware of this advantage, describes this need for Emirati Arabic speakers "... but it also gives you an advantage, because again you are the minority this is your country, they need you to know Arabic so that what they can't do, the majority of the workforce, you can do, that is why they hire Emiratis. So it is important." In the UAE, Emirati citizens are indeed a minority as more than 75% of the population is made up of expatriates and English is the main lingua franca among most of the residents of the country. Arabic, therefore has become a rare but necessary commodity in administrations and businesses. Students are now well aware of how Arabic is in demand and many have expressed their concerns about their lack of proficiency in their first language, especially those from an English medium school background. Many bemoaned their inability to write in Modern Standard Arabic, the version of Arabic used for education, and, in some cases, even to speak their local dialect fluently. Some students even called for Arabic preparation courses similar in nature to the current provision under the English Academic Bridge Programme. The following excerpt from Hala illustrates this view, "... but it's not a bad idea having the readiness taken here in Arabic as well. Because readiness here in the university is for people who are weak in English, why not make it for students who are weak in Arabic as well. It's going to be difficult of course, but it will help us." Readiness refers to the language preparation programme that students need to take in order to meet the English admission requirement. Hala is suggesting that a readiness programme in Arabic should be provided to help students with their Arabic.

***

While this is a legitimate academic need identified by a number of students facing major challenges with the academic side of Modern Standard Arabic, it also reflects a larger and more serious issue, which is the quality of the teaching of Arabic in the UAE and the overall proficiency level of Emirati students in their first language. There have been major debates at the ministerial level to put Arabic back on the list of national priorities but there has not been any tangible action at decision making or curricular levels to resurrect Arabic. In fact, while the official discourse recognizes

Arabic as the official and national language and calls for its protection and dissemination, the trend in education is going in the opposite direction, with the continuous spread of English to all levels starting at year one of primary school. For some of the study participants the suggested solution was an obvious need for the improvement of the quality of teaching Arabic at all levels and mainly at university, and the introduction of more Arabic medium content classes. This call for dual language education was made by Arwa:

> We did personally take some courses in Arabic, three courses in Arabic actually, I find them very very useful, I am not advocating English all the time. I think it is important to study in English but at the same time to have these courses that the university has done where you get the terminology translated into Arabic so you know both. I am a strong believer in being bilingual, being totally, having both.

Aysha, another participant, confirms the need for a dual language approach to the curriculum when she describes what can be done in teaching some disciplines.

> I am not against Arabic, and I think there are some courses we need to balance, and study them in Arabic such as the media writing, and that's what they are doing now in the college of communication. I feel that we should take more courses in Arabic. I know that I am weak in Arabic, but still that would help me for later in the future workforce especially in writing.

It is worth pointing out that Aysha went to English-medium primary and secondary schools, but her EMI background did not negatively influence her views about EMI.

*Challenges with EMI and coping strategies*

Data about academic challenges experienced by university students in their pre-college stage and during their specializations confirmed findings in the literature about the consequences of EMI on the quality of the students' learning experiences in content classes. There were major similarities at the level of linguistic challenges observed by Bielenberg (2002) and those recounted by some of our participants. Like most of the students in our study Bielenberg's participants are the product of public school education in the UAE, where Arabic is the medium of instruction. Upon transition to university, the students experienced a total shift in the medium of instruction and consequently a different approach to education entailing new definitions and roles for them. The salient challenges were linked to English language proficiency and the kind of academic skills required to perform well in an EMI environment. Recounting her story of the major efforts she spent on improving her English, Salwa describes how her first two years at university were marked by a struggle to cope with the demands of EMI:

> I graduated from a public school, so that was the challenge because when I took the first English course (English 145), I faced a lot of difficulties and couldn't follow up with my peers, and in the first two assignments I got very low grades but then I started to depend more on myself, and on my readings and also the instructor was taking me on a side, and looking more through my drafts, so that's the way I improved myself. But there was a big challenge for me in writing.

The students' Arabic academic background interfered with their learning of the new mode, a phenomenon observed by Osman (2009). Their major educational schemata and learning experiences are rooted in Arabic and its associated models of learning. This is well captured by the following excerpt from Selma:

> The Arabic language was the base in which I get my ideas from I didn't have a background in English books so I was more into Arabic even when I am writing in English I try to think in English but it's a bit hard not to think in Arabic. I always have the ideas in my head regardless of the grammar mistakes. Before I used to think in Arabic and try to translate my thoughts in English but now I somehow think in both English and Arabic. When I used to think in Arabic and try writing it in English, the outcome was a mess.

EMI did serve as a gatekeeper (Troudi, 2009b) to those who could not meet the challenge of achieving the required English language proficiency to be accepted in some colleges. While this has become an established educational practice in the UAE and increasingly in the Gulf the detrimental effects of EMI policies on students' educational and career choices have largely been ignored. Selma's quote illustrates this point:

> There were girls who faced problems in English even after entering the general programme and that stopped them from entering the communication and media major. They thought that since they were weak in English they wouldn't be able to do well in this major and they chose the Education major given that it may be easier for them. Thus this college uses simple English rather than the advanced English. Other majors like the business major, they use specific terms and have their own world of teaching. I think that at the beginning of entering any major, you'll face some problems but if you try to adapt it will be easier for you to learn while if you didn't you'll be facing problems until you graduate.

The literature abounds with arguments questioning the legitimacy and even the ethicality of language policies that involve exclusionary practices (Abbott, 1992; Hewson 1998; Markee, 2002; Williams & Cook, 2002). Of equal importance is the argument that EMI policies and instruction in a foreign medium is not supported by research and does not guarantee success or equivalent levels of educational achievement as when mother tongue education is in place (Bruthiaux, 2002).

In the case of the current study and the population it represents, students facing academic challenges in their majors, as a result of EMI, resorted to seeking support from available resources put in place by the university. These varied from extra tutorials by lecturers to writing centres. Students also relied heavily on dictionaries to understand main texts in their fields. Students from English medium schools also faced some challenges, but they were not attributed to English proficiency. Those who were "lucky" enough to go to private schools reported their ease with English and how comprehension of content was rarely a problem.

## Discussion

The data showed a clear division in attitudes and experiences between students based on their school background and the medium of instruction. There is a disparity in the quality of experience at university level due to English language proficiency. Perhaps the concept of a 'choiceless choice' best describes the situation of the majority of Emirati students regarding the language of instruction. Being a speaker of Arabic, an Emirati has no choice but to study his/her chosen university subjects in English. This is now a taken-for-granted reality and an uncontested practice in many Arab countries.

If one takes students' experiences into consideration and the argument of students' rights to be taught in their mother tongue (Skutnabb-Kangas, 2009), can EMI continue to prosper and can it avoid the image of English being an oppressive and dominant ideology especially in contexts with apparent differences between the local and the global? We think that in the case of the UAE and the Arab world in general, EMI needs to be engaged in self-criticism. To do so the discipline needs to adhere to some theoretical requirements. For without theorization and without awareness of the role of mother tongue and bilingual education, EMI will continue to alienate the very participants it claims to serve and empower in the first place. These are the students who have no right to choose the language of their instruction. Instead of an over-reliance on received knowledge about the status of English and fashionable trends in international education, educationists in contexts such as the UAE need to consider the quality of the learning experience of the students. Equally important are the effects of an EMI policy on the overall qualification levels of graduates in the workplace and their performance. Evaluation and research studies need to be conducted to investigate these two issues. In addition, principles of scientism were used as a mechanism to rationalize EMI. While this is a recognized strategy in introductions of educational policies there is equally a need for an interpretive and critical approach with qualitative methods to uncover the quality of educational experience under EMI policies. Without a critical approach to issues of education, the nomothetic and at times erroneous nature of the claim to scientific objectivity by educational policies such as EMI will continue to exert a lot of power and influence on the lives of generations of students. An analogy can be drawn to the debate over bilingual education in the US, which at present is still "dominated by positivistic and management models which hide their ideologies behind a demand for objectivity, hard data and scientific rigor" (Macedo, Dandrinos, & Gounari, 2003, p. 69). In fact, the claim to scientificity and neutrality used by proponents of EMI can itself be used by counter-discourses calling for interrogating such an approach. There are, up to now, no empirical studies in the Gulf region which prove that graduates of mother tongue educational programmes are outperformed by those who underwent an EMI model.

Contrary to how it is neutrally and "scientifically" presented EMI is not ideology free. What is missing is a healthy dose of self-criticism, scepticism, and contestation, which are central to the scientific approach, to avoid the fragmentation of bodies of knowledge (Macedo, et al., 2003, p. 76). If and when research studies are conducted, EMI proponents show one side of the picture which serves their ideological agenda (e.g. Jongsma & Jongsma, 2006). When linguistic challenges are mentioned they are reduced to necessary developmental stages in need of pedagogical interventions.

Can we afford to see EMI isolated from issues of socio-cultural and linguistic identity which ultimately shape the students' learning experience at the tertiary level? Neutral and pseudo-empirical discourses in education, especially in matters of language policy, can distort reality. In pursuit of performance, achievement, and employability students' faces are dehumanized and their voices silenced and the result is a distorted reality of the students' learning conditions. A critical reading of this reality is needed so we can engage with the various effects of the EMI policy. Some critical writers like Macedo, Dentrinos and Gounari (2003) warn that the wrong language of instruction policy can cause fractured cultural identities which "usually leave an indelible psychological scar experienced even by those subordinated people who seemingly have 'made it' in spite of all forms of oppression" (p. 77). The participants in this study expressed major concerns about the constant onslaught of English and its potential disastrous effects on Arabic as a language and a cultural symbol. While acknowledging the major role English plays in helping them secure employment and a career, they were aware that this is taking place at the expense of the status of Arabic, which is undergoing a perpetual reduction in its role in their educational experience at the tertiary level. Besides being the symbol of their cultural, linguistic, and religious heritage Arabic was, for the majority, the language of instruction in their first twelve years of primary and secondary education. They have experienced its rapid fall from educational grace and an almost total devaluation at tertiary level. The language of education was not anymore the language of their culture. For educational and pragmatic reasons English was widely embraced and even those who experience language difficulties often manage to seek and find academic support. But this linguistic dualism, which characterizes the situation in the UAE (Findlow, 2006) is fraught with uncertainty and unease. The relationship between English and Arabic is not based on equity or mutual coexistence and harmony. With respect to language use, this relationship remains asymmetrical with English being the dominant force. There are local and regional voices calling for the reassertion of the local and the indigenous in an attempt to resist imperialistic and neo-colonial cultural hegemony (Al-Dhubaib, 2006; Messidi, 2010). This needs to be seen within the wider socio-cultural and political climate in the region and in the aftermath of the recent political conflicts in Iraq and Palestine. In the context of this study the participants and their colleagues translated their dissatisfaction with the status of Arabic into critical action when they organized a university-wide campaign to protect Arabic.

Findlow (2005) describes how a tension between global and local interests has characterized the UAE higher education system. This tension, she argues, "mirrors the global-local tensions that underpin society as a whole, with ideas about 'cultural authenticity' formed in the tension between imitation of and resistance against colonial models" (p. 296). We hope to pursue this issue further in future research to explore the relationship between EMI and students' sense of linguistic and cultural identities.

## Conclusion

Hewson (1998) argues "learning a subject in a second language is particularly difficult when the first language is inherently very different from western-based languages. Specialized terminology, which is not necessarily congruent between the two languages, poses considerable problems for the teachers and significant learning difficulties for the students" (p. 318). This view resonates when applied to many of our study's participants.

However, as demonstrated through the data excerpts used in this study, students have managed to appropriate English to their own needs and utilitarian agendas (Canagarajah, 1999). Their sense of agency was not affected by the powerful status of EMI. In fact, an interesting finding in this study is that those students who did not see a role for Arabic as a medium of instruction did not do so on the basis of a conviction that Arabic was not a language of academia or sciences. They did not compartmentalize Arabic to certain classical domains such as Islamic studies and English to other more current or contemporary subjects like technology and sciences the way Findlow reported in her 2006 study. For our participants, Arabic was not considered an academically inferior language. The issue was more to do with the quality of education the students received in their schools and their language ability and overall comfort with Arabic. It was clear that the way these students were taught Arabic has, to a large extent, shaped their attitudes towards using it for instruction at the tertiary level. While the message of the educational system is that Arabic is not the best conduit for scientific and other academic subjects because of the demands of the global market, the students' stance on the issue is informed by more practical considerations of language proficiency and ability to comprehend and produce academic discourse without major challenges while keeping a realistic check on employability.

This study shows the complexity of EMI policies and some of its effects on students' educational experiences and career perspectives. Further studies are needed to look into how EMI shapes the students' sense of linguistic and cultures identities.

## Acknowledgements

The authors thank the students who volunteered their time for our study and showed a lot of interest in the topic.

## References

Al-Askari, S. (2002). Arabs and the Arabisation of the modern sciences? *Al Arabi*, *508*(3), 8–5.
Al-Dhubaib, A. (2006). *The Arabic language in the era of globalisation*. Riyadh, Saudi Arabia: Obeikan Publishers.
Bruthiaux, P. (2002). Hold your course: Language education. Language choice and economic development. *TESOL Quarterly, 36*(3), 275–296.
Bielenberg, B. (2004). Identifying linguistic challenges for English language learners in mathematics and IT classrooms. In P. Davidson et al. (eds), *Proceedings of the 9th TESOL Arabia Conference: English language teaching in the IT age* (pp. 109–118). Dubai: TESOL Arabia Publications.
Brutt-Griffler, J. (2002). *World English: A study of its development*. Clevedon: Multilingual Matters.
Canagarajah, S. (1999). *Resisting linguistic imperialism in English teaching*. Oxford: Oxford University Press.
Clark, M. (2006). Beyond antagonism? The discursive construction of "New" teachers in the United Arab Emirates. *Teaching Education, 17*(3), 225–237.
Creswell, J.W. (1998). *Qualitative inquiry and research design: Choosing among five approaches*. London: Sage.
Cresswell, J.W. (2009). *Research design: Qualitative, quantitative, and mixed methods approaches*. London: Sage.
Findlow, S. (2005). International networking in the United Arab Emirates higher education system: Global-local tensions. *Compare, 35*(3), 285–302.
Findlow, S. (2006). Higher education and linguistic dualism in the in the Arab Gulf. *British Journal of Sociology of Education, 27*(1), 19–33.

Guefrachi, H., & Troudi, S. (2000). Enhancing English language teaching in the United Arab Emirates. In K. Johnson (ed.), *Teacher education: Case studies in TESOL practice series* (pp. 189–204). Alexandria, Virginia: TESOL Inc.

Hewson, M.G. (1998). The ecological context of knowledge: Implications for learning science in developing countries. *Journal of Curriculum Studies, 20*(4), 317–326.

Holliday, A. (2001). *Doing and writing qualitative research*. London: Sage.

Jenkins, J. (2007). *English as a lingua franca: Attitude and identity*. Oxford: Oxford University Press.

Jongsma, K., & Jongsma, J. (2006). Teaching science and mathematics in English in grade 1 and 2 classrooms in the UAE. *International Journal of Learning, 12*(5), 226–236.

Karmani, S. (2005). Petro-Linguistics: The emerging nexus between oil, English, and Islam. *Journal of Language, Identity, and Education, 4*(2), 87–102

Kvale, S. (2007). *Dong interviews*. London: Sage.

Kvale, S., & Brinkmann, S. (2009). *Interviews: Learning the craft of qualitative research interviewing*. London: Sage.

Macedo, D., Dendiros, B., & Gounari, P. (2003). *The hegemony of English*. Boulder, Colorado: Paradigm Publishers.

Mohamed, I. (2007). Obstacles of medical translation and Arabisation of medicine. In S. Al-Askari (ed.), *The scientific culture and the foreseeing of the Arabic future* (pp. 175–215). Kuwait: Ministry of Information – Al Arabi Magazine.

Messidi, A. (2010). *Towards a new cultural awareness*. Dubai: Ministry of Culture.

Osman, K. (2009). *Emirati nursing students' experiences of studying nursing and science through English*. Unpublished doctoral thesis. University of Exeter.

Pennycook, A. (2003). English in the world/the world in English. In A. Burns & C. Coffin (eds), *Analysing English in a global context* (pp. 78–92). London: Routledge.

Perry, F.L. (2005). *Research in applied linguistics: Becoming a discerning consumer*. London: Lawrence Erlbaum Associates.

Phillipson, R. (2009). English in globalisation, a lingua franca or a lingua frankensteinia. *TESOL Quarterly, 43*(2), 335–339.

Radnor, H. (2001). *Researching your professional practice*. Buckingham: Open University Press.

Ricento, T. (2003). The discursive construction of Americanism, *Discourse & Society, 14*(5), 611–637.

Ricento, T. (2006) (ed.) *An introduction to language policy: Theory and method*. Oxford, UK: Blackwell Publishing.

Ritchie, J., & Lewis, J. (2003). *Qualitative research practice: A guide for social students and researchers*. London: Sage Publications.

Skutnabb-Kangas, T. (2009). What can TESOL do in order not to participate in crimes against humanity? *TESOL Quarterly, 43*(2), 340–344.
Tollefson, J.W. (2007). *Language policy, culture and identity in Asian contexts.* Mahwah, NJ: Lawrence Erlbaum Associates.
Tollefson, J.W., & Tsui, A.B.M. (2004) (eds), *Medium of instruction policies: Which agenda? Whose agenda?* London: Lawrence Erlbaum Associates.
Troudi, S. (2009a). English versus Arabic: Languages for sciences and academia. In B. Beaven (ed.), *IATEFL 2008 Exeter Conference Selections* (pp. 94–96). Canterbury: IATEFL.
Troudi, S. (2009b). The effects of English as a medium of instruction on Arabic as a language of science and academia. In P. Wachob (ed.), *Power in the EFL classroom: Critical pedagogy in the Middle East* (pp. 199–216). Newcastle upon Tyne: Cambridge Scholars Publishing.
Williams, E., & Cooke, J. (2002). Pathways and labyrinths: Language and education in development. *TESOL Quarterly, 36*(3), 297–322.

# Appendix

Semi-structured Interview items:

General introduction: name, where from?
Area of study? Year of study?
Story of English: When did you first learn that you would be studying for your degree in English?
What did you think about it? How did you feel about it?

At the end of your secondary education: did you receive any information about your degree? Whether you would be studying in English or in Arabic?

How would you describe your experience of studying your degree/specialisation in English?

Prompts:
How do you deal with the language of the specialisation?
Any issues of comprehension of lectures?

Any issues of comprehension of materials/ textbooks?
Any issues with writing your assignments in English?
Any challenges in oral activities [participation in class discussion] and presentations?
Any other challenges?
Ease and confidence in English?

When you have difficulties in any of the above areas how do you solve the problem? Can you get help? How?

What about Arabic?
Prompts:
What role does Arabic play in your studies?
Do you think your specialisation can be taught in Arabic?
Do you think scientific subjects can be taught in Arabic?
If you had a choice between studying your specialisation in Arabic or English what you chose? Why?

In general does studying through English have any effect/bearing on Arabic?
What do you speak at home?
Language used in following: internet, social interaction

What does Arabic represent to you?

Your relationship with English? What does English represent to you?

In general what do you think about EMI?

What English variety do you think you are using at your university? American? British? Australian? Are you aware of any other variety?

LYNNE RONESI

3   Who Am I as an Arab English Speaker?
    Perspectives from Female University Students
    in the United Arab Emirates

ABSTRACT

This qualitative study, undertaken at the American University of Sharjah in the United Arab Emirates (UAE), investigates how female university students – undergraduate writing tutors with very strong English proficiency – understand their identity as Arabs and maintain their native tongue of Arabic even as they are immersed in English on a daily basis. This research examines the students' perceptions, in part, through the analysis of their written response to the prompt "Who am I as a writer in English?" This response was a required assignment in a course that prepared these students to be writing tutors at the university. To expand and verify themes identified in the text analysis, interviews were also conducted with the students. Informed by scholarship in critical applied linguistics and second language acquisition and grounded in participants' accounts of family and educational experiences, this study contextualizes the participants' linguistic attitudes and illuminates how they negotiate the discourses and perspectives of Arabic and English to benefit their agency. The students' educational experiences and insights resulted in suggestions for changes in the instruction and promotion of Arabic that would help support its maintenance – a matter of grave importance to these young women even as English dominates their lives – and provided a strong argument for a movement to two-way bilingual education. These are significant considerations for language learning policy in the UAE and for other Arab countries in which English operates as a lingua franca.

## Introduction

"To be bilingual might be my greatest advantage. I have more words now." These simple yet powerful words were taken from a poem by an Arab student endeavouring to answer the question: Who am I as a writer in English? This question was designed to have students, who were strong in English, reflect on their identities as bilingual individuals; it constituted an assignment in a course where students with strong skills in English were being trained to serve as writing tutors at the American University of Sharjah (AUS). Like most universities in the UAE, AUS is an English-medium university. While it is distinguished by its diverse student population from over 80 countries, AUS has a large and varied population of Arab students. In recent years, there has been a growing, well-documented concern that English is replacing Arabic in the UAE (Al Gurg, 2010; Al-Issa & Dahan, 2007; Janardhan, 2007; Sankar, 2009). Many attribute this phenomenon to the presence of a large western and Asian expatriate population who relies on English instead of Arabic as a lingua franca; there is also a perception that English is emphasized over Arabic in schools, thus contributing to a lack of Arabic proficiency among young Arabs. AUS, a campus that mirrors the diversity of the UAE population, seems an optimal context for exploring this issue. This chapter investigates how female university students – writing tutors with very strong English proficiency – understand their identity as Arabs and maintain their native tongue of Arabic even as they are immersed in English on a daily basis. Accounts of participants' family and educational experiences contextualize the participants' linguistic attitudes and illuminate how they negotiate the discourses and perspectives of Arabic and English to benefit their agency. The students' educational experiences and insights resulted in specific suggestions for changes in the instruction and promotion of Arabic that would help support its maintenance – a matter of grave importance to these young women even as English dominates their lives.

## Literature review

Much has been written over the last 20 years about the hegemonistic forces of English in postcolonial countries. In two seminal works that prompted much interest and scholarly work in critical applied linguistics and pedagogy, Phillipson (1992) and Pennycook (1994) identify insidious postcolonial activities which have served to devalue local languages and culture in the interest of promulgating English as a global language. These works shed light on power structures that prevail and influence local language and English policy, direct attention to educational endeavours and language policies that do not benefit postcolonial or periphery communities, and serve to question the benefits of globalized English. Another influential work, Canagarajah's (1999) critical study on Tamil students in Sri Lanka, complicates Phillipson and Pennycook's "macro-societal" approach ... [by examining] how linguistic inequalities are effected, propagated, or played out in instructional contexts in the periphery" (p. 42). Canagarajah's micro-social perspective takes into account the individual within a societal designation, placing periphery students in a more powerful role than that of mere postcolonial subjects by highlighting issues of identity, human agency, and context as important motivators in their linguistic choices and negotiations:

> What post-colonial subjects display is the critical detachment they are able to adopt towards the cultures and communities they inhabit. The position on the hybrid subject situated in the margins of discourse and cultures is therefore creative and radical. Probing the dynamics of one culture from the spectacles afforded by the other, they are able to resist the tendency to be uncritically absorbed into a single cultural or discursive system. (Canagarajah, 1999, p. 183)

Canagarajah's study introduces the notion of *resistance* which suggests that, as hybrid subjects, postcolonial students have the power to "negotiate, alter, and oppose political structures, and reconstruct their languages, cultures, and identities to their advantage" (p. 2). Such students choose to use their local language and English in ways that empower them as they assess which discourse supports their agency best in a particular context. Canagarajah emphasizes the role of context – or *politics of location* (hooks, 1989) – as periphery students understand and evaluate the role of their local language and English in their lives. He argues that the macro-societal approach to understanding the spread of English in postcolonial communities does not validate the experiences of periphery members. "Periphery thinking has to be shaped by its own location" (1999, p. 35).

Other micro-social perspectives have highlighted the interplay of culture, context, agency, identity, and power structures in English language teaching (ELT) both within and outside of postcolonial contexts. Norton's (2000) study of immigrant women in Canada underscores the role of identity on second language acquisition (SLA). Grounding her study in part on social identity theory which characterizes identity as multiple, dynamic, and strategic, Norton posits that language learners *invest* in a particular discourse when they perceive that discourse to be useful in gaining social advantage and enhancing agency.

> The notion of investment ... conceives of the language learner as having a complex social history and multiple desires. The notion presupposes that when language learners speak, they are not only exchanging information with target language speakers, but they are constantly organizing and reorganizing a sense of who they are and how they relate to the social world. Thus an investment in the target language is also an investment in a learner's own identity, an identity which is constantly changing across time and space. (Norton, 2000, p. 11)

In later studies, Norton and colleagues explore the relationship between investment and *imagined communities*. Basing the concept of *imagined communities* on Wenger's (1998) treatment of learning on achieving membership in communities of practice, Pavlenko and Norton (2005) suggest that the choice to engage in a language is driven by the wish to enter a particular social, academic, or professional affiliation. That is, investment in a language is often driven by its perceived ability to provide membership in a desired community, leading to a desired identity (Pavlenko & Norton, 2005). Norton (2001) emphasizes that language instruction should support identity and agency development by facilitating students' access to the imagined communities in which students envision participating.

Fairly recently, these theoretical frameworks have been applied in educational settings in multicultural and postcolonial contexts. Norton and Kamal (2003) studied children at an English-medium Pakistani middle-school. The data, informed by both Canagarajah's (1999) and Norton's (2000, 2001) work, highlighted the importance of "politics of location" to understand how these children, who had experienced much political and social upheaval, perceived English not as hegemonistic but as facilitative for communicating with the world, a connection the children acknowledged as important in pursuing a peaceful future in an imagined community where technology, communication, and religion prevailed. Their Muslim values and their proficiency and respect for their native Urdu was not diminished by their appropriation of English; rather, they invested in both languages as context and agency required. At a postsecondary level, Kim (2003) investigated the effect of English on the identities of Malaysian females enrolled in a Master's degree program at the Faculty of Language Studies. Data, drawing on Norton's notion of investment, revealed that Malaysian English speakers struck a delicate balance between their Malay and English-speaking identities, choosing the language that best supported their agency depending on their purposes within the context. Moreover, the Malaysian participants valued the ability English provided to access other worldviews and to understand their own culture in a more complex way. A similar study in Turkey on prospective English teachers (Atay & Ece, 2009) investigated the impact of English on their sociocultural identities. Participants perceived their identities to be predominantly Turkish but also felt themselves as members of the western world; additionally, they understood and accommodated the differences of the two languages and cultures and felt that such knowledge permitted a more flexible and tolerant worldview which enhanced their personalities.

Over the past decade, research in line with the above theoretical perspectives has highlighted the importance of narrative, introspective, and autobiographical accounts in investigating the interaction between second language acquisition and bilingualism and negotiations of identity, agency, and environment in adult lives (Belcher & Connor, 2001; Koven, 2007; Pavlenko, 2006; Pavlenko & Lantolf, 2001). Extending this notion to multilingual and multicultural educational contexts, Grimshaw and

Sears (2008) advocate relying on personal narrative and an "interpretive and qualitative" (p. 273) approach to studying the identity negotiations of expatriate children, known also in the literature as global nomads and sometimes as "third culture kids" (Tokuhama-Espinosa, 2003). Arguing that since "movement was a defining feature in the lives of global nomads ... an appropriate research methodology would be one that traced the trajectory of the participants' lives and accounted for the strategies of identity management that they developed along the way" (Grimshaw, 2008, p. 272). Many postcolonial societies feature an expatriate workforce, and their "third culture kids" figure prominently in the educational settings.

## Context of the study

The United Arab Emirates (UAE) is such a society. Once known as the Trucial States, a protectorate of England, the UAE gained independence and achieved nationhood in 1971. As the people indigenous to the UAE – known since 1971 as Emiratis – were few in number and largely uneducated, the new oil-rich government undertook importing foreign labour to build an infrastructure. Due to the large number of expatriates, the Emirati population is a small percentage of the inhabitants. As the workforce is international and a large number come from Asian and western countries, English has become a lingua franca in the UAE. Nonetheless, a significant number of expatriates come from many Arab nations, and are generally educated professionals. These Arab expatriates generally settle in the UAE for several years and raise families here. Most of these professionals want their children to learn Arabic, but for many Arab families the most the viable options are English-medium schools, largely because many Arabic-medium schools are limited to UAE citizens, but also because these families are keen to have their children master English (Al-Issa & Dahan, 2007). Moreover, the tertiary institutions in the UAE are English-medium, and often students from Arabic-medium schools find admission, and subsequently, academic success difficult due to their lack of English proficiency. Burden-Leahy (2009), commenting on the English-based and western-style curriculum of the UAE universities, observes, "this choice by the UAE government appears to be based on the principle of modernization, of recognizing higher education as a nation-building tool and out of respect for the achievements of the western education model" (p. 532). The need for UAE universities to teach in English was recently reconfirmed by Sheikh Nahyan Bin Mubarak Al Nahyan, Minister of Higher Education and Scientific Research, largely in response to a proposal by the Federal National Council (FNC) to make Arabic the medium of instruction in state universities (Nahyan: English to stay as medium of instruction in varsities, 2009). Yet, the proposal of the FNC echoes the well-documented concerns that Arab language, culture, and identity are losing their foothold in the UAE (Al Gurg, 2010; Al-Issa & Dahan, 2007; Janardhan, 2007; Sankar, 2009) given the prevalence of English in terms of education, commerce, media, tourism, and technology.

Thus informed and motivated by the above-mentioned theoretical perspectives and research, this investigation was undertaken to shed light on the *politics of location*, and sought to understand how Arab students in the UAE understand and evaluate the role of their local language and English in their lives. This chapter investigates the following question: How do female Arab university students in the UAE, who are strong in English, interpret their ability in terms of their identity, native tongue, and culture?

## Participants

The participants were 10 bilingual female Arab students enrolled at AUS who had taken a Writing Tutors class in a prior semester. It is noteworthy that students who enrol in the Writing Tutors class were recommended by their freshman composition professors on the basis of their talent in

English writing, their interpersonal skills, and their diligence. While my initial intention was to study both men and women, even as only three men met the requirements as outlined above, I learned that one male student had transferred to a university in the United States and another had graduated, leaving only one man. While disheartened at what I considered a limitation, I made the decision to include only female students in the investigation. However, noting the young women's immense enthusiasm at the gendered nature of the study, I began feeling that this imposed limitation was rather an opportunity to investigate an unrepresented group in this research area. Indeed, as Burton (1994) – drawing from Edwards – points out, when assessing the impact of a colonial language on the fate of a local language and identity, attention must be paid to the women's experience: "[Not only is] women's experience with bilingualism ... likely to be different from that of men, [but also] these differences can be significant for the fate of minority languages because of women's role as mothers" (p. 2). Moreover, Arab women in Arab countries have received little empirical research attention in terms of bilingualism and identity.

The 10 participants, all between the ages of 19 and 21 years, were Arab females who classified themselves as belonging to one, two, and in some cases three of the following nationalities: American, Qatari, Canadian, Egyptian, Emirati, Jordanian, Palestinian, and Syrian. They represented a variety of majors in the College of Architecture, Art and Design, College of Engineering, and College of Arts and Sciences. These young women were some of the academically strongest students at the university and most, in addition to being writing tutors at AUS, were involved in extracurricular cultural associations, as often officers as members; additionally, over the years, a number of them had represented AUS in various capacities in regional or international competitions (i.e., Model UN, Festival of Thinkers, etc.). In this study, participants' autobiographical data underscored the influence of family and educational experience on the participants' negotiations of identity, culture, and languages. As insight into these areas provides a basis for understanding the complex interplay between these facets of the participants' lives, brief biographies of the participants follow. Participants' names – along with some minor details – were changed to maintain their anonymity.

## 3 Who Am I as an Arab English Speaker?

Four participants were Gulf Cooperation Council (GCC) citizens who had grown up in their own countries. Nour and Dana are citizens of the UAE. Nour, a design major, had attended either British or American schools all her life. Dana, majoring in civil engineering, had attended a private school for children from Gulf countries which taught social sciences and humanities in English, and math and sciences in Arabic. The other two Gulf citizens are Qatari: a mass communications major, Zeinab, who was taught exclusively in American schools, and a computer science major, Nauf, who bounced between English-medium and Arabic-medium schools throughout her primary and secondary instruction.

The other participants could be characterized as global nomads (Grimshaw & Sears, 2008). Three grew up in Arab countries that were not their own. Daliya, a design major, is an Egyptian who was born and raised in the UAE and studied in an English-medium school; Lama, a Palestinian, was a mass communications major who was also born and raised in the UAE; she attended American and British schools. A chemical engineering major, Rawan is a Jordanian who grew up in Saudi Arabia on a compound inhabited by mostly American and British families and was sent to an American school. The last three participants had spent a great deal of their lives in North America. Sidra, international studies major, was born in Syria, grew up in the United States, and attended a US Islamic school that taught Arabic as a subject before she moved to the UAE as a teenager and attended an American school. Layla, a Palestinian-Jordanian-American, was born in Kuwait, and lived seven years in the United States before moving to the UAE as an adolescent and attending American school. She is a mass communications major. Like Layla, Amal is a Palestinian whose family lived in Kuwait until the Gulf War forced them to return to Jordan. From Jordan, the family spent eight years in Canada before moving to Dubai.

## Data collection and analysis

Following the approach of all the above-mentioned research, this study was qualitative in nature. Data analysis revolved around text and interview review. The texts were course assignments responding to the question "Who Am I as a Writer in English?" which participants had submitted while enrolled in the Writing Tutor course. This is the first of several exploratory writing assignments in the course and requires students to respond to the question in a genre of their choice (i.e., poem, narrative, short story, essay). This assignment is due by the third week of the Writing Tutor course, by which time students have read works by multicultural and multilingual authors addressing their relationship with English communication and writing. The students' responses were analysed for information pertaining to English writing as affected by identity, first language, family, cultural, and educational issues. Participants were then e-mailed their assignments to re-read shortly before their interview with the understanding that part of the interview would address different aspects of their response. Semi-structured interviews were conducted over the course of six weeks, and each interview lasted between 60 and 90 minutes. All interviews began with the autobiographical question "How did you become bilingual?" as advocated by Grimshaw and Sears (2008). After that, each participant was asked to clarify and elaborate on selected parts of her written response to the course assignment, particularly those aspects mentioned above. To ensure data was accurate and available for iterative review, each interview was digitally taped and transcribed. The written assignment response and interview data provided an expanded context for interpreting the participants' perceptions, creating a sound basis for a response to the research question. Data reduction entailed data display, iterative examination, code generation, and conclusion drawing. To further insure the trustworthiness of the research, participants were asked to read the preliminary findings in order to ascertain whether their ideas were represented accurately.

## Findings

*Family and education in the maintenance of Arabic identity and language: Spoken Arabic*

A clear theme throughout the data was the influence of parents particularly, and to some degree, extended family, in the maintenance of Arabic identity and language. Participants indicated that at least speaking, and often, reading in Arabic were emphasized by parents. It is notable that the three participants who grew up in North America – Sidra, Layla, and Amal – had family policies about not speaking English in the home – and were strongly encouraged to read in Arabic.

> My parents always stressed, "You have to read Quran, you have to learn this and that." The importance of [maintaining Arabic language and identity] came mostly from my family. My family kept reminding me of how important it is to not lose your language and not lose your culture and not lose where you came from. At the end of the day, we are Canadian but we are also Arab. We were Arab first and we're Arab – that's the most important thing (Amal).

Many participants observed that their parents were disdainful of Arab families who spoke English to each other, as Lama, who grew up in the UAE, recalls.

> I remember my mom asking my older sister to always speak in Arabic with me, which is something we do now, naturally. But she [warned us], "Don't use English [at home]" because outside of my house, it's all English. With my siblings, my mom made sure that [we did not speak in English at home], because she saw it with the daughters – the kids of her friends – and she hated it. She [maintained], "Your language is your identity. We are Arabs. We should speak Arabic. Period." So she was very ticked off at her friends and asked them, "What you think? You're cool because you can speak English to your kids?"

And even those parents who were reported as more relaxed in the home about language use – like Nour's mother – were insistent that their daughters "rise to the occasion" in Arabic in public or more extended family venues.

> It's just this thing where if you don't speak English, then that's not good for you because that means you haven't been properly educated and that means you're not going to get a good job and so on. But then, if you speak good English like we do and it comes at the expense of your Arabic, (Nour humorously lowers voice to dramatic whisper) you're never going to get married. ... Like, if we're going to visit my mother's relatives, [my mom] says this thing – the literal translation is "Don't twist your tongue." And what she means is, "Don't talk in English."

In general, participants spoke mostly Arabic at home, often with friends, and they were able to negotiate in Arabic when needed. They were, overall, fairly satisfied with their verbal skills. For participants, speaking in Arabic is strongly linked to expressing their Arabic identity, narrowing the breadth of life down to a comfort zone where common understandings and perceptions are shared with near and dears. Zeinab and Daliya touch on this notion as they explain their feelings about Arabic in relation to English:

> Well, English is such a broad language and it breaks through different cultures but, I think for me, to be able to speak Arabic narrows it down, gives me some sort of identity. It's the connection for me with my ancestors, the land, history – that kind of thing, which is really, really important for me. Like, if I didn't know Arabic and my grandfather or great-grandfather came back to life, he'd probably have a heart attack and I'd probably lapse into one as well. I've always tried to make the family proud and I felt that that was one of the ways that I'd be able to achieve it (Zeinab).
> Talking in Arabic you tend to draw on all these different references that are so exclusive to the culture and they're so funny and they're entertaining and they're smart and it's such a pleasure being able to talk like that to someone who shares that with you. English has a different kind of humour, but in Arabic I get to tap into something that is part of a cultural identity that really connects everything in the family and everything in Egypt – it begins to come together when you start speaking like that (Daliya).

## Written Arabic

While speaking in Arabic is meaningful in terms of their investment in their cultures, reading and writing in Arabic does not appear to have the same meaning for them, even as many of the Muslim participants mentioned the importance of being able to read the Quran. While all participants can read and write Arabic at varying levels, they all feel that their levels in reading and writing are lower than those in English. Additionally, most participants rarely engage in sustained reading and writing in Arabic – an admission that was often accompanied by a sense of guilt. Nearly all of the participants attended English-medium primary and secondary schools and many studied only Arabic, Islamic studies, history and geography in Arabic. That, and the fact that all are currently immersed in English as university students in an English-medium university cannot be overlooked as significant factors in their lack of engagement with written Arabic. However, data illuminated additional issues influencing this situation. The participants felt that caretakers of Arabic – educators, scholars, and government officials – had not done their duty by the language and its learners and had failed to nurture and promulgate Arabic in pedagogically-sound ways. This, too, had contributed to a situation whereby participants could not negotiate in written Arabic at the same level as in English.

Sidra reports that her parents have identified a gap in early-learning materials in Arabic which they and a group of concerned educators are seeking to fill:

> My dad is involved in a project with a company that is trying to start up home-grown Arabic cartoons. The people that started that company realized that Arabic kids really don't have any sort of foundational Arabic programs that can initiate them into their own culture. Any cartoons we have are basically American or Japanese translated into Arabic. My mom is working on a [related] project where they're trying to take the cartoon characters in my dad's project and create all sorts of written materials for kids. There are a lot of things like that in English but I haven't seen anything like that in Arabic and apparently the people who have done research on this project have not seen anything like that either. To find something really good quality and authentically, 100% Arab – that is rare. From my own experience in terms of seeing, like, my little cousin's library at home – what's going on at home, what books they have and stuff, pretty much everything's in English, or it's translated into Arabic. There isn't that foundational stuff [to teach beginner Arabic] for younger kids.

Layla corroborates Sidra's observations as she recounts the opportunities she had to read in English in the US compared to her younger brothers' opportunities to read in Arabic in the UAE:

> So, libraries are everywhere [in the US] and you can just go and borrow books and you can borrow up to 20 books, and that's what I used to do. And then we had so many activities that encouraged us to read – the accelerated reader, for example, [where] you would read a certain amount of books and then you would answer questions on a computer and then if you got a certain amount of points then you can go to a field trip or something. Yes, there are libraries here [in the UAE]. They're very small.

Dana compares the texts of her English and Arabic classes:

> I used to enjoy English classes more because they were kind of more interactive. The English textbook itself was more interactive – the questions and everything [whereas] in Arabic it was – the text was shorter and it was a story that you already read or something that you already know and you use the text but you don't interact with it. In the English texts, they update the versions. Like every [few years] you have edition one, then edition two. But, for Arabic, it's like what I studied, my sister studied, my brother will study it and maybe by older cousin has studied it before. So, it's like you don't even have to open the book, you can hear it from your cousin, even your friends from different schools.

Nour corroborates Dana's complaint about the lack of currency in Arabic texts: "My sister who is 11 years older than me studied the same thing I studied. The books have not changed. There are mistakes in the print of the book that were not even fixed in the reprint, because nobody cares."

Dana observes: "I think even when you open the Arabic book, you can feel that not much effort was put into it." She adds,

> I would ask the Ministry for Arabic books with content that we can actually discuss. As it is, we don't read about writers – modern writers, or anything about modern life. [The content is] like something very basic. It's very specific, very simple. You just read it. That's it. And it doesn't broaden your perspective – your horizon – about any topic (Dana).

Like Dana, Nauf feels that Arabic language instruction focuses too much on history. While she acknowledges historical knowledge is important, she advises also "push[ing] the modern, just to cover both issues.... [The curriculum could actually provide knowledge about] the culture but show [students] the real world, the world they're living in right now. That would help balance the Arabic instruction."

Zeinab extends the comparison of English and Arabic classes to classroom activities:

> Arabic was like you sit down, listen to the teachers talk for an hour, write down notes, copy off the board, do your homework – or at least get someone to do it for you – bring it back, she gives you an A. All good. [On the other hand,] English had a lot more interaction in class. The teacher was always asking us for our opinions, and we'd have different activities [where] she'd relate the lesson to real life; whereas, Arabic was just, "Here's the book. Here's the assignment. Do it." It was a lot more dry.

Lama wishes she had had a better foundation in Arabic in her early years in terms of books and teachers:

> The government, the Ministry of Education, gives out the same books in Arabic, Islamic studies, and history and geography to all the schools, so it just depends on the teacher, and the students' absorption of everything. My Arabic teachers weren't that great. They didn't really care about Arabic as much as they cared that you do well in math and English. [For example,] they'd [decide], "Okay, Lama is not a very good reader in Arabic." Alright. But they wouldn't encourage me to read more. They'd just give me the standard thing. Every student reads five sentences no matter what level they are. Of course, I would imagine that if a student is weak in something, the teacher kind of helps to strengthen it. But I didn't have that and I think that that would have helped me a lot.

The participants perceived that their instruction in Arabic writing did not teach them argumentation or challenge them to use critical thinking skills. Nauf, whose writing voice in English is passionate and crackles with an incisive wit, feels she has no such similar voice in Arabic:

> It's just [that] I was trained to argue in English; I wasn't trained to argue in Arabic. I think that's the main thing. I know how to argue in English but in Arabic, it's just basically sweet talk. If I want to defend myself – defend anyone else – I have to switch to English. I can't do that in Arabic. It would just sound like – I don't know – a six-year old trying to convince someone.

Participants indicated that even advanced Arabic writing instruction was limited to description, and that students were not encouraged to explore topics from a critical stance or engage a variety of viewpoints.

> Like, for in Arabic [writing class], there's always these classic themes. They're always brought up again and again, for example, West versus East – that kind of thing. Like, if I go into a test [and I am asked] to comment on one of these things, the teachers expect you to go with the majority of the view. "Oh, the West exploits the East. The East wants to preserve its culture. The West is infiltrating it." So if you just have that argument in mind when you go into a test, you'll be okay. Whereas in English, any topic can come up and it can go either way. I think [that in English writing instruction] there's just more freedom for you to express what you really believe, not just restating things that are already perceived to be the truth (Zeinab).

Among participants, there was often a sense of inaccessibility about written Arabic. Nauf, one of the participants who had fairly in-depth instruction in Arabic, concludes, "You can never be a scholar in Arabic in my level. So I am able to talk and write in Arabic in an adequate way, not a perfect or scholarly way. I don't think anyone these days can write real Arabic." Nour points out that even if she wants to read and write in Arabic, information in Arabic feels much less easily obtainable than in English.

> If I needed to write a research paper in Arabic, I know I wouldn't be able to because there are few sources available. I mean, in English, you just type it in Google and you get like a million hits for any topic. In Arabic, you're not going to find anything because people don't bother to even post it on the internet. There aren't as many databases or journals or magazines or books or any kind of resources. Wikipedia has pages in Arabic but you look at the English page and it's huge and you click on the part that says *al-'Arabiyya*, the Arabic equivalent, it's like [only] a paragraph.

Nour wonders why the many Arab professors at the university do not publish in Arabic, citing a singular example of a photography professor who recently published the same book in Arabic that he had published in English the previous year. "Whatever [our Arab professors] are researching, they just publish it in English. Well, why aren't they publishing it in Arabic as well?"

Nour's question about Arab professors who do not publish in Arabic may seem naïve to academics who understand that tenure and promotion rely on the publication of scholarship in internationally-recognized journals which, due to globalization, are mostly in English. However, her question is an incisive and important one providing insight as to why participants are less invested in written Arabic. It is clear that participants in this study understand the following to be true: considerably less is published in Arabic than in English; their Arabic language instruction did not challenge and motivate them in the same way as their English instruction; and, in view of the literacy skills required to be a thoughtful and active participant in the twenty-first century, their Arabic instruction did not adequately prepare them. In general, even as participants praise Arabic writing and literature for its beauty, nuance, depth, and complexity, they feel that their grasp of written Arabic is adequate for their purposes, and do not invest in written Arabic to the same degree that they do in spoken Arabic.

*Agency and context in the maintenance of Arabic language and identity: The role of Arabic*

Participants have made conscious decisions to preserve – and even improve – their spoken Arabic and to engage in maintaining an Arab identity in ways that made sense to them in their linguistically and culturally complex lives. While many Arabs have expressed fear that Arab culture in the UAE is weakened by the large number of non-Arabs living in the country and the widespread use of English, participants indicated that the existence of various Arab communities therein – which include friends, family, fellow students, professors, among other groups – provide context and support for investing in Arabic and Arab identity, even as they are immersed in English every day. Exposure to these communities triggers a sense of belonging, the key to which is a common language.

Since they have moved to the UAE from North America, Amal and Layla have come to feel a stronger sense of Arab identity and an increased interest in improving their Arabic. Clearly, in the UAE context, Amal and Layla felt a keener need to engage their Arab identity, and invested in spoken Arabic as a means to do so:

> [When I first arrived to the UAE from Canada] – because I wear a *hijab* and because I look Arab – people would speak to me in Arabic and [as I couldn't understand,] they would think I was stupid. I was embarrassed. [This no longer happens to me]

> because I made a decision that I wanted to learn Arabic. And I made a lot of friends who spoke Arabic and then I would ask them to speak Arabic to me and if I didn't understand something, I would ask them, "What does this mean?" So in the past four years now, I've made big improvements. My spoken Arabic is almost fluent and very rarely do I find I don't understand someone (Amal).
>
> A lot of people don't even realize that I grew up in America because now I speak in Arabic with a lot of my friends. I didn't used to do that when I first moved to the Middle East. And now I do feel very attached to my Arabic culture and language... At home, whereas [in the US] I used to want to speak in English with my parents, now I actually enjoy speaking in Arabic with them. I like having that common language between my parents and me even though I'm one-hundred percent sure that if I speak in English, they will understand me (Layla).

Rawan, even though a bit more reticent than the other participants to speak in Arabic due, in part to "[her] funny accent," acknowledges sprinkling her conversations with sentences and phrases in Arabic when she speaks with Arabs – even her professors – to acknowledge the common bond between them.

Even though she grew up in the UAE, Daliya who, a few years earlier, felt more comfortable in English, finds herself speaking more and more Arabic: "I used to communicate in English with friends, but because most of my studio friends are Arabs, I began to get a sense that [speaking in English to them] might be creating a barrier." Yet, while she enjoys weaving in and out of Arabic and English with Arab and non-Arab friends at the university, Daliya is clearly opposed to using English in her visits to her family in Egypt:

> If I insist on not [using] Arabic to communicate better and expect [my family in Egypt] to understand English, I'm really creating barriers. The responsibility falls back to me. If I want to communicate well, I must speak Arabic. If you go back home and you're talking to your family in English, [they might assume] "Oh, she's high and mighty now." My own family doesn't take great offense to [my occasional use of English], but at the same time I feel like it's a barrier. Like, just get over yourself and speak in Arabic.

Nauf has a policy of "balance" and maintaining the integrity of both Arabic and English by not mixing the two languages:

I'm glad because I know I can balance [the two languages]. I'm not going to go to my dad and talk to him in English. Because we're Arabs, we have to communicate in Arabic. But if, in some situations, I need to use English, I need to use English. I have them both; I should use them in the situations I need. I don't mix my Arabic and English words together. Both of them have an important impact in my life and I have to use both of them in the situations I feel it's best for them to be used in.

Yet, Arabic and English are often mixed in the UAE, especially when it comes to commerce. Earlier in the year, the university had invited a Lebanese typographer, Pascal Zoghbi, to lecture and give workshops to design students. Zoghbi explained that, typically, when Arab designers are given a project for a bilingual sign or publication, they first develop the company's name in a Latin font and then create the Arabic counterpart. Most often, the Arabic font is created by cutting out pieces of the English lettering, with little regard for the integrity of traditional formation of the Arabic letters. This practice makes the Arabic words distorted and hard to read.

"Why is it that the Arabic needs to be changed to fit the Latin?" protested Nour, who had attended Zoghbi's lectures. "If I create a specific logo for a government organization, why don't I keep the Arabic the way it is and try to do something with the English to make it work with the Arabic?"

Displaying resistance (Canagarajah, 1999), Nour wants to work to release Arabic fonts from the hegemony of English, and has made it a career goal to break with this tradition by placing Arabic script at the forefront of her design work: She asserts, "Design is never fixed. You can create your own aesthetics, create your own discourses, and set your own standards and rules. As designers, we're taught to take risks. Well, this is the kind of risk I think I should take."

## The role of English

An important emerging theme in the data was the participants' use of English in negotiating an Arab identity tailored to their own specifications. Participants are conscious of stereotypes and negative perceptions of Arabs and, in an act of resistance, invest in the opportunity speaking and writing English provides to undermine parochial thinking about Arabs, relishing the opportunity to express themselves as *real* Arab women to the world. Some participants remarked on this phenomenon as a minor, though gratifying occurrence in daily life. Zeinab, for example, notes that she challenges stereotypes simply by meeting new people:

> Well for one thing, my family, in general – there's a stereotype that they try to be very Arab, Arab, Arab, Arab. So when [professors and other Arabs] see my last name, they [make assumptions about me]. When they hear how well I speak English, that's very shocking for them! Also, my writing catches them off-guard and so that means a lot for me because it's not my language.

Other participants discussed similar incidents with further-ranging implications. An event of some significance for Nour was the reaction she elicited from some of her fellow attendees at an international design workshop in France last year. After spending a few weeks interacting with designers from a number of different countries, Nour was told the following by an American participant: "You speak English so well! Whenever we see someone with *hijab* on TV, this is not what we see. We would expect that you would be very restricted and very limited and it's not like that at all."

Lama reports a similar experience when she travelled to a conference in China with her professor.

> There were people from all around the world and they were just completely shocked that I was a Muslim Arab who had a voice, who could talk, who had a personality, and not just some shot-down, embarrassed, afraid kind of little thing. And I told them that we're just girls like every other place. I mean, I would love more opportunities like that to represent Arabs. And the moment they saw my openness to discuss and explain issues, they were coming at me with questions about Islam, about Arabs, about the Middle East and about Palestine, and I loved it. Because I felt like I was doing what my duty is.

Lama's duty, as she sees it, will extend to other venues in the future. She wishes to reach out to the world via her writing, "so it's not just interaction with people, it's also getting [a better perception of Arabs] out without moving from my seat." To these participants, their English-speaking and Arabic selves are integral parts of their imagined communities (Norton, 2001). Amal and Layla have similar goals as Lama, but as future journalists. Layla notes:

> We have a lot of books about Arabs in Arabic. We have a lot of books about great people, great Arabs. We have a lot of books about Arab problems. But we don't have a lot of Arab writers who write about Arab problems from an Arab point of view in English. And the information about Arabs in English is biased and it's not really good for Arabs. It's not something that really gives the Arab point of view. So that is where I see myself in the future.

One participant who is already reaching out to the world with her writing is Sidra, a gifted writer in English who started publishing her writing while still a teenager. For several years, Sidra has had a bi-monthly contract with a magazine to write articles on Arab and American foreign policy issues, and she also writes a blog which addresses Arab and American themes.

> But this semester, I've stopped so much blogging and instead I'm trying to write some fiction dealing with Arab Americans, or with Arabs, or with Americans views of the Arab world – something along those lines. They are stories in English, and I find it so interesting to try and incorporate Arabic into these stories and dialogue. I really find pleasure in showing these two cultures together because they are, in a way, two cultures pitted against each other politically now. There are problems that America has with the Middle East – particularly the Arab world – and I like showing these two cultures in a way that is non-confrontational or in a way that might be challenging, but [which demonstrates that] those challenges can be overcome. [I want to show] there are people – and I feel that I am one of those people – who live both cultures and bring together both cultures and it's not impossible. And I think what I try to show in these stories is that we're all human. And that yeah, I speak this funny language, Arabic, with my mom or, yeah, I listen to this weird music that my parents really don't like, but I am both of these worlds, and they are both everything to me.

## *Arabic, English, and expanded identities*

Sidra's real and fictional worlds, where both ideologies and both discourses are expressed and negotiated, are more expanded and complex than the world of a monolingual speaker of either English or Arabic. Participants expressed similar attitudes towards their bilingual lives. Even though most participants acknowledged that their primarily English education had resulted in a higher proficiency in English than in Arabic, they perceived their bilingualism as an expansion in agency and identity – not a diminishment. Participants expressed this notion in a variety of ways, but all shared the sense that they were – and would be – enriched by having access to both languages, both mindsets, and their attending characteristics. In considering how English and Arabic affect her thought processes, Daliya marvels about how they seem to work in concert.

> It's strange because I'll be thinking something in English and then the next minute I'll be thinking something in Arabic and they both move together at the same time and I don't feel any sort of conflict. I don't feel any sort of confusion. Maybe the reason I feel the need to move in between is because I feel one sort of covers something that the other doesn't. Really they complement each other in some way. They *don't* conflict with each other. They *don't*. (Daliya's emphasis) I make a distinction between Arabic and its assumptions and the way of thinking that comes with it. And English and its assumptions and the way of thinking that come with it. And maybe I know how to manage both well and that's why they're seamless. Maybe it's just in the way I manage them. I guess it all comes down to how aware you are of the language.

In more specific terms, Rawan notes that the protocols in Arabic speaking, which vary depending on the age and status of the person one greets, are cognitively more demanding than in English and "teach you to how to be perceptive and to understand others from their actions or words." In her estimation, negotiating the various demands of two disparate languages like Arabic and English makes one better able to cope with the complexity of life. Similarly, Lama perceives that her competence in her internship is enhanced by her ability to access both languages and mindsets:

> Being an Arab is important here in the media industry because the people who are selling their thoughts, the TV networks, are Arab and so we have to communicate and negotiate in Arabic. And our ads, for example, have to be in the lifestyle of an Arab for our Arab market, and it actually helps me to be part of that market, too. I speak in Arabic mostly but there are a lot of Asians and my boss is from New York. So, I get to speak both [languages]. And it's cool.

Amal is grateful that she understands two groups of people who are understood as being polemic and sees that this ability will be invaluable in her career as a journalist.

… 3 Who Am I as an Arab English Speaker? 71

> When someone talks about a certain thing or argues a certain thing, I can see it from many different perspectives as opposed to just one. And I'm glad for that. For example, [it's clear that Arabs and westerners] don't really see eye-to-eye. The western people will say, "How can these people have their daughters living with them until they're married? That's why their women are so dependent," and all of that. And the Arabs will say, "How can they let their daughters go out on the streets dressed like that?" But I can see both points of view and I understand both. I really feel like it's a very positive thing in regards to journalism because Arab journalists and Arab media always want the western point of view so I have that. But at the same time, I can write English and offer the Arab point of view as well so it's very good to have both.

## Discussion

This study investigated how female university students – writing tutors with very strong English proficiency – understood their identity as Arabs and maintained their native tongue of Arabic even while immersed in English on a daily basis. It was clear from the data that these students felt strongly about their Arab identity despite the wide use of English in the UAE, constant exposure to western thought and images, and their English-medium education. Their sense of identity was strongly linked to parental support and promotion of their culture and language – insistence that Arabic be spoken at home, encouragement for reading, engagement of Arabic tutors, and, for some, participation in community Islamic classes. The participants' attachment to their language and culture was most demonstrated by the participants' emphasis on both maintaining and, in some instances, working to improve their spoken Arabic. To the participants, *amiya*, the term for the spoken Arabic used in daily discourse, was understood as the primary means by which they remained grounded in their culture, through language steeped with meaning and local understandings that linked them and their interlocutors in a unique bond reflecting family, religion, tradition, history, humour – all the aspects that make them Palestinian, or Egyptian, or Emirati – or more broadly, Arab.

Yet, despite parental emphasis on Arabic and the participants' own engagement with the spoken language, participants understood their Arabic knowledge to be incomplete in terms of their proficiency with written or scholarly Arabic. Data highlighted the dilemma that Arab parents face when choosing schools for their children in the UAE. The lack of emphasis on English at Arabic-medium schools reduces students' chances for admission and success in the UAE's English-medium postsecondary institutions; however, Arabic instruction offered to children enrolled in English-medium schools was characterized by a weak curriculum and poor pedagogical practices. Subsequently, participants were less able, and, therefore, less motivated to practice or engage with written Arabic in a scholarly or professional way – an attitude reinforced by the perception that written Arabic did not figure prominently in professional life. While the participants believed their proficiency in written English to be sufficient for their futures, they understood that in contexts where the use of written Arabic, and to some degree, formal spoken Arabic, would be critical for civic or professional participation, they – even as intelligent young women – would have a more limited voice.

In evaluating these circumstances in terms of the globalization of English, participants did not feel that the English language had impinged upon their Arabic language, but that custodians and educators of Arabic had failed them: "So they just [neglected] the beauty of the actual language and the skills they could teach us, and they just taught us the bare minimum." This view – and many of the participants' specific points regarding poor pedagogical practices, poorly trained and paid Arabic teachers, uninspiring texts, lack of presence on the internet, scarcity of research and resources published in Arabic – are corroborated in several different treatments concerning the promotion of Arabic language and knowledge (Knowledge & Human Development Authority, 2009; Sankar, 2009; United Nations Development Programme, 2003; Watson, 2004). It seems clear that the current approach to Arabic instruction and the subsequent lack of investment in written Arabic, as perceived and expressed by the participants, does not promote the use of Arabic as a vibrant and viable language of communication in the twenty-first century.

Nonetheless, as participants revealed, being Arab and using English in many parts of their lives did not constitute a contradiction; these young women saw themselves as Arabs who could use English to express themselves, even their Arab selves, and reported engaging in acts of resistance to undermine entrenched ideas about Arabs. Moreover, English and its associated assumptions and mindsets did not encroach on and subvert their identity as Arab women; instead, data indicated these young women "challenge the negative subject positions offered by [English] by appropriating ... and infusing [English] with their own values to serve their interests and aspirations" (Canagarajah, 1999, p. 183). As feminist postcolonial scholar Hasna Lebbady (2004) points out, "it is by getting inside [English] that [Arabs] can begin to take a more active role in [their] own representation, which need no longer be a matter of simple exclusion and opposition to the 'West'" (p. 13).

Moreover, this study illuminates the role of investment and imagined communities (Norton, 2000, 2001) in language learning and language choice. Data illustrated how participants invested in those aspects of their two languages that supported their agency and identity; additionally, this study extends the notion of investment – which has been traditionally applied to second language learning – to first language use and learning. Participants demonstrated how those aspects deemed as agency-enhancing in one's first language – in the case of our participants, spoken Arabic – or not, as in written Arabic – can be developed or abandoned. Yet, as features of the participants' professional and social imagined communities required Arabic and English, they invested in both in accordance with perceived need.

These participants, young bilingual and bicultural Arab women, are the very individuals Edward Said (1993) refers to as "the political figures between domains, between forms, between homes, and between languages" (p. 332). Said, echoed by Canagarajah (1999), suggests such individuals "have the potential to resist the forces of uniformity and hegemony" (p. 183). In view of the polemic situation between the West and the Arab world, these young women can be viewed as socially and politically influential in terms of their ability to counteract and complicate western notions of Arabs and Arab notions of westerners. While Arabic and English might be described as competing discourses with vastly different rhetorics and contrasting values, these female bilinguals did not see these differences as creating dissonance; rather, the dissimilarity of the two languages and mindsets expanded the students' world and supported their expression as human beings of depth and complexity.

*Pedagogical implications*

Data from this study suggests that the state of Arabic / English bilingualism should be understood as desirable precisely because the languages and associated cultural assumptions are so dissimilar. From a political view, as acknowledged by the participants, the Arab world and the western English-speaking world are "two cultures pitted against each other." Yet, these bilingual participants saw in themselves the means to connect these worlds, to clarify misinterpretations, to demonstrate how perceived differences might be overcome. Moreover, from a cognitive – and cultural – viewpoint, participants understood the disparate cognitive demands of both languages as enhancing their critical thinking and complexity of thought, especially as concerns their social and cultural lives – a notion supported by bilingual research (see Benet-Martínez, Lee, & Leu, 2006).

Such understandings are strong arguments for the promotion of a dual language or two-way immersion Arabic / English bilingual educational approach, which employs a 50:50 model – half the day in one target language, half the day in the second target language (Frengel, 2003); additionally, this model has the prosocial goal of "promot[ing] linguistic and ethnic equity among the children ... bridg[ing] the gaps between cultures and languages that ... divide ... society (Garcia, 2008, p. 329). Such a policy would be an effective way of celebrating the hybridity of UAE society, where Arabic and English would not be understood as opposing discourses, artificially separated in school, but as discourses that complement learner goals and realities (Canagarajah, 2005). The potential for a dual language educational approach is further supported by the demographics in the UAE, whereby the numerous native Arabic speakers and English speakers could populate such schools in accordance to their enrolment aims, which call for equal numbers of native speakers of each target language. Recently, the first US Arabic / English dual language model opened at the FAME Charter school in Fremont, California (Noguchi, 2009); the progress of this school could be observed and analysed, and if found to be regionally-appropriate, serve as a model for the development of similar schools in the UAE.

However, before such a model could be developed, Arabic language pedagogy needs to be reconsidered and strengthened. The urgency of this endeavour is underscored here as this study highlights an unfortunate result of weak Arabic instruction – a lack of investment in scholarly Arabic by extremely intelligent and capable Arab women who cherish their Arab identity. Arab educationalists – along with parents, students, and government officials – need to work together to begin revisiting and updating curriculum, creating engaging language resources, developing children's language programs, and encouraging "cognitive learning, critical thinking, problem solving and creativity" in Arabic (United Nations Development Programme, 2003, p. iv). In addition, teacher training programs that focus on bilingual pedagogy and address socio-political aspects of language learning should be standard offerings at the various UAE universities. Language teachers who are cognizant of the political, cultural, and social implications of their work can promote critical understanding of periphery-based issues and support learner identity and agency development (Canagarajah, 1999; Norton, 2000, 2001) as well as create "awareness and valorisation of linguistic diversity amongst their students" (Huguet & Lasagabaster, 2007, p. 238). It would certainly be a great achievement if all students in the UAE, like the student quoted in the first sentence of this chapter, understood Arab and English bilingualism to be one of their greatest advantages.

*Final thoughts*

The 10 female participants in this study are exceptional by any standard and in any society. As their narratives demonstrate, they are intelligent, sophisticated, critical thinkers, and extremely articulate. Their comments reveal awareness of the interaction between language, identity, and culture. They clearly understand the value of bilingualism. Also, these bright young women are caring and civic-minded, having elected to share their talents with their peers as writing tutors. As such, this sample is not representative of all the students in the UAE in terms of attitudes and capability. While this study's atypical sample might be considered a limitation, this insight into high-calibre students is extremely important as it depicts a "near" ideal: intelligent Arab students with strong Arab identities who are bilingual in Arabic and English – but whose literacy skills in Arabic have suffered due to a litany of weaknesses surrounding Arabic curriculum and instruction. This suggests that among Arabs who share the values and insights of these young women, Arabic identity and culture *might* withstand the onslaught of global English; however, advanced Arabic literacy will *not* be sustained if poor Arabic pedagogical practices continue.

To complicate these results and establish a more complete understanding of the impact of global English on Arab society, more regional studies should be undertaken with diverse samples. Certainly, studies treating the effect of global English on students who were sent to Arabic-medium school would contribute different insights into the issue. Also, research attention should address the impact of global English on the unfortunate and all-too-common phenomenon of students with poor literacy skills in both Arabic and English.

At the conclusion of our interviews, I asked participants if they wished their parents had elected to send them to Arabic-medium schools in view of the subsequent outcomes in terms of their Arabic literacy skills. No students reported regretting their parents' choice. These young women felt that their ability to communicate in English was a precious gift that enhanced their lives and would help secure their futures, even if being thus educated compromised to varying degrees their skills in written Arabic. Yet, this was a question that I wished I did not have to ask. Parents should not have to choose between English and Arabic, or any mother tongue, when considering their child's education. Certainly, it is ingenuous to deny that global English allows the world to share ideas. However, as this study illuminates, grounding in one's culture and language affects the calibre of ideas shared in English or in any other second language. It is already evident that this grounding – along with their bilingual experience – has enriched the contributions these young Arab women are beginning to make to their world.

## Acknowledgements

The author wishes to express her gratitude to the 10 participants in the study who enthusiastically shared their time and their stories. The author would also like to acknowledge the assistance of Miss Anna Ray who cheerfully transcribed the interviews and shared her insights.

## References

Al Gurg, M. (January 15, 2010). Cultural uniformity isn't a good thing. *Gulf News*, p. 10.

Al-Issa, A., & Dahan, L. (2007). Globalization, English language, and Muslim students in the United Arab Emirates. *Educational Awakening: Journal of the Educational Sciences*, *4*(2), 147–163.

Atay, D., & Ece, A. (2009). Multiple identities as reflected in English-language education: The Turkish perspective. *Journal of Language, Identity, and Education*, *8*(1), 21–34.

Belcher, D., & Connor, U. (eds). (2001). *Reflections on multiliterate lives*. Buffalo, NY: Multilingual Matters.

Benet-Martínez, V., Lee, F., & Leu, J. (2006). Biculturalism and cognitive complexity: Expertise in cultural representations. *Journal of Cross-Cultural Psychology*, *37*(4), 386–407.

Burden-Leahy, S.M. (2009). Globalisation and education in the postcolonial world: The conundrum of the higher education system of the United Arab Emirates. *Comparative Education*, *45*(4), 525–544.

Burton, P. (1994) Women and second language use: An introduction. In P. Burton, K. Kushari Dyson, & S. Ardener (eds). *Bilingual women: Anthropological approaches to second language use* (pp. 1–29). Providence, RI: Berg Publishers.

Canagarajah, A.S. (1999). *Resisting linguistic imperialism in English teaching.* Oxford, UK: Oxford University Press.

Canagarajah, A.S. (2005). Accommodating tensions in language-in-education policies: An afterword. In A.M.Y. Lin & P.W. Martin (eds). *Decolonisation, globalization: Language-in-education policy and practice* (pp. 194–201). Buffalo, NY: Multilingual Matters.

Frengel, J. (2003). Two-way immersion programs in the United States. In T. Tokuhama-Espinosa (ed.). *The multilingual mind: Issues discussed by, for, and about people living with many languages* (pp. 47–61). Westport, CT: Praeger.

Garcia, E.E. (2008). Bilingual education in the United States. In J. Altarriba & R.R. Heredia (eds). *An introduction to bilingualism: Principles and processes* (pp. 321–343). New York: Lawrence Erlbaum Associates.

Grimshaw, T., & Sears, C. (2008). "Where am I from?" "Where do I belong?" The negotiation and maintenance of identity by international school students. *Journal of Research in International Education, 7*(3), 259–278.

hooks, b. (1989). *Talking back: Thinking feminist, thinking black.* Boston: South End Press.

Huguet, A., & Lasagabaster, D. (2007). The linguistic issue in some European bilingual contexts: Some final considerations. In D. Lasagabaster & A. Huguet (eds). *Multilingualism in European bilingual contexts: Language use and attitudes* (pp. 234–251). Buffalo, NY: Multilingual Matters.

Janardhan, M. (February 27, 2007). UAE: Debate grows over modernity's effect on Arab values. *Global Information Network,* p. 1.

Knowledge & Human Development Authority. (2009). *Dubai Schools Inspection Bureau (DSIB) Annual Report.* Retrieved February 22, 2009, from <http://www.khda.gov.ae/en/DSIB/InspectionBureau.aspx>

Koven, M. (2007). *Selves in two languages: Bilinguals' verbal enactments of identity in French and Portuguese.* Philadelphia, PA: John Benjamins Publishing Company.

Lebbady, H. (2004, Winter). An anglophone Moroccan? *Tingis: A Moroccan-American Magazine of Ideas and Culture,* 12–13.

Lee, S.K. (2003). Multiple identities in a multicultural world: A Malaysian perspective. *Journal of Language, Identity, and Education, 2*(3), 137–158.

Nahyan: English to stay as medium of instruction in varsities (November 22, 2009). *Gulf News.* Retrieved February 22, 2010, from <http://gulfnews.com/news/gulf/uae/education/nahyan-english-to-stay-as-medium-of-instruction-in-varsities-1.530758>

Noguchi, S. (November 2, 2009). K-12 program would be first English-Arabic dual immersion. *Mercurynews.com*. Retrieved February 15, 2009, from <http://www.famecharter.org/downloads/press/Fremont_Charter_Hopes_to_Start_SJMN_2009.pdf>

Norton, B. (2000). *Identity and language learning: Gender, ethnicity, and educational change*. New York: Longman.

Norton, B. (2001). Non-participation, imagined communities and the language classroom. In M. Breen (ed.). *Learner contributions to language learning: New directions in research* (pp. 159–171). Harlow, England: Pearson Education.

Norton, B., & Kamal, F. (2003). The imagined communities of Pakistani school children. *Journal of Language, Identity and Education, 3*(4), 301–317.

Ortiz, A.M. (2000). Expressing cultural identity in the learning community: Opportunities and challenges. In M.B. Baxter Magolda (ed.), *Teaching to promote intellectual and personal maturity: Incorporating students' worldviews and identities into the learning process* (pp. 67–79). San Francisco: Jossey-Bass.

Pavlenko, A. (ed.). (2006). *Bilingual minds: Emotional experience, expression, and representation*. Buffalo, NY: Multilingual Matters.

Pavlenko, A., & Lantolf, J.P. (2000). Second language learning as participation and the (re)construction of selves. In J.P. Lantolf (ed.), *Sociocultural theory and second language learning* (pp. 155–177). New York: Oxford University Press.

Pavlenko, A., & Norton, B. (2005). Imagined communities, identity, and English language teaching. In J. Cummins & C. Davison (eds), *Kluwer handbook of English language teaching*. Dordrecht: Kluwer Academic Publishers.

Pennycook, A. (1998). *English and the discourses of colonialism*. New York: Routledge.

Phillipson, R. (1992). *Linguistic imperialism*. New York: Oxford University Press.

Said, E. (1993). *Culture and imperialism*. New York: Alfred Knopf.

Sankar, A. (December 3, 2009). Arabic lessons leave pupils tongue-tied. *Gulf News*. Retrieved February 22, 2010, from <http://gulfnews.com/news/gulf/uae/arabic-lessons-leave-pupils-tongue-tied-1.545557>

Tokuhama-Espinosa, T. (2003). Third culture kids: A special case for foreign language learning. In T. Tokuhama-Espinosa (ed.). *The multilingual mind: Issues discussed by, for, and about people living with many languages* (pp. 165–169). Westport, CT: Praeger.

United Nations Development Programme (2003). *UNDP Arab human development report 2003: Building a knowledge society*. New York: United Nations Publications. Retrieved February 18, 2010, from <http://www.arab-hdr.org/publications/other/ahdr/ahdr2003e.pdf>

Watson, D.T. (2004). *The role of English in the provision of high quality education in the United Arab Emirates*. Unpublished master's thesis, University of South

Africa, South Africa. Retrieved February 18, 2010, from <http://etd.unisa.ac.za/ETD-db/theses/available/etd-07252005-125945/unrestricted/dissertation.pdf>

Wenger, E. (1998). *Communities of practice: Learning, meaning, and identity.* Cambridge: Cambridge University Press.

FATIMA BADRY

# 4  Appropriating English: Languages in Identity Construction in the United Arab Emirates

## ABSTRACT

This chapter contributes to the homogeneity-heterogeneity debate within globalization studies through an exploration of the impact of global English on the local cultural identity of the young generations in the United Arab Emirates (UAE). The unique demographic makeup of the UAE, where around 80% of the population is expatriate, the adopted developmental strategies embracing globalization and educational policies which have made English the language of instruction at all levels make the UAE an interesting locality to examine the impact of globalization on cultural and linguistic identity. Survey data supplemented by ethnographic explorations reveal participants' increasing appropriation of outer layers of western cultural behaviours but a clear sense of belonging to Arabness. Their embrace of globalization does not seem to be an imposition but a choice that has impacted their lifestyles but not their core cultural values, which they consider to be similar to their parents'. Participants' linguistic behavior is predominantly open and porous across social spaces. Their stated linguistic preferences support bilinguality with a distribution running along the modern/traditional axis. English is preferred for intellectual/modern domains while Arabic is the preferred language to express affective/traditional activities. The linguistic and cultural behaviours and perceptions expressed by the participants in this study lend support to a non-essentialist approach to identity, but also suggest a decreasing role of Arabic in their linguistic repertoire.

## Introduction

We no longer have to be displaced geographically and live in other places in order to be exposed to other cultures. The other is with us in our society, our schools, and our homes. Globalization has contributed to familiarizing and making commonplace, otherwise far away and unfamiliar behaviours from foreign places. "Almost everywhere in the world, experience is increasingly 'disembedded' from locality and the ties of culture to place are progressively weakened by new patterns of 'connexity' ... For most people, most of the time the impact of globalisation is felt not in travel but in staying at home" (Morley, 2000, p. 14). One of the pervasive agents of this global connexity that has brought the foreign into the local psyche is the English language, the de facto global medium accepted as the means to modernization. The world over, English has become a lingua franca in transnational exchanges. English is the language of international communication in business, media, and research everywhere including in former European colonial powers, such as France, Belgium and the Netherlands (Cornillie, Lambert & Swiggers, 2009; Helot & Young, 2006; Shohamy, 2006). Because globalization affects every aspect of human life, it has become the focus of multidisciplinary approaches which have contributed to a plethora of definitions and assumptions about its effect on human relations. As Scholte (2000) points out:

> [The term] globalization ... has become a heavily loaded word. People have linked the notion to well-nigh every purported contemporary social change, including an emergent information age, a retreat of the state, the demise of traditional cultures, and the advent of a postmodern epoch. In normative terms, some people have associated "globalization" with progress, prosperity and peace. For others, however, the word has conjured up deprivation, disaster and doom (p. 14).

Definitions of globalization vary depending on the domain being examined and the ideological perspectives adopted (Germain, 2000; Scholte, 2000; Wells, 2001). For some, globalization in its most basic sense refers to simply internationalization resulting from multinationals' activities beyond their own states (Breton & Reitz, 2003). For others, it is equivalent

## 4 Appropriating English: Languages in Identity Construction

to liberalization of relations between states leading to the integration of economic activities (Martin, 2000; Shuey, 2001). Others choose to focus on its universalization aspects leading to "planetary synthesis of cultures" in a "global humanism" (Scholte, 2000). For those critical of western dominance, globalization is defined as westernization/modernization of the world which has led to a hegemonic dominance of the US and its multinationals (e.g. McDonald's and CNN) over the world (see Wells, 2001). According to Scholte, defining globalization as any of these processes is redundant and does not advance our understanding of the concept. He suggests instead examining globalization in terms of its "deterritorialization or supraterritorialization" which captures better the essence of what globalization means today because it draws attention to

> a far-reaching change in the nature of social space. The proliferation and spread of supraterritorial ... connections brings an end to what could be called "territorialism", that is, a situation where social geography is entirely territorial. Although, ... territory still matters very much in our globalizing world, it no longer constitutes the whole of our geography (Scholte, 2000, p. 46).

In addition to debates about how to define globalization, researchers also disagree on its impact on societies. This second debate is about whether globalization leads to homogeneity or heterogeneity of cultures and societies around the world. Proponents of the homogeneity platform argue that globalization is progressively leading to uniformity across nation-state borders, killing in its way local cultures, identities and ways of life (Garcia & Skutnabb-Kangas, 2006). Such uniformity is a consequence of multinational corporations' control of finance, production and information flow, and the dominant use of English in all their global transactions. Some go even further to consider the spread of English around the world an extension of imperialism at the linguistic level which is progressively threatening the survival of many local languages across the world (Mohanty, 2006; Phillipson, 1992, 2000, 2001; Phillipson & Skutnabb-Kangas, 1996; Skutnabb-Kangas, 1999, 2000). From this perspective it is argued that "[g]lobalisation introduces a single world culture centred on consumerism, mass media, Americana, and the English language. Depending on one's perspective, this homogenization entails either progressive cosmopolitanism or oppressive imperialism" (Scholte, 2000, p. 23). Those who believe that globalization leads to heterogeneity argue that local cultures and modes of production are able to appropriate the global into the local (Appadurai, 1996; Brutt-Griffler, 2005; Kraidy, 2005; Pennycook, 2007) by transforming, molding, and blending the global into local to result in "glocalization," a term initially used by Robertson (1992). Furthermore, global agents themselves contribute to this heterogeneity by adapting to the different local contexts in which they operate to make themselves more marketable to specific populations (e.g. McDonald's offering of McArabia burgers and Pizza Hut's Shawarma Pizzas in the Arabian Gulf region).

An ancillary question raised within this perspective relates to the validity of the idealized notion of cultural and linguistic purity in the first place. Many researchers have emphasized that in the cultural arena, "cultural forms are hybrid, mixed, impure, and the time has come in cultural analysis to reconnect their analysis with their actuality" (Said, 1994, cited in Kraidy, 2005, p. 70). Hybrid and creolized new cultural forms "of meaning, identity and community" have resulted from "countless new combinations and blurring distinctions between nations and between civilizations" (Scholte, 2000, p. 24; see also Bhabha, 1994; Nederveen Pieterse, 1995). In their discussion of the problematics of the concept of identity itself, Brubaker and Cooper (2000) argue that categorizing people into fixed groups is no longer possible due to the porous and ambiguous nature of geographic, cultural, and social boundaries. From their analysis of an example of the Hungarian/Romanian boundaries in Transylvania, the authors point out why the concept of identity referring to some unitary homogeneous reality is no longer applicable and conclude that classifying Hungarians and Romanians in Transylvania as two distinct identities "obscures as much as it reveals about self-understandings, masking the fluidity and ambiguity that arise from mixed marriages, from bilingualism, from migration, from Hungarian children attending Romanian-language schools, from intergenerational assimilation (in both directions), and – perhaps most important – from sheer indifference to the claims of ethnocultural nationality" (p. 27).

Culture blending and creolization resulting from globalization have also been highlighted in linguistic studies describing the need to recognize several standards of English and move away from the dominant paradigm of an idealized Standard English whose norms are dictated by the Anglo-American canons (Brutt-Griffler, 2002; Kachru, 1996; Mazrui, 2004; Saraceni, 2009).

This chapter explores the impact of "Global English" on the local cultural and linguistic identity of the young generations in the United Arab Emirates (UAE). In the UAE, English has become the language of communication in all domains as a result of its adoption as a medium of instruction throughout the educational system and the demographic makeup of UAE society with over 80% expatriate residents for whom English is the lingua franca. These educational and demographic realities, together with the country's economic and developmental orientations, combine to produce a global society, par excellence, and a rich site to examine the impact of globalization on cultural and linguistic identity. The evidence from the study reported on in this chapter is aimed at contributing to the homogeneity-heterogeneity debate within globalization studies by arguing that young Arabs appropriate global English as part of their Arab identity. Increasingly, young Arabs are living along a biliguality continuum where their identity as Arabs no longer centres on the Arabic language alone as its core. Before discussing the study, an overview of how identity has been conceived in the Arab context as well as recent discussions of the relation between identity and language in bilingual contexts is sketched out, followed by an overview of the socio cultural context of the UAE relevant to the questions raised in the study.

## Identity and language

Arab identity has generally been conceived and imagined, both by insiders and by outsiders, as relying essentially on language (e.g. Al Husri, 1985; Hourani, 1983, cited in Suleiman, 2003; Tütsch, 1965). According to Al Husri, what matters most in Arab national identity are a common Arabic language and shared history. The emphasis on language being at the heart of Arab national identity is well captured in Al Husri's declaration that "every Arabic-speaking people is an Arab people, [and every] individual belonging to one of these Arabic speaking peoples is an Arab" (quoted in Suleiman, 1994, p. 6). Arabic was able to play this role because it was perceived "not only [as] a mere instrument of communication or container of ideas and feelings; [but also as]... the embodiment of a whole culture and the guarantor of linkages across time and space" (Barakat, 1993, p. 34).

The Pan Arab nationalist movement relied on Arabic for "maintaining the internal cohesion of the group and in guarding its identity" (Suleiman, 2003, p. 23). In his discussion of the development of Arab nationalism, Suleiman (2003) traces the linkage between Arabic nationalism and the Arabic language back to the Napoleonic expeditions in Egypt in 1798. To emphasize the difference between the Turks and the Arabs and play down the religious ties holding the Ottoman Empire together, Napoleon made his first proclamation in Arabic to underscore the difference between Turks and Arabs. In the history of Arab nationalism, the Arabic language was used as a boundary setter against the other, and functioned as an instrument to develop Pan Arab nationalist sentiments. The dependence on the Arabic language in the construction of Arab national identity both within each state and in the Pan Arab nationalist movement was strengthened further at different times in the nineteenth and twentieth centuries because of, or in reaction to the different colonizers, first the Turks and later the Europeans (see Suleiman, 2003, for more details about the historical development of Arab nationalism). During the colonial era, Arabic was viewed as a symbol of national identity and the banner of Pan Arab unity.

Total dependence of Arab national identity on the Arabic language came under questioning in the twentieth century (Tütsch, 1965). The sociopolitical realities of the Arab world during the post colonial era led to a weakening of the role of Arabic shifting it to the periphery of what it means to be an Arab. Many factors may be called upon to explain this shift including the strengthened presence of global English (and French), state nationalism, an upsurge of local linguistic identities and a weakening of Pan-Arabist sentiments. Modern Arabs no longer consider Modern Standard Arabic (MSA) as their only language of literacy. Dialectal varieties, frowned upon in the past, are becoming accepted in written and digital media and the use of a European language along with Arabic is widespread. Barakat (1993) correctly argues that "a definition of Arab identity rooted primarily or solely in language tends to ignore several aspects of the present state of the Arabic language, such as the continuing gap between written and spoken Arabic, the different Arab dialects, the bilingualism in some Arab countries, and the limited literacy of the Arab masses" (p. 35). Barakat identifies several composites around which the sense of belonging to Arab identity revolves. They include shared culture, shared language, common place in history, common experiences, geography, social formations, shared economic interests, ethnicity, religion, and shared external challenges and conflicts. Moreover, he warns against the fallacy of looking at identity as fixed and suggests that "under certain specific conditions that must be consciously created by Arabs themselves, old identities may fade, and new ones emerge" (p. 33). Such views seem to be gaining ground in identity research and signal that in "both the sociological and the linguistic literature there are references to a paradigm shift" (De Oliveira, 2002, p. 245).

Identity studies today are largely based on the notion that both individual and social identities are made and remade depending on external factors, present affiliations, and future outlooks, rather than being strictly tied to a common past, common language, and common territory (Le Page &Tabouret-Keller, 1985; Norton, 1997; Ryan, 1997; Urciuoli, 1995). When it comes to the role of language in identity, "in many instances, language and identity are not isomorphic and people do not always see language vitiating their cultural identity. Any sense of mapping language onto culture and culture onto national identity and thus onto [territorial] border, must be mediated through macro-micro interstices in relationships" (Urciuoli, 1995, p. 533). Rather, identity is "how people understand their relationship to the world, how that relationship is constructed across time and space, and how people understand their possibilities for the future" (Norton, 1997, p. 410). From this perspective, individuals are said to be enacting "acts of identity" depending on several factors which include either the desire to belong or distinguish oneself from a particular group (Le Page & Tabouret-Keller, 1985). Identity formation is also influenced by one's desire to access material resources that can help him/her become affiliated with the desired group (Bourdieu, 1982). In multilingual contexts, identity is increasingly defined in terms of its fluidity, hybridization, and contextual adaptability, where individual agency and collective pressures play a major role in one's self and social identification. Multilinguals express facets of their identity through particular languages and cultures; their linguistic repertoires allow them to enter into group memberships without necessarily feeling identity fragmentation or living this multiplicity in negative terms (Badry, 2007). This is particularly the case when individuals feel a sense of ownership of *their* languages and cultures.

Depending on the desired self projection, individuals locate themselves at different places on the culture/language continua and identify themselves using relevant factors to achieve their desired image. For example, in her analysis of self-identification strategies of Spanish/Portuguese town representatives, De Oliveira (2002) found that although both localities were situated at the periphery, identity was expressed differently (local versus regional) by the two town representatives. She concluded that individuals' identity orientations reveal a "non-essentialist view [and that] neither 'identity' nor the social variables from which identity derives, are viewed as constants. Instead, they are viewed as constructs which individuals create through their social and linguistic behaviour" (p. 245). Similarly, Zakharia's (2010) study of high school students in Beirut, Lebanon revealed that Lebanese youth hold "both a strong connection to Arabic as well as a strong multilingual ideology" (p. 166). Her data suggest that while the young Lebanese defended the need to know Arabic to be Lebanese and Arab, they also felt that "Arabic was not necessarily equated with being Arab, nor was it solely equated with being Lebanese" (p. 169).The discourse around Arabic that emerged from participants in her study is best captured in one of her participants statement that "if you love this land, then language doesn't matter" (student interview, in Zakharia, 2010, p. 170). For the youth interviewed, the discourse around global English shows that not only is English seen as important to secure future opportunities, but is also lived as a modern identity marker. Zakharia points out that while the practice of emphasizing the foreign language in Lebanon's educational system has not changed from the colonial period when French was the prestigious language, the ideological discourse has. She argues that "[b]y articulating the centrality of Arabic in *ideological* terms and the importance of French and English in *practical* terms, the tripartite language policy suggests a break from a discourse of linguistic-cultural allegiance regarding foreign languages towards one of linguistic instrumentality" (p. 162) (emphasis in original).

Increasingly, studies of identity in bilingual contexts suggest that the depiction of identity choices as discrete – either/or – classifications is inadequate in today's globalization in its suppraterriorial sense. Some researchers go even further to question the adequacy of the concept of a fixed identity in capturing how people identify themselves in a world that is progressively intertwined and in flux (Brubaker & Cooper, 2000). In addition, unlike colonial English (or other colonial languages), global English is appropriated by its non native speakers as *their* instrument to reach various goals including new identity projections. Bi/multilinguals situate themselves towards one end or the other of the traditional/modern continuum depending on the act of identity desired in a specific context and with a particular audience. These transformations also point to the need to analyse the constructs that make up identity and their interactions from a more dynamic perspective that allows for fluidity and agency at the level of individuals' self-identification in response to changing social variables brought about by globalization, their desire to get integrated into specific groups, and the groups' willingness to accept new memberships.

Globalization has brought about transformation at all levels of humanity that require new theoretical paradigms that move away from static dichotomies of speakers as native/ non native, which are often disconnected from language users' own relationships to multiple languages or language varieties. Leung, Harris, and Rampton (1997), and Nero (2005) have argued that individuals' language identities and linguistic behaviours point to the need for a new postmodern paradigm in studying agency in identity construction that goes beyond the static pigeonholing of individuals into discrete categories.

## The UAE context

A federation of seven Emirates since 1971, the United Arab Emirates is situated in the Southeast part of the Arabian Peninsula. It has the world's sixth largest oil reserves and is one of the most developed economies in the Middle East. In the past four decades, the UAE, spearheading other Arabian Gulf countries, has embarked on a rapid modernization process that has been set in motion by its oil wealth and bolstered by the state's strategies embracing globalization. As Khalaf (2002) describes it, "[t]he rapid integration of post-oil Gulf societies within the global system is evident in the flows of strategic resources such as oil, migrant workers, technological know-how, finance and other globally oriented corporate services" (p. 15). To enable this growth, the UAE has had to import a large expatriate population from all over the world. Today the population is estimated at 6 million from less than 200,000 in 1969. This has resulted in the UAE nationals being a minority in their own country, making up less than 20% of the total population. Other residents of the UAE come from other Arab countries (15%), Iranians (8%), South Asians (50%), and Europeans, North Americans, Australians, and East Asians (8%) of the total population (Population). This demographic composition has led to the "far-reaching change in the nature of social space" considered to be a key characteristic of globalization. Such a context provides the social science researcher with a context to explore the role of language in identity construction and examine how changes in "the character of a society's map" will lead to changes in "its culture, ecology, economics, politics, and social psychology" (Scholte, 2000, p. 46).

One of the areas where these changes are far reaching is the UAE's linguistic map. The linguistic space in the UAE offers continually changing configurations of social spaces with the intersection of different linguistic varieties. In addition to Modern Standard Arabic, the official language, several dialects of Arabic, Persian, Hindi, Urdu (World Factbook, 2010), and many varieties of English are widely used in the UAE depending on the speakers' national background and context of communication. However,

English, and not Arabic, has become the engine of the state's efforts to be part of the global world. It is the primary language of communication outside the home and progressively inside the home as well. One cannot get by without English in urban centres whether at the supermarket, the movie theatre, or in shopping malls. At home, parents import nannies that communicate with children in English, nurseries are immersing children in English to give them a head start, and middle and upper class Arab parents are proud to showcase their offspring's communication skills in English. More significantly, English is used as the medium of instruction in private schools and more and more public schools are moving in the same direction introducing English in the early grades.

## Concerns about loss of Arab identity due to globalization

This mobility of English into the everyday spaces raises questions about how linguistic globalization, perceived as essential for development, is affecting the identity of the young generations of Arab nationals and residents in the UAE, and what role language plays in identity construction (Gulf News, 2008; Issa, 2008; Mohammed, 2008). Many voices are sounding the alarm about how accessibility to western media is changing the cultural identity of UAE society and how the survival of Arabic as the national language is at risk. There are also fears that the dominance of English in education, government, and business is as an agent of disembedding from local culture and threatens UAE identity as an Arab and Muslim nation (Al Lawati & Al Najami 2008; Al Saayegh, 2008; Ismail & Saffarini, 2008; Youssef, 2008). To assuage these concerns, the government reaffirmed that the Arabic language is "the official language in all federal authorities and establishments" (Al Baik, 2008a). Other prominent Emiratis, such as Ahmad Humaid Al Tayer, Chairman of the National Human Resources Development and Employment Authority, have gone further to advocate the use of Arabic in all business contracts, invoices, restaurant menus, and billboards (Al Baik, 2008b). Proponents of the use of Arabic as the national and official language argue that language and identity are tightly linked and that the decreased use of Arabic threatens the Arab and Islamic identity of the UAE (Salama, 2010). Worries that the infiltration of English has gone too far were summarized by Al Kitbi (a UAE intellectual) who declared to *Gulf News* that "there is no nation that allows an invasion of foreign languages in government institutions the way we did in the UAE" (Al Baik, 2008a). To respond to these concerns, several symposia were organized in the country to discuss best practices to preserve UAE national identity and the year 2008 was declared as the year of national identity by the president of the UAE (Al Baik, 2008a).

## The study

This study examines the impact of globalization, as manifested through the adoption of English as an agent of modernity in the UAE's linguistic and cultural spaces, on young Arabs' sense of belonging to Arabness. Participants were students between the ages of 19 and 25 years attending a private American educational model university where the medium of instruction is English. Given the comparatively high tuition fees, most students attending the university belong to a relatively high socioeconomic background. The selection of such an institution to conduct this study may at first seem to be less neutral, as one would expect these students to be more open to English and globalization than students attending public universities. It may be argued that findings may not be representative of university students in the UAE. The rationale behind the choice of this population, however, was predicated on two considerations: First, English is prevalent everywhere in UAE higher education, including public universities, and is becoming the medium of instruction in most of the UAE secondary educational system. Second, one of the objectives of the study was to explore the resilience of Arab identity under maximum exposure to English conditions. The sample in the study represents this condition.

## Methodology

The main instrument used to collect data was the student survey in Appendix A, supplemented by findings from an earlier faculty survey and group discussions with 30 Arab students enrolled in a course on the sociolinguistic context of Arabic. The student survey consisted of a 33 item questionnaire in English designed specifically for this study. The questions were designed to elicit responses to four major issues. First, the use of English and Arabic in different communicative contexts was addressed in scale questions 15, 16, 17, 18, 19, 22, and 30. Second, students' preferences regarding the use of English and Arabic were elicited by questions 5, 23, 24, 25, 26. Third, their preference of outward cultural artefacts by questions 21, 27, 28, and 31. Fourth, the degree to which participants feel they belong to Arab culture and whether they think there is a change in their identity was the focus of questions 6, 7, 8, 9, 10, 11, 20, 32 and 33. Finally, students' attitudes towards the West were elicited by questions 12, 13, 14, and open ended questions 34 and 35. The questionnaire also collected biographical information about participants' nationality, age, gender, mother tongue, and educational background.

The survey was distributed to a convenience sample of over 200 university students attending required general education courses in the subjects of English composition and Arabic heritage with English as a medium of instruction. Two colleagues in the department of languages and literature agreed to distribute the surveys to all enrolled students in their classes during the fall 2006 semester. Their teaching load totalled eight sections with an average of 22 students per section. All completed forms were returned to the researcher. Incomplete surveys as well as surveys completed by non Arab students were set aside and not included in the analysis. Data were tabulated and percentages were calculated using Minitab statistical package.

## Results

The 105 Arab students (19–25 years old) who completed the surveys were from different parts of the Arab world. Given the small number of participants from each country, they were grouped based on larger geographic regions recognized as major groupings in the Arab world (see Table 1): 38 participants were from the Arabian Peninsula (Bahraini, Emirati, Iraqi, Kuwaiti, Omani, Saudi, and Yemeni); 37 were from the Levant (Jordan, Lebanon, Palestine, and Syria); 12 students were from Egypt; and eight participants were from Libya, Somalia, and Sudan. In addition to these four geographic groups, eight students identified themselves as dual Arab-American citizens. Two students did not fill in their nationality.

| Group 1: Arabian Peninsula | Group 2: Levant | Group 3: Egypt | Group 4: Dual citizens | Group 5: Other | undeclared |
|---|---|---|---|---|---|
| Bahrain; Emirates; Iraq; Kuwait; Oman; Saudi Arabia; Yemen | Jordan; Lebanon; Palestine; Syria | Egypt | Arab Americans (US and Canada) | Libya; Somalia; Sudan | |
| 38 | 37 | 12 | 8 | 8 | 2 |

Table 1 Participants' national background

An equal number of female (53) and male (52) students responded to the survey. Eighty per cent of the students had attended private secondary schools and 20% graduated from public schools. All participants considered themselves bilingual Arabic English speakers. To be admitted to a major in the university, all students must have a minimum TOEFL score of 530. In addition, their English writing proficiency is assessed by the English Placement Test (EPT) for placement in freshman composition courses. No Arabic proficiency assessment is required for admission into UAE universities; however, all participants in the study are speakers of a dialectal variety of Arabic.

Results are presented and discussed under the following sections: (a) English and Arabic use in different communicative contexts; (b) language preferences and linguistic identification; (c) outward cultural artefacts favourites; and (d) perceived degree of belonging to Arab culture and change in local identity. Since there were no major differences between male and female responses, the gender variable was not included in the data analysis presented here. Regional differences are discussed whenever they occur.

*English and Arabic use in different communicative contexts*

Findings show that students' choice of language use is determined by their audience and context of interaction. Inside the home, Arabic still prevails in interactions with parents for over half of the participants (57%) with one third (33%) of the respondents using both languages. Just around 10% of the respondents report using English exclusively when communicating with their parents. These percentages are reversed in communications with siblings. When conversing with their siblings, 57% reported using both languages and 37% responded that they relied on Arabic exclusively in these interactions.

Outside the home, bilingual usage is the norm even when interactions are among Arab speakers. The majority of students reported using both Arabic and English at university (88%), with friends (85%) and with strangers (84%). Only 8% responded that they never use English with their friends and rely on Arabic only in their communications with them (see Table 2).

| English Use | Parents (%) | Siblings (%) | Friends (%) | Strangers (%) | University (%) |
|---|---|---|---|---|---|
| Always | 10 | 6 | 7 | 13 | 11 |
| Never | 57 | 37 | 8 | 4 | 1 |
| Both | 33 | 57 | 85 | 83 | 88 |

Table 2  Uses of English

These findings reveal a linguistic behavior that is predominantly bilingual. Alongside Arabic, English is present in the private space of the family home and across generations. The use of English and Arabic with parents, by over a third of the participants, suggests that no space seems to be the exclusivity of Arabic anymore. However, the use of English with parents varies according to regional background. English is used the least with parents by Somali, Libyan, and Sudanese students. Seventy five per cent of this group (6 respondents) stated that they never use English with their parents as compared to 61% (n = 23) from the Arabian peninsula (Saudi, Emirati, Bahraini, Omani, Yemeni, Iraqi, and Kuwaiti). Over half (54%) of the Levant respondents (n = 20), 50% (n = 6) from Egypt and 43% (n = 3) dual citizens never use English with their parents. It is also interesting to note that 25% of Egyptians declared using English all the time with their parents as opposed to 3% of the respondents from the Levant region.

Patterns of communication inside the home revealed unequal use of Arabic between the regional groups. The limited use of English with parents by the Somalis, Libyans, and Sudanese may be due to lower literacy rates among the older generations in these countries. The higher percentage of English use with parents within the Egyptian group is puzzling and cannot be interpreted based on the small sample of Egyptian students in the study. However, additional background information about religious affiliations and other socio-economic variables may be needed to understand these patterns. It should also be noted that none of the dual citizens responded that they communicated in English only with their parents, which could be due to the desire of Arab American expatriates to reconnect with their Arabic roots.

In fact, Arab American parents generally allude, in casual conversations, that providing an Arabic cultural background for their children was a major reason for them to leave America and move back to the Arab world.

The demographics of the UAE may be partly used to explain the extensive use of English outside the home. The UAE population is a truly supraterritorial population with a mix of people from all linguistic backgrounds, which makes English the default language. In addition, although the majority of the students' social networks are from Arab backgrounds, they speak different dialects of Arabic, which at times makes comprehension difficult. Given these dialectal differences and at times unspoken rivalries as to which local/regional dialect is superior, reverting to English for communication between speakers of different Arabic dialects may be felt as a more neutral ground and requires less effort to adapt to the other's dialect.

*Language preferences and linguistic identification*

The tendency towards the dual use of English and Arabic discussed above is further supported by the respondents' stated preferences for language overall. Nearly two thirds (63%) of the respondents said they prefer both languages as opposed to 23% who stated a preference for Arabic and 14% a preference for English. When asked about which language they think in, participants were equally divided with around one third finding it easier to think in English, one third in Arabic and one third in both. Similar percentages were obtained for preferences in terms of expressing feelings, with a slightly higher percentage for Arabic 38% as compared to 28% who prefer to express their feelings in English. About 34% indicated their preference for both languages. The results are not as equally distributed when it comes to which language is considered better for studying. Overall, 63% believe it is easier to study in English as opposed to 31% who find studying in English to be difficult. Only 6% are equally at ease in either language. However, 43% of the respondents selected Arabic as the language that better expresses who they are and as a symbol of linguistic identity as compared to 22% who opted for English, and 1/3 felt that both languages equally express who they are (see Table 3).

| Language | Overall Preference | Thinking | Feelings | Studying | Linguistic identification |
|---|---|---|---|---|---|
| English | 14 | 33 | 28 | 63 | 22 |
| Arabic | 23 | 33 | 38 | 31 | 43 |
| Both | 63 | 34 | 34 | 6 | 35 |

Table 3  Language preferences

Students' responses presented in Table 3 show a preference for English for what may be termed extrinsic/intellectual functions such as studying (63% prefer to use English compared to 31% who prefer Arabic). Arabic is still preferred for intrinsic/affective functions such as expressing ones' feelings and a symbol of linguistic identity. However, it is worth noting that about one third of the respondents express bilingual preferences for both intrinsic and extrinsic functions, except in studying where there is a clear preference for English. Similar preferences were also expressed by students in my Arabic sociolinguistics class. English is clearly the favoured language for study. As one student put it, "I cannot imagine myself solving a mathematical problem in Arabic now, even though I studied mathematics in Arabic in high school. It is just easier for me to do it in English" (Jordanian male student majoring in engineering).

These preferences seem to be aligned with the discourse prevalent in language planning approaches in UAE education policies that promote the use of Arabic for traditional and religious subjects and English for modern sciences, technology, and mathematics. Nonetheless, although English seems to be gaining ground in the academic fields and social interactions, participants still perceive Arabic as the language that is closely tied to their identity, which points to a distinction between the functional and symbolic roles of language. Here too regional differences were quite marked regarding overall language preference and self-identification as presented in Table 4.

## 4 Appropriating English: Languages in Identity Construction

|  | Language preference | | | Self-identification with language | | |
|---|---|---|---|---|---|---|
| Region | Arabic | English | Both | Arabic | English | Both |
| Arabian Peninsula | 24 | 13 | 63 | 42 | 30 | 28 |
| Levant | 33 | 5 | 62 | 60 | 5 | 35 |
| Egypt | 8 | 25 | 67 | 8 | 42 | 50 |
| Arab American | 0 | 25 | 75 | 38 | 25 | 38 |
| Other | 25 | 25 | 50 | 25 | 25 | 50 |

Table 4  Language preference and self-identification by region

Percentages presented in Table 4 show that for the Arabian Peninsula and Levant students, Arabic remains an important marker of their identity even if they like to use both languages. Pragmatic and symbolic choices seem to point to opposite directions. While only 24% of the students from the Arabian Peninsula prefer the use of Arabic overall, 42% still believe that Arabic expresses better who they are (i.e., linguistic identification). This trend is the same among students from the Levant (33% and 60% respectively). However, Egyptian and other students' responses do not reveal this divergence and reveal a concordance between which language they prefer and its role in their identification. The two languages seem to play a similar role in their preference and identification. Although none of the Arab Americans prefer to use Arabic, over 38% think that Arabic better expresses who they are. These results are also important in that they show that all groups favour the use of both Arabic and English (from 50% to 75%) while, except for the Egyptian and 'Others' groups, 38% to 60% maintain that their identity is tied more to Arabic (see Table 4). The relatively high percentage (30%) of respondents from the Arabian Peninsula who feel that English is important in their self identification compared to (5%) of the Levant group is worth noting. The stronger impact of English on the young generations in the Arabian Peninsula may be attributed to several factors which include the absence of a tradition of generalized education in Arabic before the embrace of the modern system which promotes literacy in English, the perception of English as a status language, the rapidity of social transformations from very traditional societies to global ones in a short period of time, and the prevalent official discourse stressing the advantages of learning English as a shortcut to development.

## Outward layers of cultural artefacts

As in many other parts of the world, Arabs who consider themselves modern have appropriated western dress, western music and other forms of entertainment as part of their own cultural baggage. Since identity construction is generally built, not only on language but also on other cultural artefacts (Barakat, 1993), the following section examines whether observed changes in these outer layers of culture reflect changes in Arab cultural identity. The questions on this issue elicited participants' responses regarding their preferences in terms of clothing, music, TV channels, and food. These responses shed additional light on how respondents situate themselves on the local/global continuum and how they choose to represent themselves to the other, given that "culture is a fuzzy set of attitudes, beliefs, norms, and basic assumptions and values that are shared by a group of people" (Spencer-Oatey, 2000, p. 4).

Results in Table 5 indicate a clear preference for western dress with half of the respondents (51%) choosing western clothes exclusively and 38% stating that they like both Arab and western dress. Around 11% prefer the 'disdasha' (men's white traditional dress) and 'abaya' (women's black long cape-like coat).

| Culture | Clothing | Music | Food | TV |
|---|---|---|---|---|
| Western | 51 | 26 | 17 | 27 |
| Arabic | 11 | 25 | 61 | 20 |
| Both | 38 | 49 | 14 | 53 |
| Asian | | | 8 | |

Table 5  Preference of outward layers of culture

However, a wide variation from one regional group to the other was revealed. Western dress was preferred by Egyptian students overwhelmingly (82%) in comparison to other groups. Sixty per cent (60%) of the Levant participants, 57% of the dual citizens, 50% of "Others" and 32% of Gulf students stated a preference for western dress. Traditional dress was favoured by 19% among the Arabian Peninsula group, 14% among Arab Americans, 13% among "Others", and 6% among the Levant groups. None of the Egyptians expressed preference for traditional dress.

It is worth noting here that in most countries of the Arabian Peninsula, traditional dress is mandated by the government for work and official occasions for their nationals. For example, in ID photographs for passports and other identification documents, nationals must wear their traditional dress, including the head gear, for both men and women. Also, for many Arabs who wear western dress regularly, traditional dress remains a strong marker of national identity and is the dress of choice on special occasions and for religious activities. Moreover, the interpretation of the national dress as a sign of tradition that is antithetical to modernity has changed. In his study of national dress and the construction of Emirati cultural identity, Khalaf (2005) traces changes in attitudes towards "Emirati national dress from rebellious rejection of traditional dress in the 1960s and 1970s to a total embrace of the national dress to distinguish the nationals from all other expatriates and symbolize their new state of wealth" (p. 254). In addition, in countries like the UAE, many nationals wear the traditional dress to express their identity as local and distinguish themselves from others who are in the majority since being identified as a local usually entitles one to privileged treatment in society.

In their responses to questions about music and media preferences, nearly half (49%) of the Arab students surveyed enjoy both western and Arab music, but preference for western music seems to be gaining ground as those who prefer it (27%) slightly outnumber those who selected Arabic music as their number one choice (25%). The same trends are also evident in students' choice of newspapers and TV channels. These results are not surprising given the clear dominance of the airwaves and the media scene by global cable TV and internet where English and American products are dominant.

Contrary to this trend, Arabic food remains the favourite food for the majority of the survey participants (61%). Only 17% of the respondents stated that they preferred western food and 14% liked both. This preference for Arabic food may explain the menu adaptations of global fast food chains, which offer western food with local flavours such as McArabia burgers by McDonald's and shawarma pizzas by Pizza Hut.

## Degree of belonging to Arab culture and change in local identity

Responses suggest that participants believe that there can be change in one's lifestyle without it reflecting change in one's culture. While around 56% of the respondents think that their culture is either the same or very similar to that of their parents, only 28% think the same about their lifestyles.

| Similarity | Culture | Lifestyle |
| --- | --- | --- |
| Exactly the same | 12 | 6 |
| Somewhat similar | 44 | 22 |
| Somewhat different | 31 | 39 |
| Very different | 13 | 33 |

Table 6  Similarity to parents' culture and lifestyle

Percentages represented in Table 6 suggest that respondents feel that their adoption of the outer layers of cultures, which give them a different lifestyle from that of their parents, does not change their core cultural values, which most continue to share with their parents.

An investigation of whether the use of English has resulted in changes in students' attitudes towards their families, their identity, and the way they relate to Arab culture and the West, reveals that 73% believe that using English as a medium of communication has definitely not or has barely changed how they relate to their families. Similarly, 71% report that learning English has not changed their sense of having an Arab identity, and 68% think that it has definitely not or not really affected their attitude towards

## 4 Appropriating English: Languages in Identity Construction

Arab culture. Learning English however is perceived to have contributed to changing respondents' interpretation of world events (72%) and their own outlook towards the future (69%) as illustrated in Table 7.

| Change | Relating to family | Arab identity | Relating to Arab culture | Interpretation of world events | Outlook on future plans |
|---|---|---|---|---|---|
| Definitely | 6 | 10 | 6 | 44 | 41 |
| Somewhat | 21 | 18 | 26 | 28 | 28 |
| Not really | 43 | 1 | 33 | 22 | 20 |
| Definitely not | 30 | 71 | 35 | 6 | 11 |

Table 7 Changes resulting from learning English

Based on the findings discussed above, it may be concluded that the majority of the respondents have appropriated many layers of western culture in their daily lives and exhibit a behavior that meshes tradition and modernity to construct a new Arab identity. They use both English and Arabic in their daily interactions, watch Arabic and English media, and prefer to dress in western clothes. However, over 70% of the respondents considered themselves to be mainly Arab as compared to only 19% who claimed to belong to both cultures. Here too there are important regional differences between Egyptians on one side and the other four groups on the other. Only 42% of the Egyptians responded that they considered themselves Arabs as opposed to 63% to 79% for the other groups.

Responses to questions eliciting students' perceptions of how globalization and the adoption of English have impacted Arab culture and identity, reflect the ambivalence usually felt by multilingual/multicultural individuals towards their belonging to more than one culture and language (see Table 8). Although most respondents (94%) acknowledged the positive impact of English and globalization on Arab culture, 62% felt that the effects of learning English and globalization is not really positive on Arab identity and 28% asserted that it was definitely not positive.

| Effect | On Arab culture | On attitude towards Western culture | On Arab identity |
|---|---|---|---|
| Definitely/somewhat positive | 94 | 45 | 30 |
| Not really positive | 4 | 40 | 62 |
| Definitely not positive | 2 | 15 | 28 |

Table 8 Effect of learning English and globalization

For the surveyed students, speaking the other's language and adopting some of the other's cultural artefacts does not necessarily lead to identifying with him nor necessarily developing a positive attitude towards the West. When asked whether the adoption of English is a good or a bad idea for Arabs, 10% thought it was a good idea and 29% thought it was a bad idea compared to the majority (62%) who stated that it was neither good nor bad, thus lending further support to the interpretation that English serves a primarily instrumental function. These attitudes are reminiscent of attitudes towards colonial languages during the colonial period. In many cases, the colonized learned the colonizer's language to use it as an instrument of resistance rather than obedience. Fanon describes how the perception of French during the Algerian struggle for independence changed from the language of colonialism and oppression to an instrument of reform and change. He stated that:

> In the earlier phases of the struggle, national resistance and identity was pegged exclusively to Arabic, and the use of French was virtually regarded as an act of cultural treason. Later, however, confronted with the reality of combat on a day-to-day basis, the Arabic language came to be stripped of "its sacred character, and the French language of its negative connotations" (Fanon cited in Mazrui, 2004, p. 115).

These changing perceptions of languages' strict association with national identity seem to be at play under globalization as well. While in the post independence era, local languages were perceived as the symbol of national identity and authenticity, in the age of globalization, "many languages are becoming progressively detached from national cultures as a new language ecology is emerging worldwide, where language function seems to be changing from symbolic to pragmatic, from representing national identity to providing access to world markets" (Dahbi, 2004, p. 629).

## Discussion

For the Arab bilingual youth, the desire to be part of modernity through English, and the affirmation of one's identity as an Arab are not felt to be in opposition. In discussions with my students in a course on the sociolinguistic context of Arabic (fall of 2007), many expressed the opinion that modernity and Arabness are not necessarily lived as two discrete points in a continuum but rather as intertwined parts of a whole. The 30 students in the course were from all parts of the Arab world. The group discussions were focused on examining the role of Arabic in Arab identity. Their initial opinion was to define an Arab as someone who speaks Arabic as his/her mother tongue. However, further analysis of this one-to-one mapping conception of Arabic and Arab identity led them to acknowledge that although they definitely consider themselves Arabs, English has taken over important functions in their academic thought processes and everyday interactions. They admitted that they could no longer function exclusively in Arabic, nor carry out certain intellectual activities such as solving mathematical problems in Arabic (most students were from the engineering and business schools). Moreover, they all had *Arab* friends or knew other *Arabs*, who grew up in the West and who did not speak Arabic. During these discussions, students also pointed out that one of the barriers to speaking Arabic with friends was the existence of regional differences between the various Arabic dialects. They felt that it is sometimes difficult to communicate in Arabic with other Arabs from different dialectal backgrounds, particularly between the Maghreb (West) and the Mashreq (East) regions. In the end, students reached consensus. They agreed that what makes an Arab, Arab is his/her feeling of belonging to Arabness and that using Arabic as one's main language is no longer the necessary and sufficient condition for belonging to Arabness. This sense of belonging transcended linguistic and territorial boundaries and was believed to be grounded in sharing a common past, coming together against common threats and looking towards an imagined common future (Anderson, 1983; Barakat, 1993).

Additional support for the weaker link between Arabic and identification with Arabness was also expressed in an earlier survey of Arab American faculty who had moved from the West to the Arabian Gulf. Many stated that a major reason for their return to the Arab world was to raise their children in an Arab culture. However, for them Arab identity lies more in the values that are part of Arab culture, which need to be preserved, than in which language is dominant. In response to a question about defining cultural identity a female faculty member wrote, "My emotional being is very Arabic, yet my logic (mind) is westernized somehow." Here too, we have a discourse expressing the intertwining of traditional values, associated with Arabness, and modernity, associated with English in the construction of Arab identity among Arab American expatriates.

Researchers have pointed out that young Arabs today live their linguistic and cultural duality along a continuum where the Arabic language and culture symbolize authenticity and certain nostalgia for the past, while English or French symbolize modernity, status, and cosmopolitanism (Dahbi, 2004; Findlow, 2006; Gill, 1999; Zakharia, 2010). For Arabs who live "at home", both the desire to be part of today's global culture, to which English opens the doors, and the feeling of belonging to Arabness coexist. They do not feel they have to make a choice and are comfortable with being both depending on their audience and setting (Badry, 2007). This acceptance of duality suggests that the influence of a second language on native culture and identity must be reinterpreted outside of the earlier paradigms which placed language at the core of cultural identification. Using Hofstede's (1993) "onion metaphor" language has moved away from the centre of the onion to become one of the intermediate layers that can be peeled off. The multilayered onion metaphor is a useful construct because it allows us to explain changes that can occur at some layers and not at others. Furthermore, the embrace of other cultures and languages is a choice that has impacted the young generations' lifestyles but not their core cultural values, which they consider to be similar to those of their parents.

This cultural blending is not a recent phenomenon. The tendency to think of globalization as a twentieth-century phenomenon ignores that contact between cultures or what Morley (2000) calls "transculturation" has been the norm rather than the exception throughout human civilizations.

## 4 Appropriating English: Languages in Identity Construction

History clearly shows that human development has, in fact, been predicated on blending rather than purity of knowledge. Blending of different languages and cultures has helped many languages develop and stay alive and has led to the greatest achievements of human civilizations throughout history. Morley (2000) offers what he calls "a progressive notion of home …which does not necessarily depend, for its effective functioning, on the exclusion of all forms of otherness, as inherently threatening to its own internally coherent self-identity. Clearly, in this respect, internal hybridity is the necessary correlative to a greater openness to external forms of difference, and is thus the condition of a more porous and less rigidly policed boundary around whatever is defined as the home community" (p. 15). Cultural flows must not be seen as "processes of homogenization but as part of reorganization of the local" (Pennycook, 2007, p. 7), where local cultures take up from global forms to produce new forms of glocal identifications. As Campbell (1999) argues, "increased coherence and integration in the mounting global traffic in people and meanings" encourages individuals to be actively engaged in reconstructing an identity which is both global and local. At the same time that uniformity stretches across geographical borders, there is also locally "an increase in the scale and importance of 'neo-tribes' – instances of multiple local acts of self-identification with the tags of ethnic and geo-cultural allegiance … together with self-recruitment to a great variety of other imagined and self-constructed communities" (Campbell, 1999, p. 1). Under these conditions, resistance to adopting new ways of speaking becomes low because people do not see their performances in different vernaculars as a threat to their identity, but rather as an added value and enriching experience.

The linguistic and cultural behaviours and perceptions expressed by the students in this study lend support to a non essentialist approach to identity. Identity is not constant across time or space; it involves individuals' tolerance of ambivalence and friction between the local and global especially if that means creating more opportunities and opening up desired spaces associated with the other. According to Canagarajah (2005) some of these tensions about the place of the colonial languages are a result of tensions between decolonisation and globalisation. While non-western communities were busy working on one project (decolonisation), the carpet has been pulled from under their feet by another project (globalisation). It is as if one historical process got subsumed by another before the first process was complete. There are significant differences in the project of both movements: decolonisation entails resisting English in favour of building an autonomous nation state; globalisation has made the borders of the nation state porous and reinserted the importance of the English language for all communities, through multinationals, market forces, pop culture, cyber space, and digital technology. ... People are not prepared to think of their identities in essentialist term (as belonging exclusively to one language or culture), their cultures as monolithic (closed against contact with other communities), and their knowledge forms as pure (uniformly local or centralised). (pp. 195–196)

While it is clear that participants in the study seem to have welcomed global English into their personal lives and made it part of their identity, it is equally important to remember that "often the construction of identity ... is not an individual or exclusively personal thing. Selves are neither made nor changed in isolation" (Ryan, 1997, p. 42). Identity choices and boundaries within which we move are set by the social milieu we belong to. These boundaries, as Giroux (1991) argues, are "socially organized with maps of rules and regulations that serve to limit or enable particular identities, individual capacities and social forms" (quoted in Ryan, 1997, p. 43). The dominant ideology in the UAE, espousing globalization to achieve rapid modernization and assigning high value to English, may have predetermined what choices young Arab residents of the UAE make in order to improve their future prospects.

In addition, the attractiveness of English as a preferred choice is also bolstered by factors relating education policies, curricular, and pedagogical practices associated with the teaching of Arabic. First, adopted language-in-education policies do not address the impact of the complex diglossic nature of Arabic. The exclusive use of MSA in literacy development with young learners ignores important differences between the dialectal variety spoken at home and the MSA used in school. The traditionally prescriptive approach used to teach MSA as the only form of Arabic has not succeeded in promoting literacy in Arabic. A biliteracy continua that advocates the need to promote different literacies, using multiple linguistic varieties (Hornberger, 2003) and establishing a transition from dialectal varieties to the standard form may ease learners into the literate form and motivate them to learn it. Second, in many Arab countries the use of Arabic as a medium of instruction only for what is perceived as "traditional subjects" as opposed to the use of English (or French) for what is considered "modern subjects of sciences, mathematics and technology" has been used to explain students' lack of motivation to learn Arabic. As Zakharia (2010) argues, "In devaluing the Arabic language, schools also devalue the knowledge passed on in that language" (p. 173). For example, in a study examining language-in-education policies in Lebanese high school she found that "[a]dministrators, teachers, and students complained about students' misbehaviour in Arabic classes almost across the board" (p. 171). Students reported being bored and demotivated in Arabic classes. These disciplinary problems were attributed to students' and parents' undervaluation of Arabic. However, the author points out that the structure of the curriculum, pedagogical approaches, and content taught in Arabic are also responsible for the relative lack of interest in Arabic literacy. Under these conditions, and while waiting for Arabic teaching to improve, English (or French) becomes the more efficient way to acquire the required know how to be part of the global world.

## Summary and conclusion

Participants in this study displayed a linguistic behavior that is, for the most part, open and porous across social spaces. They reported using both English and Arabic in most of their interactions, although their use of English was more prevalent outside family circles than with their parents and siblings. Their stated linguistic preferences also revealed a bilingual behavior with a language distribution running along the modern/traditional axis. English was preferred for intellectual/modern domains while Arabic was the preferred language to express affective/ traditional activities. Participants' responses also confirmed an increasing appropriation of western cultural behaviours in dress and entertainment, but a clear preference for Arabic food. In terms of identification and sense of belonging respondents identified themselves as belonging to Arabness despite their acknowledgment of the increased role of English in their life. Participants recognized that English has had a major impact in their outlook for the future and how they interpreted world events, but did not feel that it affected the way they related to either Arab culture or their families. Moreover, over half of the respondents did not think that learning English has given them a positive attitude towards the West. In fact, an overwhelming majority considered that globalization has had a positive influence on Arab culture (94%) as compared to around 30%, who believed that globalization impacted Arab identity in a positive manner. The degree to which they self-identified themselves with the Arabic language varied from one region to the other. However, the limited background information collected from participants and the small sample make it impossible to explain these differences. Additional data focusing on regional differences is necessary to assess their extent.

The linguistic and cultural behaviours and perceptions expressed by the participants in this study lend support to a non essentialist multifaceted view of identity and point to an appropriation of English in the construction of an Arab identity that is not centred around language. Based on these findings, personal experience, and observations, it can be concluded that global English and globalization have resulted in behaviours that appear to support the homogeneity perspective in that people in the UAE and elsewhere are increasingly adopting certain American ways of life such as clothing, music, pop culture, and the use of English. However, these same "Americanisms" show different levels of appropriation of localisms leading to heterogeneity. The English spoken reflects local flavours through codemixing and translanguaging, blue jeans and t-shirts are worn under the traditional Abaya, the dishdasha is worn with a baseball cap, rap music is sung in Arabic, and the hamburger is served with Arabic flavours. The adoption of English as a medium of communication is lived as expressing the modern side of a mainly Arab identity even among populations that predominantly use English in their daily lives. Identity is allowed to be more open to external influences and this openness is not perceived as a threat.

## 4 Appropriating English: Languages in Identity Construction

In the Arabic context, discourses about Arab identity reveal a multilayered conception of identity that includes on the one hand, a sense of belonging to the imagined Arab nation (al qawmiyya al 'arabiya), reminiscent of Anderson's "imagined communities" (Anderson, 1983), which transcends political borders and relies on MSA as its symbol. MSA is held onto as the thread uniting the increasingly divergent Arab nations that make up the Arab world. On the other hand, the national dialectal variety symbolizes a national identity (al qutriya). The country's dialectal variety is used in everyday interactions and is the language of affect and citizenship. Both forms, the standard and dialectal varieties, represent intertwined acts of authentic linguistic identity and combine with English (or French) to express the modern/global facet of a modern Arab identity.

Bilingual and multilingual communities around the world have always lived their lives through more than one language (see for example Mohanty's (2001) description of the Indian context). What is particular to the UAE context is the rapidly decreasing role of Arabic in literacy and media contexts, which must be addressed if Arabic is to remain one of the languages in its future (Khaled, 2010). The limited role of Arabic locally is not necessarily due to the presence of suppraterritorial English but to the type of educational policies in place which do not promote a truly bilingual approach. Campbell's (1999) description of life under globalization as "a duplex or semi-detached mental habitat, one half of which is global and the other local and which must be linked if the habitat is to survive" (p. 1) captures well the mental and affective state of young generations all over the world including the young Arab generations. What is needed is a balance between the two halves of the duplex, which can be achieved by going beyond lip service to Arabic literacy. A serious reflection on the diglossic nature of Arabic and how it impacts literacy development, an overhaul of the Arabic curriculum and its pedagogy, and an emphasis on teacher training are all urgently called for to maintain bilingualism and strengthen the Arabic act of identity in the UAE.

The ambivalence regarding how young Arabs feel about their constructed Arab identity reflects ideological and political discourses prevalent all over the Arab world today. In the UAE, as elsewhere, the desire to preserve an authentic Arab identity and the perceived inevitability of adopting English as the fastest way towards success are two sides of an identity that has appropriated the global language to serve its needs. However, appropriation of English does not have to be at the expense of the national language. For Arabic to remain part of the identity of young and future generations in the UAE (and elsewhere in the Arab world), the same efforts exerted in teaching English must be brought to bear in improving the teaching of Arabic.

## References

Al Baik, D. (10 March 2008) UAE makes Arabic official language. *Gulf News*. [government]. Retrieved January 11, 2011, from <http://gulfnews.com/news/gulf/uae/government/uae-makes-arabic-official-language-1.90822>

Al Baik, D. (16 March 2008). It is not acceptable to drop Arabic language from our lives. [The Nation: Heritage and culture] *Gulf News*. Retrieved January 11, 2011, from <http://gulfnews.com/news/gulf/uae/heritage-culture/it-is-not-acceptable-to-drop-arabic-language-from-our-lives-1.91564>

Al Lawati, A., & Al Najami, S. (20 March 2008). In depth: Sorry, I don't speak Arabic. [The Nation: Education]. *Gulf News*. Retrieved January 11, 2011, from <http://gulfnews.com/news/gulf/uae/education/in-depth-sorry-i-don-t-speak-arabic-1.92415>

Al Najami, S. (18 October 2007). Bilingual education hangs in the balance for schools. [The Nation: Education]. *Gulf News*. Retrieved January 11, 2011, from <http://gulfnews.com/news/gulf/uae/education/bilingual-education-hangs-in-the-balance-for-schools-1.207122>

Al Saayegh, F. (27 May 2008). How can we maintain a national identity? *Gulf News*. Retrieved January 11, 2011, from <http://gulfnews.com/news/gulf/uae/general/how-can-we-maintain-a-national-identity-1.107008>

Anderson, B. (1993). *Imagined communities: Reflections on the origins and spread of nationalism*. London: Verso.

Appadurai, A. (1996). *Modernity at large: Cultural dimensions of globalization*. Minneapolis, MN: University of Minnesota Press.

Arabic is at the heart of UAE's identity [editorial]. (11 March 2008). *Gulf News*. Retrieved January 11, 2011, from <http://gulfnews.com/opinions/editorials/arabic-is-at-the-heart-of-uae-s-identity-1.90955>

Badry, F. (2007). Positioning the self, identity and language: Moroccan women on the move. In S. Ossman (ed.), *The places we share: Migration, subjectivity, and global mobility* (pp. 173–186). New York, NY: Lexington Books

Barakat, H. (1993). *The Arab world: Society, culture and state.* Berkeley, CA: University of California Press.

Benhabib, S. (2002). *The claims of culture: Equality and diversity in the global era.* Princeton, NJ: Princeton University Press.

Bhabha, H. (1994). *The location of culture.* London and New York: Routledge.

Blackledge, A., & Pavlenko, A. (2001). Negotiation of identities in multilingual contexts. *The International Journal of Bilingualism, 3,* 243–257

Block, D., & Cameron, D. (2002). *Globalization and language teaching.* London: Routledge.

Bodley, J.H. (1994). *From cultural anthropology: Tribes, states, and the global system.* <http://www.wsu.edu:8001/vcwsu/commons/topics/culture/culture-definitions/bodley-text.html>

Bourdieu, P. (1982). *Ce que parler veut dire: l'economie des echanges linguistiques.* Paris: Fayard.

Breton, R., & Reitz, J.G. (2003). Introduction: Rethinking the impact of globalization processes-differentiation as well as convergence. In R. Breton & J.G. Reitz (eds), *Globalization and society: Processes of differentiation examined* (pp. 1–10). London: Praeger.

Brubaker, R., & Cooper, F. (2000). Beyond "identity". *Theory and society, 29,* 1–47.

Brutt-Griffler, J. (2002). *World English: A study of its development.* Clevedon, UK: Multilingual Matters.

Brutt-Griffler, J. (2005). "Globalisation" and applied linguistics: Post-imperial questions of identity and the construction of applied linguistics discourse. *International Journal of Applied Linguistics, 15* (1), 113–115.

Campbell, J.R. (1999). *Identity and affect: Experiences of identity in a globalising world.* London: Pluto Press.

Canagarajah, S.A. (2005). Accommodating tensions in language-in-education policies: An afterword. In A.M.Y. Lin & P.W. Martin (eds), *Decolonisation, globalisation: Language-in-education policy and practice* (pp. 194–201). Clevedon, UK: Multilingual Matters.

Cornillie, B., Lambert, J., & Swiggers, P. (2009). Linguistic identities and language shifts in their ecolinguistic setting. In B. Cornillie, J. Lambert, & P. Swiggers (eds), *Linguistic identities, language shift and language policy in Europe* (pp. 9–24). Paris, France: Peeters.

Dahbi, M. (2004). English and Arabic after 9/11. *The Modern Language Journal, 88*(4), 628–631.

De Oliveira, S. (2002). Discourses of identity at the Spanish/Portuguese border: Self-identification strategies of centre and periphery. *National identities, 4*(3), 245–256.

Findlow, S. (2006). Higher education and linguistic dualism in the Arab Gulf. *British Journal of Sociology of Education, 27* (1), 19–36.

Garcia, O. & Skutnabb-Kangas, T. (eds). (2006). *Imagining multilingual schools: Language in education and glocalization.* Clevedon: Multilingual Matters.

Germain, R.D. (2000). Globalization in historical perspective. In R. Germain (ed.), *Globalization and its critics: Perspectives from political economy.* New York: St Martin's Press.

Gill, H. (1999). Language choice, language policy and the tradition-modernity debate in culturally mixed postcolonial communities: France and the francophone Maghreb as a case study. In Y. Suleiman (ed.), *Language and society in the Middle East and North Africa: Studies in variation and identity* (pp. 122–136). Surrey, UK: Curzon.

Hansen, J.G., & Liu, J. (1997). Social identity and language: Theoretical and methodological issues. *TESOL Quarterly, 31*(3), 567–576.

Helot, C., & Young, A. (2006). Imagining multilingual education in France: A language and cultural awareness project at primary level. In O. Garcia & T. Skutnabb-Kangas (eds), *Imagining multilingual schools: Language in education and glocalization* (pp. 69–90). Clevedon, UK: Multilingual Matters.

Hofstede, G. (1994). *Cultures and organizations: Software of the mind.* London: Harper Collins.

Hornberger, N.H. (ed.). (2003). *Continua of biliteracy: An ecological framework for educational policy, research and practice in multilingual settings.* Clevedon, UK: Multilingual Matters.

Issa, W. (27 November 2008). Isolation won't protect identity. *Gulf News.* Retrieved January 11, 2011, from <http://gulfnews.com/news/gulf/uae/employment/isolation-won-t-protect-identity-1.145088>

Ismail, M., & Saffarini, R. (01 March 2008). Globalisation of the English language. *Gulf News.* Retrieved January 11, 2011, from <http://gulfnews.com/life-style/education/globalisation-of-the-english-language-1.87117>

Kachru, B.B. (1996). World Englishes: Agony and ecstasy. *Journal of Aesthetic Education, 30*(2), 135–155.

Khalaf, S. (2002). Globalization and heritage revival in the Gulf: An anthropological look at Dubai Heritage Village. *Journal of Social Affairs, 19*(75), 277–306.

Khalaf, S. (2005). National dress and the construction of Emirati cultural identity. *Journal of Human Sciences*, Bahrain University, *11*, 230–267.

Khaled, A. (20 May 2010). Parents seeing to promote language want Arabic equivalent of Harry Potter. *The National.*
Kraidy, M. (2005). *Hybridity, or the cultural logic of globalization.* Philadelphia, PA: Temple University Press.
Le Page, R., & Tabouret-Keller, A. (1985) *Acts of identity: Creole-based approaches to language and ethnicity.* Cambridge, UK: Cambridge University Press.
Leung, C., Harris, R., & Rampton, B. (1997). The idealized native speaker, reified ethnicities, and classroom realities. *TESOL Quarterly, 3* (3), 543–560.
Martin, W. (2000). Why this hatred of the market? In F.J. Lechner & J. Boli (eds), *The globalization reader.* Malden, MA: Blackwell.
Mazrui, A.M. (2004). *English in Africa: After the cold war.* Minneapolis: University of Minnesota Press.
Mohammed, E. (17 April 2008). Arabic is key to national identity. *Gulf News.* Retrieved January 11, 2011, from <http://gulfnews.com/news/gulf/uae/heritage-culture/arabic-key-to-national-identity-1.98255>
Mohanty, A.K. (2006). Multilingualism of the unequals and predicaments of education in India: Mother tongue or other tongue? In O. Garcia & T. Skutnabb-Kangas (eds), *Imagining multilingual schools: Language in education and glocalization* (pp. 262–283). Clevedon, UK: Multilingual Matters.
Morley, D. (2000). *Home territories: Media, mobility and identity.* London: Routledge.
Nederveen Pieterse, J. (1994). Globalisation as hybridisation. *International Sociology, 9*(2), 161–184.
Nero, S.J. (2005). Language, identities, and ESL pedagogy. *Language and Education, 19* (3), 194–211.
Norton, B. (1997). Language identity and the ownership of English. *TESOL Quarterly, 31*(3), 409–429.
Pennycook, A. (1995). English in the world/the world in English. In J.W. Tollefson (ed.), *Power and inequality in language education* (pp. 34–58). Cambridge, UK: Cambridge University Press.
Pennycook, A. (1998). *English and the discourses of colonialism.* London: Routledge.
Pennycook, A. (2007). *Global Englishes and transcultural flows.* London: Routledge.
Phillipson, R. (1992). *Linguistic imperialism.* Oxford, UK: Oxford University Press.
Phillipson, R. (2000). (ed.), *Rights to language equity, power, and education.* Mahwah, NJ: Lawrence Erlbaum Associates.
Phillipson, R. (2001). English for globalisation or for the world's people? *International Review of Education, 47*(3/4), 185–200.

Phillipson, R., & Skutnabb-Kangas, T. (1996). English only worldwide or language ecology. *TESOL Quarterly, 30*(3), 429–452. Retrieved January 11, 2011, from <http://www.jstor.org/stable/3587692>

Population to rise in 2010 to 7.5 million. Retrieved from <http://www.uaeinteract.com/docs/UAE>

Robertson, R. (1992). *Globalization: Social theory and global culture*. London: Sage.

Ryan, J. (1997). Student communities in a culturally diverse school setting: Identity, representation and association. *Discourse: Studies in the cultural politics of education, 18*(1), 37–53.

Said, E. (1994). *Culture and imperialism*. New York: Knopf.

Salama, S. (21 April 2010). Law to protect Arabic to be enacted soon. *Gulf News*. Retrieved January 11, 2011, from <http://gulfnews.com/news/gulf/uae/government/law-to-protect-arabic-to-be-enacted-soon-1.615367>

Saraceni, M. (2009). Relocating English: Towards a new paradigm for English in the world. *Language and Intercultural Communication, 9*(3), 175–186.

Scholte, J.A. (2000). *Globalization: A critical introduction*. New York: Palgrave.

Shohamy, E. (2006). Imagined multilingual schools: How come we don't deliver? In O. Garcia & T. Skutnabb-Kangas (eds), *Imagining multilingual schools: Language in education and glocalization* (pp. 171–183). Clevedon, UK: Multilingual Matters.

Shuey, R. (2001). Globalization: Implications of US national security. In G.J. Wells, R. Shuey, & R. Kiely (eds), *Globalization* (pp. 37–51). New York: Novinka Books.

Skutnabb-Kangas, T. (1999). Linguistic human rights – are you naïve or what? One world, many tongues, special issue on language policies, *TESOL Journal, 8*(3), 6–12.

Skutnabb-Kangas, T. (2000). *Linguistic genocide in education – or worldwide diversity and human rights?* Mahwah, NJ: Lawrence Erlbaum Associates.

Spencer-Oatey, H. (2000). *Culturally speaking: Managing rapport through talk across cultures*. London: Continuum.

Suleiman, Y. (1999). (ed.), *Language and society in the Middle East and North Africa*. Richmond, Surrey, UK: Curzon.

Suleiman, Y. (2003) *The Arabic language and national identity: A study in ideology* Washington, DC: Georgetown University Press.

Tajfel, H. (1974). Social identity and intergroup behavior. *Social Science Information, 13*, 65–93.

Tomlinson, J. (1999). *Globalization and culture*. Chicago: University of Chicago Press.

Tütsch, H. (1965). *Facets of Arab nationalism*. Detroit, MI: Wayne State University Press.

Urciuoli, B. (1995). Language and borders. *Annual Review of Anthropology, 24*, 525–546. Retrieved January 11, 2011, from <http://www.jstor.org/stable/2155948>

Wells, G.J. (2001). The issue of globalization: An overview. In G.J. Wells, R. Shuey & R. Kiely (eds), *Globalization* (pp. 1–36). New York: Novinka Books.

World Factbook. (2010). Retrieved January 11, 2011, from <https://www.cia.gov/library/publications/the-world-factbook/geos/ae.html>

Youssef, M. (11 March 2008). Use of Arabic will preserve our cultural identity – intellectuals. *Gulf News*. Retrieved January 11, 2011, from <http://gulfnews.com/news/gulf/uae/heritage-culture/use-of-arabic-will-preserve-our-cultural-identity-intellectuals-1.90978>

Zakharia, Z. (2010). Language in education policies in contemporary Lebanon: Youth perspectives. In O. Abi-Mershed (ed.), *Trajectories of education in the Arab world* (pp. 157–184). London: Routledge.

# Appendix

Students' survey
Language and identity research

---

Please fill out this survey by ticking or circling the most appropriate choice. Your answers are confidential. Thank you for agreeing to participate.

1. Age group *(please tick one)*
   ☐ 18 or younger     ☐ 19–25     ☐ 26 and over

Major_____ Freshman_____ Sophomore_____ Junior_____ Senior_____

2. Gender: *(please tick one)* ☐ Male     ☐ Female

3. Arab and any acquired other Nationality: *(please fill in the blank)* _____
   Mother tongue _____

4. Did you attend a private____ or public school? ____

5. What is your preferred language in everyday communication?

|   | Arabic |
|---|---|
|   | English |
|   | Both English and Arabic |
|   | Other |

6. If you had to compare your culture with that of your parents would you say it is
   Exactly the same   Somewhat similar   Somewhat different   Very different

7. If you had to compare your lifestyle with that of your parents would you say it is
   Exactly the same   Somewhat similar   Somewhat different   Very different

8. Learning English has affected my interpretation of world events
   Definitely   Somewhat   Not really   Definitely not

9. Learning English has affected my plans for my future
   Definitely   Somewhat   Not really   Definitely not

10. Speaking English has affected the way I relate to my family
    Definitely   Somewhat   Not really   Definitely not

11. Speaking English has affected my attitude towards Arabic culture
    Definitely   Somewhat   Not really   Definitely not

12. Speaking English has affected my attitude positively towards western culture
    Definitely   Somewhat   Not really   Definitely not

13. Globalization has changed Arab culture
    Definitely   Somewhat   Not really   Definitely not

14. Speaking English all the time is a very good idea
    Definitely   Somewhat   Neither good not bad   Definitely not

## 4 Appropriating English: Languages in Identity Construction

15. With my friends I speak
    | | | | | |
    |---|---|---|---|---|
    | English | All the time | Most of the time | Sometimes | Never |
    | Arabic | All the time | Most of the time | Sometimes | Never |

16. With my parents I speak
    | | | | | |
    |---|---|---|---|---|
    | English | All the time | Most of the time | Sometimes | Never |
    | Arabic | All the time | Most of the time | Sometimes | Never |

17. With my brothers and sisters I speak English
    | | | | | |
    |---|---|---|---|---|
    | English | All the time | Most of the time | Sometimes | Never |
    | Arabic | All the time | Most of the time | Sometimes | Never |

18. With strangers I speak
    | | | | | |
    |---|---|---|---|---|
    | English | All the time | Most of the time | Sometimes | Never |
    | Arabic | All the time | Most of the time | Sometimes | Never |

19. At the university I speak
    | | | | | |
    |---|---|---|---|---|
    | English | All the time | Most of the time | Sometimes | Never |
    | Arabic | All the time | Most of the time | Sometimes | Never |

20. When it comes to my culture I consider myself
    | | | | |
    |---|---|---|---|
    | Mainly Arab | Equally Arab and western | More Western than Arab | Neither western nor Arab |

21. I feel most myself when I wear

    | | |
    |---|---|
    | | Western clothes |
    | | Traditional Arab clothes |
    | | Equally in both |

22. I prefer to read newspapers in

    | | |
    |---|---|
    | | Arabic |
    | | English |
    | | Both English and Arabic |
    | | Other |

23. I find that I think better when I use

|   | Arabic |
|---|---|
|   | English |
|   | Both English and Arabic |
|   | Other |

24. When it comes to expressing my feelings, I prefer to use

|   | Arabic |
|---|---|
|   | English |
|   | Both English and Arabic |
|   | Other |

25. Overall, the language that really expresses who I am best is

|   | Arabic |
|---|---|
|   | English |
|   | Both English and Arabic |
|   | Other |

26. Using English in my studies

|   | allows me to express my ideas more easily |
|---|---|
|   | doesn't make a difference |
|   | makes it difficult for me to fully express myself |

27. My favourite music is

|   | Arabic |
|---|---|
|   | Western |
|   | Both |

28. My favourite food is

|  | Arabic food |
|--|--|
|  | European food |
|  | Asian food |
|  | American food |

29. To be part of today's Modern world Arabs should

|  | adapt English for business and science |
|--|--|
|  | revive their traditions and Arabic culture through Arabic |
|  | recognize the superiority of English |
|  | modernize Arabic to be used in Business and science |

30. List 4 of your favourite TV channels

Arabic channels_____

_____

English channels_____

_____

31. Does the way you dress express who you really are?

| Yes |  |
|--|--|
| No |  |

32. I consider myself belonging to both Arab and western cultures

| Yes |  |
|--|--|
| No |  |

33. I consider my identity to be mainly an Arab identity

| Yes | |
|---|---|
| No | |

If yes, in what ways?
___

34. What do you think of the US government position towards the Arab world?
___

35. What do you think of the Palestinian and the Iraq issues?
___

Thank you

HASSAN R. ABDEL-JAWAD AND ADEL S. ABU RADWAN

## 5 The Status of English in Institutions of Higher Education in Oman: Sultan Qaboos University as a Model

### ABSTRACT

This chapter presents the results of an investigation into the role and use of English in institutions of higher education in Oman, focusing on Sultan Qaboos University, Oman's only public university, as a model. The study shows that English is seriously competing with Arabic and gradually is overtaking its role in users, usages, and domains. English is the dominant language of interaction, discussion, deliberation in official meetings, and among faculty, staff, and some cases students. Moreover, English is not only the language of instruction in most departments and colleges but is also acting as a competing official language, since most, if not all, documents such as basic laws, by-laws, regulations, and minutes of meeting are originally issued in English and then translated into Arabic. Publications of various types, including magazines, newsletters, and flyers are commonly published in English or in both languages. In addition, high proficiency in English is a basic university admission requirement not only for postgraduate programs but also for undergraduate programs. Quite recently, the Ministry of Higher Education issued a decision to adopt a general Foundation Program in all higher education institutions in Oman. This program includes four areas of learning: English language, mathematics, computing, and general study skills, with the noticeable absence of Arabic. Moreover, financial and human resources allocated to the promotion of English vastly outweigh the resources allocated to teaching the native language despite frequent complaints made by instructors about students' weakness in Arabic.

## Introduction

Over the last few decades, English has been serving as a lingua franca in many international circles, and accordingly has achieved the status of a "global language". Evidence of the powerful status of this lingua franca is manifested in many domains and fields. According to Crystal (1997), most of the scientific, technological, and academic information in the world, and over 80% of all information stored in electronic retrieval systems are created in English. Moreover, scientific journals in most fields worldwide are published in English more than any other language, and the most influential databases in the world are extracted from English-language journals. English is also the dominant and sometimes the sole language at conferences, symposia, programs, and international gatherings. According to Hersh and Zhang (1999), English is basically the working language in international medical circles, and advancement in this particular field requires knowledge of the language. Furthermore, higher education programs in many non-English speaking countries adopt English as the language of instruction and research writing. Zughoul (2003) states that English has become the main language of research and instruction in institutions of higher education in the Arab world, especially in faculties of medicine, science, engineering, and business.

The global spread of English has stirred strong intellectual, social, cultural, and even political debates in many countries. While English is perceived by many as a means of progress, democracy, modernity, technology, and information, it is seen as by others as a hegemonic and colonial agent which threatens their indigenous languages and cultural identities (Hoogstad, 2008). This debate has generated several new concepts such as "killer language", "linguistic imperialism", "language globalization", "globalization of language", "language hegemony", and "perfidious plot". Some view this insatiable spread of English as an imperial hegemony which is deeply embedded in a set of cultural, social, economic, and political relations (Phillipson, 1992, 2003). On the other hand, others emphasize the naturalness and neutrality of the spread of English (Kachru, 1986; Pennycook,

1999, 2001). Pennycook (2001) argues that English is bound to the world and the world is bound to English. He, therefore, adopts the "functional perspective" which stresses choice and usefulness of English as an explanation for its global spread. This spread, though it may have been initiated by colonialism, has actually been "an accidental by-product of global forces" and accordingly is "the property of the world" (p. 79). Moreover, it has been beneficial to humanity since it gives people access to tremendous resources available only in English.

The hegemony of English has become an issue of deep concern internationally, regionally, and locally, as people have increasingly felt that their cultural values and linguistic practices are at risk. For example, in non-English speaking western countries, there is a growing concern that English is expanding at the expense of internationally-recognized languages like French and German, which have historically been languages of scientific, administrative, and educational activities (Phillipson, 2003). Similarly, in the Arab world, especially in the Arabian Gulf countries, the wide spread use of English, perceived by a great majority as a hegemony, is raising great concerns in intellectual and political circles to the extent that several seminars, symposia, and conferences have been held to address this specific issue (e.g., Qatar February 2009 regional conference on "Language and identity: The danger of the hegemony/domination of English"). Many intellectuals believe that English is posing a great threat to Arabic (see e.g., Al-Qubaisi, 2009; Al-Sheikh, 2009). In this regard, Suleiman (2004) states that "Gulf intellectuals ... talk about how Arabic is under attack, how it is in grave danger of being overrun by other languages on its home ground, and how it is under siege and abandoned by its native sons and daughters who seem to prefer the lure of other tongues, mainly English" (p. 35). He adds that they feel that Arabic has become like "a small island that is in danger of being submerged by the foreign linguistic flood" (p. 35).

These intellectuals have often raised questions about whether English in any way represents a threat to the Arabic language and culture, and whether it challenges the position and/or role of Arabic in the Gulf. This project presents the results of an investigation into the role and use of English in institutions of higher education in Oman, focusing on Sultan Qaboos University (henceforth, SQU), Oman's most prestigious and only public university, as a model. The study explores the status, use, and spread of English at SQU, focusing on users, usages, and domains. Specifically, the study addresses the following research questions:

1. What is the status of English at SQU?
2. Is English encroaching on Arabic at SQU in terms of roles, functions, domains, and users?
3. Is English replacing Arabic in the domains that are traditionally reserved for Arabic?

To answer these research questions, it is critically important to understand the wider socio-political and cultural context in which SQU is located, the Sultanate of Oman at large. Thus, the next section provides an overview of the status of English in the Sultanate of Oman. The following section describes the situation at SQU, focusing on language use in official documents, meetings, publications, employment, interaction, admissions, and instruction. This will be followed by a discussion section, and finally a conclusion.

## Historical background

To trace the historical roots of the English language in Oman, Al-Busaidi (1995) gave a brief survey of the nature of the relations between Oman and Britain. Although Oman had never been a British colony, a Protectorate or a Mandated territory, Britain had been directly related to and involved in Omani affairs since at least 1800 and had signed a number of trading, commercial and friendship treaties and agreements in which Britain was granted favourable trading opportunities in the country. Consequently, English was the key operating language, especially among expatriates, mainly Indian medical and health services staff and British military personnel, who used to run most of the governmental institutions. In fact, a good command of

English was a basic requirement to get an official job (Al-Busaidi, 1995). Furthermore, what promoted the high status of English was a trend among the elites to use English in their daily interactions. Thus, "Oman is unique in its relationship with Britain ... [and] it readily accepted English in the running of its institutions in 1970" (Al-Busaidi, 1995, p. 86). The stage, thus, was set quite early for the dominance of English. In fact, up to 1970 and even after, there was a total dependency on non-Arabic speaking expatriates, who were the dominant workforce, with English being not only the language of wider communication among them but also the main official language for them.

Another historical factor which has contributed to the promotion of English in Oman is the return of great numbers of Omanis who were fluent in English from Zanzibar, resulting in a major increase in the use of English. Al-Busaidi (1995) remarks that "perhaps no other linguistic group had been more influential in this process than the Swahili speaking Omanis" (p. 95).

Moreover, the presence of a large Indian community and the great number of other foreign workers in Oman has contributed significantly to the spread and promotion of English (Poole, 2006). This linguistic diversity has been encouraged by Oman's policy of tolerance, which has tolerated the spread, use, and maintenance of other languages.

## Factors promoting the spread of English: Official policies

In addition to the various historical factors mentioned above, the special status of English in Oman has further been promoted by the Omani government's official policies. Al-Busaidi (1995) mentions that English has been receiving legislative power from the state and has been institutionalized in various domains. This has been corroborated by many Omani researchers (e.g., Al-Balushi, 1999, 2001; Al-Busaidi, 1998; Al-Issa, 2002, 2006a, 2006b, 2006c, 2007; Al-Seyabi, 1995; Al-Toubi, 1998). Al-Issa (2006a) states that

English receives all forms of official support, e.g. political, economic, social, and legislative, from the government and that "English in Oman has institutionalized domains like business ... media and education and is therefore a powerful tool for modernization, national development, and Omanization" (p. 220). Contrary to expected norms, where the national language (in this case Arabic) is usually adopted in the implementation of national policies, English is perceived by policy makers to be the key to the success of the national policy of Omanization, i.e. the process of replacing foreign workforce with Omani nationals. These policy makers maintain that English must be the medium of education and training in technology, industrialization, commerce and business, oil industry, and in running and maintaining the country's natural resources (Al-Busaidi, 1995). Thus, English is perceived as a nation-building language. Similarly, Al-Balushi (2001) writes that "English came to be perceived by many Omani officials and authorities as the second language through which all economic, technological, vocational, educational, and communicative functions could be conducted" (p. 5)

In the document, Reform and Development of General Education, published in 1995, the Ministry of Education in Oman recognizes the great importance of English as the global language of science, technology, business, banking, world economy, communication, and telecommunications networks. Consequently, the Omani Government "opted for English as its only official foreign language," and required it to be taught in schools from the first grade and to be used as the medium of instruction in higher education institutions (Al-Issa, 2006a, p. 4).

## General atmosphere and attitudes

These official policies and the dominant positive stand towards English have contributed to its spread to the extent that it has covered a wide spectrum of functions and domains, thus encroaching upon the status of the national language. English is the main language of the labour market since the foreign workforce that runs much of Oman's economic machinery uses it as a lingua franca. Moreover, English predominates in many organizations and institutions of higher education including bilingual private schools, community private schools, technical colleges, and companies such as Petroleum Development of Oman, Oman Refinery Company, Oman Air, Oman Aviation Services, and others. Moreover, "all key economic centres and social services were developed with English as the language of internal and external communication" (Al-Busaidi, 1995, p. 132). This has created a linguistic division of labour, i.e. *diglossic situation*, where traditional, local, tribal, and religious affairs and domains are associated with Arabic, while novelty, nationalization, modernization, industrialization, business, technology, and development are generally associated with English. This has led to a recession of the role of Arabic to a closed class of functions and domains and to the rise and expansion of English to an open class of functions and domains. Accordingly, Arabic signifies local identity, solidarity, and traditions while English stands for high socio-economic status and high vitality.

This expansion in the role of English has further been promoted by a very dominant and positive attitude toward the language by Omanis in general. In fact, this attitude echoes a wider and a more universal trend which identifies English as a language that opens doors for development, modernization, information, and even democracy, and considers it as "a key to better life for the poor and the underprivileged" (Pennycook, 1999, para. 1). In a recent edition (October 1999, No. 237) of the *El Gazette* ("English Language Journal Opening Doors Across the World") Pennycook refers to a quote in the editorial about the importance of English, which says that "for many of the world's poorest people, English can hold the key to escape from grinding poverty." No wonder then that "parents around the world are demanding greater access to English, and therefore to provide more English at the primary level will enhance development" (Pennycook, 1999, para. 3).

At the Omani local level, while the overwhelming majority of children acquire Arabic as their first language, a small yet influential percentage of the population prefers to use English as a first language at home. Many

Omanis, besides seeing English as a gate to development, progress, and modernization, believe that it is a key to success in their professional lives. For those coming from the more upwardly mobile professional class, the use of English has often become an assertion of alignment with the above-mentioned global context. Thus, English has been primarily perceived as a symbol of prestige and an assertion of a superior social status. Similarly, for the young generation, being young, forward-looking, modern, technologically advanced and enlightened is usually associated with speaking English. Al-Jurf (2004) showed a similar pattern among Saudi and Jordanian university students in the language and scientific colleges. This association may have stemmed from the young generation's overall dissatisfaction with the local cultures, products, and even languages, and at the same time empathy towards western values, cultures and language. This has been a general trend not only in Oman but also in the Arab world in general. In this regard, El-Shibiny (2005) mentions that

> Arab thinkers and governments are worried by the infatuation of large numbers of young Arabs with western civilization. They are dazzled by western culture as presented through television, satellites and radio programs, and fascinated by western music, films, magazines, books, recreational games, etc. In addition, they are overwhelmed by western history in arts and literature, economics and science. (p. 106)

Moreover, the absence of any negative attitudes towards the language, since there is no association with colonization contrary to many other countries in the region, has fostered this evident affinity to English in the Omani context.

In conclusion, it is evident from the above discussion that both the global and national levels are conducive to the promotion of English, thus creating a more favourable and positive environment for the predominance of the language at various entities within the wider national context. One of these important and prestigious entities is Sultan Qaboos University. In the next section, the use and spread of English at SQU will be investigated, taking into consideration different domains, functions, usages and users.

## English at Sultan Qaboos University

SQU was established in 1986 to offer higher education to Omani youths, and it commenced with five colleges: Medicine, Engineering, Science, Education, and Agriculture. In 1987, the College of Arts and Social Sciences was established, followed by the College of Commerce and Economics in 1993. The College of Law joined the university in 2006, and finally the College of Nursing was established in 2008. According to statistical information obtained from the Deanship of Admissions and Registration, the student population in academic year 2009/2010 was 16,288, of whom approximately 99% are Omani nationals. SQU is a co-education institution with enrolment split almost evenly between the two genders (8,042 women and 8,246 men). The majority of students are enrolled in undergraduate programs (13,611), and the rest are enrolled in various postgraduate programs including master's and PhD degrees.

The main objectives of SQU, as stated in the University Law issued by Royal Decree 71/2006, give, whether explicitly or implicitly, a bigger role for English than Arabic in all aspects of university affairs. Of the 17 objectives listed, only two of them imply direct usage of Arabic while the remaining objectives require knowledge and use of English for their fulfilment. The following is a sample of these objectives:

1. Provision of specialists and experts of Oman in diverse fields, taking into account the changing need of the marketplace and working within the framework of state policy on resource development.
2. Constant modernization of the educational process at the undergraduate and postgraduate levels.
3. Preparation of Omani scientists, researchers and experts capable of undertaking organized, systematic and innovative work in diverse areas of science, arts and technology.
4. Interaction with international academic experience in all areas of thought, science and culture.
5. Cooperation with leading international universities and institutions

At the practical level, a quick survey of the use of English in different contexts conspicuously shows that English is not only used as a foreign language, but it has acquired the status of a second language, competing with, and in many cases encroaching on, the roles, position, and status of Arabic. In the following sections, the use of English in areas like official documents, publications, meetings, admissions, and instruction will be investigated.

## Official documents

The University Basic Law does not explicitly make any reference to an official language as Arabic is considered the official language of the university in conformity with all other state entities in the Sultanate of Oman. Accordingly, all official documents such as the University Charter, laws, by-laws, provisions, regulations, and decisions which carry the seal and signature of the University Vice Chancellor must be in Arabic. However, since a sizable number of the university staff is made up of non-native speakers, these documents are usually translated into English. Since its inception and until recently, the majority of the university advisors, deans, heads of departments and centres were non-native speaking expatriates. In such a context, documents produced by these administrators were originally drafted in English and then translated into Arabic. Therefore, English texts represented the *source texts* and the Arabic ones were the *target texts*. In principle, it is likely that the target text may never be as authentic and natural as the source one.

One very important type of official document is the contract, which includes employment, business, and international contracts. All employment contracts are produced in two versions: one in Arabic for Arabic speaking employees and the other in English for all non-native speaking expatriates. The Arabic version is considered the legal and reference document for the first group, while the English one is used for the second group.

On the other hand, business contracts such as procurement, construction, and maintenance contracts are generally produced in English, since most of the companies and entities engaged in any business with the university often adopt the global business language: English. These contracts are translated into Arabic, and in case of any dispute, the reference version is determined by mutual agreement as stated in each contract individually. International contracts, agreements, and memoranda of understandings are produced in three versions: one in each official language of the contracting parties, i.e. one in Arabic, one in the official language of the second contracting party, and a third version in English. The English version is the reference one in case of any dispute. Accordingly, it is evident that English is competing with Arabic as an official language in terms of all official documents.

## Publications, notices, and advertisements

Publications of various types, media and scientific, are commonly published in English or in both languages. In the university, there are five local media publications, four of which are published in Arabic and the fifth in English. In terms of scientific publications, the university publishes five academic journals produced by the Colleges of Engineering, Medicine, Science, Agriculture, and Arts and Human Sciences. While the first four journals are published entirely in English, the latter is a bilingual journal. It is important to note that while authors of articles published in the journal of the College of Arts and Social Sciences are required to produce abstracts in English for articles written in Arabic, the other Colleges do not require authors to translate their abstracts into Arabic.

With regard to announcements, advertisements and notices, English is competing with Arabic, if not dominating this area. A quick survey of all university bulletin boards shows that local advertisements are published equally in both languages. The same applies to advertisements about jobs/vacancies, sales, seminars, and workshops. Moreover, all announcements and public notices produced by the university administration, particularly the Public Relations Office, are bilingual. Advertisements about jobs/vacancies are often published in international chronicles, papers, and websites where English is the dominant language. In all these advertisements, proficiency in English is stated as a basic requirement for all jobs, even for colleges where the dominant language of instruction is Arabic, such as the College of Arts and Social Sciences and the College of Education. A good example of this trend is the academic year 2010–2011 advertisements regarding openings in the College of Arts and Social Sciences. In this particular advertisement, fluency in English is stated as one condition for all vacancies, including the ones in the Arabic Department. Moreover, the applicants are required to have experience in teaching in English or at least be able to teach in English. In contrast, none of the advertisements published by other colleges in the university demands knowledge of Arabic as a basic requirement for getting a teaching position. Again, the dominance of English over Arabic in these functions is readily apparent.

## Internet

The fact that English has a powerful global status has made it the dominant language of the internet, thus giving it more power, diffusion, and global status. It has become "the lingua franca of [the internet]. All other languages, irrespective of their status ... in their countries, will be local languages in that 'glorious global village'" (Mallikarjun, 2003, heading 22, para 3). At SQU, both students and staff use English extensively in all internet activities including, emailing, chatting, searching for information, and conducting various other operations. Among many factors, what promotes the extensive use of English in the cyber world is a lack of availability of most professional and specialized on-line sources of information in Arabic. Evidence of this is can be found on the university's main library website, where almost all electronic journals are available exclusively in English. A one-question random survey of 200 students at the university was conducted by the researchers. The students were asked about the most common language they use on the internet. More than 95% of the respondents reported that they use English almost exclusively when they are on-line.

## Language of meetings

In the meetings of all councils at the university, college and departmental levels, with the exception of the Colleges of Arts, Education, and Law, English is the working language. Accordingly, the minutes of these meetings are mainly recorded in English and subsequently translated into Arabic. Likewise, minutes of the Arabic-medium colleges are usually recorded in Arabic and often translated into English. Similarly, English predominates as the language of agendas, deliberations, and minutes in the meetings of most committees at all levels (e.g., university promotion committees, standards committee, quality assurance, and accreditation committees). Additionally, English acts as a lingua franca in the great majority of local, regional, and international conferences held at the university. Proceedings of these conferences are overwhelmingly published in English.

## Employment

Knowledge and a good command of English are always stated as a basic requirement for employment at the university. Employees can be classified into the following categories: administrative and support, academic, and technical. According to statistical information provided by Department of Planning and Statistics at the university, the number of administrative and support staff, as of December 2008, was 1023, of which 917 were Omanis.

It is true that the language of communication for the majority of them is Arabic; however, for all of them some knowledge of English is required, as they often have to interact and communicate with non-native speakers of Arabic. Furthermore, some of these Omani employees do not speak Arabic natively; thus, they frequently switch to English for communication.

The number of academic staff is 1,107 members, of whom 363 are non-native speakers of Arabic, coming from 43 nationalities, excluding Arab countries. English is used by these non-native speakers as a lingua franca in their daily interactions with all other employees. At the academic level, all faculty members are strongly encouraged to publish their research in international journals, which are predominately published in English. In fact, in order to be promoted, all faculty members are required to publish in such international journals. Interestingly, while the faculty in humanities are required to publish part of their work in English, those in the other colleges are not required to do the same in Arabic-based journals, thus creating some form of imbalance between the two languages.

The university employs 499 technical staff members, of whom 426 are Omanis whose native language is Arabic. However, due to the nature of their work, they usually use English more frequently than Arabic. The university hospital employs 2,010 staff members, of whom 997 are Omanis. Taking into account the nature of work and the fact that more than half the hospital employees are non-native speakers of Arabic, it follows that English is the predominant language there, both as a working language and as a language of interaction. In conclusion, it is evident that English is the dominant language for employment among employees and seems to be encroaching on the native language.

## Admission requirements

High proficiency in English is a basic university admission requirement not only for postgraduate programs but also for the undergraduate programs. Upon admission to the university, all undergraduate students must take an entrance test administered by the Language Centre, which is the largest academic unit in the university, consisting of 206 staff members, approximately 20% of the university faculty members. The main objectives of the Language Centre as stated in the university laws and regulations of 2006 are "to prepare students of the university to meet the rigorous demands of instruction in a foreign or second language.... [and to] ultimately develop the students' full potential as participants in a modern bilingual society, or for success in English-medium professional careers."

Based on the entrance test, students are placed in one of five non-credit proficiency levels (levels 2–6). Each proficiency level is an eight-week intensive English course during which students spend an average of 20 hours a week taking different language skills (reading, writing, speaking, and listening). A simple mathematical calculation reveals that, for instance, a student placed at level 2 has to take a total of 800 contact hours of non-credit intensive English before s/he can be admitted into his/her program of study. Once students complete level 6 successfully, they can join their own departments; however, they are required to take at least two English for Specific Purposes (ESP) courses in their respective specializations. These ESP courses, which are also given in the Language Centre, consist of 60 contact hours each per semester. In contrast, there is no similar intensive Arabic language program to prepare students for the rigor of academic study in Arabic-medium programs despite students' apparent difficulties in the use of academic Arabic, supposedly Modern Standard Arabic (MSA), as frequently voiced by many faculty members (personal communication, March, 2010).

Quite recently, the Ministry of Higher Education issued a decision regarding the Foundation Programs in all higher education institutions in Oman (*The Decision of the Higher Education Council No.13/2008, HE the Minister for Higher Education issued Ministerial Decision No.72/200*) stating that the General Foundation Programs should be adopted by all public and private higher education institutions operating in the Sultanate of Oman. These programs must include four areas of learning: English language, mathematics, computing, and general study skills, with the noticeable absence of Arabic.

The language admission requirements for postgraduate programs require a minimum of 550 on the TOEFL examination or level 6 in IELTS. Students with a score of 500 on the TOEFL or level 5 in IELTS must register for an advanced course in English and must graduate with a "B" average. Failure to achieve the target grade results in non-admission into the program. With regard to programs where Arabic is the language of instruction, the different programs set their own Arabic and English language admission requirements, which currently demand a minimum score of 500 on the TOEFL or level 5 in IELTS.

The language requirements for both the undergraduate and graduate programs show unequivocally a heavy focus on English language requirements and at the same time a noticeable absence of any Arabic language requirements. It may be argued this imbalance is due to the fact that English is the language of instruction in most colleges, and thus, students need to be properly prepared in English to achieve success in their studies. However, this same argument holds true for Arabic-medium programs, where many faculty members often complain bitterly and continuously about their students' inadequate command of Modern Standard Arabic.

## Language of instruction

In many Arab universities, it is often explicitly stated that the official language is Arabic, and hence it is the language of instruction, with a relatively few exceptions. However, as mentioned above, SQU's basic law does not refer to any specific language to be used as the official language of the university or as the language of instruction. This situation has given the different colleges and departments a considerable degree of freedom in determining their language of instruction. Since a sizable percentage of the staff members in the university are non-native speakers of Arabic who usually use English as a lingua franca, and since the university has been vigorously seeking international accreditation and recognition in order to achieve higher standards and to ensure quality, English has been adopted as the most viable option in this context. Accordingly, English has been adopted as the only language of instruction in all colleges, with the exception of the colleges of humanities and social sciences, which themselves have recently been promoting bilingual education in many of their departments.

Given that students are the entity which is directly influenced by this linguistic choice, their attitudes and opinions about this issue are of paramount importance. In view of this, a questionnaire (see appendix A) was designed to elicit information about their responses to this serious issue. The questionnaire, which consisted of 17 items, was randomly distributed to 128 students (62 males and 68 females) from the colleges which have adopted English as the language of instruction.

Students' responses to the questionnaire reveal several important points relating to the use of English at SQU. First, 31% of the respondents evaluated their proficiency in English before joining the university as weak, 65% as fair, and only 4% as good. Second, based on the Language Centre entrance test, 23% of the respondents were placed in the lowest level (i.e., level 2), and consequently had to go through the maximum number of intensive English courses (i.e., 5 levels), 16% were placed in level three and had to take 4 levels of intensive English, 16% in level 4 who had to take 3 intensive levels, and 45% in level 5 who had to go through 2 levels only. Despite this intensive English training, it is quite interesting that about 34% of the respondents reported that they had not benefited from the foundation courses in English and 55% of them reported that they had. The other 11% were exempted from the intensive courses.

With regard to language of instruction, the responses reveal the following results: first, 45% of the respondents indicated that they had encountered language problems in taking courses in their major, while 44% reported no problems, and 11% sometimes encountered problems. The majority of respondents (77%) indicated that they faced no difficulty in understanding teachers' lectures in class while 17% had some difficulty, and only 6% said they had serious difficulties. This may be attributed to the fact that a high percentage of the instructors are of Arab origin and in many cases when difficulty exists, they tend to switch to the native language. The same pattern applies to understanding questions both in class and during exams: 76% indicated they faced no problems, while 15% reported facing some problems, and 9% reported facing serious problems. However, when it comes to understanding texts, only 48% of the respondents had no difficulty in understanding the texts while 23% often had problems, and 30% always had difficulty. In line with this answer, 53% preferred to have the textbooks in English, 39% in Arabic, and 8% reported no language preference. However, when asked about whether they would perform better if the textbooks were in Arabic, 60% answered positively, while 37% answered negatively and 3% reported no effects for language of the textbooks. This same pattern also applies to class discussions.

When asked about preparation for examinations, 34% of the respondents reported that they spend more time on understanding language and content, 23% on language, and 40% on content only. In taking examinations, 30% of them indicated that they had difficulty understanding the questions because of language and 20% of them reported some difficulty, while 49% reported no language difficulties at all. Nevertheless, when asked if the use of Arabic in writing questions and answers would improve their performance, 65% of them reported it would, while 35% indicated it would not, and 5% showed no difference. When asked about the language which they will use at work after graduation. Sixty-four per cent of them reported that they will use English while only 27% mentioned they will use Arabic and 9% indicated they may use both languages.

Overall, when students were asked about their preferred language of instruction, 51% of them preferred English, 44% Arabic, and 5% indicated no language preference. It is evident that despite all the difficulties reported above, English is preferred over Arabic by more students. This same question was given to another group consisting of 132 students who were randomly chosen from the same colleges and who were also asked to give their justifications for their preferences. Fifty-seven per cent of the respondents preferred English and 43% preferred Arabic, a result which corroborates those reported by the first group. The justifications given by students in the second group are quite revealing, as they show the dominant trend in institutions of higher education in Oman. Interestingly, the explanations reveal a division of labour between the two languages, an idea alluded to earlier. Those who chose English gave the following justifications for their choices:

## 5 The Status of English in Institutions of Higher Education in Oman

- English is a global and international language.
- English is the dominant language in the marketplace.
- A big percentage of the faculty are non-native speakers of Arabic, and even those native speakers of Arabic do not appear to be competent to teach their specialization in Arabic.
- References, textbooks, manuals and other materials are available almost exclusively in English.
- English is the language of science and technology; thus, it brings them closer to developments and advances in their field of study.
- Scientific specializations are difficult to be taught in Arabic.
- Learning in English is a way for them to learn a second language, which is required if they opt to continue their higher education abroad.
- It is more beneficial to access information in the source language because translation of these sources into Arabic will result in loss of information.

As for those who selected Arabic, they provided the following reasons for their choice:

- Arabic is their native language, and it gives them pride to use it in learning.
- It is a way of maintaining their identity as Arabs and Muslims.
- It is easier to understand the subject, participate in discussions and give good answers if Arabic is used as the language of instruction. They pointed out that use of English hinders them from actively participating in class discussions.
- Learning in Arabic saves time as they spend more time trying to figure out the English texts.
- Arabic is the language of the society and they are more likely to use it when they graduate from the university.
- Arabic has been their sole language of instruction prior to joining the university, and switching to another language is an abrupt change, which is likely to affect them negatively in their educational pursuit.
- Many of their friends failed in their initial major due to language difficulties, and accordingly had to transfer to Arabic-based specializations.

Overall, these explanations show that the first group of students (those who prefer English) strongly believes that English is more practical and easier to use in their fields of study than Arabic. Moreover, they seem to perceive it as a more prestigious and superior language, which they often associate with higher level functions and domains. In addition to that, the majority of them are instrumentally motivated to learn the language because it gives them an advantage in their professional life and in the society after they graduate from the university. On the other hand, the second group of students (those who prefer Arabic) emphasizes the integrative nature of language use, as they prefer to use the language of the community for ease of communication and identity marking, which are more associated with domestic domains and functions.

In addition to the questionnaire, personal interviews were conducted with a large number of students and instructors individually and in groups to probe their views and feelings about the status of English at SQU. In these interviews, the overall attitude of the students was favourable towards English. The majority of them see English as a means to obtain scientific and technological information and to attain a good job. Moreover, they stressed that English is the dominant language of their constituencies and professions all over the world. Since English is the dominant language in their fields, survival outside the university after graduation necessitates using English in their daily communication. This apparent enthusiasm in using English is not hindered by the difficulties they encounter in their use of this foreign language, difficulties which they and their instructors emphatically expressed. These include difficulties in understanding textbooks and teachers' lectures, and in participating in class discussions, since their lack of a good command in English constrains their abilities to engage in class discussions. The difficulties are more evident in examinations because students encounter problems, not only in understanding the questions but also in writing the answers, especially for essay-type questions, which eventually results in low performance and low grades. Being aware of these difficulties, instructors usually tend to overlook the language problems and focus more on content. According to the instructors interviewed, this situation has resulted in the creation of a new variety of a highly technical working language which students use in their classes, exams and professional interactions.

Interestingly, the students pointed out that the general foundation courses offered in the Language Centre were of little help to them in coping with the linguistic demands of their specializations. However, they did remark that the English for Specific Purposes courses were directly relevant to their education, and thus were very beneficial to them. Many students mentioned that the difficulty associated with the language of instruction has led many students to transfer from English-medium colleges to Arabic-medium specializations. As for many others, they overcome the language difficulties by relying on summary notes and slides provided to them by their instructors. On a different issue, the interviewed students were divided on the rationale for using English. One group questioned the value of using English as the language of instruction because they argued that, after graduation, they are likely to work in public schools or in other government sectors where Arabic is the dominant language. The other group stressed the importance of English as a vehicle for them to obtain a good position in the industry and the private sector. In this regard, only a small percentage of the interviewees expressed any interest in the western culture or way of life.

In conclusion, students' views expressed in the two questionnaires and interviews seem to point to a distinctive case of divided loyalty. On the one hand, there is a strong attachment to the native language as it is associated with domestic and national values such as pride, identity, history, and religion to the extent that some of them prefer to use it over English as the language of instruction. On the other hand, a great majority of them, despite their evident weakness in English, have a strong, favourable, and positive attitude towards English not only as the language of technology and science, but also as the key to better jobs, a wider marketplace, and future professional development. In general, the student body at SQU is very receptive and welcoming to this foreign language.

## Discussion

The favourable attitude towards English in Oman at all levels has strengthened the position of the language in institutions of higher education like SQU, and has given it a distinct status. This situation is attributed to the fact that English in Oman is not tied to any colonial past since the country has never been under British rule. On the contrary, Britain has always been seen as a friendly country which has continuously offered support to Oman in various domains. In this context, English is considered a vital language with no negative associations. This receptive attitude has steadily promoted English without any tangible social, national, or even official resistance. It is a welcomed and beneficial product necessary for modernization, Omanization, and the building of the country. This line of argument echoes the discourse provided by advocates of the hegemonic status of English, yet it may differ in intention. In this regard, Phillipson (1992, p. 8) contends that "the discourse accompanying and legitimating the export of English to the rest of the world has been so persuasive that English has been equated with progress and prosperity." He also emphasizes that despite the fact that English has a hegemonic position in many countries, many accept it as "the natural state of affairs." In this situation, we strongly believe that regardless of the intentions of the sender/promoter of the language, the attitude of the receiver/consumer makes a major difference in how this language is viewed. In Oman in general and at SQU in particular, the collective attitude towards English is more appropriately explained from a functionalist perspective, which, according to Pennycook (2001, p. 79), "stresses the choice of English for its usefulness rather than its association with any colonial, political, and cultural issues," rather than from Phillipson's imperialist point of view.

What spurred the use and spread of other languages, particularly English, in Oman is the official policy of tolerance which comprises among many things, linguistic tolerance. Such a policy has always promoted the spread, use, and maintenance of many languages including English. Furthermore, the existence of a great number of non-native Arabic speaking expatriates working and living in Oman is another factor that promoted the use of English as a lingua franca. As was shown above, a sizable percentage of staff at SQU is Arabic non-native speaking expatriates, a situation that necessitates the use of English as the wider language of communication.

The results mentioned in the previous sections show that SQU is becoming a truly bilingual community though there exist some imbalances in the relationship between Arabic and English, favouring English. This imbalance is evident in the following: (a) English is the language of instruction in more colleges than Arabic; (b) publications in English outnumber Arabic publications; (c) admission requirements focus on competence in English, and they totally overlook competence in Arabic, even in the newly proposed foundation program, despite the fact that some students are not competent speakers of Arabic; and (d) finally, the financial and human resources allocated to the promotion of English vastly outweigh the resources allocated to teaching the native language.

The status and power of English at the global and local levels give it high linguistic vitality. Although Arabic serves as an essential marker of Omani Arab national identity, English is seen as more vital not only internationally and globally but also at the local business, commercial, technological, educational, and social fronts. Thus, it can safely be concluded that English is not only competing with the native language, but also overtaking more of its domains and functions. Arabic is relegated to domestic and traditional domains, functions, and usages, signifying in-group and national identity, solidarity and traditional values. On the other hand, English symbolizes high socio-educational status, and high competence and prestige, a clear case of *diglossic division of labour*.

The results obtained in this study show that there is a high demand for English and that knowledge of the language is seen as the gateway to success, progress, democracy, better job opportunities and life. Phillipson (1992) asserts that such a huge demand for English may have been intentionally created and that education and educational policies adopted by institutions of higher education have a very active role in the spread, domination, and ultimately hegemony of English. In this regard, Ibrahim (1985, p. 11) warns of the dangers of using a foreign language as the language of instruction in institutions of higher education. He states that "students who study through a foreign language come to the university unprepared for the task since all of their pre-university education is done in Arabic." In fact, one of the main and frequent complaints echoed by our informants is that throughout their pre-university schooling they used Arabic in learning. As a corollary, switching to a new language has proven to be extremely difficult, leading many of them to transfer to Arabic-medium departments. Aware of this issue, the university established the Language Centre whose primary function, as stated in its objectives, is to "prepare students of the university to meet the rigorous demands of instruction in a foreign or a second language." According to the Language Centre records, in 2009, around 2522 new students took the placement test. Of these, 834 were qualified to take a more advanced test, i.e. an exit test which exempts those who pass it from taking any intensive English courses. Only 322 of them passed this test and the rest (512) did not pass it, which means they had to be placed in Level 5 and had to take level six afterwards. The rest of the students (1688) who did not qualify to take the exit test had to be placed in one of the 5 intensive language levels as follows: level 1, 192 (7.6%); level 2, 247 (9.8%); level 3, 566 (22.4%); level 4, 344 (13.6%); and level 5, 339 (13.4). In general, those students who are placed in the first 2 levels have the bare minimum of language knowledge; while those placed in level 3 and 4 may have very rudimentary knowledge of the language. Taking into consideration that this cohort of students represents the top 5% of the high school graduates in the Sultanate, one may wonder about the English proficiency of the other students who failed to join SQU and who will likely join many other state and private higher institutions in the Sultanate. It is certain that preparing these students to meet the demands of study in a foreign language will be an arduous task, both financially and in terms of human resources. Despite the Centre's extensive effort as reflected in the many intensive courses offered there, a good percentage of our informants reported that they continue to struggle with their courses as a result of instruction in a foreign language.

Ibrahim (1985) warns of another serious danger associated with using a foreign language as a medium of instruction including suffering from low self-esteem because of unsatisfactory performance and low expectation of learning. He adds that a foreign language may lead students to develop some bad learning habits such as "copying texts without understanding them", "rote memorization, spotting", etc. Moreover, "the use of English is a barrier which prevents students from participation in class discussions" (Ibrahim, 1985, p. 12). Our informants reported such serious problems as many of them mentioned that they usually do not read the textbooks because they find them difficult to understand and usually have to spend much more time trying to figure out the meaning of new words. Alternatively, they resort to copying teachers' and other students' note as well as teachers' slides as the main sources of information. Additionally, many reported that they tend to memorize the material rather than understand it, and some of them tend to translate texts using the Google translator, which often results in wasting time, or loss of information as a result of miss-translation. Ironically, despite the students' evident struggle to cope with the demands of study in a foreign language, a fairly high percentage of them still favour English over Arabic.

## Conclusion

The patterns of linguistic behavior at SQU regarding the use of Arabic and English reflect asymmetrical power relations between the two languages, resulting in a new form of diglossic pattern where Arabic has become subordinate to English in science, technology, publications, instruction, and often interaction. The wide use of English seems to be in conflict with the expected supremacy of the native language, since English is dominating Arabic, the national language. Thus, English seems to be acquiring the status of a second language rather than a foreign language. Overall, it is evident that Arabic is in the heart while English is in the mind. In fact, English has become "an evil we cannot do without." In the face of this hegemony, one may wonder what the future holds for the native language.

# References

Al-Balushi, R. (2001). ELT in the Sultanate of Oman. *RELO Newsletter, 5*, 5–6.
Al-Balushi, O. (1999). *The internet and Omani students' English language learning problems: Critical study.* Unpublished master's thesis. University of Manchester.
Al-Busaidi, K. (1995). *English in the labour market in multilingual Oman with special reference to Omani employees.* Unpublished doctoral dissertation, University of Exeter.
Al-Busaidi, S. (1998). *An investigation of teachers' and students' attitudes towards the use of mother tongue in the English foreign language classrooms in Oman.* Unpublished masters' dissertation. University of Reading.
Al-Issa, A. (2002). *An ideological and discursive analysis of English language teaching in the Sultanate of Oman.* Unpublished doctoral thesis. University of Queensland, Australia.
Al-Issa, A. (2006a). The cultural and economic politics of English language teaching in the Sultanate of Oman. *The Asian EFL Journal 8*(1), 194–218.
Al-Issa, A. (2006b). Ideologies governing teaching the language skills in the Omani ELT system. *Journal of Language and Learning, 4*(2), 218–231.
Al-Issa, A., (2006c). Language problems facing Omani learners of English. *ORTESOL Journal, 24*, 19–26.
Al-Issa, A. (2007). The implications of implementing a "flexible" syllabus for ESL policy in the Sultanate of Oman. *RELC Journal, 38*, 199–215.
Al-Jurf, R. (2004). اتجاهات الشباب نحو استخدام اللغتين العربية و الإنجليزية. في التعليم. ديوان العرب
Al-Qubaisi, A. (2009). إشكاليات التعليم باللغة الانجليزية فى دول مجلس التعاون"التعليم باللغة الانجليزية و آثاره التربوية و الثقافية "ورقة مقدمة لندوة اللغة و الهوية في. دول مجلس التعاون أنموذجا، التي عقدها المجلس الوطني للثقافة و الفنون و التراث في الدوحة من 15-17 يناير
Al-Seyabi, F. (1995). *Identifying the English language needs of science students in the College of Science and College of Education and Islamic Studies at Sultan Qaboos University.* Unpublished master's dissertation. Sultan Qaboos University.
Al-Sheikh, G. (2009). 2009/11/13 طغيان اللغة الإنجليزية يههد اللغة العربية و أجيالها المقبلة. جريدة الغد،
Al-Toubi, S. (1998). *A perspective on change in the Omani ELT curriculum: Structural to communicative.* Unpublished master's dissertation. University of Bristol: UK.
Crystal, D. (1997). *English as a global language.* Cambridge: Cambridge University Press.

El-Shibiny, M. (2005). *The threat of globalization to Arab Islamic culture*. Pittsburgh, PA: Dorrance Publishing Company.

Hersh, W., & Zhang, L. (1999). Teaching English medical terminology using the UMLS: Metathesaurus and world wide web. Retrieved April 26, 2010, from <http://skynet.ohsu.edu/~hersh/amia-99-chinese.pdf>

Hoogstad, M. (2008). English as a lingua franca. *Voices*, January-February.

Ibrahim, M. (1985). *Communicating in Arabic: Problems, prospects*. Paper presented at the symposium on adopting vernacular languages to the demands of modern communication, Bad Hamburg, Frankfurt, June 12–15, 1985.

Kachru, B. (1986). *The alchemy of English: The spread, functions, and models of non-native English*. Oxford: Pergamon Press.

Mallikarjun, B. (2003). Globalization and Indian languages. *Language in India, 3*. Retrieved April 26, 2010, from <http://www.languageinindia.com/feb2003/golobalization.html>

Ministry of Education. (1995). *Reform and development of general education*. Sultanate of Oman.

Pennycook, A. (1999). *Development, culture and language: Ethical concerns in a postcolonial world*. Paper presented at the 4th international conference on language and development, October 1999. Retrieved April 26, 2010, from <http://www.languages.ait.ac.th/hanoi_proceesings/pennycook.htm>

Pennycook, A. (2001). English in the world/the world in English. In A. Burns & C. Coffin (eds), *Analyzing English in a global context* (pp. 78–89). London: Routledge.

Pennycook, A. (2003). Islam, English and 9–11: An interview with Alastair Pennycook conducted via email during the months of October and November 2003. *TESOL ISLAMIA*.

Phillipson, R. (1992). *Linguistic imperialism*. Oxford: Oxford University Press.

Phillipson, R. (2003). Linguistic imperialism 10 years on. An interview with Robert Phillipson, based on an interview conducted in Abu Dhabi in 2004. *TESOL ISLAMIA*.

Poole, B. (2006). Some effects of Indian English on the language as it is used in Oman. Distinctive developments in an Arab sultanate. *English Today, 88*, 421–424.

Suleiman, Y. (2004). *A war of words: Language and conflict in the Middle East*. Cambridge: Cambridge University Press.

Zughoul, M. (2003). Globalization and EFL/ESL pedagogy in the Arab world. *Journal of Language and Learning, 1*(2), 1–29.

# Appendix

## Questionnaire

Major _____    Male / Female

Year _____    Average in Secondary Certificate _____

1. How do you evaluate your English before joining the university?
    a. weak    b. fair    c. good    d. excellent

2. How many courses did you take at the Language Centre? _____

3. Do you feel that you have benefited from the courses you took at the Language Centre for your present study?
    a. Yes    b. No    c. somehow    d. Other: specify _____

4. In taking the courses in your major, do you have any language problem?
    a. Yes    b. No    c. Sometimes

5. Do you understand the teachers' explanation?
    a. Yes    b. No    c. Sometimes

6. Do you understand the questions?
    a. Yes    b. No    c. Sometimes

7. Do you have difficulty in understanding the texts you read?
    a. Yes    b. No    c. Sometimes

8. Would you prefer to have the textbooks in English or Arabic?
    a. English    b. Arabic    c. No Difference

9. Do you think that if the texts were in Arabic you would perform better?
    a. Yes    b. No    c. No Difference

10. Do you think that if the class discussions were in Arabic you would be able to perform better?

    a. Yes               b. No              c. No Difference

11. In preparing for the exams, do you spend more time on understanding content or language or both?

    a. content          b. language          c. both

12. In taking exams, do you think that you have difficulty in understanding the questions because of language?

    a. Yes               b. No              c. Sometimes

13. Do you think that if the questions were written in Arabic you would have performed better?

    a. Yes               b. No              c. No Difference

14. Do you think that if your answers were written in Arabic you would perform better?

    a. Yes               b. No              c. No Difference

15. Overall, would you prefer the language of instruction in your major to be English or Arabic?

    a. Yes               b. No              c. No Difference

16. When you graduate, what language you are more likely to use in your work?

    a. English           b. Arabic           c. Both

SILVIA PESSOA AND MOHANALAKSHMI RAJAKUMAR

# 6 The Impact of English-medium Higher Education: The Case of Qatar

## ABSTRACT

While the spread of English has led to the increasing development of world bilingualism and all its benefits, in recent years the colonial heritage of English as the language of western cultural domination has come under scrutiny alongside the rise of globalization. Qatar is no exception to these tensions, particularly as it has invited and encouraged the promotion of English-medium education in order to participate in the era of globalization. While the spread of English in Qatar is in tandem with its modernization and rapid development, some fear that progress is in contradiction with Muslim culture and that the spread of English may cause Arabic language loss. Despite this reality, there has been little documented research on youth attitudes towards English in Qatar because it is generally assumed that the young embrace all signs of modernity without any reservations. This chapter reports on a pilot study examining undergraduate students' perspectives on the impact of English-medium education on Arab and Muslim culture, language, and identity through a survey, self-assessments of language abilities, focus groups, and personal interviews. Fifty students from Carnegie Mellon University in Qatar and Qatar University were surveyed and a sample participated in a focus group or an individual interview. The findings indicate that while academic and professional uses of Arabic may be lost in the future, students understand the complexity of their reality embracing their bilingualism and cultural hybridity, using Arabic at home and as a link to their culture and English for practical purposes.

## Introduction

In the last 10 years, the State of Qatar has undergone tremendous development and modernization in various sectors, which may have impacted Qatari culture. In the education sector, with the establishment of various English-medium private schools and English-medium independent schools as a result of the Qatari education reform, the transition of Qatar University from Arabic to English-medium, and the birth of Education City (EC) with six American universities, English has become a part of daily Qatari life. While knowledge of English is a commodity that carries with it various economic and social benefits (Baker, 2006), the spread of English in Qatar and throughout the world has created various tensions. Some question whether the spread of English in the world has led to global bilingualism or English imperialism, and particularly in Qatar, whether the emphasis on English-medium education may lead to the loss of Arabic and the preference for western ideas and practices rather than Muslim values and traditions. In line with the objectives of this volume, these are important questions that this chapter addresses through a pilot study of 50 college students from Education City and Qatar University. Specifically, the research question underlying this research is the following: How does global English impact university students in Qatar in terms of their native language, identity, and culture?

## Background

Historically, the English language established its dominance in the international sphere primarily as a result of its colonial history and, most recently, as the language of globalization (Crystal, 1997). The colonial era laid the foundations for English to preside over other languages as a lingua franca, a language widely spoken globally and beyond the population of its native speakers. In recent years the colonial heritage of English as the language of western cultural domination has come under scrutiny alongside the rise of globalization (Brutt-Griffler, 2002; Canagarajah, 1999; Pennycook, 1994; Phillipson, 1992, 2009). What some nations fear is the challenge English presents to the maintenance of traditional language practices and cultural identity. As Baker (2006) notes, "Where English has rapidly spread, the danger is that it does not encourage bilingualism but rather a shift towards English as the preferred language, especially in schools" (p. 90).

The potentially negative impact of the English language on local cultures stems from the fact that language and identity are intrinsically connected, and through education language can be a powerful tool in shaping identity. As Baker (2006) points out "Learning a second language is not just about language. It is also about who we are, what we want to become, and what we are allowed to become" (p. 137). Consequently, "[a]n understanding of language without consideration of identity can never hope to be complete" (Joseph, 2004, p. 40). The importance of language in forming identity is further explored by Gellner (1964) who posits that colonial education leads to the erosion of identities and language shift. Because of the major role of education in nation building, in the formation of national identity, and in the transmission and reinforcement of cultural values, the adoption of English on a major scale in the education system inevitably raises questions on the status of the indigenous language and local cultures (Fishman, Conrad, & Rubal-Lopez, 1996).

The Arabian Gulf is no exception to these tensions. Bilingualism has been present in Arabic speaking nations since colonial contact with the British Empire. Today, the Gulf States have recognized the importance of the inclusion of English in their education systems and are committed to improving language education in their countries. However, little is known about the impact of English-medium education and western educational practices on the languages, identities, and cultures of the youth in the Gulf. Some efforts have been made to document this phenomenon in the Gulf countries. In Saudi Arabia, various studies conducted from the 1940s to the 1990s with Saudi Arabian males with higher education degrees show their disagreement about the fact that learning English indicates following, imitating, and adopting western patterns of behavior (Al-Abed Al-Haq

& Smodi, 1996). In addition, the studies show that "the respondents were ideologically and sentimentally attached and practically committed to Arabic" as 70% showed disagreement in educating their future children in English-medium schools and emphasized the need to use Arabic (Al-Abed Al-Haq & Smodi, 1996, p. 469). In contrast, in a video produced at the Dubai Men's College (2007), an English-medium university in the United Arab Emirates, the overwhelming majority of students showed a clear preference for using English over Arabic. Despite Arabic being their mother tongue, the students find it difficult and unnatural speaking in Arabic as most had attended English-medium schools. The generational shift in attitudes presented in both cases stem from the global proliferation of English in most schools in Gulf nations, as is the case with Qatar.

Qatar has invited and encouraged the promotion of English-medium education at all levels in order to participate in the era of globalization. At the primary and secondary school levels, the transition to English-medium education came about through the establishment of more private or international schools and the establishment of independent schools as a result of the Qatari educational reform in 2002. Under the name "Education for a New Era," the reform established government-funded gender segregated independent schools where math and science are taught in English with the goal of preparing students to enter the American universities in Qatar and later a globalized workforce, especially in Qatar where more than two thirds of the 1.5 million population are foreigners. In Education City, funded by the Qatar Foundation (<http://www.qf.org.qa>) and established in 1995, the implementation of six co-educational American universities taught solely in English is a revolutionary step in modernizing Qatar's educational system. In these institutions both female and male students learn alongside each other in English taught by mostly western male and female professors. Qatar University, the public university founded in 1973, started an education reform in 2003, which involves transitioning to English-medium education.

The introduction of English as a language of instruction is not a stand alone practice but is also accompanied by other pedagogical and value changes which introduce new methods of teaching and learning in the classroom. These processes affect the ways that students interact with faculty and think of themselves as learners, thereby reinforcing students' perception of change in Qatar with the teaching of English. The long term impact of these institutions is yet to be seen and will need at least a generation of graduates in order to ascertain the full scope of these changes, but in the present, this study begins to answer some of the pressing gaps amongst this pivotal population that has been the recipient of several stages of these transformations.

These transformations, fuelled in many instances by the English language and western practices, have generated various responses around the world. From the three Islamic responses to English proposed by Rahman (2005 cited in Baker, 2006) which include the following: (a) acceptance of English and assimilation in Anglophone culture, (b) rejection and resistance based on religion and preferred identity and values, and (c) pragmatic utilization so as to share power and knowledge, raise wealth and social status, and "learn the language of your enemy" (p. 90); social acceptance due to pragmatic utilization seems to be the response to English in Qatar. However, little is known about how the adoption of English-medium education for practical purposes will impact the language, identity, and culture of the youth living and studying in Qatar, many of whom are Muslims and Arabic speakers.

Despite the importance of the potential impact of this phenomenon in Qatar, no major investigation has been conducted on this topic. Amna Al Thani's (2008) thesis from Carnegie Mellon University in Qatar investigating the linguistic preferences of undergraduate college students, who attended independent schools in Qatar, is one step toward documenting this phenomenon. Based on a survey of 36 students from Education City and Qatar University, Al Thani's results indicate that linguistic preferences depend on the communicant and the discussion topic, with Arabic being preferred for communicating with family and about informal topics and English being chosen for more academic uses. In between, a "hybrid linguistic identity" is developed when code-switching with friends (p. 31). Despite the great merits given to this undergraduate student work, Al Thani's study fails to address the impact of English-medium education directly, as all the questions in her survey were only related to linguistic preference and only *inferences* were made with regard to identity.

Clearly, there is a need to learn more about this situation and its current and future impact. This pilot study directly addresses these issues through local perceptions of the impact of English-medium education and how it affects the individual and the country's construction and maintenance of self-identity, traditions, and culture. Currently, there is no available data for evaluating the impact of English-medium education on the students attending these schools. To the best of our knowledge, there has been no documented research on youth attitudes towards English, identity, or culture in Qatar despite the increasing research on these areas in other countries of the Gulf. Perhaps because it is generally assumed that the youth embrace all signs of modernity without any reservations, this has not yet been a focus of investigation. However, our research reveals that students feel more tension about the choices before them than perhaps their parents' generation because the choices they make are seen to impact the future citizens in a Qatar where the nationals are a minority.

Modernity for the Qatari young person can be a very vexing question because it represents opposing values to that of traditional Gulf culture. These traditions are often sources of national and familial pride; the juxtaposition of language and modern/western practices against those of family, home, and country put the young person at a paradoxical interchange between consumption of modern goods and services (including state funded English education) as well as restraint in terms of behavior, dress, and conduct as they adhere to values rooted in a Muslim/Arab/Arabic speaking culture. This study goes directly to the heart of this contradiction by interviewing students and perhaps, for the first time in a formal structure setting, listening to how they face these challenges.

## Methodology

In the spring of 2007 and 2008, one of the researchers taught a course on bilingualism at her institution that revealed students' interest in discussing the impact of English-medium education on their native language, culture, and identity. More specifically, in this course, through discussion board postings and classroom dialogues, students addressed questions related to language maintenance and shift and the impact of the spread of English in Qatar and its consequences, and wrote final papers investigating various aspects of language, identity, and culture. This pilot study draws on data from students' written discussion board postings and final papers.

Building on the work of the students in this course, the researchers conducted a pilot study to learn more about students' perspectives on the impact of English-medium education in Qatar. During the period of January through March 2008, 50 students at Carnegie Mellon University in Qatar, who had enrolled in the bilingualism course taught by Pessoa and 20 students at Qatar University, who had taken a writing course with Rajakumar in 2006, were invited to complete an online survey about attitudes toward English-medium education and its impact. Fifty students completed the survey, 40 from Carnegie Mellon and 10 from Qatar University. Fifty per cent of the students were Qataris and 50% of diverse Arab backgrounds including Egyptians, Lebanese, Jordanians, and Palestinians. Thirty-two per cent attended Qatar University and 68% attended Carnegie Mellon-Qatar. Thirty per cent of the students were educated in government schools in Arabic, 50% in independent schools in English and Arabic, and 20% in private schools in English. The survey results were aggregated and analysed descriptively (see survey in Appendix A).

Survey respondents were invited to participate in a focus group or a personal interview to give feedback regarding their perceptions about the spread of English in Qatar and its impact on language, culture, and identity. Using an interview and focus group protocol (see Appendix B), three individual interviews and 10 focus groups were conducted. Careful verbatim notes were taken during the focus groups and interviews, and were subsequently analysed in terms of recurrent themes that emerged from the conversations with the students.

## Findings and discussion

The most salient finding from the study is the students' desire to learn to be fully bilingual, that is use western practices for future opportunities but also maintain the Arabic language and the values of traditional Arab and Muslim society. These are not necessarily in opposition to one another, but often raise interesting questions at the level of the individual and for the future of the State of Qatar's population. Reflecting on the spread of English in Qatar through education and commerce, one third-year female Qatari student wrote:

> I believe that Arabic in the Gulf will be maintained because of culture and religion. To practice Islam, knowing Arabic is vital. Also, the general culture encourages the use of Arabic between parents and relatives. However, business is international, and in the Gulf business is becoming more westernized. We're seeing way more British and American companies here than ever before, and if you don't know English, you can't participate in this development. But no matter how westernized the Gulf becomes, or "English-influenced," The Arabic language will still never die because of the Quran, and the need to understand and read it in Islam.

The need to maintain Arabic as a link to Islam is echoed by various students, as this third-year female Qatari student wrote:

> Although I think English is considered a very valuable commodity in a world where it is used in almost everything, I believe that Arabic, for the most part, will not be lost in this part of the world for various reasons. One of the most important ones is that Islam is the main religion in this country.

University students in Qatar remain bilingual and embrace their Arab and Muslim identity through the use of Arabic at home and with friends, and as a link to their religious identity; however, many have not developed Arabic for academic and professional purposes due to their education in English. Students in English-medium universities have very limited exposure to written Arabic and voiced their concerns about their ability to conduct themselves academically and professionally in Arabic. Amongst those who attended English-medium primary and secondary schools, 55% believed that this has directly decreased their ability to use Arabic. Eighty-five per cent of the students agreed that education in English decreases the use and knowledge of Arabic. Similarly, 80% believed that academic and professional uses of Arabic may be lost in the future, despite Arabic's importance for Islamic practices. As a matter of fact, 90% indicated that knowledge of and use of Arabic will never be lost because of Arabic's importance for Muslim religion. The findings demonstrate the widening gap between the use of Arabic in students' personal and academic lives. Eighty per cent felt their spoken Arabic was excellent, but only 47% felt their written Arabic levels were excellent. This disparity between spoken and written language abilities in Arabic reflects the use of Arabic in their daily lives. Students are more comfortable with speech and dialectical use than they are with the formal conventions of writing because most of their academic training is in English.

In reflecting on the influence of English on Arabic, one sophomore female Qatari student indicated, "Now, if you want to say the word in Arabic; you think of the word in English. We translate from English." Once a foreign or second language in Qatar, English is gaining more prevalence in the country to the point of students relying on English for coming up with words in Arabic. Not only do students rely on English out of necessity but also because of the prestige and popularity of English. For example, one second-year male Egyptian student wrote:

> Nationals of Qatar and those who grow up speaking Arabic tend to shift towards English in different domains since it is found to be popular and prestigious. We find many Arabs unable to read Arabic and some of them actually have low fluency as well.

Similarly, a second-year student of Palestinian origin wrote:

> As people are learning English, they are letting go of Arabic. Many people now talk to their Arabic-speaking friends, siblings, or family members in English. [...] Some Qatari children cannot speak a word of Arabic. This shows that people do not use the language [English] when they only need to, like when talking to an English speaker, but instead they use it all the time, which over time causes them to forget many of their first language's words and expressions and gradually lose their true identity.

Interestingly, the results point to differences among first- and fourth-year students with fourth year students being more pessimistic about their Arabic language abilities. With the emphasis placed on English-medium education, this situation is expected to intensify with fewer and fewer students being able to use their Arabic professionally in the future. Despite their perceived low levels of academic Arabic skills, the participants reiterated their commitment to use Arabic as a cultural link to traditional values and culture, but seemed unsure of how to accomplish these personal goals in light of the professional training they were receiving.

In reflecting about the status, use, and level of Arabic skills of students in Qatar, one second-year female Qatari student voiced her concerns about the potential loss of Arabic by her generation due to continuous education in English. In this regard, she explained that:

> The Arabic language is being neglected. I forgot how to write papers in Arabic. My spelling became much worse; I don't know how to spell words anymore; I asked my cousins who are 10 for the spelling; it's embarrassing. I haven't written [in Arabic] in two years. We should learn in English but we should not forget our Arabic.

Interestingly, this student is concerned about Arabic "being neglected" and not being forgotten, but she concludes by saying that "We should learn in English." Clearly, students see the value of education in English, but some have strong feelings about not neglecting their Arabic. This student also points out the fact that she has to ask her younger cousins for the spelling of words in Arabic. Her cousins may be educated in government schools in Arabic in Qatar and as a result may have Arabic fresher in their minds, but this is not the case for the majority of children in Qatar. With the implementation of independent schools and the transition to English, more and more Qatari children are now schooled in English. As a matter of fact, many students talked about speaking in English with their siblings, especially their younger siblings, and how the younger generation may be losing its Arabic. Some even discussed the fact that Arabic-speaking parents choose to speak English with their children in order for the children to be better prepared to enter English-medium schools. In this regard, one sophomore male Qatari student indicated, "My cousin is four years old and since he was born his parents have been talking to him in English, so that he doesn't have problems with English."

Although the students in general feel that education in English is not a threat to their local culture and identity, the situation may change in the next generation. In responses to how English-medium education affects them, 90% indicated that they remain who they are despite being educated in English and that English-medium education has not affected them negatively. In contrast, when thinking of the younger generation, some students feel that the younger generation will be greatly impacted by western culture to the point of losing their language, identity, and culture. For instance, one second-year female Qatari student indicated that:

> The young ones, I think, will be very different; they will be like Americans. They are going to lose their values; they are not being taught. Women [mothers] are not good; they are leaving all the teaching to schools. Schools are not teaching all the values they [children] need to know. I think that mothers should be more engaged in the house and teach their children how to deal with this change. Children are just learning what they are giving to them. Children don't know what's right or wrong. If they are going to an English school, they are going to adapt [to the West].

The comment by this student points to various complex issues voiced by the students in regard to the impact of English-medium education on students' culture and identity. This student feels that the future generations "will be like Americans," viewing this in a negative light as apparently being "like Americans" means losing "their values." This particular student blames parents, particularly mothers for "leaving all the teaching to schools" rather than being actively involved in teaching their children their culture's values. Perhaps this student's concern reflects the current situation in Qatar with school-aged children; however, this did not seem to be the case for the majority of the students surveyed and interviewed. In the survey results, 80% indicated that English-medium education is appreciated for its practical purpose and parents are responsible for instilling Muslim values in their children, something most students surveyed believed their parents did despite their English-medium education.

Despite the concern of the potentially greater impact of English-medium education on the younger generation, 80% of the students surveyed indicated that they would send their future children to English-medium schools because of the benefits of such schooling. 65% of the respondents believed there should be more English-medium schools because they prepare students to compete in international institutions. American or British universities were listed as having more prestige than Arab institutions. In order to compete for the best opportunities, students felt English proficiency was not negotiable. In reflecting about the emphasis on English-medium schooling in Qatar, one first-year male Qatari student indicated no concerns with the supposedly negative spread of English in Qatar, stating that:

> I think that schools should focus more on English because now more jobs are in English and it's better to study in English than Arabic. Most business is in English. I think this is good. It's better for the Qatari government and the culture and the society.

Common feelings of appreciation for English-medium education were voiced by the majority of the students. The students indicated they had positive experiences as a result of their schooling in English. These students felt they have greatly benefited from the emphasis on certain skills such as the development of critical thinking and being more tolerant of diverse opinions.

Such comments by the students reveal the impact that English-medium education has on students beyond language and starts to shed light on complex issues of culture and identity. With English-medium education come certain practices and values, such as critical thinking that students embrace in order to participate in today's knowledge-based globalized society. However, many participants indicated that their parents or extended family members felt that English-medium education may cause them to become "too westernized and modern." In this regard, a second-year female Qatari student stated, "As we speak in English, we do act more westernized. It forces you to act as an English-speaking person." Acting more like an "English-speaking person" or "like an American" may be seen as conflicting with Muslim values and culture. In more general terms, one female third-year Lebanese student wrote:

> People show a negative response to the spread of English in the Islamic world because they believe that it threatens their culture. The more you are able to speak a language, the more you are able to integrate into the culture and become part of it. Since the English-speaking cultures tend to be seen as having a negative, less conservative effect on the Islamic world so does the language itself.

These views were echoed by other Education City students. For instance, a first-year male Qatari student stated, "I know many students who study here, their religion has been affected a lot; but me, I'm still resisting. It depends on the person himself, if his roots are strong." "Resisting" the temptations of western practices and culture was echoed by various students who criticized female students for not fully covering or not wearing the *abaya*, and male students for not wearing the traditional *thobe*. References to students' "roots" and the Muslim values instilled by parents to help them remain attached to their cultural values were recurrent in the focus groups and interviews.

However, the fear of youth in Qatar acting more westernized was also a concern among parents, as 16% of the students surveyed indicated that their parents regret having sent them to English-medium schools. In reference to this, one second-year female student indicated:

> Until now they [my parents] regret me coming to Education City. They said that my personality changed [...]. Before I came to Education City, I was very shy with boys. Now I just don't care. I'm not as shy anymore. Before, I didn't accept the idea of friendship between boys and girls. Before I thought it was impossible to happen [...]. Now you can be friends with boys. But I don't mention this at home. They [my parents] started saying I got ruined because of this school. I really don't know what they are talking about. I'm friends with boys but I don't tell my family. It's not worth getting into a big argument with them. My mother thinks I'm more open, that I accept the western culture more, and I am more lenient about my views than before. There are some things that we used to consider very bad; this is the difference, I used to think things were very bad and criticize them and now I don't.

Two important aspects of the potential cultural impact of English-medium and western education on the culture and identity of Muslim students in Qatar emerge from this comment. First, this comment addresses the concerns of parents who see changes in the personality, behavior, and values of their children, especially their female children, as a result of attending an American university in Education City. This particular student is described by her parents as being "more open" and "more lenient" to the point of being "ruined" by western cultural practices such as being friends with boys. Clearly, in the minds of Muslim parents, these are not labels for their Muslim daughters to be associated with.

Second, the comment by the student points to issues of personal development and change and cultural conflict for Muslim young women being educated in American educational contexts in Qatar. It is important to note that for the female Qatari students, attending a co-ed American university in Education City can be a challenging task at first and a great source of conflict which they eventually get used to. For instance, one female student explained, "I was crying at the beginning; I didn't want to go to a mixed university, but I got used to it." The negative reputation that Education City holds among some of the most conservative sectors of the Qatari population creates a great burden for female students. In various focus groups with female Qatari students, they discussed the negative reputation of Education City among some people in Qatar, for example, "English schools don't have a good reputation here; girls went and started going out with boys and parents didn't want that."

Like the student in the extended comment above, the female students in the focus groups explained how they managed to navigate between the outside world and community pressures and their own perspectives of tolerance and acceptance of a changing Qatar. One student indicated that, "The reputation of EC is not very good; people say bad things. But now I accept it. If I see something, I don't say anything. Now we accept seeing friends having relations." At times, this involved having what some referred to as a "double identity" or "double personality," which involved interacting and working closely on school projects with male students but ignoring them outside of Education City if they met by chance in a shopping mall or restaurant. For other female students, coping with these changes and cultural conflict is taken in a lighter fashion and is seen as a natural progression in Qatar's development. In this regard, one first-year male Qatari student indicated, "All the country has changed; we are a developed country; everything has changed; even if our parents didn't change, you need to cope; you can be with boys."

Perhaps this last comment best summarizes the state of this issue in Qatar. The youth studying in higher education in Qatar understand the changes in Qatar and have learned to "cope" or embrace these changes for practical purposes while maintaining their language, culture, and identity. The comment "you can be with boys" does not mean female Muslim students will start engaging in western practices of dating men, but instead in the changing society in which they live, society will have to understand that for the country to continue to develop men and women must work hand in hand without breaking the Muslim laws of the country. In this regard, one third-year female Qatari student wrote:

> Sheikah Mozah's initiative to start educational institutions of world-class reputation is ample proof of her dedication to bringing the best education into the region. However, the balance is evident. The Arabs have been able to completely maintain their cultural and social identity, influenced strongly by the established fundamentals of their religion. They've successfully incorporated the positive elements of the western culture and know their limitations.

Similarly, another third-year female Qatari student wrote:

> There's nothing wrong with English being the medium of instruction in schools. Cultural roots at home are still very strong at home, so I don't think there's any compromise here. The professional job market does demand English as a major prerequisite, but I don't think that it is the lifeline of the economy.

As can be seen from the vibrant student responses, there is much interest in addressing issues regarding the spread of English in Qatar among the young generation. While all recognize that English is spreading fast in Qatar, the majority of the students do not think that Arabic will be lost due to the cultural and religious value of the language. What may be at risk are academic uses of Arabic, which students are aware of and accept as competent bilingual individuals who use English for academic and professional uses and Arabic in personal and social domains.

As a result, the students conclude that while it is important to learn English for educational and professional purposes, it is crucial to preserve other languages and local cultures and to maintain the first language. First language maintenance can be achieved through institutions (e.g. family, schools) that embrace the benefits of bilingualism and use both languages in non-academic and academic domains.

## Conclusion

The findings from this pilot study and subsequent conversations and class discussions with students have, in a way, changed our perspectives on the impact of English-medium education in Qatar. We started our inquiry into this issue with the hypothesis that the emphasis on English-medium education is greatly threatening the maintenance of the Arabic language in Qatar and Arab culture and identity. While the findings show a decrease in the use of Arabic for academic and professional purposes and the students' concerns for their inability to use Arabic for these purposes, many of the participating students have proven to be ahead of us in their understanding of English as a lingua franca for the practical benefits it provides them with in this era of globalization. Students embrace their knowledge of English for academic and professional uses and maintain their link to their culture and religion through Arabic. Although academic and professional uses of Arabic may not be as developed as the students' English abilities, students are aware of these complexities and embrace their bilingualism and cultural hybridity for what it is and for what it allows them to accomplish in a continuously developing Qatar.

As linguists have long acknowledged, it is rare to find bilingual individuals with equal proficiency in two languages as bilingualism usually depends on exposure and use in different domains (Baker, 2006). Some students would like to have more exposure to academic and professional uses of Arabic and the universities in Education City understand the value of promoting more balanced bilingualism. As a result, at least two of the six universities in Education City offer advanced courses in Arabic for native speakers including literature courses and business Arabic. These initiatives are bound to help students to continue to develop their Arabic language skills, which many would like to, as proven by the large participation of Qatari students in advanced literature courses in Arabic offered at Carnegie Mellon in the 2009–2010 academic year.

Nevertheless, the students' concerns about the threat of English to their native language and culture, and their own inability to use Arabic cannot be ignored. This is particularly important as 80% of the students surveyed indicated that they would send their future children to English-medium schools. Even among those who are the most concerned about the impact of English on Arabic and Arab culture, would send their future children to English-medium schools. If this generation that was partially schooled in Arabic is concerned about their inability to use Arabic, we must question what will happen to the future generation of Qataris who are likely to receive most of their education in English and be even more immersed in English due to technology and globalization. What could prevent Arabic from being lost is, as the students' mentioned, its use as a link to Arab and Muslim culture and its prevalence as an identity marker that helps students to show "resistance" to western practices and values. Interestingly, those who emphasize this "resistance" are in agreement with the general view among the students that Arabic is the language of their home and their culture, and English is the practical language of education and business. With this clear division, the uses of both Arabic and English are likely to continue to be channelled toward different uses, and sadly some may lose their ability to use Arabic for academic and professional uses, but will still use it informally as a link to their culture.

Despite the potential loss of academic and professional Arabic in Qatar, the language will most likely be maintained in the near future as it is used as an identity marker and a link to their culture, with English having its own uses and domains. As Crystal (1997) argues, our students view English "as a valuable instrument enabling people to achieve particular goals" (p. 24). In reference to local languages and in line with the students' perspectives, Crystal argues that:

> Local languages continue to perform an important set of functions (chiefly, the expression of local identity) and English is seen as the primary means of achieving a global presence. The approach recognizes the legacy of colonialism, as a matter of historical fact, but the emphasis is now on discontinuities away from power and towards functional specialization. It is a model which sees English playing a central role in empowering the subjugated and marginalized, and eroding the division between the "haves" and the "have nots". (p. 24)

Thus, we would like to see a Qatar that guarantees access to good quality English-medium education in order to use English as a language of opportunity and empowerment, while maintaining Arabic. It is acknowledged that, "Both principles demand massive resources" (Crystal, 1997, p. 28), which Qatar and the Gulf countries in general have. We surely hope that these resources are used effectively for Qatar to continue to invest in effective bilingual education for all.

# Future work

Being the first of its kind, this pilot study is an important contribution to understanding complex issues of language, culture, and identity in Qatar. In the future, we aim to conduct an expansion of the pilot study with the specific aim of examining the perspectives of an estimated 500 undergraduate Arabic-speaking students longitudinally using both quantitative and qualitative methods. This prolonged observation through the students' four years of college education will help track the development of attitudes regarding the emphasis on English-medium education and western educational practices, as well as the impact of such emphasis on self-perception, cultural values, and language ability. The survey on which this pilot study is based is essentially a synchronic one, in that it captures the characteristics, experiences, and perspectives of a particular individual at a particular point in time. The data collected in the diachronic, longitudinal design complements the primary design of the pilot study. In order carry out this component of the study, a modified version of the initial survey will be administered to all first year student participants (estimated at 200) once a year throughout the four years of their college education. The yearly survey will track the progression of attitudes, perceptions, and reactions to the collegiate experience in English.

In addition to the yearly survey, a sample size of 30 first-year students will be followed during their entire four years of college education in a more comprehensive manner. Key variables in deriving this purposive sample will include nationality, gender, type of secondary school attended, and native language, and ability in the native language. These are variables that yielded interesting results in our pilot study. For instance, female students, and in particular Qataris, had stronger opinions about the impact of English-medium and western education on their self-perception and what others thought of themselves, emphasizing the need and importance to "hang on" to the Arabic language and Muslim values despite their immersion in English. In this future study, each of the 30 students, 15 from Qatar Foundation and 15 from Qatar University, will be asked to complete questionnaires, participate in focus groups and personal interviews, and complete language assessments and writing samples.

It will also be important to assess students' language abilities in English and Arabic through systematic assessment and the analysis of student writing in order to triangulate the data from the self-assessment of the students' language abilities. The assessment of students' Arabic competence is important to address potential first language attrition in the population under study, something which we deem of great importance given the emphasis on English and the potential marginalization and loss of Arabic.

# References

Al-Abed Al-Haq, F., & Smodi, O. (1996). The status of English in the Kingdom of Saudi Arabia (KSA) from 1940–1990. In J.A. Fishman, A.W. Conrad, & A. Rubal-Lopez, *Post-imperial English: Change status in former British and American colonies, 1940–1990* (pp. 457–484). New York: Mouton de Gruyter.
Al-Thani, A. (2008). *Bilingualism: The fusion of native and foreign culture and language.* Unpublished Senior Honour's Thesis. Carnegie Mellon University in Qatar.
Baker, C. (2006). *Foundations of bilingual education and bilingualism* (4th edn). Tonawanda, NY: Multilingual Matters Ltd.
Brutt-Griffler, J. (2002). *World English: A study of its development.* Clevedon: Multilingual Matters.
Canagarajah, S. (1999). *Resisting linguistic imperialism in English teaching.* New York: Oxford University Press.
Crystal, D. (1997). *English as a global language.* Cambridge: Cambridge University Press.

Fishman, J.A., Conrad, A.W., & Rubal-Lopez, A. (1996). *Post-imperial English.* New York: Mouton de Gruyter.
Gellner, E. (1964). *Thought and change.* London: Weidenfeld and Nicolson.
Higher Colleges of Technology, Dubai Men's College. (2007). [DVD video production]. Dubai, UAE.
Joseph, J. (2004). *Language and identity: National, ethnic, religious.* New York: Palgrave Macmillan.
Pennycook, A. (1994). *The cultural politics of English as an international language.* New York: Longman.
Phillipson, R. (1992). *Linguistic imperialism.* New York: Oxford University Press.
Phillipson, R. (2009). *Linguistic imperialism continued.* New York: Routledge.

# Appendix A

### Survey: English-medium Education in Qatar and Its Impact

This survey is part of a pilot study that aims at gathering preliminary data on the impact of English-medium education on the youth living and studying in Qatar. Your participation is voluntary and the data collected will remain confidential.

1. Gender:       1. Male       2. Female

2. Age:

3. Nationality (as indicated in passport):

4. Ethnic/Country affiliation (if different from nationality):

5. Religion:

6. Languages spoken:

7. Which language(s) do you consider to be your native/first language(s):

8. Names of schools attended from year 1 to year 12, years spent in that school, city/country, and main language of instruction.

# 6 The Impact of English-medium Higher Education: The Case of Qatar

|   | Name of school | Years | City/Country | Language |
|---|---|---|---|---|
| 1. | | | | |
| 2. | | | | |
| 3. | | | | |
| 4. | | | | |
| 5. | | | | |
| 6. | | | | |

9. Name of university attended, years spent in that school, and main language of instruction.

|   | Name of university | Years | City/Country | Language |
|---|---|---|---|---|
| 1. | | | | |
| 2. | | | | |
| 3. | | | | |

10. How would you rate your ability to use spoken Arabic?
    1. Excellent   2. Very good   3. Good   4. Poor   5. Very poor

11. How would you rate your ability to use written Arabic?
    1. Excellent   2. Very good   3. Good   4. Poor   5. Very poor

12. How would you rate your ability to use spoken English?
    1. Excellent   2. Very good   3. Good   4. Poor   5. Very poor

13. How would you rate your ability to use written English?
    1. Excellent   2. Very good   3. Good   4. Poor   5. Very poor

*Please indicate to what extent do you agree or disagree with the following statements on a scale of 1–5 where 1 is Strongly Agree and 5 is Strongly Disagree.*

14. The overall quality of education in Qatar is improving.
    1. Strongly Agree   2. Agree   3. Neutral   4. Disagree   5. Strongly Disagree

15. Education in the government schools in Arabic is better than education in the private schools in English.
    1. Strongly Agree   2. Agree   3. Neutral   4. Disagree   5. Strongly Disagree

16. Education in private schools in English is better than the education in government schools in Arabic.
    1. Strongly Agree   2. Agree   3. Neutral   4. Disagree   5. Strongly Disagree

17. The national educational reform project benefits the general population.
    1. Strongly Agree   2. Agree   3. Neutral   4. Disagree   5. Strongly Disagree

18. The independent school initiative has the potential of improving the quality of education in Qatar.
    1. Strongly Agree   2. Agree   3. Neutral   4. Disagree   5. Strongly Disagree

19. The introduction of English as the language of instruction in independent schools in Qatar is important for the future academic success of the students.
    1. Strongly Agree   2. Agree   3. Neutral   4. Disagree   5. Strongly Disagree

20. There is too much emphasis on English education in the national educational reform project.
    1. Strongly Agree   2. Agree   3. Neutral   4. Disagree   5. Strongly Disagree

21. Education in English decreases the knowledge of and use of Arabic, especially in the younger generations.
    1. Strongly Agree   2. Agree   3. Neutral   4. Disagree   5. Strongly Disagree

22. With the emphasis of English education in Qatar, academic and professional uses of Arabic might be lost in the future.
    1. Strongly Agree   2. Agree   3. Neutral   4. Disagree   5. Strongly Disagree

23. Knowledge of and use of Arabic will never be lost because of Arabic's importance for Muslim religion.
    1. Strongly Agree   2. Agree   3. Neutral   4. Disagree   5. Strongly Disagree

24. I believe there should be more English-medium schools in Qatar.
    1. Strongly Agree   2. Agree   3. Neutral   4. Disagree   5. Strongly Disagree

25. Education in English separates people from their native culture and identity.
    1. Strongly Agree   2. Agree   3. Neutral   4. Disagree   5. Strongly Disagree

26. English-medium education may be a threat to the local culture and identity.
    1. Strongly Agree   2. Agree   3. Neutral   4. Disagree   5. Strongly Disagree

27. It is impossible to separate western ideas from the English language.
    1. Strongly Agree   2. Agree   3. Neutral   4. Disagree   5. Strongly Disagree

28. Education in English makes people too westernized.
    1. Strongly Agree   2. Agree   3. Neutral   4. Disagree   5. Strongly Disagree

29. Education in English does NOT affect local culture and identity.
    1. Strongly Agree   2. Agree   3. Neutral   4. Disagree   5. Strongly Disagree

30. I believe all teachers should be Muslims in elementary and high schools to promote Muslim values and traditions.
    1. Strongly Agree   2. Agree   3. Neutral   4. Disagree   5. Strongly Disagree

31. I believe there should be more Arabic-speaking schools in Qatar.
    1. Strongly Agree   2. Agree   3. Neutral   4. Disagree   5. Strongly Disagree

32. There should be an equal emphasis on bilingual education in English and Arabic in Qatar's schools for students to continue to develop both English and Arabic.
    1. Strongly Agree   2. Agree   3. Neutral   4. Disagree   5. Strongly Disagree

33. Education in English is necessary to better prepare students for English-medium universities.
    1. Strongly Agree   2. Agree   3. Neutral   4. Disagree   5. Strongly Disagree

34. Education in English should be appreciated for its practical benefits but efforts must be made by parents to instil religious values (e.g. Muslim values) on their children.
    1. Strongly Agree   2. Agree   3. Neutral   4. Disagree   5. Strongly Disagree

35. In the future, I will send my children to attend English-medium schools.
    1. Strongly Agree   2. Agree   3. Neutral   4. Disagree   5. Strongly Disagree

36. In the future, I will send my children to English-medium schools but teach them religious values (e.g. Muslim values) at home.

    1. Strongly Agree    2. Agree    3. Neutral    4. Disagree    5. Strongly Disagree

37. In the future, I will send my children to Arabic-medium schools where they will learn religious values (e.g. Muslim values).

    1. Strongly Agree    2. Agree    3. Neutral    4. Disagree    5. Strongly Disagree

*If you have ever attended an English-medium school, or if you are attending an English-medium university now, please answer the following questions.*

38. My experience in English-medium education has been positive.

    1. Strongly Agree    2. Agree    3. Neutral    4. Disagree    5. Strongly Disagree

39. My experience in English-medium education has benefited me.

    1. Strongly Agree    2. Agree    3. Neutral    4. Disagree    5. Strongly Disagree

40. English education has contributed to the development of my critical thinking.

    1. Strongly Agree    2. Agree    3. Neutral    4. Disagree    5. Strongly Disagree

41. My knowledge and use of Arabic has decreased due to my education in English.

    1. Strongly Agree    2. Agree    3. Neutral    4. Disagree    5. Strongly Disagree

42. My knowledge and use of Arabic has NOT been affected due to my education in English.

    1. Strongly Agree    2. Agree    3. Neutral    4. Disagree    5. Strongly Disagree

43. English education has changed the way I understand myself and my culture.

    1. Strongly Agree    2. Agree    3. Neutral    4. Disagree    5. Strongly Disagree

44. I remain who I am regardless of having been educated in English.

    1. Strongly Agree    2. Agree    3. Neutral    4. Disagree    5. Strongly Disagree

45. English education has made me more critical of my culture.

    1. Strongly Agree    2. Agree    3. Neutral    4. Disagree    5. Strongly Disagree

46. English education has affected my religious views.

    1. Strongly Agree    2. Agree    3. Neutral    4. Disagree    5. Strongly Disagree

47. English education has had no effects on my religious or cultural views.
   1. Strongly Agree   2. Agree   3. Neutral   4. Disagree   5. Strongly Disagree

48. English education has made me more tolerant in my forming own ideas and about other people's ideas.
   1. Strongly Agree   2. Agree   3. Neutral   4. Disagree   5. Strongly Disagree

49. I wish I were not educated in English.
   1. Strongly Agree   2. Agree   3. Neutral   4. Disagree   5. Strongly Disagree

50. My parents regret sending me to an English medium school because they say it makes me more modern and westernized.
   1. Strongly Agree   2. Agree   3. Neutral   4. Disagree   5. Strongly Disagree

51. My parents are pleased with the English education I received.
   1. Strongly Agree   2. Agree   3. Neutral   4. Disagree   5. Strongly Disagree

52. Regardless of my education in English, my parents instilled in me our ethnic/local values (such as Muslim values).
   1. Strongly Agree   2. Agree   3. Neutral   4. Disagree   5. Strongly Disagree

Thank you for answering the questions in this survey. If you would like to participate in a follow-up interview for the purposes of this study, please state your complete name, e-mail address, and cell phone number.

# Appendix B

## Interview & Focus Group Protocol: Impact of English Education Interview

1. Please, describe your schooling experiences from grade 1–12: Name of school, type of school (government, independent, private, monolingual, bilingual) language of instruction, quality of education, teachers, learning/social environment.

2.  What were the reasons for your parent's choice of schooling for you? For example, why did your parents decide to enrol you in an Arabic/English, monolingual/bilingual, government/independent/private school? What were the reasons for your parents' or your choice of attending a university in Education City/Qatar University? What does your extended family think about your parents' and your schooling decision? For students in Education City, what does your extended family think about you being educated in English in an American university in Education City?

3.  To what extent are you or your parents satisfied with your schooling decisions? What did you and your parents like about your schooling experiences and what didn't you like? What was beneficial to you about your schooling experiences and what was not?

4.  How do you think your schooling experience impacted your knowledge and use of Arabic and English? For example, do you feel your Arabic is better than the Arabic of students who were schooled mostly in English? Or do you think your Arabic is weaker due to your schooling experience in English? How do you think this linguistic impact will affect your future life?

5.  How do you think your schooling experience impacted you as an Arab Muslim individual? To what extent do you think your schooling impacted your Muslim values and identity (how you see yourself?).

6.  For students in Education City, could you describe your first experiences when you started university in Education City? How did it feel at first to be in a mixed gender context? How does it feel now?

7.  To what extent do you think there is too much emphasis on English education in Qatar? How do you think English education might impact Qatari culture and identity?

8.  What do you think will happen to knowledge and use of Arabic to the next generation of Arabs living in Qatar with the emphasis on education in English?

9.  How do you think English-medium western education will impact Qatar's future generation in terms of their culture and identity?

10. Is there anything else you would like to add about the impact of English-medium and western education in Qatar?

FATMA FAISAL SAAD SAID

# 7 "*Ahyaanan* I text in English *'ashaan* it's *ashal*": Language Crisis or Linguistic Development? The Case of How Gulf Arabs Perceive the Future of their Language, Culture, and Identity

## ABSTRACT

Gulf Arabs are perceived as the most advanced of the Arabs in terms of state wealth, living standards, quality of life, education, and literacy levels for both men and women and overall opportunities availed to them by virtue of being citizens. In order for this advancement to have taken place the Gulf had to find a way of educating its people to international standards. One such way was the introduction of English in the education system at all levels and most importantly in higher education. Foreign workers from Europe, America, Canada, and Australia were brought in to assist in this modernization process and the language of common communication became English. After two or three decades, there are now calls to revive Arabic and reduce the effect and impact of English, not only in the education system but in the everyday lives of Gulf Arabs, where the use of English in non-formal situations has become the norm. Some quarters are claiming that the Arabic language is at the beginning of its death and soon will have no speakers, if English continues to be promoted over Arabic, in the media, through domestic South Asian maids and nannies, and in the education system. Through the collection of countless forum discussions (mostly Gulf *muntadayaat*) and blog pages, ten online articles/newspapers, and short interviews with students from the Gulf studying in London, we begin to understand through personal first-hand experiences how Arabs view the loss of their language, culture, and identity.

> *"I remember back to a time when everyone neglected me and left me all alone; they doubted me and considered me useless in their lives. I urged my people to come back and activate me but they ignored me. My enemies accused me of impotence at the peak of my youth; I wish I was barren so that their words would not hurt me ... I see people of the west powerful and mighty and how many people have achieved power and might through the power of their language."*
> — HAFEZ IBRAHIM, "The Arabic language laments it fate", 1937

## Introduction

A lamentation it is indeed, coming from a poet dubbed the "Shaa'ir al wattaniya ... the nationalist poet" (Khalil, 1979, p. 597), it seems that no heed was taken and Arabic still laments its fate today as it did then, in the first half of the last century. The author of the above excerpt, Egyptian poet Hafez Ibrahim (1871–1932) was noted for his love of the Arabic language and his strong views against introducing the local variety (*ammiyah*) into schools and education, as a medium of instruction. He felt that this was an insult to the pure, high, and unpolluted language of the Quran, the language of the forefathers of the Arabs and a language by which a people – a great people in his opinion – were defined (*Al Ahram Weekly*, 2003). In this very famous extract, Ibrahim is the mouthpiece for the Arabic language, speaking on its behalf through personification in the way he knows best: poetry. Symbolic words that are used here are significant since, as will be shown in the following, they are the same words that appear in the blogs and during the interviews. The idea of "useless," "neglect", "doubt", and "unproductive" are all recurring themes that are representative of the worries and complaints of how Arabic today is seen by Gulf Arabs.

In these verses, Arabic complains that its people (Arabic speakers) no longer see a need for it and that they (the speakers) and the enemy (invading languages) see Arabic as an unproductive member of the language community and one that is void of all words and expression. The expression in Arabic and the choice of words and suggestions and even the style and metres of verse almost juxtapose the accusations made about the language's incompetence. Anybody who understands Arabic poetry and reads the Arabic will see the deliberate use of over-styling and deep almost artificial eloquence overtly employed by Ibrahim in the poem, a clear and obvious protest against the very accusations made against Arabic. In other words, the level of the Arabic in the verses is testimony to its completeness and uniqueness as a language and one that can withstand modernity and technology. Ibrahim chooses an interesting word to describe the accusation made against Arabic, that of "impotence", a meaning and connotation so strong that it touches the very essence of any man and here the very being of the Arabic language; it is being denied the qualities that would make it a language by definition of the word. It is through its ability to form new words, and through the production of eloquent phrases and sentences that a language is seen as usable and its speakers feel confident to use it under all circumstances and in all phases of time. Arabic here is marginalized in the mind of the poet; other languages want to take over and see Arabic as an enemy; stoically, Arabic stands its ground and is not made to feel less than its enemies.

Is Arabic seriously under threat? With over 400 million speakers in the world (Encarta, 2006) is it really justified to worry about the disappearance of a language with this many speakers? Many different groups, such as the Arabic Language Protection Association (ALPA) and the National Council of Culture (NCC), are airing their concerns about the future of this language, what is the reality of this fear? Is it founded or simply an overreaction? In this chapter, I present the opinions of Gulf Arabs on why they predict Arabic is declining and its future is bleak; and as a consequence why this will impact negatively on their identity and culture (Al-Issa & Dahan, 2009; Fishman, 2001; Hourani, 1991; Rouchdy, 2002; Smart, 1990; Spolsky, 2004; Suleiman, 2004).

## Data sources

Three types of data were used in gathering information for this chapter. These were blogs and forums, online newspaper articles, and a group focus interview with 10 students in London. These students were from the Gulf region (UAE, Yemen, Kuwait, Qatar, Bahrain, and Saudi Arabia); there were four women and six men. The interview was conducted in central London, and completed over a period of two hours in one sitting, with all the students present. The aim of the interviews was to raise the following specific questions: Is the Arabic language and culture under threat? And if it is how and why is it under threat? The questions were posed and all the students in turn aired their views. Part of the aim here was to create an environment in which dialogue could take place whilst discussing such a sensitive issue. All participants requested they remain anonymous and only their countries and occupations be mentioned. It was seen as most appropriate to first consult what was expressed on the internet, then review those arguments in professional online articles/news pieces, and finally to consolidate and compare the results with what Gulf students thought. Would all three data sources share the same sentiments or would there be a contradiction in the findings? The findings of this chapter show that, in fact, all three data sources raised exactly the same issues and they all shared the same anxieties and fears.

## "Lughati huwwiyati": Linguistic reflections of frustrated bloggers

The internet, or more precisely blog pages and forums, have become a place in which young Arabs are able to express themselves without fear of being judged, misunderstood, or imprisoned for their views. Most of the bloggers use pseudonyms to avoid identification, and often the frustration, on any number of issues, felt by the youth is evident in these pages (Deibert et al., 2010; Sadiki, 2009; Sakr, 2009; Seib, 2009). The internet becomes an important information source for a researcher because of its naturally occurring spontaneous nature in the expression of opinions and views. The usual laws of discussion are completely changed because the nature of the internet allows a person to express him- or herself with confidence because he or she is not being judged or is not known to others (Cavanagh, 2007; Holt, 2004; Rockwell, 2003; Weigand, 2009). One topic that many Arab youth discuss is their feelings about the Arabic language, its current predicament, and how they currently feel disconnected from it for a number of reasons, chiefly, they claim, because of the prevalence of English.

In the 100 blog pages surveyed in relation to the topic of language, culture, and identity, the first recurring theme was that the Arabic language is gradually being lost along with its culture and identity. The title of this subsection, "Lughati huwiyyati", is an expression used in many of the blogs and it literally means "my language my identity". The bloggers (montada. com) here equate language to identity, explaining that "my language makes me and without it I do not belong". One blogger (arabayah.blogspot.com) says, "... our language is dead, people Arabic died and we buried her". This is very pessimistic and other contributors on the page echo his sentiments. Others (aluae.net/vb) agree and complain that they can no longer make their identity distinct because they are losing themselves and their roots by losing their language. There is discussion on the site (aluae.net/vb) of the various student bodies across the Middle East who hold small fairs titled "my language, my identity" and the aim is to highlight the importance of the Arabic language to young Arabs (forum.wow-uae.net). Apparently, such an event took place in Egypt (egy-press.blogspot.com) with much success and the blogger presents photographs of the various student-led speeches and panels regarding this issue. Other bloggers say they will also do something similar in their countries and one student in Kuwait (fwasel. com/vb) says he has secured the approval of his university to hold such an event. Clearly, such anxiety over losing themselves has moved the students to act in the easiest and most effective way they see fit: through student bodies. A blogger (omania2.net/avb) who calls himself "Ameer" adds that the reason Arabic has died is that it is no longer useful for modern life in a modern world. This echoes Hafez's words in his poem of the accusations made against Arabic that it is "useless" and its speakers have no confidence in using it anymore. In over 50 of the blogs surveyed, similar, if not exact, comments and sentiments were expressed.

A blogger (z27z7z.comvb) calling himself "MaXmAx" not only declares the death of Arabic but posits that the Quran is the only reason Arabic is still spoken today. He unapologetically writes "... Arabic died and the Arabs now lament her and cry over her everyday, they hold on only to the remnants of Arabic, and if it wasn't for the Quran, the Arab would have been forgotten in history and left to rot in the desert like a dead camel." This is a powerful feeling and a reflection of how Arab youths feel about their language. The negativity is so profound that one is forced to consider such a statement with a degree of seriousness. Is it possible that without the Quran the Arabic language would be non-existent? The one part of this statement that stands out is the author's claim that had it not been for the Quran, Arabic would be extinct. The other bloggers (z27z7z.comvb) agree and go on to express dissatisfaction with how Arabic is used and blame this on the use of their vernaculars (*ammiyah*) and accuse the older generations for not having honoured Arabic enough by teaching them the "pure" language. Nazri (2010) claims the following quite strongly:

> From a linguistic point of view, the revelation of the Quran was the most important event in the history of the Arabic language. It was an event with far reaching and lasting consequences, for the Quran gave Arabic a form it had so far lacked. In fact it was due to the desire to preserve the Quran that efforts were made to develop and refine the Arabic alphabet. (p. 12)

Quite unequivocally, Nazri makes it clear that Arabic is preserved because of the Quran and that without the Quran Arabic would not be a language of today. It is for this reason that Quranic Arabic is not in danger of being lost, due to the fact that it is the liturgical language of Islam. With over a billion followers, many Muslims try to learn Arabic, whether at advanced or basic levels, in a bid to understand the words of God without the barrier of translation (Jaspal & Coyle, 2010; Jeppie, 2007; Kung, 2006; Langlaude, 2007; Mann, 2004; Tayob, 1995). Arabic of the Quran has survived for over 1,400 years and continues to survive in its pure unpolluted form, and in

7 *"Ahyaanan I text in English 'ashaan it's ashal"*  185

places where it was not even a national language and does not even count towards statistics. Any history book will demonstrate the well-preserved Arabic writing tradition, most notably in West Africa, and how this strong Arabic literary tradition found its way to the Americas when the slaves were taken there (Austin, 1984; De Roo, 1900; Diouf, 1998). The Arabic that is in danger is the people's local spoken vernacular, along with its culture and regional idiosyncrasies. The efforts exhausted in the first few decades of Islam to preserve the Quran pushed Arab language scholars to explore and document unique aspects of the Arabic language. Such close study and scrutiny of the Quran, not merely in an endeavour to understand the words and meanings, but to also understand why, as a book, it was unique led to the flourishing of other disciplines in a short amount of time. These are the fields of grammar, eloquence, stylistics, the difference between prose and poetry, and narrative style (Ba'albaaki, 2008; Nouryeh, 2008; Ostler, 2005; Safi, 2008; Wansborough, 2004; Versteegh &Versteegh, 1997).

Can a language be seen as living or as an entity that can die? What are the motivations behind such claims? Does the study of linguistics view language in this way?

## Language death: But do languages live?

Language is what makes a human being. Though this sounds simple, it is a fact that without language there would be an absence of a highly organized world as we know it; and this is because language communication (whether sign or otherwise) allows for such high complex systems to exist. It is the single most defining characteristic that sets human beings apart from everything else in existence (Enfield & Levinson, 2006). Aitchison (1998) refers to human beings as the articulate mammals in documenting the advantage language gives human beings over other species, an advantage discussed at length as far back as Aristotle (Allan, 2004). One of the ways in which language and the human ability to speak is advantageous is in its central function to act as a medium of communication between people. It is a very effective, efficient, economical, and easy way of externalizing the internal to others. There are many definitions for the meaning of "language" and one such definition is: "a systematic means of communicating by the use of sounds or conventional symbols" (Encyclopaedia Britannica, 2010).

It must be understood however, that language has a more important function that goes beyond mere communication. This factor is the way that it encapsulates histories, memories, ideas, worldviews, and the thoughts of its speakers. I am not taking on the Sapir-Whorf hypothesis (Boroditsky, 2003; Gumperz & Levinson, 1996; Levinson, 2000; Pinker, 1994; Sapir, 1959; Whorf, 1940) in its determinist view that a language condemns its speaker to think and see the world in one way, which is different to a speaker of another language. Rather, here we see each language as unique from another in a way that it affords its speakers concepts that are perhaps not found in other languages. For example, in Arabic the concept of honour (*sharaf*) and respect (*hishma*) is not only understood in a different way than that same concept in, for example, English; but even the way that speakers of the language will reflect this in their proverbs, literature, and action will be different from that of the English speakers. The use of address terms and the overt reflection of hierarchy that is present in the Arabic language and culture is not the same as it is in the English culture and language. Such characteristics of languages influence the way in which people think and treat one another and it is because of these idiosyncrasies that language death means the death of a thought-frame or a worldview, which future generations will never know about. Nazri (2010) says, "... the Quran introduced a host of new themes and linguistic forms not only to the Arabic language but to the Arab mind as well" (p. 13). Here she links language to the mind, the idea that the language of the Quran offered more than words to the Arabs and the Arabic language; it offered a new way of looking at the world.

*The New York Times* (Wilford, 2007) describes the current worry among linguists about the rapid rate at which languages die; a rough estimate is about one every ten days. Wilford (2007) quotes David Harrison (2007) an associate professor of linguistics at Swarthmore, in the United States, as saying that, "... their loss leaves no dictionary, no text, [and] no record of the accumulated knowledge and history of a vanished culture" a true loss. The author continues and writes about the impact of Spanish and/or Portuguese on native languages in Bolivia and indicates that one of the dying languages is "a secret tongue mainly for preserving knowledge of medicinal plants, some previously unknown to science" and that this would be a serious loss for mankind if no action were taken to preserve it.

No other human possession apart from language, can capture experience, invoke feelings, and induce action. It is for these reasons that when a language is deemed as endangered efforts are made to document the words and linguists strive to find all the speakers of that language. One such language documentation body, The Hans Rausing Endangered Languages Project, has the following motto: *"Because every lost word means another lost world ..."* It is this code that people fear to lose and most people, the world over, feel that their lives, histories, beliefs, and understanding of the world are all locked inside language and words and that losing it results in losing oneself. For any language to survive and remain in use, it must be used appropriately and correctly and if changes are made these should be administered in a systematic fashion. Languages can die and their death is at the hands of their own speakers, but even before a language dies there are signs and warnings of its demise. From the findings in this chapter the prevalent view is that the Arabic language is in this situation leaning towards language shift and some blogs report language death.

Language shift, according to Fishman (1991), is a situation in which the language community shifts from using their default (original) language to using another language. This shift, if not corrected, can eventually replace the mother tongue and in most cases results in language death. Fishman (1991) argues that in order for there to be a successful reverse in language shift, intergenerational language transmission is very important and without it language will shift faster and inevitably die. This means that parents or grandparents need to speak with their children or grandchildren in their native language in order for it to remain viable. This important measure needs to be taken and it is a major key in helping overcome the possibility of Arabic loss, which is a concern in the Gulf today. The bloggers (z2z7z7.comvb) who blame their parents for not sharing the heritage of Arabic further accuse their governments of complacency, which has resulted in the loss of the Gulf culture and language.

Many philologists and linguists view language as an entity that can "live" and "die" (Einsenlohr, 2004). There is, however, recent criticism about the simplification of language as a living entity (Edwards, 2009), because some scholars believe that language is not as predictable as living organisms; and therefore does not have to necessarily go through the same cycles of survival or death. They do not deny, however that language has features that make it look like and at times behave like a living organism, in the biological sense. The implications of looking at language as a living entity, is that it must be used in order to survive; the language must be developed over time and if neglected may be forgotten or lost all together. Al Twaijiri (2010) says that

> Like any living being, language is subject to contingencies and prone to the vicissitudes of time caused by developments, changes, and novelties. Language life is part of its speaker's life. It becomes strong when they become strong and falls weak as they yield to weaknesses. (p. 7)

If speakers do not maintain their language, then it may be susceptible to misuse and eventually loss, a living entity needs to be kept alive, and the nourishment for language is constant use. Einsenlohr (2004) says, "... the large number of languages reported to be abandoned by their speakers are often explicitly compared to biological species, whose demise would constitute an irreplaceable loss for humanity as a whole" (p. 22). This "loss" is in line with the idea that a language also encodes, beyond mere vocabulary and phrases and grammar, an entrenchment of culture and identity. If this is lost then the new generations do not have the opportunity to understand the world, as it was understood by their forefathers. Hornberger (1998) reiterates this idea of language as a living entity and how it must compete with others in order to survive, similar to the lament of Arabic in Hafez's poem. Hornberger says, "... parallels are drawn between endangered languages and endangered species; in each case, the endangered ones, fall victim to predictors, changing environments or more successful competitors" (p. 442). There is also a view of language as an entity that has to survive among all other life forms, it must compete and it is a matter of survival of the fittest. If another language has more interested speakers or a better opportunity for speakers to learn it, then it takes over and gains more speakers and, eventually, the smaller weaker languages are marginalized and even lost.

Educational policy makers usually design a structure of education and learning that will ensure that a chosen language(s) at all levels is (are) used correctly (Edwards, 2009). This way young people grow up not only speaking their language, but they also relate to all those who speak that language and share a history, an experience, a certain view of the world (in the broad sense), and a sense of belonging with its fellow speakers. Speakers of a language usually foster a linguistic identity and a cultural identity when they have knowledge of the language and all that relates to it. Most education systems relate to and support the aims of an education policy, young people are taught language in formal classes together with history and culture or in some countries religious studies. It must be stressed, however, that this is not an easy or straightforward exercise (Edwards, 2009). This type of comprehensive system allows not only for language learning but also for children to understand their own culture and values taught in their own language. The speaker needs to live the language and be part of it by way of education, media (audio, visual, and written), and everyday interaction and communication. As this chapter will illustrate, there are many inconsistencies in the Gulf with respect to a uniform clear system of language education and culture according to the inhabitants of the Gulf, who have experienced education in both Arabic and English. It is a human right that a people's language is protected so that they can use it freely and without a feeling of inferiority when using it. As Abdusalaam (1998) says, "Islam considers language a human right that has to be guaranteed and protected for every member of the human race because of its advantageous effects on socio-cultural relations in a society" (p. 52). In addition to that, UNESCO (1981) recognizes the right that people have to use their language without fear or discrimination, because it understands the value a language offers to its speakers. The declaration made by UNESCO is that all must be done to "... ensure the right to use the mother tongue and the official language (or one of them) of the country of residence" (Phillipson, 1992, p. 96). This is an excellent declaration and it ensures that people in different countries feel at ease speaking and teaching their languages.

In conclusion, language is viewed as a living entity and anything living needs some type of nourishment by which to survive. Without nourishment it may malfunction, become disabled and not be as useful as it could be, and may eventually die. Efforts should be made to save any language from death and, because of the important abstract notions that language can encapsulate, it is of paramount importance that these entities are looked after through proper use and promotion. Language can consequently be revived and brought back to life if its speakers see a unique value in it.

## Identity and culture: Are they really related to language?

This section will briefly outline some key concepts on how language relates to culture and identity in general. Further reading of more specialist works and arguments and counter-arguments can be found elsewhere (see Auer, 1984; Austin, 1975; Cameron, 2001; Edwards, 2009; Le Page & Tabouret-Keller, 1985; Nino-Marcia & Rothman, 2008; Piller, 2002; Romaine, 1999, 2000, 2004a). With reference to this chapter and theme of the book, I propose that language is a clear and overt marker that reflects both the culture and identity of its people at both the internal and superficial level.

Culture and identity are the two aspects that are related to language in such a way that they really cannot be separated. The question often posed is the following: does culture influence language or does language influence culture? As a notion, culture is usually defined in many ways and there is no single set definition on which everybody agrees. In 1952, Krober and Kluckhohn collected 164 definitions for the concept of culture, which reveals why there really has been no agreement. Below is a definition that seems to be favourable and captures much of what anthropological linguistics might consider as culture. Ifte Choudhary (2010) on his faculty website gives the definition as, "... the cumulative deposit of knowledge, experience, beliefs, values, attitudes, meanings, hierarchies, religion, notions of time, roles, spatial relations, concepts of the universe, and material objects and possessions acquired by a group of people in the course of generations through individual and group striving". Earlier I maintained that language captures some of these aspects, such as experience, beliefs, and values. I therefore conclude that language captures culture. It is through the vocabulary and available grammatical forms that a culture of a people is captured and, to reiterate, losing language is losing culture and losing culture is losing one's identity.

People are usually socialized into their culture through communal action and learn from the actions of their parents and community, Baldwin et al. (2006) describes this process in the following way, "... the total set of experiences in which children participate so that they eventually cease to be totally confused and instead become respected members of a culture" (p. 107). Language plays an important part in this process, as it is the medium by which customs and practices are explained to children or novices so that they understand the background to their culture and reasons behind particular acts and ways of being. Schieffelin and Ochs (1986) address the role of language in socialization by stating, "Language socialization is a concept [...] taken to mean both socialization through language and socialization to use language. [...] [C]hildren and other novices in society acquire tacit knowledge of principles of social order and systems of belief (ethnotheories) through exposure to and participation in language-mediated interaction" (p. 2). The key in this definition is the central and crucial role language plays in socializing the children or novices into their culture; no other human ability has the capacity to take on this effective role. Although the Sapir-Whorf hypothesis is usually criticized for its extreme deterministic approach, the authors do appreciate Sapir's recognition of the important role language plays in socialization. Sapir said that "language is probably the greatest force of socialization that exists" (Schieffelin & Ochs, 1986, p. 3). It is therefore important for a nation to decide through which language its people will be socialized into its culture(s), and at what stages the language(s) will or will not be used.

In terms of identity, it has usually been the sociolinguistic branch that has looked closely at the notion of identity as it relates specifically to language. This is a topic that generates much debate; here I aim to present the notion at its basic level in an effort to show the relationship between the language and identity of a speaker. Through the different types of variationist studies (Labov, 1966) to the more recent analytical viewpoints and non-static understanding of identity (Auer, 1984; Austin, 1975; Le Page &

Tabouret-Keller, 1985) the field of sociolinguistics has established itself as the centre of such study. It is from the viewpoint of sociolinguistics that this chapter will view identity as it relates to language and language use.

The concept of identity is viewed in two ways: the essentialist view and the constructionist view. Essentialism (Popper, 1969) claims that an entity is defined by certain characteristics it possesses and by which it is recognized, and therefore it cannot be mistaken to be other than that entity. With this viewpoint there is an absence of flexibility and it is difficult to apply such a theory to social reality, especially where this concerns language and its various manifestations in identity and culture. Such characteristics are viewed, by many sociolinguists, as rigid, never-changing, non-negotiable, and created only once, hence such an ideology imagines the, "... 'other' as homogeneous and static" (Nino-Marcia & Rothman, 2008, p. 15) as opposed to fluid.

On the other hand, the constructionist model views identity as fluid, non-static, negotiable, re-negotiable, in a constant flux, and, most importantly, not fixed. Identity construction and display is viewed through "doing" or "performing" (Nino-Marcia & Rothman, 2008, p. 15); therefore it is through actions and speech that a person establishes his identity rather than through his physical being and characteristics (Butler, 1998; Cameron, 2001; Edwards, 2009; Jaffe, 1999, 2007; Piller, 2002; Romaine, 1999, 2000, 2004a).

A person assumes the culture and identity of his primary language through the proper learning and using of his language. Although it is important for a child to first learn one or two languages very well and be socialized into their worldview, before being exposed to other languages and value systems. This is not the place for a discussion on first language acquisition, but these issues relate to the idea that the primary language (s) a person speaks plays a role in who he/she is (Finegan, 1994; Klein, 2003; Mantero, 2007; Nelde, 1990; Villarreal, 2008). Even though the writers on the blogs are not linguists, they are correct to connect the loss of language with that of culture and identity. They clearly state in the blogs (for example, almotamar.net, manhal.net, awraq-uae, and fwasel.com/vb) that to be a true Arab you *must* speak Arabic; to be an Arab, Arabic must be your language.

7  *"Ahyaanan I text in English 'ashaan it's ashal"*

## What defines an Arab?

The definition of an Arab is important if we are to understand the frustration and fear of the Gulf Arabs with respect to their language. The best way to understand this is through the Arab League's own definition, since this is the body that "serves the interest of the Arabs" (Yale Law School, 2001) and that definition is as follows, "... a person whose language is *Arabic*, who lives in an *Arabic* speaking country, and who is in sympathy with the aspirations of the *Arabic*-speaking peoples" (avalon.yale.law.edu). The word Arabic has been italicized intentionally to highlight the repetition of this one word in a very short sentence. One key phrase in the definition is "whose language is Arabic". This was obviously formed some time after the inception of the League and seems to be a simplistic, natural, and obvious way of describing an Arab: by his tongue. The results of the findings in this chapter may suggest that perhaps many of the inhabitants in the Gulf may not after all be "Arab" by the definition of the Arab League. If they cannot speak Arabic in the true sense of speaking the language, with confident ability and profound knowledge of all the rules, then either the Arab League needs to change the definition of an Arab or the Gulf Arabs need to learn the Arabic language. All people are defined first and foremost by their language and then culture and tradition, but language is first in line of all possible characteristics by which a person is defined.

The other issue about the definition is that it did not foresee or appreciate that an Arab living in England, America, Canada, or Australia can be more of an "Arab" than an "Arab" in the Gulf, an Arab region. Some of these Arabs living outside (often referred to as *mughtaribeen*) have a strong command of the language, grammar, literature, and history and maybe are "in [more] sympathy with the Arabic speaking peoples" than those who live in an Arab country itself; here specifically, I refer to the Gulf region. It seems that in order to assume an Arab identity, speaking Arabic is what allows membership into that community and without it one cannot be counted as an Arab. Hence the fear that the Arabs have over their identity, as far as language is concerned, is well-founded and not an overreaction. Language defines like nothing else.

## Real people, real experiences and real fears: Gulf students in London

The discussions among the students highlighted the anxiety, disappointment, and at times anger at the way they perceived the neglect of Arabic language in their respective countries. The third data source includes 10 online articles and news items about the issues of language and the identity crisis in the Gulf, as seen by all levels of society. For the purposes of this chapter, I concentrate on two more main issues in addition to the fear of language death discussed above: educational policies and how Arabs no longer see Arabic as a language to use in modern life.

## Language policy and language planning in the Gulf

The most popular topic of discussion was the education system and how the Arabs – both the students in London and bloggers – were dissatisfied with the neglect of the Arabic language in the education sector. There was an overall feeling that the Arabic language had been neglected and, in turn, the English language was promoted as the language of tomorrow and as the language of information. Their outcry was not because of the status of Arabic; rather it was at the fact that in the long-run they felt as though they had lost their language.

One of the interviewees said poignantly, "I can't even construct a sentence in Arabic without making a grammatical mistake, and Arabic is supposed to be my language." When prompted as to why this was, without hesitation and with agreement from the other students, the answer was, "... because I was not taught properly at school." So the blame here is solely on the school and not on their family or society. Other participants felt that English was so powerful in schools that students were speaking English amongst themselves instead of using their common language and mother tongue. In one of the blogs (www.aluae.net/vb) an Arabic teacher in the UAE writes, "... language is a means of expression and thought and it is what forms an independent identity for the child, and it ingrains a feeling of national belonging in him/her ... when a child is exposed to a language he is also exposed to its culture and thought ..."

Like any educational system in any country, Gulf teachers must deliver the curriculum, but the frustration with the current situation is not at all pleasing to them. One aspect that is clear in complaints such as the above is the profound understanding of what language genuinely is, and its importance in the lives of Arabic speakers. Usually such analyses are expected to emanate from linguists and not teachers in school; perhaps this reflects the overt obvious and rapid loss of Arabic among school children, as observed by their teachers. However, the blame of language policies and how they connect to the education system is not one mentioned only by students; it is seen as a valid and serious issue among some Arab academics as well. Al-Jazeera (2008) reports this issue by citing findings of a 2006 conference held in Egypt that addressed this very concern. It was titled "Egyptian Experts: Arab Identity Is in Danger because of the School Curriculum". In the conference, each expert pointed out how the Arabic language was a marginalized subject in school and that students were given far more English lessons than Arabic. There was also an emphasis that Arab history, as a separate subject, was not being taught in detail and in some schools this subject was replaced by English language classes instead. The experts fear that without these two subjects Arab children will in the future not have a sense of themselves, or have a well-defined identity, and this may cause psychological problems and well-being will not be promoted.

Language planning is defined in the following way by the pioneers in this field of research, Kaplan and Baldauf (1997) as, "... a deliberate effort to influence the function, structure, or acquisition of a language or language variety within a speech community ..." (p. 4). It is a process that needs to be thought out very carefully and one, if accomplished well, can serve to help its speakers excel in all spheres of life and not just that of language. It has not been possible to have a look at the education or language policy of any of the Gulf countries, though according to Spolsky (2004) all Arab countries are monolingual and have Arabic as the sole official language.

This means that "... one language is associated with the national identity [while] others are marginalized", so here Modern Standard Arabic (MSA), or at least that is the assumption, is the main language with the varieties or vernaculars not documented or given special status (p. 60). There is evidence, though, that at times certain dialects are preferred and seen as better, such as the case wherein the Shiites of Bahrain adopt the Sunni dialect and in that way get better jobs and more opportunities (Holes, 1984, 1986). Or the Palestinian-Jordanian case where Palestinian men started using the [g] sound in place of their glottal stop [ʔ] (Suleiman, 2004). So from /ʔamar/ 'moon' the pronunciation became /gamar/ and this allows the speakers to feel a certain air of sophistication when they speak in this way. The common factor in these two simple cases, whose true nature cannot be addressed here, and in other cases across the Arab world is that no single dialect takes its place alongside the official language of Arabic (MSA); the rest are all unofficial. With a complex, unique, and intricate case of Arabic aside from political reasons and tribal confrontations this is a very wise move to make and it does unite and unify each country with another that has Arabic as its main language, at least theoretically. This type of policy does allow and promote the learning of a new language and these could be promoted through the availability of options students may have in school to learn French, German, Italian or any other available language. With such a policy in place one would assume that the speakers excel in language acquisition and proficiency of the official language to a very advanced level and that they have a profound understanding of the culture. Language policies can be re-written, re-designed, and implemented as and when a government or a legal organization decides so.

On a relevant note, the UAE has recently (2008) announced that the official language of their country is Arabic and that entails all people using Arabic in public buildings, government buildings, the news, any official broadcasts, and the parliament. The thought that comes to mind is the following: can this really be enforced? (Gulfnews.com, 2008; Tristam, 2008). This announcement seems to be out of place since it seems strange that an Arab country should decide in 2008, more than 30 years since its inception, to make Arabic its official language. This announcement has generated a lot of discussion on the internet and google.com makes

## 7 "Ahyaanan I text in English 'ashaan it's ashal"

available 239,000 pages under the search "UAE makes Arabic its official language". All types of people, both linguists and non-linguists, discuss what this means. One blog (uaecommunity.blogspot.com) from the UAE commented on the news and a contributor calling themselves ProudEmarati writes the following,

> The title is not accurate because Arabic is already the official language of the country. The new decision is to confirm that Arabic is the language to be used in transactions in all federal governmental institutions and agencies. Which is pathetic if you ask me considering that we shouldn't have gone to this level in the first place. Arabic should be the language to be used without any argument!! Either way, this decision doesn't [sic] worth the paper it has been printed in [sic] unless it is applied in the local governments too. I don't see the point of asking the federal government to apply such decision [sic] while letting the local governments speak whatever language they want. (Nov. 2009)

If we ignore the mistakes in English (we will address the poor level of English among Gulf students below), the frustration and perhaps an air of shock can be read from this message; an Emirati cannot believe that this "pathetic" decision has been taken. A reflection of the current state of Arabic also becomes clear from the words "... considering that we shouldn't have gone to this level in the first place," which is perhaps a reference to the fact that there has been no pride in Arabic, by the government or the people. They also assertively insert, "Arabic language should be the language to be used without any argument!!" The exclamation marks in the written discourse make for a vivid realization of how the writer and others like him or her feel about their language. This was no surprise since the same sentiments were made clear by the participants in London.

If the policies are already in place then these should be implemented; other participants continue and remark that the law "means nothing" and everybody will continue to speak their own language. The language policy needs to make clear the role of Arabic and the role of English and where each one is to be used; it needs to be void of confusion in order for it to be implemented.

The language, in which children are educated, is one way in which that particular language can be promoted and taught well. Abu-Libdeh, commenting on this issue with regards to the UAE (1994), says that

"... government officials do not often base language decisions on language data either out of ignorance or because political considerations are given precedence ..." (p. 2). This is a strong statement to make about how language policies are made and on what grounds their contents are motivated.

One of the students during the interviews also noted that English in the Gulf schools is introduced very early on in the education process. She says that in her native Kuwait there are some nurseries (kindergartens) that only communicate with the children in English. Other students reported similar occurrences in their countries and they thought this was not at all positive since the children would only be four years old at the time, most coming from a home of spoken dialect Arabic with a maid who either spoke Pidgin English or broken Arabic. They claimed this caused confusion, and then after a year or two when the children enter formal school they are expected to learn MSA as the language of "education." When asked why all this was so wrong, since MSA was the official written and read language of all Gulf countries, they all agreed that the pressure to learn Arabic correctly was too great. They explained that most children speak dialect Arabic at home, and their maids speak Pidgin Arabic or Pidgin English to them, and in school they are expected to learn a correct form of Arabic and English. This pressure is exacerbated by the lack of excitement and useful up-to-date resources in the Arabic classrooms. Most books are up to 10 years old, one Arabic teacher from Qatar, now reading a master's specializing in language acquisition, tells me that there are no smart-board/ interactive board programs for Arabic language. Ten years, he says, in the education sector is a long time; it is enough time for an organization to change its complete educational system and even change the way in which students are graded, "so how can we have books that old?" He understands the frustration of his students as he notes, "... the students are always complaining that it is all about rules, and not fun and they even tell me, sir who needs Arabic?" He reports this with some degree of frustration. He continues adding that "without my language I am nothing ... how can I study in school in a completely new language alien to me ... I'd rather study Arabic". However, his students clearly do not see it that way and will never see it that way unless they understand the importance of their language to them, in terms of their own culture and identity. Until that is made clear to them, Arabic will never be useful or important to them now or in the future.

## 7 *"Ahyaanan I text in English 'ashaan it's ashal"*

All the interviewees, who were teachers, made clear that their quarrel was not with the governments or education systems, but with the inability to have a body in place that ensured Arabic had a clear place in the educational system and in other spheres of life. The students discussed the use of Arabic in the workplace, arguing that if there is no Arabization at the education level, whereby the workers/ students are taught up-to-date information in the language they understand most comfortably, how will they conduct meetings and write memos in the workplace? "Not in Arabic for sure" remarks a Saudi PhD student, "English will always feel for them as the language of sophistication and enterprise". This is why the title of this chapter *"Ahyaanan* I text in English *'ashaan* it's *ashal"* was chosen because it means "sometimes I text in English because it's easier"; here "easier" refers to English being easier than Arabic to write. It is an expression similar to those used in many of the blogs, where young people were making the point that because they learn so much English, writing Arabic becomes a chore (for example, saw4.tau.ac.il, forum.wow-uae.net, almotamar, and manhal.net). It seems that overall the issue of language and how that relates to nearly all spheres of life is a serious concern to these students. I am also told that they are all studying in the UK to the highest levels in international education, whether MAs or PhDs, and yet when they return to their countries they will teach their specializations in English. There is no up-to-date or agreed upon corpus for effective Arabization to take place at such technical levels. Most of these bodies, which are said to be working on a corpus, are never really seen and their presence in the media and education planning and policy is void.

Another important factor to mention here is that although there is a fear that the Arabic language is in danger of being taken over by English, the fact of the matter is that even the levels of English among the students are appalling. Abu-Libdeh (1994) says, "Unfortunately, the level of students' performance and teaching practices is both low (Ministry of Education)" (p. 6). This was over 15 years ago and yet in conferences and from the participants themselves there is still a confirmation that the situation has not changed much. This means that in actual fact these students are not competent communicators, writers, or speakers of either of the two languages. Pragmaticians, I am sure, can already see the problems that may arise because of this. What intrigued me about this is that one of the students said, "... you are confused because you think most Gulf Arabs speak very crisp American English with all the latest expressions ... but when you ask us to write we cannot." He continued to say that in his native Qatar he studied English for many years and when he comes to England he still must take the pre-session classes for "English-for-academic purposes". He adds poignantly, "So what was I doing all these years?" This is a point that was taken quite seriously and one that explains the frustration amongst English teachers generally in Gulf schools. One of the participants, who is also a TESOL teacher from Oman, informs me that in her class (of 15-year-olds) none of the students could spell adequately. She explains that at the start of her class she likes to give spelling tests of new words that they have already been covered in the previous class and that none of the students ever score half the mark. What type of linguistic situation is in play here? What inhibits proper language learning? It seems the Gulf is an ideal place to conduct research related to acquisition or rather non-acquisition of language.

To conclude, the matter of a clear, unified, uniform, and agreed upon language policy as far as and especially as it relates to education, needs serious revision if any linguistic forms of identity are to be formed or defined by the speakers and members of the concerned societies. Edwards (2009) says that "Consequently, all planning ... touches upon notions of identity. This psychosocial aspect is often part of a larger enterprise fuelled more directly and transparently by practical imperatives" (p. 225). His idea here is that any planning will affect the identity of the speakers and refers to identity as a "psychosocial" aspect that needs to be supported practically. Such protective measures ensure the sustainability of cultures and norms within a given linguistic society. This is very relevant to the reality of Arabic currently in the Gulf. A clear policy and implementation needs to be completed to ensure overall well-being and avoid cultural confusion among young Arabs.

## How Gulf Arabs have no confidence in using Arabic as a language of today

Arabs as a people in the Gulf region, specifically, although not every Arab, do not see the value of Arabic as their language, according to the interviewees. The preference is for English. One of the students mentioned that in her native Oman, when a child speaks English the parents are praised and seen as exemplary in how they have prepared their child for the future. Abu-Libdeh (1994) says expressively, "On the one hand they [Arabs] recognize it as an instrument for modernity and development (Fishman, 1971) and on the other hand they perceive it as a colonial heritage" (p. 5). Is there a double-function for English, one of need and the other of resentment perhaps?

In relation to this, the participants point out that in order for there to be good language use by citizens of the Gulf, they need role models. People in powerful, well-known positions need to use Arabic in the correct way, and that way not only children but adults will be encouraged to want to at least speak in the same language. They inform me that the problem is two-fold: if the Arabic is used, even by leaders, presidents, or actors the grammar is wrong and no linguistic competence is shown. Secondly, if Arabic is used it is heavily unbalanced through code switching with English at both the word and sentence levels. The point is that these people could have used Arabic but chose not to. Hence, they paint a picture that English is the language to speak in all spheres of life, not just in business or education. There is no incentive for young people to use Arabic, since all their role models do not seem to approve of it by virtue of their choice to use English in its place, often unnecessarily.

An Al-Jazeera presenter by the name of Dr Faisal al Qaasim (2009) writes an article titled, "When will the Arab leaders learn the Arabic language?" (www.marebpress.net, 2009) and protests at the constant mistakes these leaders make during their speeches and interviews on local and satellite television. He writes with sarcasm and frustration,

> Why don't the speech writers for these leaders tell them, "By God! You have shamed us in front of all humanity by your crocked speech and Picasso-like talk whereby the head cannot be distinguished from the leg or the nose from the ear. Your use of Arabic is shameful not eloquent by any standards, not words, or sentences, or pronunciation or syntax dear wonderful leaders! If Sibawayhi was to hear you he would turn in his grave, the man died saying that his heart was preoccupied by a grammatical issue … when will you our beloved leaders decide that part of your greatness is measured on part by the greatness in your speech? You appear uneducated in the eyes of those watching you …"

The writer here equates the greatness of leaders with their ability to use language in a defined, refined, and correct manner. This echoes Ibrahim's poem quoted at the opening of this chapter in which he says, "I see people of the West powerful and mighty and how many people have achieved power and might through the power of their language". A reoccurring theme that proper language use equals political or maybe ideological power and that those in leadership positions need to master language if they are to be seen as truly powerful, is repeated here. The criticism is almost a plea from the writer, advising the leaders that they are not taken seriously because of their lack of proper language use. He reminds them that the Arabic language is a language of rules and regulations by saying that Sibawayhi (the father of Arabic grammar and author of the canonical work *al-Kitaab*, which is a comprehensive reference for Arabic grammar still in use today) would turn in his grave if he was to hear their speech. Little wonder then, the participants inform me, that there is no emphasis in language policies or educational policies to cater to Arabic since the leaders themselves do not care for grammar or eloquence. The participants say that in the Gulf region the ruling families are usually great role models for the young boys and men, and whatever they do, say, wear, or drive all the young boys and men want to be seen doing the same thing. The examples they present are as follows: if a prince or sheikh or amir (leaders) grow their hair to a certain length and is seen on television like that, then within a month all the young boys will do the same. If the leaders wear a certain colour *thowb* (long garment famously worn by men in the Gulf, usually white and accompanied by a red or black headdress) like gold or brown, then these colours become so popular that some shops run out of that colour within a week. The point made by the participants is that if the leaders take pride in their language, this will empower the youth to take pride in their language and it will be an incentive for them to use Arabic and still look "cool".

Al Qaasim (2009) cites his experience of living in the UK for a number of years and how he saw language being used by the then prime minister Tony Blair in comparison to how the Arab leaders use language. He says that the prime minister, the Members of Parliament, and all government representatives never made grammar mistakes in English at all and they were all clear in the way they explained their points. He gives an example, "they would never say, 'I likes your country.' In all my time of over a decade in England I can't remember a time when huge grammatical mistakes were made ... on the other hand the Arab leaders toss and throw around the rules and regulations of the Arabic language" (marebpress.net). He makes the point that in order for a desired meaning, on part of the speaker, to be achieved certain rules must be applied and mixing of dialect with MSA is not the way forward; Arabic in public discourse needs to be maintained in its true form.

Another worried blogger (arabya.blogspot.com) complains that when these famous people are on television they like "to mix English words, phrases and structures into the language." This, for him, is a worry because this way he sees that the language will be lost and young people will not see any value in speaking Arabic. The participants also add that English is seen as the "gateway" to success and a better life and career prospects, so the more English you speak the closer you get to your goals in life. Many young people think that Arabic is "useless" and not "up-to-date" enough for the present day, which echoes Ibrahim's poem. The same accusations made over a century ago are being made again today.

In sum, people need incentives to use their languages well and often look to their role models, people like leaders and actors. These role models give the overall impression, even if unintentional, that Arabic is not important and neither is learning it. The people feel that using English presents them as sophisticated individuals and that Arabic has a place only in religion and religious discourse and not in everyday "worldly" life.

## Recommendations

This is not a prescriptive section of the chapter nor will it solve all the complaints raised by the Gulf Arabs; however, it is a superficial attempt at exploring ideas that may start a discussion about these issues. In this section I present some simple ideas of how experts in the Gulf and around the world approach good language learning, planning, and what promotes acquisition. One should not forget that even if a brilliant, accurate, and up-to-date language policy is put in place that will not erase the current anxiety about the loss of Arabic language, culture, and identity. The Gulf Arabs themselves must believe that Arabic as a language is their language and instead of expressing dissatisfaction that they are losing the language, they should make efforts at both individual and group levels to promote the use of Arabic. We must not, however, forget that there are those Arabs who do not see Arabic as their language and believe that English can offer them better economic and holistic satisfaction and that Arabic should be left for religion. This type of person will not be affected by any language policy or the promotion of one language over another in the education system since there are many other ways in which English can be promoted in their lives. Any recommendations made here are in the interest of those who want Arabic to be promoted and express anxiety over its loss.

One such recommendation, made by Dr Reima al-Jaraf, is that perhaps those in the education policy and planning department need to understand the issues of initial and second language acquisition in young children. They need to understand and explore the issues relating to the optimum age of acquisition of a second language. At what age does a child need to be formally introduced to a second language, with regards to grammar, writing, and comprehension? The aims and objectives of these policies need to be made clear and the desired outcomes need to be considered.

Hornberger (1998) presents a certain number of scenarios in which language planning has played a pivotal role in the revitalization of local languages. She concludes that there is "... consistent and compelling evidence that language policy and language education serve as vehicles for promoting the vitality, versatility and stability of these languages, and ultimately promote the rights of their speakers to participate in the global community on and IN their own terms" (p. 442). A language policy is one that takes into consideration the identity, culture, and language abilities of its people. The outcomes are a vision into the future of perhaps how the next generation will use the language.

On another note, serious thought needs to be given to the growing number of immigrants in the Gulf countries and how this will or will not affect the use of Arabic of the local population. There should be no imposition on how the foreigners use their languages, but the public language needs to be Arabic; as it is in Britain and America. Both nations have citizens who speak many other languages, but the public language is English; other language schools exist and coexistence is the norm, but English is not marginalized. If Arabic is to be sustained as a language of the future, a serious corpus needs to be introduced and Arabization needs to be an item acted on and not one that takes up journal or book pages alone. The influence that the media has on language, culture, and identity cannot be ignored, and it should be used to assist in maintaining Arab culture. If Arabic is to seriously take its place back among the Arabs, then educational policy is one area in which Arabic as a language can be reinstated as the language of the Arab people.

## Conclusion

This chapter has demonstrated, through three main data sources, that most Gulf Arabs are anxious about the future of their language, culture, and identity. They feel this way for many reasons; however, this chapter addressed the three major reasons: the neglect of Arabic as a language, the absence of a unified uniform language policy, and the lack of role models for young people to speak in Arabic.

Arabic is a language that is unique in the sense that it has remained in its original form for over one thousand years without changes in grammar or style. It is very possible for one to read a text from as far as back 500 years ago and still understand it without the need of a more diluted Arabic or translation. This is a living language by all standards of the word, but it is the Gulf Arabs who need to move towards using the language. There is no crisis for Arabic as a language, as a way of seeing the world, or as a set of rules, the crisis is that the speakers will lose out on their Arabic through lack of use.

There is a struggle for the need to learn English as a language of education and the need to preserve Arabic as a distinct language marker. To achieve this would be a balancing act and would require that the Arab people together with their governments work to achieve this systematically, whether this is through extra Arabic classes, or a unified uniform language policy or an agreed upon corpus for Arabization. The governments and the people need to work together to preserve Arabic language, culture, and identity; otherwise, the Gulf could soon have Arabic as a second language. This problem is solvable; all that is perhaps needed is for those in power and those in the position of writing language policies to take the issue seriously and spend the next decade implementing these changes. Incentives need to be offered to citizens to encourage them to use Arabic.

# References

*Primary and secondary texts*

Abdusalam, A.S. (1998). Human language rights: An Islamic perspective. *Language Sciences 20*(1), 55–62.
Aitchison, J. (1998). *The articulate mammal: An introduction to psycholinguistics.* Oxon, UK: Routledge.
Al-Issa, A., & Dahan, L.S. (2009). Globalization, English language, and Muslim students in the United Arab Emirates. *Educational Awakening: Journal of the Educational Sciences, 4*(2), 147–163.

Allan, K. (2004). Aristotle's footprints in the linguist's garden. *Language Sciences, 26*(4), 317–342.

Al Twaijiri, A.O. (2010) Future of the Arabic language. Publications of the Islamic Educational, Scientific and Cultural Organization – ISESCO. Retrieved January 18, 2011, from <http://www.isesco.org.ma/english/publications/Marabic/P4.php/>

Auer, P. (1984). *Code-switching in conversation: Language, interaction and identity.* London: Routledge.

Austin, A. (1984). *African Muslims in antebellum America: A sourcebook.* New York: Garland Press.

Ba'albaaki, R. (2008). The legacy of the Kitab: Sibawayhi's analytical methods within the context of the Arabic Grammatical Theory. *Studies in Semitic Languages and Linguistics, 51.* Netherlands: Brill

Baldwin, J.R., Faulkner, S.L., Lindsley, S.L., & Hecht, M.L. (eds) (2006). *Redefining culture: Perspectives across the disciplines.* Mahwah, NJ: Lawrence Erlbaum Associates.

Bassiouney, R. (2010). Redefining identity through code choice in *Al Hubb fi al manfa* by Baha Tahir. *Journal of Arabic and Islamic Studies, 10,* 101–118.

Boroditsky, L. (2003). Linguistic relativity. In L. Nadel (ed.), *Encyclopedia of cognitive science* (pp. 917–922). London: Macmillan.

Cameron, D. (2001). *Working with spoken discourse.* Oxford, UK: Sage.

Cavanagh, A. (2007). *Sociology in the age of the internet.* Maidenhead, UK: Open University Press.

Choudhury, I. (2010). *Meaning of culture.* Texas A&M. Retrieved from <http://www.tamu.edu/classes/cosc/choudhury/culture.html>

Deibert, R., Palfrey, J., Roholinski, R., & Zittrain, J. (2010). *Access controlled: The shaping of power, rights and rule in cyberspace.* Boston, MA: MIT Press.

De Roo, P. (1900). *History of America before Columbus.* London: J. Lippincott.

Diouf, S.A.(1998). *Servants of Allah, African Muslims enslaved in the Americas.* New York: New York University Press.

Edwards, E. (2009). *Language and identity.* Cambridge: Cambridge University Press.

Ferguson, C. (1972 [1959]). Diglossia. *Word, 15* (pp. 325–340) reprinted in P.P. Giglioli (ed.), *Language and social context.* Harmondsworth, UK: Penguin.

Fishman, J.A. (1991). *Reversing language shift: Theoretical and empirical foundations of assistance to threatened languages.* Clevedon, UK: Multilingual Matters.

Fishman, J.A. (2001). *Can threatened languages be saved?* New York: Multilingual Matters.

Fishman, J.A. (2001). *Handbook of language and ethnic identity*. New York & Oxford: Oxford University Press.

Gumperz, J., & Levinson, S. (eds). (1996). *Rethinking linguistic relativity*. Cambridge: Cambridge University Press.

Holes, C. (1984). Bahraini dialects: Sectarian differences exemplified through texts. *Zeitschrift fur Arabische Linguistik, 13,* 27–67.

Holes, C. (1986). The social motivation for phonological convergence in three Arabic dialects. *International Journal of the Sociology of language, 61,* 33–51.

Holt, R. (2004). *Dialogue on the internet: Language, civic identity and computer mediated communication*. Westwood, CT: Greenwood Publishing Group.

Hornberger, N. (1998). Language policy, language education, language rights: Indigenous, immigrant and international perspectives. *Language in Society, 27,* 439–458.

Hourani, A. (1991). *A history of the Arab peoples*. New York: Warner Books.

Ibrahim, H. (1972). *Diwan Hafez Ibrahim*. Cairo: Dar al Kitaab.

Jaspal, R., & Coyle, A. (2010). "Arabic is the language of the Muslims – That's how it was supposed to be": Exploring language and religious identity through reflective accounts from young British-born South Asians. *Mental Health, Religion and Culture, 13*(1), 17–36.

Jeppie, S. (2007). *Language, identity, modernity: The Arabic study circle of Durban*. Pretoria, South Africa: Human Sciences Research Council Press.

Kaplan, R., & Baldauf, R. (1997). *Language planning from practice to theory*. Clevedon, UK: Multilingual Matters.

Kroeber, A.L., & Kluckhohn, C. (1952). *Culture: A critical review of concepts and definitions*. Cambridge: Peabody Museum of American Archaeology and Ethnology.

Kung, H. (2006). *Tracing the way: Spiritual dimensions of the world religions*. New York: Continuum.

Labov, W. (1966). *The social stratification of English in New York City*. Washington, DC: Centre for Applied Linguistics.

Langlaude, S. (2007). *The right of the child to religious freedom in international law*. International Studies in Human Rights. Netherlands: Brill.

Le Page, R.R., & Tabouret-Keller, A. (1985). *Acts of identity: Creole based approaches to language and ethnicity*. Cambridge: Cambridge University Press.

Levinson, S.C. (2000). Yeli dyne and the theory of basic colour terms. *Journal of Linguistic Anthropology 10* (1), 3–55.

Mann, M.A. (2004). *Science and spirituality*. Bloomington, IN: AuthorHouse.

Mikhail, M. (1979). Iltizam: commitment and Arabic poetry. *World Literature Today*, *53*(4), 595–600. Oklahoma: Oklahoma University Press. Retrieved January 18, 2011, from <http://www.jstor.org/pss/40133014>

Nahir, M. (1977). The five aspects of language planning. *Language planning problems and language planning 1*, 107–123.

Nazri, N. (2010). *Linguistic miracle of the Quran: Science of the Quran*. Retrieved January 18, 2011, from, <http://www.scribd.com/doc/27564351/Lingustic-Miracles-of-the-Quran/>

Nino-Marcia, M., & Rothman, J. (2008). *Bilingualism and identity: Spanish at the cross-roads*. Amsterdam: John Benjamins.

Nouryeh, C. (2008). *The art of narrative in the holy Quran: A literary appreciation of a sacred text*. Lampeter, UK: Edwin Mellen Press.

Ostler, N. (2005). *Empires of the word: A language history of the world*. Hammersmith, UK: HarperCollins.

Piller, I. (2002). *Bilingual couple talk: The discursive construction of hybridity*. Amsterdam: John Benjamins.

Pinker, S. (1994). *The language instinct*. Harmondsworth, UK: Penguin.

Popper, K.R. (1969). *Conjectures and refutations: The growth of scientific knowledge*. London: Routledge.

Rockwell, G. (2003). *Defining dialogue: From Socrates to the internet*. Amherst, NY: Humanity Books.

Romaine, S. (1999). *Communicating gender*. Mahwah, NJ: Lawrence Erlbaum Associates.

Romaine, S. (2000). *Language in society: An introduction to sociolinguistics*. Oxford: Oxford University Press.

Romaine, S. (2004). The bilingual multilingual community. In T.K. Bhatia & C.W. Ritchie (eds), *The handbook of bilingualism* (pp. 385–405). Oxford: Blackwell Publishing.

Rouchdy, A. (2002). *Language contact and language conflict in Arabic: Variations on a sociolinguistic theme*. London: Routledge Curzon.

Sadiki, L. (2009). *Rethinking Arab democratization: Elections without democracy*. Oxford: Oxford University Press.

Safi, L.M. (2008). *The Quranic narrative: The journey of life as told in the Quran*. Westport, CT: Praeger.

Sakr, N. (2007). *Arab media and political renewal: Community, legitimacy and public life*. New York: Palgrave Macmillan.

Sapir, E. (1958 [1929]). The status of linguistics as a science. In D.G. Mandelbaum (ed.), *Culture, language and personality selected essays by Edward Sapir* (pp. 65–77). Berkeley, CA: University of California Press.

Seib, P. (2009). *New media and the new Middle East.* New York: Palgrave Macmillan.
Schieffelin, B., & Ochs, E. (1986). Language socialization. *Annual Review of Anthropology, 15,* 163–191.
Smart, B. (1990). Modernity, postmodernity and the present. In B.S. Turner (ed.), *Theories of modernity and postmodernity* (pp. 14–26). London: Sage.
Spolsky, B. (2004). *Language policy.* Cambridge: Cambridge University Press.
Suleiman, Y. (2004). *A war of words: Language and conflict in the Middle East.* Cambridge: Cambridge University Press.
Tayob, A. (1995). *Islamic resurgence in South Africa: The Muslim youth movement.* Cape Town, South Africa: University of Cape Town Press.
Versteegh, K., & Versteegh, C.H. (1997). *Landmarks in linguistic thought III: The Arabic linguistic tradition.* New York: Routledge.
Wansborough, J.E. (2004). *Quranic studies: Sources and methods of scriptural interpretation.* Amherst, NY: Prometheus Books.
Weigand, E. (2009). *Language and dialogue.* Amsterdam: John Benjamins Publishers.
Whorf, B.L. (1940). Science and linguistics. *Technology Review 42*(6), 229–231.
Zuckermann, G. (2009). Hybridity versus revivability: Multiple causation, forms and patterns. *Journal of Language Contact, 2,* 40–67.
Zuckermann, G. (2009). Let my people know! *Jerusalem Post,* May 18. Retrieved January 18, 2011, from <http://www.jpost.com/Opinion/Op-EdContributors/Article.aspx?id=142577>-

## Websites

<http://www.alarabnews.com/alshaab/gif/12-12-2003/a6.htm>
<http://aljazeera.net/news/archive/archive?Archiveid=1093354>
<http://marebpress.net/articles.php?id=3361>
<http://forum.te3p.com/292288.html->
<http://arabyah.blogspot.com/2008/05/2009.html>
<http://www.bbc.com/newsforums/ >
<http://www.montada.com/showthread.php?t=631159->
<http://forum.te3p.com/99886.html>
<http://www.aawsat.com/details.asp?section=17&article=434796&issueno=10502/>
<http://www.aluae.net/vb/archive/index.php/t-13812.html>
<http://www.aljazeera.net/news/archive?archiveid=1058605>

<http://www.awraq-uae.com?p=72>
<http://www.islamonline.net/arabic/arts/2002/03/article1.shtml>
<http://www.annabaa.org/nbanews/50/310.htm>
<http://sawa4u.tau.ac.il/index.php?option=com_content&task=view&id=39&itemid=64->
<http://www.arabicstory.net/forum/ofiversion/index.php/t12041.htm>
<http://www.fwasel.com/vb/showthread.php?t=84277>
<http://www.omaniyat.com/vb/showthread.php?t=13289>
<http://www.arabrenewal.org/articles/4094/1/caaUE-caUNEiE-aacDc-ai-Yi-ION/OYIE1.html>
<http://www.omania2.net/avb/showthread.php?p=11025599>
<http://forum.wow-uae.net/t721.html>
<http://www.almotamar.net/news/37195.htm->
<http://www.metransparent.com/old/texts/salim_jubran_arabic_language.htm->
<http://www.z7z7z.comvb/t1452.html>
<http://www.alsoyoti.com/vb/showthread.php?p=2016>
<http://www.aljazeera.net/NR/exeres/58679E86-DBDE-45A6-5803E93946ED-frameless.html->
<http://forum.amrkhaled.net/showthread.php?t=35151->
<http://www.bab.com/full_article.cfcm?id=5173 – >
<http://www.yem22.com/vb/showthread.php?t=388 – >
<http://www.ktaby.com/book-onebook-19113.html->
<http://www.nabanews.net/2009/18501.html->
<http://www.manhal.net/articles.php?action=show&id=2713->
<http://egy-press.blogspot.com/2008/06/blog-spot.7963.html>
<http://www.voiceofarabic.net/index.php?option=com_content&view=article&id=498:2009-06-02-05-14-28&catid=99:blog&Itemid=131>
<http://www.languageonthemove.com/blog/2009/12/20/where-is-the-arabic/> Ingrid Piller
<http://avalon.law.yale.edu/subject_menus/mideast.asp/> – 1945 Pact of the Arab league states March 22. Yale Law School – The Avalon Project (Documents in Law, History and Diplomacy) The Middle East 1916–2001: A documentary record.
<http://middleeast.about.com/b/2008/03/09/uae-makes-arabic-its-official-language.htm>Pierre Tristam
<http://www.nytimes.com/2007/09/19/health/19iht-19language.7561402.html> Languages die, but not their last words, John Noble Wilford
<http://www.guardian.co.uk/world/2009/feb/20/endangered-languages-unesco

http://www.highbeam.com/doc/1G1-217261742.html> Arabic language will protect our identity (Abu Dhabi)

<http://www.hrelp.org/- The Hans Rausing Endangered Languages Project

http://www.zawya.com/Story.cfm/sidWAM20100221011011281/Ruler%20of%20 Sharjah%20to%20attend%20Arabic%20Language%20National%20Day/> Arabic language Protection Society Sharjah UAE

<http://www.khaleejtimes.com/DisplayArticle.asp?xfile=data/theuae/2005/December/theuae_December37.xml&section=theuae&col=> Arabic in decline in its own lands (2010)

ELIZABETH S. BUCKNER

# 8 The Growth of English Language Learning in Morocco: Culture, Class, and Status Competition

## ABSTRACT

English usage has been growing rapidly throughout Morocco, as the country further opens to the larger world and youth seek out better educational and employment opportunities. This chapter examines the growth of English in Morocco's complex linguistic landscape. It argues that unlike French and Spanish, English does not have a colonial legacy in Morocco and in fact, seems to represent something different – a language of future opportunity. Based on 15 months of fieldwork in Morocco, including 453 surveys with young Moroccans, and 50 writing responses, this chapter argues that although English is widely welcomed in Morocco, young Moroccans seem to distinguish their individual identities and personal pursuit of economic status from their national identity as Moroccans. Specifically, while still valuing Arabic as a national language, surveys find English language learners are less likely than control students to consider Arabic a favourite language or an important language for their future lives. This chapter further argues that English is becoming a new means for socio-economic competition in Morocco, by appealing to upper and lower classes alike. Upper classes view English as a way to maintain their privilege as Morocco opens itself to the global economy. In contrast, many lower class Moroccans, who are weak in French, see English as a means to access public sector teaching positions, a traditional channel of mobility, or to sidestep the power of French entirely and engage directly with the global economy on their own terms as low-paid labour in Morocco's tourist industry and informal economy.

## Introduction

Language has always been more than spoken or written words; it is how we understand and express our fundamental humanity. It is a form of identity, a signifier of social status, and a medium of communication. Perhaps nowhere in the Arab world have language, status, and identity been grafted together by history in such complex and nuanced ways as in Morocco.

Morocco has a long history of multilingualism with three dialects of Amazighe (Berber), Modern Standard Arabic, Moroccan dialect, French, and Spanish all commonly spoken regionally or nationally. While French and Spanish are both international languages, they are also the languages of Morocco's colonizers and their power in the country is based on a history of political, cultural, and linguistic imposition. In contrast, English does not have a colonial legacy in Morocco and in fact, seems to represent something different – a language of future opportunity. Over the past decade, English has become increasingly important in all realms of life in Morocco, including economics, politics, tourism, education, and employment. Consequently, enrolments in English language programs have been growing exponentially over the past five to ten years.

While the rapid rise of English in Morocco is not in question, we know very little about how the language fits into the linguistic ecology of the country, or what role it plays in Moroccans' lives. This chapter aims to contextualize the growth of English within Morocco's complex linguistic environment, while summarizing empirical research on the growth of English as it relates to young Moroccans' conception of social status and national identity.

The first section examines the legacies of various languages in Morocco to contextualize the growth of English in the nation. The second section will examine the surge of English that the country has experienced over the past decade and the multiple factors that are fuelling its growth. Third, a review of prior literature on English in Morocco is presented, summarizing students' motivations for learning English, while pointing out the need for more research on how English relates to students' perceptions of social status and national identity. The fourth section will outline my conceptual framework, while the fifth overviews the research methodology and data collection. Section six discusses findings from more than 400 surveys with Moroccan youth. Lastly, I conclude with interpretations of how English may be differentially affecting young Moroccans lives by arguing that different classes of Moroccan youth may be envisioning different uses for English based on their future aspirations.

## The legacies of language in Morocco

In Morocco, bilingualism has been a fact of life for a millennium, as Arabic and Amazighe (Berber) dialects have intersected and influenced one another since the Arabs invaded North Africa in the tenth century AD. While Arabic was the language of commerce in the metropoles of Fes and Rabat, the Amazighe languages were dominant in rural areas. They survived because of, not in spite of, their marginalization in rural areas; without roads, schools, or media, Arabic never fully succeeded in ridding Morocco of its indigenous languages. The three dialects of Amazighe are still the mother language of nearly a third of Moroccans and have recently been experiencing a cultural and linguistic resurgence, despite their overall decline in usage as a result of official Arabization policies (Daniel & Ball, 2009; Ennaji, 2005; Howe, 2005; Marley, 2004).

For the past one hundred years, however, another language has dominated Morocco's economic and political realms. French has been the dominant foreign language in Morocco since the early twentieth century, imbued with a connotation of western modernity, economic wealth, and cultural superiority that came from political and economic imposition. In 1912 France officially colonized Morocco, incorporating the country into their protectorate and exiling Sultan Mohammed V. As soon as the French took control of Morocco, French became the national language, used in all public and political arenas. The significance of this linguistic imposition was not simply that it lowered the status of Arabic, but that its presence and importance remained long after the French themselves did. French continued to dominate many aspects of the education system, governmental affairs, and economic and social life for nearly two decades after independence (Benmamoun, 2001; Daniel & Ball, 2009; Ennaji, 2005; Redouane, 1998a).

Since its independence in 1956, however, the Moroccan government has enforced an explicit policy of Arabization, aimed at reclaiming their linguistic heritage and improving the status and usage of Arabic within the nation. The former ruler, King Hassan II, clearly stated that the threat of French was the impetus behind the Arabization policy, "the dominance of the French language is likely to sap the foundations of our personality and thus, the unity of our country by destroying our mother tongue, and cultural unity, which is based on the national language, the language of the Quran" (Redouane, 1998b, p. 2). Arabization was seen as the way to fight the harmful effects of French colonialism by asserting a distinct and worthy Moroccan identity as an Arab-Islamic state. This process of Arabization was seen as the cultural compliment to Morocco's political and economic independence. This historical emphasis on language is not surprising, considering the widely recognized connection between language and national identity formation in newly independent nation-states (Anderson, 1983).

The educational system was seen as a primary focus for implementing the process of Arabization. Redouane (1998a) explains that "a basic objective has been to restore Morocco's pre-colonial culture through a development of the national, culturally unique educational system – one that provides an education that is Moroccan in its thinking, Arabic in its language and Muslim in its spirit" (p. 198). The past five decades have witnessed mixed success of the official Arabization policy in both educational and governmental realms. Many have argued that while Arabic has now been entrenched in the Moroccan educational system from primary schools to universities, abandoning French has closed doors for many Moroccans seeking a western education, and further cemented class inequalities by denying the lower classes full proficiency in French (Marley, 2004).

## 8 The Growth of English Language Learning in Morocco

This chapter argues that as a result of Morocco's long and complicated history of language imposition and incorporation, the role of English in Morocco is distinct from that of other countries of the Middle East. In Morocco, English is not a second language, but a third or fourth language for many residents. With each new wave of colonization and cultural blending, it seems that Moroccans do not lose a language, but simply add another one to their linguistic tapestry. With centuries of Arab-Amazighe bilingualism and the colonization of the French and Spanish, English is only the latest in a long line of foreign languages to take root in Morocco. As a result, the relationship between English and Arabic in Morocco differs in important ways from other countries of the region. Specifically, English may be prized for its instrumental value as a key to the outside world, without carrying the baggage of cultural imposition that colonization brings. And even while the recent emphasis on learning English may be undermining Moroccans' interest in Arabic, it still may not be perceived as a threat to Arabic, as much as a threat to other foreign languages, namely French and Spanish.

## The growth of English in Morocco

While Arabization has limited the official role of French, the language is still the economic language of power in the country and an important key for Moroccans who hope for social mobility, and it further acts as the nation's linguistic gate to the West. Nonetheless, English has been growing rapidly in status and usage throughout Morocco for the past decade, and is now in a position to compete with French in many realms of Moroccan society (Ennaji, 2005).

Currently, English is taught at the secondary and tertiary level of the public education system. In 1999, Morocco enacted comprehensive educational reform that introduced English education at the lower secondary level (Commission Spéciale Education Formation, 2000). Likewise, there are a number of private educational centres that teach English, the largest of which are well-established language centres including American Language Centres, the British Council, and AMIDEAST. Enrolments in private centres have been growing rapidly over the past decade and many English language centres reported growth of more than 20% annually in 2005–2007.

English benefits from widespread support socially and from the government. In fact, the former Governor of Rabat-Sale made the case for teaching English to all Moroccans, and specifically emphasized its importance in business (Ennaji, 2005; Zughoul, 2002). English also enjoys much cultural prestige. Fatima Sadiqi (1991), the well-known Moroccan scholar of gender and language, reports that in a survey she conducted in 1991, "87% of respondents welcome the idea of seeing [English] spread in Morocco" and 81% "think that English is useful for Moroccans" (p. 108). It has been nearly two decades since Sadiqi's study, and the presence and importance of English has only continued to grow.

In fact, one of the most striking changes to occur over the past fifteen years has been the dramatic growth of English-language television programs, music, and written materials. In her 1991 article Sadiqi states, "English television programs and films are translated into French" and "the people living in Rabat, the capital, have the opportunity to watch three foreign television channels: TV5, RAI, and especially an American channel, World Net, (two hours a day)" (p. 103–105). Today, however, we note the overwhelming presence of the television, the DVD market, and the satellite dish, which have dramatically increased exposure to American television shows and movies. These are the effects of globalization, which lead Fatima Hilali-Bendaoud (2000) to state that English's "prestige is very high, especially among youngsters who like it for its music, songs and films" (p. 14). Certainly, Morocco's efforts to liberalize telecommunications, expand Internet access, and diversify its economy since 2000 have contributed to this surge in exposure to the English language and the resulting demand for English language education.

Despite the widespread interest and general support for English in Morocco, little empirical research has been conducted on the growth of English in Morocco and its expanding influence and role in the country.

## 8 The Growth of English Language Learning in Morocco

Nonetheless, there is a growing body of literature on students' motivations for studying English (Buckner, 2008; Ennaji, 2005; Sadiqi, 1991). In general, these studies have found that Moroccans' motivations for studying English are primarily instrumental, as English is required both to pass the high school graduation exam and makes youth more competitive in the labour market. Other important reasons for Moroccans' interest in English include: to pursue higher education abroad or at Al-Akhawayn, Morocco's elite English-medium university, to access the internet, and to communicate with tourists and foreigners. There are also important cultural elements to students' motivations for learning English, as many Moroccan youth seek to understand American media and become familiar with foreign cultures.

Due to its widespread support, many believe that English is now in a position to compete with French in Morocco and North Africa generally (Zughoul, 2002). Even 20 years ago, Sadiqi (1991) pointed out that English had begun to catch up to French in terms of its prestige, stating that "English has certainly started to compete with French in Morocco ... given that French is offered from the primary school onward, in addition to its predominant use both in and outside school; it would thus be expected to be chosen by more students" (p. 111). Some scholars attribute positive attitudes towards English as a negative reaction towards French for this phenomenon. Sadiqi (1991) states that "being a colonial language, French has inevitably been considered a symbol of political and cultural dependence, although this is not explicit. The rather negative attitude toward French indirectly increases the popularity of (and hence the positive attitude toward) English, a language without any colonial connotations" (p. 111). Nearly two decades have passed, and the role of English has only expanded. Is English still considered "the lesser of two evils" or has the growth of English started to threaten Moroccans' sense of national identity? This study aims to answer that question, by understanding how the various languages of power in Morocco – Arabic, French, and English – are intersecting in young people's conceptions of national identity and their pursuit of economic mobility and social status.

## Conceptual framework

This research is based on the premise that language fulfils various roles in people's lives; specifically, it allows them to project a specific class, cultural, religious, or national identity, serves as a communicative tool, and reflects a certain level of social status. Additionally, this research assumes that a given language's role changes depending on the individual and the situation. This section outlines the conceptual ideas that frame my study of Moroccans' language attitudes.

First, language is a social phenomenon that contributes to the creation of group and individual conceptions of self. Specifically, language facilitates communication between members of the same ethno-linguistic, national, or class groups and shapes their shared experiences in society. These common experiences contribute to creating bonds and help constitute an imagined community (Anderson, 1983; Schmidt, 2000). Building off of the idea of community, Mohammed Ennaji (2005) explains that language is a means of expressing a cultural identity. As he describes, "culture is what basically characterizes a society as an identifiable community; it encompasses language, history, geography, religion, the political system, literature, architecture, folklore, traditions, and beliefs" (p. 24). He further explains that culture is closely linked to other features of individuals, including their gender, family background, citizenship, and class. All of these ideas help shape individuals' life experiences and thus, help constitute individual and group identities. As Ennaji (2005) explains, "languages, and more particularly mother tongues, are important for identity-building. They have a symbolic role as they represent cultural elements that affect the first identity of individuals" (p. 24). Thus, language and culture are closely entwined in individuals' conceptions of identity.

Because language norms are transferred to individuals through their participation in socially constituted collective groups, language acts as what Durkheim (1982) calls a "social fact", or a "condition of the group repeated in individuals because it imposes itself upon them ... a product of shared existence, of actions and reactions" (p. 56). Consequently, the ability to speak a language or exhibit certain speech patterns becomes synonymous

## 8 The Growth of English Language Learning in Morocco

with the characteristics shared by members of the group, such as geographic identity or social class. This becomes important in the Moroccan context, as many English students want to be considered upwardly mobile, educated, future oriented, western, modern, or any other attributes associated with speakers of the language.

The idea that language constitutes identity is the premise of social identity theory, which argues that individuals and groups strive for positive self-identification and cultural recognition (Schmidt, 2000; Taylor, 1992). It is in this context that studying language attitudes is important. As Ennaji (2005) explains, "A positive attitude toward a language would create a positive cultural identity, and this contributes to the maintenance and promotion of the language. On the other hand, a negative attitude would inhibit and crush identity, and eventually leads to language loss" (p. 25). Given the global rise of English and the language's economic, cultural, and political power, understanding Moroccans' attitudes towards both English and Arabic becomes critical. Specifically, we might worry if Moroccan young people's interest in English is accompanied by negative attitudes towards Arabic.

To complicate the analysis of language as a form of identity, however, we must understand language is not just a form of acquired identity proscribed by others or a static understanding of ourselves; instead it is flexible and context-dependent. As a result, everyday language decisions are used to emphasize desired identities, depending on the situation and perceived group affiliation (Fairclough, 2003). In this way, language can also be a marker of social status or a way that individuals project their social position.

Second, language is a form of social power, meaning that it is a marker of social status and the means by which structures of power are negotiated. Because different language practices are associated with distinct groups, who have differentiated social status and power in society, language becomes a means of attaching status and power to an individual or group. Although Arabic is the mother tongue of the majority of Moroccans, and the only official language of Morocco, for the past one hundred years, the language of power in Morocco has been French because of its colonial legacy and economic and state power. By their nature, languages of power become a means by which sub-dominant groups are denied access to structures of power or social services. In Morocco, the poor quality of the public school system, which promotes a rote-memorization approach to language learning, has prevented lower class Moroccans from truly mastering French, often denying them high status professional positions.

While no specific language system is inherently better than another, the language of the elite is instituted as that which is standard or considered superior. This hierarchy of languages is not arbitrary; it is a function of how power works in society. Gramsci's notion of hegemony can help us understand how power manages to shape truths about language. His understanding of hegemony is based on the idea that those in power control cultural means of production as well as the economic means (Carnoy, 1984). Hegemony, the control or dominance of the ruling group, functions when the internalized norms of a society reinforce the status quo. Hegemony is the idea that "civil society is permeated by a system of values, attitudes, morality and other beliefs that passively or actively support the established order and thus the class interests that dominate it" (Chavez, 2001, p. 45). Once internalized, hegemonic norms shape the way that people perceive and interpret their world. "Common sense, for Gramsci, is the largely unconscious and uncritical way of perceiving the world that is widespread in any given historical epoch" (Chavez, 2001, p. 45). The concept of hegemony helps explain how dominant classes can not only hold power in society but can also ensure that this social arrangement is naturalized and accepted as inevitable. Specifically, in Morocco, French remained the language of power long after the French themselves had left, because of its hegemonic power. Gramsci's theory of hegemony and common sense help explain how ideologies of linguistic superiority and inferiority are internalized and reinforced through linguistic hegemony. It is not only those in power who believe their language is superior; rather, all members of society come to recognize certain language practices as superior and to recognize other practices – often their own – as illegitimate, improper, and sub-standard. Similarly, even those Moroccans who do not speak French or English recognize these languages' status as economically and culturally powerful and may aspire to learn foreign languages, possibly at the expense of their mastery of Arabic.

# 8 The Growth of English Language Learning in Morocco

Another important consideration is the economic power of language. Language abilities and linguistic styles often determine to which jobs an individual has access. Paulston (1994) states that "one can even argue that the most important factor influencing language choice ... is economic, specifically one of access to jobs" (p. 5). The economic significance of language is an important consideration for Moroccans, who believe that speaking English will give them access to better jobs. Building off of these ideas of identity and status, the following sections of this chapter will describe findings from a survey with Moroccan young people that examined how English fits into Morocco's linguistic landscape, and more specifically, how English fits into young people's construction of their identities as Moroccans, their perceptions of themselves, their futures, and their pursuit of social status.

## Methodology

To gather information on attitudes and perceptions toward language, while also trying to capture as many different types of students as possible, I employed a mixed-methods approach, combining a survey instrument with smaller focus groups and interviews. The population of interest was urban Moroccan youth between 15 and 30 years old. This population was targeted because they are those most likely to be affected by the rise of global English as well as those most likely to be in the process of planning for future education and employment. Moreover, because of their exposure to, and facility with, new communication technology, they are also the most likely to be influenced by western media, music, and culture, all of which have contributed to Moroccans' growing interest in English.

The main research instrument was an Arabic-English bilingual survey, which was composed of multiple choice and write-in response questions in both English and Arabic (see Appendix for the English Version). Respondents were able to respond in either language. The survey gathered three major types of information: demographic information (i.e. age, nationality, and native language); language background (i.e. foreign languages studied, years studying English); and language attitudes (i.e. attitudes towards national languages and the importance of languages as compared to the past). The format of questions was based on previous studies examining student attitudes to multilingualism in Morocco (Bentahila & Davies, 1992; Marley, 2004).

With the cooperation of English teachers, I individually administered all surveys in English language classrooms. I used a convenience sample of willing English teachers to gain access to students. Overall, teachers were very willing to have a guest lecturer and researcher enter their classrooms, and none of the teachers I contacted refused me access. The sample aimed to draw students from a wide array of backgrounds – including students at elite private universities, private language centres of varying costs, public universities, Master's programs, as well as students sponsored by their employers to study English, and economically disadvantaged students, who had been given scholarships to study English by the US State Department.

The survey was administered to 347 English language learners at private language centres, public universities, and private higher education institutions from 23 classrooms at seven different institutions. Specifically, the data was gathered from three Moroccan cities: Rabat, Kenitra, and Ifrane. In Rabat, data was collected from classrooms in two private language centres and two classrooms at Mohammed V University, the oldest and among the most well reputed universities in Morocco. In Kenitra, data was collected from a Master's level class in English literature and a first-year university classroom. In Ifrane, data was collected from Al-Akhwayn, Morocco's only elite private university where English is the medium of instruction.

Only students with Moroccan citizenship were included, which left 324 Moroccan English language learners. The response rate for the survey as a whole was 100% because surveys were administered directly with students in classrooms. The response rate varied on individual questions from 80% to 100%.

I also administered a control survey to Moroccan students who were not actively studying English outside of their high school curriculum. I gathered surveys from 156 Moroccan university students from a variety of faculties at Mohammed V University in Rabat, including Chemistry and Physical Sciences, Arabic Literature, Law, Economics, and Education. While all of the students had studied English in high school, and many continued with a few hours weekly as part of their university program, none were choosing to major exclusively in English. Unfortunately, my control population was not as discriminating as I would have liked, and included students who, while not majoring in English at the university, may have studied English at a private language centre. Consequently, I eliminated all students who had studied at a private language centre, leaving 97 control students. The total number of students examined in the study was 421. Table 1 shows the sample population, broken down by age, gender, and group.

The mean age of all the students was 21.7. In terms of gender, 52.6% were female, 45.4% male and 2.1% declined to respond. While not necessarily representative of all Moroccan youth, both the control and survey samples are balanced in terms of age and gender, and draw from the population of interest, i.e. urban, young Moroccans. This allows us to be relatively confident that the two samples draw from the same general population with respect to age-gender distribution. In my sample, the mean number of years students had studied English was 5.15. The median was also 5, suggesting a balanced distribution.

The survey asked a number of questions about student perceptions of the importance of English in relation to other foreign and national languages and how language plays a role in Moroccans students' lives. Specifically, the four sets of questions this study examined were the following:

(A) What languages should all Moroccans learn?
(B) What are Moroccans' attitudes towards languages and the roles they play in their lives?
(C) How important are foreign languages in young people's lives?
(D) Is the importance of various foreign languages changing?

| Breakdown of Sample Locations by Gender and Institution Type | | | | |
|---|---|---|---|---|
| | Male | Female | Unreported | Total |
| Private University | 25 | 20 | 0 | 45 |
| Public University | 47 | 54 | 0 | 101 |
| Private Language Centre | 77 | 84 | 4 | 165 |
| Public Graduate Level Program | 7 | 6 | 0 | 13 |
| English Language Learners Total | 156 | 164 | 4 | 324 |
| Control Students | 44 | 51 | 2 | 97 |
| Total | 200 | 215 | 6 | 421 |

Table 1

| Demographics of Survey Populations | | |
|---|---|---|
| | ELL | Control |
| Age | 21.55 | 21.71 |
| Female | 51.1% | 54.2% |

Table 2

# Findings

This section examines student responses to each sub-set of questions. After collecting my survey data, I coded all survey results numerically using a scale of 1–5 for agreement and then calculated summary statistics. I also conducted a series of $t$-tests and chi-squared tests to test for differences in opinion between English language learners and students in the control group.

## 8 The Growth of English Language Learning in Morocco

### A. What languages should all Moroccans learn?

This section focuses on which languages Moroccans consider important languages for their society, i.e. which languages they think should be widely taught. All respondents were asked to measure their level of agreement to the statement: *All Moroccans should learn (Arabic, French, Amazighe, English)* on a scale of 1–5, with 5 representing strong agreement and 1 representing strong disagreement. If we assume that the level of agreement represents a continuous scale of agreement, then we can average student responses, as shown in Table 3. The differences in mean level of agreement is immediately clear – young Moroccans tend to agree that Arabic, French, and English are all important languages for Moroccans. The indigenous Amazighe language is the only language that young, urban Moroccans believe is not important nationally.

| | Mean Level of Agreement that Given Language is Important for All Moroccans | | | |
|---|---|---|---|---|
| | Arabic | Amazighe | French | English |
| Control | 4.52 | 2.77 | 4.03 | 3.99 |
| ELL | 4.45 | 2.76 | 3.97 | 4.22 |
| Total | 4.50 | 2.77 | 4.01 | 4.05 |

1. Based on a Likert Scale: 1 (*strongly disagree*) to 5 (*agree*)

Table 3

Table 3 suggests both English language learners and other university students overwhelmingly believe that all Moroccans should learn Arabic (an average value halfway between "agree" and "strongly agree"), followed by strong support for learning English and French (an average value equivalent to "agree"). While the difference between French and English is statistically insignificant, the difference between both foreign languages and Arabic is statistically significant at a 0.001 level. In short, we have good reason to conclude that Moroccans view Arabic as the most important language for Moroccans as a whole, but do not distinguish between French and English in terms of their importance for all Moroccans. Nonetheless, on average, Moroccans seem to believe that both French and English are important for all Moroccans to learn.

Tables 4 and 5 show the breakdown of Moroccans' level of agreement by percentages. As Tables 4 and 5 indicate, 90.1% of all surveyed youth believe that Arabic is important for all Moroccans; in comparison, 82% think that English is. A series of chi-squared tests indicate that there are no statistically significant differences in opinion between the control group and the English language learners, suggesting that Moroccan youth have similar attitudes towards the importance of various languages regardless of whether they study English or not. This research is consistent with previous studies on languages in Morocco; Ennaji (2005) reports that English is the most popular foreign language for students at the high school and university level.

| Level of Agreement that "All Moroccans Should Learn Arabic" | | | |
|---|---|---|---|
| | ELL (%) | Control (%) | Total (%) |
| Strongly Disagree | 1.56 | 2.17 | 1.69 |
| Disagree | 1.56 | 2.17 | 1.69 |
| Neutral | 6.23 | 3.26 | 5.57 |
| Agree | 24.61 | 30.43 | 25.91 |
| Strongly Agree | 66.04 | 61.96 | 65.13 |
| Total | 100 | 100 | 100 |
| Chi-squared test for differences between ELL and Control: $p = .632$. | | | |

Table 4

| Level of Agreement that "All Moroccans Should Learn English" | | | |
|---|---|---|---|
| | ELL (%) | Control (%) | Total (%) |
| Strongly Disagree | 2.50 | 2.17 | 2.43 |
| Disagree | 6.56 | 2.17 | 5.58 |
| Neutral | 10.94 | 6.52 | 9.95 |
| Agree | 48.12 | 47.83 | 48.06 |
| Strongly Agree | 31.87 | 41.30 | 33.98 |
| Total | 100 | 100 | 100 |
| Chi-squared test for differences between ELL and Control: $p = .217$. | | | |

Table 5

## B. What are Moroccans' attitudes towards different languages?

Language is an important form of identity and is often used by individuals to accentuate aspects of their identity or project a socially affirmed status. I hypothesized that the importance of a given language among Moroccans will depend on the situation. To investigate Moroccans' attitudes and preferences for languages in different situations, following the methodologies of Bentahila and Davies (1992), I asked respondents to write in the language that they used in different situations or which language they considered the most important for certain aspects of life. Because the questions were open-ended, many respondents wrote in more than one language. As shown in Tables 7 and 8, results from the survey suggest that English language learners and students in the control group value languages differently.

| | Percentage of Respondents Listing Following Languages as "My Language" | | | |
|---|---|---|---|---|
| | Arabic (%) | Amazighe (%) | French (%) | English (%) |
| ELL | 80.8 | 4.5 | 14.9 | 6.9 |
| Control | 89.7 | 4.1 | 5.2 | 1.0 |

1. Row sums can add up to more than 100% because some students wrote in more than one response.
2. Percentages are calculated from those who answered the question. Thirty-five ELL students left the question blank and three control students did.

Table 7

| | Percentage of Respondents Listing Following Languages as "Favourite Language" | | | |
|---|---|---|---|---|
| | Arabic (%) | Amazighe (%) | French (%) | English (%) |
| ELL | 21.2 | 1.6 | 29.0 | 54.1 |
| Control | 35.1 | 0.0 | 43.3 | 19.6 |

1. Row sums can add up to more than 100% because some students wrote in more than one response.
2. Percentages are calculated from those who answered the question. Seventeen ELL students left the question blank and two control students did.

Table 8

It is clear from the responses that English language learners are less likely to say that Arabic is "their language" and much more likely to say that French is than students in the control group. This could be due to class status, as many wealthy Moroccans are raised bilingually or in francophone homes and these students are also more likely to pay to attend private language centres. Students learning English are also more likely to list English as "their language" than are those in the control group. No previous research has investigated this topic; however, more than a fifth of English language learners select a language other than Arabic as "their language." Given the importance of language in constituting the Moroccan sense of national identity, this large number of students, who do not personally identify with the Arabic language, could indicate a decoupling of Arabic from these youths' conception of their identities.

Table 8 shows that English language learners are much less likely to choose Arabic and French as their favourite language and more likely to choose English. More than half of English language learners select English as their favourite language, with French second and Arabic much less favoured. This finding is consistent with previous survey research that finds Moroccans generally have very positive attitudes towards English (Ennaji, 2005; Sadiqi, 1991). In comparison, students in the control group list French as their favourite language followed by Arabic, with English a distant third. However, it is important to note that while students from all types of educational institutions are more likely than students in the control to list English, the actual percentage that do so varies significantly between institutions. As Table 9 shows, students in public universities drive the average upward with their overwhelming preference for English; 70% of students majoring in English at university state that English is their favourite language.

## 8 The Growth of English Language Learning in Morocco

Percentage of ELL Students Listing English as a Favourite Language by Type of Institution (%)

|  | Private University | Public University | Private Language Centre | Master's Program | Total Count |
|---|---|---|---|---|---|
| English Not Listed | 51.11 | 29.70 | 58.18 | 69.23 | 158 |
| English Listed | 48.89 | 70.30 | 41.82 | 30.77 | 166 |
| Number of Students | 45 | 101 | 165 | 13 | 324 |

Table 9

Moreover, among both English language learners and students in the control group, Arabic is not a favourite language of even a plurality of students. Instead, students seem to have very positive attitudes towards the foreign languages of English and French. Ennaji (2005) contends that a lack of positive attitudes towards a language can be a concern to the spread and vitality of the language. While Moroccans in general believe that Arabic is a nationally important language, they nonetheless, did not select it as a favourite language. Moreover, those who study English are even less likely to select Arabic as a favourite language than those not studying it; this could be a concern in the future, as English continues to grow in Morocco.

In prior studies of students' motivations, many Moroccans expressed their desire to learn English in order to communicate with foreigners, understand American songs and films, as well as work in international corporations or businesses. Recognizing the importance of a language may vary depending on the situation, I also asked Moroccan youth about which languages they found most useful in a variety of situations. Tables 10, 11, and 12 show the languages that students find most useful in their daily lives and expect to find useful in the future.

|  | Responses Selecting Language as "Most Useful Language for Daily Life" | | | |
| --- | --- | --- | --- | --- |
|  | Arabic | Amazighe | French | English |
| ELL | 60.8 | 2.9 | 35.7 | 26.0 |
| Control | 85.3 | 4.2 | 25.3 | 3.2 |

1. Row sums can add up to more than 100% because some students wrote in more than one response.
2. Percentages are calculated from those who answered the question. Nine ELL students left the question blank and two control students did.

Table 10

|  | Responses Selecting Language as "Most Useful Language for the Future" | | | |
| --- | --- | --- | --- | --- |
|  | Arabic | Amazighe | French | English |
| ELL | 3.5 | 0.0 | 27 | 89.1 |
| Control | 7.4 | 0.0 | 52.2 | 64.9 |

1. Row sums can add up to more than 100% because some students wrote in more than one response.
2. Percentages are calculated from those who answered the question. Thirteen ELL students left the question blank and two control students did.

Table 11

|  | Responses Selecting Language as "Most Useful Language for Employment" | | | |
| --- | --- | --- | --- | --- |
|  | Arabic | Amazighe | French | English |
| ELL | 5.0 | 0.0 | 57.9 | 57.6 |
| Control | 11.9 | 0.0 | 85.9 | 7.6 |

1. Row sums can add up to more than 100% because some students wrote in more than one response.
2. Percentages are calculated from those who answered the question. Forty-seven ELL students left the question blank and three control students did.

Table 12

From the tables, we can clearly see that students in the control group are more likely to say that Arabic is more useful to their daily lives than are the English language learners. A full third of English language learners said that French was the language most useful in their daily lives; while only 60% said that Arabic was one of the languages most important to their daily lives. In contrast, more than 80% of Moroccans in the control group said that Arabic was the most important language for their daily life. Again, this is most likely a function of class; whereby, the higher classes in Morocco tend to use French more often, and are also more likely to be able to afford private language classes. Table 10 also reports the curious finding that a fourth of English language learners find English a language most useful in their daily lives. This is because the survey sample includes students from Al-Akhawayn, a private university in Morocco where all courses are taught in English and students interact daily with native English speakers in dorms and on campus. Because this could bias the result upward, I also calculated the statistic by type of educational institution. While Al-Akhawayn students did exhibit the highest percentage of students reporting English useful in daily life (28.9%), the percentage of students in public universities and private language was comparable, as 23.7% of private university students and 25.4% of students in private language centres report English being useful in daily life.

We also see that Moroccan young people in both the control and sample group say that English will be the language most important for their future. Approximately 65% of students in the control group say this, while nearly 90% of English language learners report the same. The control group, however, is twice as likely to choose French as being important for their future than are English language learners (52.2% to 27%, respectively). Similarly, the control group is overwhelmingly more likely to choose French as the language most important for their job; whereas, a large percentage of English language learners designate English as the language most important for their future career.

While very little research has investigated youth attitudes to the role that different languages play in Morocco, we do know that until recently, jobs requiring English were generally limited to the educational sector in Morocco (Ennaji, 2005). Today, the rise of tourism in Morocco, with the country aiming to attract millions of new tourists over the next five years, and the growth of international trade, facilitated by Morocco's Free Trade Agreement with the US, are bringing new job opportunities to Morocco that increasingly require English skills. Nonetheless, given the fact that none of the students in the control group are actively studying English, it is curious that a majority states that English will be important in their futures. Gramsci's theory of hegemony helps us understand this finding, by suggesting that through its global hegemonic power, the superiority of English is a widely accepted idea, adopted by both those who have access to English, and those who do not.

For those concerned about the status of Arabic, the findings are not optimistic. Only 7% of the control group and an even smaller percentage, 3.4%, of English language learners list Arabic as the most important language for their future. The percentage of students selecting Arabic as important for their future employment is also very low (5.0% for English learners and 11.9% for the control group). These statistics simply do not reflect the widespread use of Arabic in Morocco, which is by far the most commonly spoken language in the country and is undoubtedly important in the vast majority of Moroccan workplaces. These statistics may suggest, however, that youth aspire to the types of jobs that require additional language skills, such as professional positions in organizations and businesses where French and English are highly valued. Such positions have high status in the labour market. In light of Gramsci's theory of hegemony, it makes sense that young people aspire to high-status professional careers, regardless of whether or not they can attain them. Nonetheless, these statistics also suggest that as Morocco professionalizes its workforce and continues developing its human capital for a knowledge-based economy, the role of Arabic may increasingly be relegated to low-paid or informal sector positions. There is no doubt that labour market stratification exists in Morocco today based on language ability; incorporation into a global economy may only exacerbate this segmentation.

Despite this growing importance of English, both the control group and the English language learners believe that French is the most important language for Morocco by an overwhelming percentage. Moreover, the percentages are nearly identical, with 80.9% of English language students

## 8 The Growth of English Language Learning in Morocco

and 81.4% indicating French. This suggests that while English is growing in importance, it is not, in fact, going to replace French in the near future.

| | Respondents Selecting Language as "Most Important Foreign Language for Morocco" | |
|---|---|---|
| | French | English |
| ELL | 80.9 | 25.0 |
| Control | 81.4 | 18.6 |

1. Row sums can add up to more than 100% because some students wrote in more than one response.

Table 13

In short, the second section of the survey suggests that there are real differences between students in the control group and English language learners in terms of which languages they expect to be important in their futures. I argue that theories of bilingualism and cultural capital can help us interpret these findings. Additive theories of bilingualism were initially formulated by Lambert (1974), who argued that additive bilingualism is when a member of a majority group learns the language of a minority group, with no concomitant loss of language or culture. In contrast, subtractive bilingualism occurs when individuals of a minority group must give up aspects of their home language and cultural identity to learn the language of the majority group (Lambert, 1974). We can extend this analysis from majority/minority groups to the economic realm, where the dominant group is made up of those who have the access to a language of power and the marginalized group does not. In this case, if an individual speaks a language of power natively, a second, foreign language is additive. If, however, the individual speaks a language other than the language of power as a native language, his or her bilingualism is not considered additive, but rather, necessary for social and economic integration, and potentially a negative trait, if he or she speaks the language of power with an accent. Bourdieu's (2001) theory of linguistic and cultural capital offers a similar analysis, arguing that the upper classes socialize their children with linguistic discourses that are imbued with high status in a given country (Bourdieu). Given that a larger per cent of English language learners list French (the economic language of power in Morocco) as "their language," than those in the control group, English must be considered an additive foreign language for them, and thus, is highly favoured by them. In contrast, the theory of subtractive bilingualism would suggest that the many Moroccans, who speak Arabic as a native language and have not fully mastered French, might feel pressured to first master French. For this reason, French is more highly favoured and considered a more important part of their future lives.

## C. *What is the importance of foreign language learning for Moroccans?*

Given that Morocco has historically been a multilingual country, we expect Moroccans to be open to learning foreign languages. We might hypothesize, however, that Moroccans seem to distinguish between what is good for Moroccans as a whole, and what is good for them individually. This is particularly true given the economic power and social status that foreign languages hold in Morocco. This study asked students targeted questions about the value of Arabic as compared to foreign languages, both for Moroccans generally and for themselves specifically. If we consider agreement to be a continuous variable (rather than discrete) based on a Likert scale of agreement, we can average student responses to questions on their level of agreement with certain statements about language learning. Table 14 shows the mean level of agreement with a variety of statements on the importance of different languages, on a scale of one (lowest) to five (highest). A series of t-tests compared how likely it is that the two means came from the same underlying population of students. The null hypothesis is that the means are the same and that both English language learners and university students in the control group have the same opinions on the importance of Arabic in their lives.

| Mean Agreement (1–5) on the Importance of Different Languages | | | |
|---|---|---|---|
|  | ELL | Control | $p$ |
| It is possible to learn many foreign languages well | 3.68 | 3.63 | .724 |
| Moroccans should not learn foreign languages at the expense of Arabic | 3.18 | 3.24 | .720 |
| A mastery of Arabic is more important to me personally than learning foreign languages | 2.41 | 2.72 | .029* |

1. Based on a Likert Scale: 1 (*strongly disagree*) to 5 (*strongly agree*)
2. $H_0$: Group means are equal.
\* $p < .05$; \*\* $p < .01$; \*\*\* $p < .001$ ($p$ based on two-sided $t$-test)

Table 14

We can see from Table 14 that Moroccans generally agree that it is possible to learn many foreign languages well and that Moroccans generally should not learn foreign languages if it detracts from their ability to master Arabic. In addition, looking at the results of our $t$-tests, we cannot reject the null hypothesis that the mean from English language learners and the control group is actually the same. Essentially, both groups of students have generally the same opinions on the possibilities of language learning and its value for Moroccans as a whole.

However, when asked about their individual intentions, Moroccans tended to disagree that learning Arabic was more important than learning foreign languages for themselves personally. The English language learners tended to disagree more often and more strongly than students in the control group. Moreover, results from the t-test suggest that these two means are very unlikely to actually be the same. In other words, we have evidence to conclude that English language learners are less likely to agree that a mastery of Arabic is more important to them than are students in the control group. Students who study English are less likely to value Arabic in their own lives than are students who are not studying English intensively on their own.

Table 15 shows the breakdown of percentages concerning the importance of mastering Arabic in young people's lives. As the table shows, English language learners are somewhat more likely to disagree or be neutral as to the relative importance of Arabic in their lives than control group students. In comparison, students in the control group are much more likely to strongly agree that a mastery of Arabic is a priority. The results of the chi-squared test indicate that it is very unlikely English language learners and control group students actually have the same breakdown of opinions.

| "A Mastery of Arabic is More Important for Me Personally than Learning Foreign Languages" | | | |
|---|---|---|---|
| | ELL | Control | Total |
| Strongly Disagree | 17.55 | 18.48 | 17.76 |
| Disagree | 48.28 | 43.48 | 47.20 |
| Neutral | 16.30 | 5.43 | 13.87 |
| Agree | 11.29 | 13.04 | 11.68 |
| Strongly Agree | 6.58 | 19.57 | 9.49 |
| Total | 100.00 | 100.00 | 100.00 |

Chi-squared test for differences between ELL and Control: $p = .001$.

Table 15

How might we interpret these mixed messages Moroccan youth are sending about the relative importance of different languages in their lives? Based on their strong support for Arabic, we might infer that Moroccans believe that the Arabic language is an integral part of Moroccans national identity, religion, and culture. Yet it seems that they distinguish between themselves and all Moroccans in order to give themselves an economic or social advantage. It seems as though they presume a mastery of foreign languages will give them the advantage they seek, and hence label a mastery of foreign languages as more important for them personally than learning Arabic.

While Moroccans' consistent insistence that Arabic is an important language nationally and it is important for all Moroccans to learn, young Moroccans are affirming the importance of Arabic, which is closely linked to the Moroccan nation and its cultural and religious legacy. Nonetheless, these students repeatedly seem to reject the importance of Arabic in their own lives. Not only did a very small percentage of Moroccans list Arabic as an important language for their future generally or their employment, a majority of them actually disagree that a mastery of Arabic is more important than foreign languages. Instead, it seems as though English, French, and other more economically powerful languages are more important to their individual lives than is Arabic. This raises the question of whether individuals from different backgrounds and with different opportunities and aspirations in life will tend to place different levels of importance on the many languages in their lives, a question not yet answered in the scholarship.

### D. Is the importance of different foreign languages changing?

In Part D, all respondents were asked whether English is more, equally, or less important than in the past. Essentially, this question asks Moroccans about how they perceive change in their language environment, while also evaluating the current and future status of English.

As Table 16 shows, with respect to the importance of English, there seems to be a sharp contrast in the opinions of English language learners and control group students. While a clear majority of both control group students and English language learners agree that English is more important now than in the past, English language learners are much more likely to think this. Nearly nine out of ten English language learners believe English is more important now, compared to only two thirds of control group students. Moreover, three out of ten control group students do not seem to perceive a growing importance of English, indicating instead that English is equally important now as it was in the past.

| Respondents Opinions of Importance of English Compared to Past | | |
|---|---|---|
| | ELL | Control |
| Less Important | 5.35 | 2.17 |
| Equally Important | 5.97 | 30.43 |
| More Important | 88.68 | 67.39 |

Table 16

Although the results of the survey are somewhat nuanced, it is clear that large majorities of youth find English more important today than in the past. Nonetheless, it does appear that English language learners are more likely to find English more important now than are students in the control group; they are also more likely to find French only equally or less important than are control group students, the majority of who believe French is more important today.

## English and status competition

In Morocco, the growth of English is but another chapter in the nation's long history of multilingualism. The survey results summarized above suggest that young people, whether studying English or not, tend to have positive feelings towards the growth of English, a finding consistently reported in the literature. Young people overwhelmingly believe that English is more important now than in the past, and a majority state that it will be important for their future lives. Moreover, eight in ten Moroccans believe that all Moroccans should learn English. Studying English, however, is correlated with a lower appreciation for Arabic and less of a desire to master the language, which is a concern for the future of Arabic in Morocco.

Given Morocco's complex linguistic history, I argue that the problem of cultural imposition that English often brings to many developing nations does not seem to be a major concern for many Moroccan youth. This is most likely the result of Moroccans' high regard for languages generally, as well as English's status as a foreign, not colonial, language. As one student, fluent in English, explained to me, when asked to clarify his pro-English stance, "Nowadays, nothing you do won't affect your culture, given the spread of English movies, media, Facebook. But English is not a cultural threat because Moroccan culture was already ruined by the French." He continued, "Moroccan culture – a huge part of it is already lost – the French didn't leave that much for English to take away. We already do a lot of things that westerners do, follow their calendar, celebrate their holidays, and watch soap operas that target American or European audiences." As this student makes clear, Moroccan culture is not threatened more today than it was during the era of colonization. Moreover, given Morocco's relatively low level of development, English is highly valued for its utilitarian purposes. Rather than being perceived as a threat, it seems that for many young Moroccans, where youth unemployment is extremely high, combating the rise of English in the name of cultural heritage seems like a luxury of the rich. As another student, when asked whether he was concerned about losing his cultural identity, articulated, "What do I need with culture? Culture can't buy me bread."

Instead, it seems as though English is becoming the newest site of linguistic and class competition in Morocco, a country where language has always been intricately tied to social status. I argue that while the upper and middle classes see English as important for maintaining their preferred socio-economic status and as a prerequisite for Morocco's integration into the global market, the lower and lower-middle classes view English quite differently, but no less crucial to their futures. To complement my surveys, I also conducted a series of free-response questions in seven classrooms in private language centres and public university classrooms. Specifically, I asked students to discuss why they are studying English and what role the language will play in their lives. Drawing on their responses, I argue that young Moroccans from lower and lower-middle classes view English as a key to social mobility that allows them to bypass the constrictive influence and colonial legacy of French, which remains the dominant foreign language of the country, but one that they cannot seem to master through the public education system. For these lower class Moroccans, many of whom aspire to migrate, English now opens up a veritable new world of Anglophone destinations, while also offering possibilities for employment in Morocco's growing service and tourism sector.

In students' free responses, the most widely reported response to the question of why they are studying English was a very general answer – because it is an international language. However, the second most widely reported response was because English will help them find future employment. In every single class, except for a small class of Master's students in English literature, more than half of all students mentioned future employment as the reason they are studying English. While students rarely mentioned specific examples of the future careers they hoped to pursue, when they did mention specifics, their aspirations revealed distinct differences based on social class. In an undergraduate English class in a university outside Rabat that serves mainly poor students from the semi-rural, and poorly developed areas around the capital, two-thirds of the students mentioned the importance of English in helping them find employment, but only two jobs were mentioned by name: *a middle school English teacher* and *a tourist guide*. A sampling of students' responses reveals that their options for the future are quite limited, but studying English helps them dream of a better future and a stable job, "My expectation from English in the future is actually just to gain knowledge for my mind and if there is an opportunity to be a middle school teacher, why not?"[1] Another student was much less optimistic about his future, but said that becoming an English teacher offered the best possible future for him, "I really don't know why I am studying English, I just realized that it is the best thing I can do. I expect that maybe one day I'll be an English teacher, not because that's what I want to do, but because that's the only thing you can become." The only other career mentioned by name was a tourist guide, which allows Moroccans to make a living in Morocco's growing tourist industry with no real qualifications other than strong language skills. As one student said, "I dream to be a guide of tourism." Another said, "I could be a teacher, why not? Or I could work as a tourist guide, or in a hotel." All of these students

---

1   Responses lightly edited for clarity and grammar.

came from poor backgrounds and many were too poor to afford an English dictionary, despite majoring in English. Nonetheless, they overwhelmingly viewed English as a means to social mobility, either in the public education system, or the booming tourist industry.

In contrast, while only two students in the Master's program mentioned a specific job, both stated they wanted to be English professors at the university level. Similarly, the students from private centres, which cater to upper-middle class students and charge sizable tuition fees (ranging between 50% and 100% of Morocco's average annual per capita income for a 6-week session), also mentioned the importance of employment, but with much higher ambitions. One student said, "English will help me in my studies because I want to be an engineer. English will help me to find a job in a big and international company." Another said, "I study English because I use it to work to communicate with our business partners and it will help me get my MBA." Others mentioned wanting to be a flight attendant or to work in huge companies. One individual said, "In the future, English will allow me to work in international relations in a big organization, and I can use it when I travel." Clearly, their ambitions are significantly higher than the students at the public universities. These findings suggest that different classes of students view the role of English in their lives quite differently. Lower classes – who have not mastered French – see English as a way of circumventing the language of power and seeking another future for themselves. In contrast, for upper class students, who may already possess strong skills in French, English will help them advance their economic position in the global arena, in international companies and firms.

## Conclusions

This chapter has argued that students' perceptions of English are nuanced. While English is widely welcomed in Morocco, it seems as though Moroccans distinguish their individual identities and their personal pursuit of economic status from their national identity as Moroccans. This is an important and potentially disconcerting finding. Specifically, if young Moroccans distinguish between what is good for them and what is good for their compatriots, then the Arabic language may not be considered Morocco's unifying national language in the future, if in fact, it ever was. Moreover, there is reason for concern over the fact that English language learners are much less likely to consider Arabic a favourite language or an important language for their futures. It seems likely that the continued economic reforms to open Morocco's economy, which will inevitably be accompanied by a growth in English, will contribute to the marginalization of Arabic in the labour market to low-wage jobs or those in the informal economy.

In addition, I argue that English is becoming a new means for socio-economic mobility in Morocco. The middle and upper classes view English as a way to maintain their privilege as Morocco opens itself to the global economy, where English is highly valued. In contrast, many lower class Moroccans, who are not bilingual speakers of French, see English as a means of sidestepping the power of French. English allows them to engage with the global economy on their own terms as low-paid labour in Morocco's tourist industry, or opens up access to secure jobs in the public sector as English teachers. Thus, English permits them access to a secure and respected middle-class profession that many of their parents only dreamed of, while doing nothing to diminish Morocco's class inequalities.

## References

Anderson, B. (1983). *Imagined communities* (Rev. ed.). London: Verso Books.
Benmamoun, E. (2001). Language identities in Morocco: A historical overview. *Studies in the Linguistic Sciences, 31*(1), 95–106.
Bentahila, A., & Davies, E. (1992). Convergence and divergence: Two cases of language shift in Morocco. In W. Fase, K. Jaspaert, & S. Kroon (eds), *Maintenance and loss of minority languages* (pp. 197–210). Amsterdam: John Benjamins Publishing Company.

Bourdieu, P. (2001). The forms of capital. In M. Granovetter & R. Swedberg (eds), *The sociology of economic life* (2nd edn, pp. 96–111). Boulder, CO: Westview Press.

Buckner, E. (2008). *English language learning in the context of globalization: Insights from Morocco.* Paper presented at the 28th Moroccan Association of Teachers of English Conference, El Jadida, Morocco. Retrieved June 15, 2010 from <http://www.mate.org.ma/EljadidaProceedings.pdf>

Carnoy, M. (1984). *The state and political theory.* Princeton, NJ: Princeton University Press.

Chavez, L. (2001). *Covering immigration: Popular images and the politics of the nation.* Berkeley, CA: University of California Press.

Commission Spéciale Education Formation, C. (2000). "Charte Nationale d'Educación et Formación, Royaume du Maroc." Retrieved November 21, 2008, from <http://81.192.52.38/NR/rdonlyres/CAF0FEC1-2E4D-4A54-9C6A-9CB26780C33F/0/Chartenationale.htm>

Daniel, M., & Ball, A. (2009). The Moroccan educational context: Evolving multilingualism. *International Journal of Educational Development, 30*(2), 130–135.

Ennaji, M. (2005). *Multilingualism, cultural identity, and education in Morocco.* New York, NY: Springer Science + Business Media, Inc.

Fairclough, N. (2003). *Analysing discourse: Textual analysis for social research.* New York: Routledge.

Hilali-Bendaoud, F.Z. (2000). *Cohesion and coherence in EFL writing: The case of Moroccan university students.* Unpublished Dissertation. Mohammed V University, Department of English.

Howe, M. (2005). *Morocco: The Islamist awakening and other challenges.* New York: Oxford University Press.

Lambert, W.E. (1974). Culture and language as factors in learning and education. In F.E. Aboud & R.D. Meade (eds), *Cultural factors in learning and education* (pp. 91–122). Bellingham, WA: Western Washington State University.

Marley, D. (2004). Language attitudes in Morocco following recent changes in language policy. *Language Policy, 3*(1), 25–46.

Paulston, C. (1994). *Linguistic minorities in multilingual settings: Implications for language policies.* Philadelphia, PA: John Benjamins Publishing Co.

Redouane, R. (1998a). Arabisation in the Moroccan educational system: Problems and prospects. *Language, Culture and Curriculum, 11*(2), 195–203.

Redouane, R. (1998b). De la dualité et la complèmentarité: Le cas du bilinguisme au Maroc. *Language Problems and Language Planning, 22*(1), 1–18.

Sadiqi, F. (1991). The spread of English in Morocco. *International Journal of the Sociology of Language, 87*(1), 99–114.

Schmidt, R. (2000). *Language policy and identity politics in the United States*. Philadelphia, PA: Temple University Press.

Taylor, C. (1992). *Multiculturalism and the politics of recognition: An essay*. Princeton, NJ: Princeton University Press.

Zughoul, M. (2002). *The language of power and the power of language in higher education in the Arab world: Conflict, dominance and shift*. Paper presented at the MATE Annual Conference, Language Planning: Planning Equity, Fez, Morocco. Retrived June 15, 2010, from <http://matemorocco.ifrance.com/issue2002c.pdf>

## Appendix

Dear Student,
The following survey will ask you about your language background, your experience studying English and your language attitudes and beliefs. It should take between 20–30 minutes to complete. All of your responses are anonymous and confidential. While we ask that you answer all the questions, please feel free to skip questions that you do not feel comfortable answering.

This survey is part of a nationwide study examining the state of English language education in Morocco. We thank you in advance for your participation; your responses will help us better understand the role of English in Morocco and will hopefully help improve the state of English teaching and learning.

I. Demographic Information

1. Age:
2. Gender:
3. Nationality:
4. Native Language:
   Moroccan Arabic
   Amazighe
   French
5. What foreign languages (other than English) have you studied (check all that apply)?

French
Spanish
German
Italian
Other (Please specify):_____

6. How well do you speak each of these languages:

Scale:
1 = Elementary proficiency (1–2 yrs. study)
2 = Limited working proficiency (2+ yrs. study)
3 = Professional working proficiency
4 = Full professional proficiency
5 = Native or bilingual proficiency

| Language | Years Studied | Speaking (1–5) | Listening (1–5) | Reading (1–5) | Writing (1–5) |
|---|---|---|---|---|---|
| MSA | | | | | |
| French | | | | | |
| English | | | | | |
| Other | | | | | |

II. English Language Background

7. How long have you studied English?

8. Where have you studied English previously, and for how long you did you study there?

Private language centre ☐
Public secondary school (high school) ☐
Private secondary school (private high school) ☐
Public University ☐
Private university or post-bac program ☐

8a. If you attend a private language centre, please select who pays for your courses:

Me or my family ☐
My employer ☐
Moroccan or American government ☐

9. What is your current level of English?

   Beginning ☐
   Intermediate ☐
   Advanced ☐

10. Why are you currently studying English?

    My current employer wants me to study English ☐
    To improve future employment opportunities in Morocco ☐
    To improve future employment opporunities outside Morocco ☐
    To study in an English-speaking country ☐
    To communicate with English-speaking relatives ☐
    To meet and interact with English-speaking tourists or students ☐
    To meet and communicate with English-speaking peers online ☐
    Because I like English language and literature ☐
    To travel or live in an English-speaking country ☐

11. How many hours of class do you have a week?

12. How many hours of homework do you have a week?

13. Do you study on your own time? (Yes/No)

    13a. If yes, how many hours do you study?

    13b. How do you study?

    Watch TV/movies in English ☐
    Read English books/journals/Internet sites ☐
    Study grammar/do review exercises ☐

## III. Language Attitudes

### A. Please Fill in the Blank

14. Of all the languages I know, the language I consider mine is:

15. My favourite language is:

16. Of all the languages I know, the most beautiful language is:

17. The language I feel most comfortable speaking is:

18. The language that is most useful for daily life:

19. The language that will be most useful to me in the future:

20. The language that is most useful for my job:

21. The easiest language for me is:

22. The hardest language for me is:

23. The most important foreign language for Moroccans is:

### B. Please choose the answer that most represents how you feel about each statement below.

24. I think all Moroccans should have to learn French.

   Strongly Agree   Agree   No Opinion   Disagree   Strongly Disagree

25. I think all Moroccans should have to learn Arabic.

   Strongly Agree   Agree   No Opinion   Disagree   Strongly Disagree

26. I think all Moroccans should have to learn Amazighe.

   Strongly Agree   Agree   No Opinion   Disagree   Strongly Disagree

27. I think all Moroccans should have to learn English.

   Strongly Agree   Agree   No Opinion   Disagree   Strongly Disagree

28. It is possible to master many foreign languages equally well.

   Strongly Agree   Agree   No Opinion   Disagree   Strongly Disagree

29. Moroccans should not learn foreign languages at the expense of Arabic.

   Strongly Agree   Agree   No Opinion   Disagree   Strongly Disagree

30. A mastery of Arabic is more important for me personally than learning foreign languages.

   Strongly Agree   Agree   No Opinion   Disagree   Strongly Disagree

C. Please circle an answer that most accurately reflects your opinion.

31. For you, is learning English more, equally, or less important than learning French?

   More important       Equally important       Less Important

32. How important is it for Moroccans to master many foreign languages?

   Very Important   Somewhat Important   Not Very Important   Not Important at all

33. Is it more, equally or less important for Moroccans to learn foreign languages now than it was in the past?

   More important       Equally important       Less Important

34. It is more, equally or less important for Moroccans to learn French now than it was in the past?

   More important       Equally important       Less Important

35. Is it more, equally or less important for Moroccans to learn English now than it was in the past?

   More important       Equally important       Less Important

36. Is it more, equally or less important for Moroccans to learn Spanish now than it was in the past?

   More important       Equally important       Less Important

IV. Language Learning

Please circle the most approproate response.

37. The most difficult aspect of learning English for me is (please select all that apply):
    Reading      Writing      Speaking      Grammar/Spelling      Listening

38. The easiest aspect of learning English for me is (please select all that apply):
    Reading      Writing      Speaking      Grammar/Spelling      Listening

39. In English, the most useful skill for me to learn is:
    Reading      Writing      Speaking      Grammar/Spelling      Listening

40. I think learning English is fun.
    Strongly Agree      Agree      No Opinion      Disagree      Strongly Disagree

41. I like my English teacher.
    Reading      Writing      Speaking      Grammar/Spelling      Listening

42. My English teacher teaches in a way that helps me learn a lot.
    Strongly Agree      Agree      No Opinion      Disagree      Strongly Disagree

43  I find our textbook/worksheets useful and challenging
    Strongly Agree      Agree      No Opinion      Disagree      Strongly Disagree

44. I consider myself a good student of English.
    Strongly Agree      Agree      No Opinion      Disagree      Strongly Disagree

45. I am satisfied with my English courses.
    Strongly Agree      Agree      No Opinion      Disagree      Strongly Disagree

46. My English courses are challenging.
    Strongly Agree      Agree      No Opinion      Disagree      Strongly Disagree

47. My English course moves at the appropriate pace.
    Strongly Agree      Agree      No Opinion      Disagree      Strongly Disagree

48. Studying English is an investment in my future.

    Strongly Agree     Agree     No Opinion     Disagree     Strongly Disagree

49. My favourite ways to learn are (please select all that apply):

Lectures from the teacher
Small Groups Discussions
Worksheets and Grammar exercises
Conversation practice with a partner
Giving presentations
Using the computer/Internet
Writing essays/journal entries
Games/Songs
Studying for Tests/Quizzes
Reading

50. Please think of your English class, would you like to see more, less, or the same of each of the following:

    Scale:
    1 = Elementary proficiency (1–2 yrs. study)
    2 = Limited working proficiency (2+ yrs. study)
    3 = Professional working proficiency
    4 = Full professional proficiency
    5 = Native or bilingual proficiency

        Lectures from the teacher
        Small Group Discussions
        Worksheets and Grammar
        One on One conversation practice
        Giving Presentations
        Using the computer/Internet
        Writing essays/journal entries
        Games/Songs/Drawing
        Studying for Tests/Quizzes

RAGHDA EL ESSAWI

# 9  Arabic in Latin Script in Egypt: Who Uses It and Why?

## ABSTRACT

This study examines handwritten texts produced by Egyptian bilinguals wherein Arabic and/or Arabic – English mixtures are produced using Latin script. The goal of examining this hybrid language – as Cook (2004) calls it – include the following: (a) to show how texts using such varieties came into existence, (b) to show who is using them, why, and whether such forms of writing represent a standardized and socially accepted form of communication, (c) to look into what the incursion of such hybrid variety indicates about the change in the status of the other varieties that used to fill these spaces, and how all of this relates to the growing hegemony of English in the Egyptian society. In addressing the first goal the paper analyses samples of handwritten texts where Latin script is used to trace the effect of computer mediated communication (CMC), which is where such forms are claimed to have first appeared. The paper discusses the effect of communication technology versus the effect of global English speaking culture on the production of such varieties. The second goal is achieved by presenting a sample of 34 Egyptian bilinguals with a questionnaire that detects who is producing such hybrid texts, when, and why they are being produced using Latin script. Finally the paper uses the results of the questionnaire to reflect on the changes in status of the different varieties used by Egyptian bilinguals especially Modern Standard Arabic (MSA) and how this relates to the increased dominance of English language in that society. However the paper also emphasizes that the increased usage of hybrid varieties that started with and gained momentum through CMC does not necessarily mean that any of the varieties traditionally used in Egyptian society are doomed to relinquish their privileged position to hybrid varieties. The paper suggests that language planning and technology could be used to check and reverse the changes happening to the linguistic scene in Egypt and other Arab countries, as has been done with other languages in other parts of the world.

"*Happy birthday 3oba 1000000 sana.*" (Happy birthday. May you live till you are a 1000000 years).
Context: A handwritten birthday greeting that appeared on a birthday card.

"*ana walahy kalmet _____ manaftalkeesh but she did not answer me i will cal her tom walhy don't worry insha2allah.*" (I *have* phoned _____ (I did not ignore your request) but she did not answer me. I *will* call her tomorrow. Don't worry.)
Context: A short note written by one student to a colleague during class time.

"*Rasulak said alnas who make u remember Allah when u see thm are 7'iyar elnas*" (Your prophet said that People who remind you of Allah are the most benevolent)
Context: A note written by an anonymous writer on a school desk.

"*sa7ini 2saa3a sab3a*" (wake me up at seven).
Context: A note written by a 15-year-old to her mother and hung on her bedroom door.

The above language, which includes mixtures of English and colloquial Arabic or colloquial and Modern Standard Arabic (MSA) written in Latin script, represents a specimen of the type of handwritten exchanges that more and more young bilingual people in Egypt (and maybe other regions of the Arab world) are now using. Writers of such texts are born in Egypt, raised by Egyptian parents, had some exposure to English within the family, but started learning it at school at the age of four (i.e., English was their second language). It would seem, however, from the above exchanges that this language variety (whose distinctive feature is the usage of Latin script to write colloquial Arabic and English) is a variety they prefer to use to express themselves compared to other choices available to them (English, MSA, colloquial Arabic in Arabic script, mixtures of MSA and colloquial Arabic in Arabic script, mixtures of English written in Latin script and Arabic in Arabic script). The contexts in which these language stretches were written, reflect that users feel at home with this variety and therefore are using it in contexts that require intimacy of expression and speed of production. The peculiar mixture that we see here seems to fit into what Cook (2004) refers to as "hybrid language varieties" (p. 111). "Hybrid" here refers to varieties "best known for their incorporation of lexical material from different languages, extensive code switching, and a young urban orientation" (Cook,

2004, p. 109). Cook, who refers to studies of language change in African cities, has related this type of language specifically to youth, urban contexts, and to language change presented by youth. Although literature includes other definitions of language *hybridization*, this chapter will use the one presented by Cook (2004), since it is more pertinent to issues being studied here. Hassan (2010), does not simply refer to hybridization as a sign of language change, but considers hybridization as a threat to the Arabic language caused by excessive borrowing from English. He points out that hybridization adds to the complexity of the language situation in the Arab world since it adjoins the emerging hybridized spoken and written forms to the already existing multiplicity of levels that mark the multi-glossic situation in the Arab world. Explanations offered by Hassan (2010) for this process of hybridization are "communicative convenience" and "social prestige."

With the increase in production of hybridized texts and their incursion into contexts that are usually related to strong Arabic language traditions like religious contexts (as the above samples show), a need arose to further understand this process of hybridization and indications. This study will therefore attempt to answer the following questions:

1. How did such hybridized varieties come in to existence?
2. Who is using them? Why? Do such forms of writing represent a standardized and socially accepted form of communication?
3. What does the increase in their usage indicate about the present status of the Arabic language in relation to the growing English language hegemony in Egyptian society?

The initial part of this paper will attempt to look into the first question by analysing a limited number of samples of the "hybrid language varieties" (Cook, 2004, p. 111) that Egyptian youth use today while writing. It will also look into social contexts in which such varieties are used. The goal here is to study linguistic features that mark such a process of hybridization, as well as what they reveal about its origin. In the second part of the paper the results of a questionnaire given to Egyptian bilingual participants are presented and discussed in order to gather information about issues suggested in the second question. The questionnaire is used to find out more information about who uses such varieties the most (age groups), why they are being used in handwritten messages, whether such forms of writing are standardized, and the social contexts in which they appear. Finally, the third part of the paper will discuss what the existence of such varieties indicates about the effect of the English language on Arab speakers.

## How did such varieties come into existence? What are their distinguishing linguistic features?

Interviews with producers of examples of the hybrid language presented above have revealed that this type of language is mainly used in computer mediated communication (CMC) and SMS messaging. In other words, users of this variety in handwritten texts have clearly indicated that this form of writing (or maybe this genre) originally belongs to CMC, but is now used by many in handwritten communication too. This is further verified by comparing linguistic features that mark those hybridized varieties with research done about features of written texts in cyber space in different languages. A brief review of the research pertaining to this issue is presented to show how and why written texts produced in cyber space are marked with new linguistic features, and gives a description of such features. This will then be related to hybridized texts produced by Egyptian youth.

Generally speaking, research about communication technology especially computer mediated communication, instant messaging (IM) and SMS messages has shown that such forms of communication have led to the incorporation of new linguistic conventions within written texts (Baron, 2001; Merchant, 2001; Segerstad, 2002). In fact, according to Merchant (2001), CMC has "radically chang(ed) the face of literacy" (p. 294). Users of the net have adapted written language to the needs of the new modes of communication by producing written texts that fall somewhere between the written (at a distance) and spoken (face-to-face) modes. In other words, the instantaneous nature of communication technology that has changed

## 9 Arabic in Latin Script in Egypt: Who Uses It and Why?

the "monologue of writing" into a "dialogue" (Baron, 2002, p. 410) has led to the appearance of written texts that are closer to *written talk* (i.e., a hybridized text that includes the relaxed informal style of talking combined with formal features of written texts) leading to "new stylistic conventions" (Baron, 2002, p. 404). These conventions included the following: (a) the use of non-alphabetic characters to construct icons, (b) simple abbreviations in which initial letters are used as short hand, (c) combinations of numbers and letters to create an approximate phonetic rendering, and (d) phonetic spelling (Merchant, 2001). It has also necessitated the use of emoticons and other types of graphical representations to replace facial expressions or sounds that would have been present in face to face communication but are not available in messaging (for example, LOL to mean "laughing out loud" or :) to mean smiling). All of the above has resulted in a form of hybridization of formal and informal features of language or features of the written and the spoken as pointed out by Tagliamonte and Denis (2008). With the appearance of such conventions, it seemed like boundaries that separate speech from writing were falling down, leading to "the collapse of the control associated with written language" (Flusser, 1989, cited in Benczik, 2003). The tendency towards communication in what might be called *written speech* is – according to Tagliamonte and Denis (2008) – part of a general move closer to the informal end of the language (any language) or what they consider "the emerging tendency for written genres to be more like speech, a process referred to as *colloquialization*" (p. 8).

Much of the above mentioned features were revealed in the language used by Egyptian youth in cyber space as demonstrated by the following message:

> mabrook ya _____ ... salli rak3eten shokr wts7i bokra tshteri masr belfiha cuz you deserve it ya da77a7a.
> (Congratulations, Pray (to thank God for your success); and tomorrow you buy yourself all that Egypt (has to offer) because you deserve it. You book worm).

This typical message reveals one form of abbreviation (cuz) where – as Merchant (2001) points out – initial letters are used as short hand. Furthermore, combinations of letter and numbers are used "to approximate phonetic rendering" of Arabic letters that do not exist in English. However, the co-existence of more than one language here (English and colloquial Arabic) reveals a much more complex process of hybridization compared to those used by English speakers using the net, since it is in fact "an utterance that belongs, by its grammatical and compositional markers to a single speaker, but that actually contains mixed within it two utterances, two speech manners, two styles, two 'languages', and axiological belief systems" (Bakhtin, 1981, cited in Hassan, 2010, p. 10). In the above message, we have features that mark the sender as Muslim *salli rak3eten shokr (prayer)*, next to those marking him as a young person teasing the receiver of the message *ya da77a7a (you book worm)*, plus that which marks him as a bilingual speaker *cuz you deserve it*. It is also interesting to note that the concept of getting what you deserve or being rewarded for hard work is the part expressed in English, as compared to the part congratulating the recipient of the message on her/his success.

I would assume however that – like the English language – this process of hybridization is not caused by the technology used for communication, but is the result of a process of adaptation to the instantaneous nature of these modes of communication. In other words, users of this technology, like users around the world, are writing in a manner that simulates speech. With the resulting fall of the boundaries between spoken and written language, the hybridized (English/Arabic) colloquial that existed in bilinguals' speech (in fact the speech of all educated people in Egypt according to Hassan, 2010) is also reflected in their writing in cyber space. In the case of Arabic (again like other languages), technology may not be regarded as the only cause for the existence of hybridized colloquial written texts in cyber space, but is just reflecting language features that already existed in bilinguals speech. For as Baron (2003 cited in Tagliamonte & Denis, 2008) points out "technology often enhances and reflects rather than precipitating linguistic and social change" (p. 8). It must be mentioned here, however, that usage of this process of hybridized colloquialization of written texts in cyber space, has led to an increase in the social acceptability of written hybridized texts in and out of cyber space. Thus, making their usage more widespread and more widely socially accepted. This will be further discussed when reviewing the results of the questionnaire used by this study.

# 9 Arabic in Latin Script in Egypt: Who Uses It and Why?

In order to trace features of colloquialization, hybridization, and features transferred from norms of CMC, an analysis of samples of hybridized handwritten language will be presented. But more importantly the analysis will look into the wide array of contexts in which such samples are used. The goal at this stage is not to establish the extent to which this variety is accepted or used (since this will be done in the following section of this paper), but to exemplify how hybridized colloquialization takes place and how it is used to serve various communication purposes in the different contexts (even those that were previously limited exclusively to MSA).

Samples to be included in this analysis are limited since they are used only to demonstrate what exactly is meant by hybridization and give some idea about the contexts in which it appears. Thus, in the following section a list of handwritten hybridized texts are presented (i.e., texts that were not exchanged through CMC or SMS messaging but by using pen and paper), their translation, and the contexts within which they appeared:

1) *"Happy birthday ya _____ wa 3obal 1000000 sana."* (Happy birthday. May you live till you are a 1000000 years).
This is a birthday greeting written by a 14-year-old girl to her mother on a birthday card.

2) *"ana walahy kalmet _____ manaftalkeesh but she did not answer me i will cal her tom walhy don't worry insha2allah."* (I have phoned _____ – I did not ignore your request – but she did not answer me. I will call her tomorrow, God willing. Don't worry.)
This is a note exchanged by two students while their teacher is explaining a new lesson. It was written in a class notebook in pencil.

3) *"Rasulak said alnas who make u remember Allah when u see thm r 7'iyar elnas"* (Your prophet said: People who make you remember Allah are the best of people.)
A note written by an unknown person on a school copybook.

4) "sa7ini 2saa3a sab3a" *(Wake me up at seven).*
A note written by a 15-year-old girl to her mother specifying the time she wants her mother to wake her up. The note was hung on the girl's bedroom door.

5) *"Early Christian:*
Instead of Bismilah al ra7man 2l ra7him they say 2abana 2alathy fel samawat w besm 2al 2ab wal 2bn wal ro7 2l Kodos.
2aham makan fel kenisa (al mathba7) → altar 'al haykal'.
3amalo 2l plan bshakl 2l cross we fel intersection 7atto al dome.
2l 7awareyoon kano 12 wa7ed fa dayman fi fel kenisa 12 3amood wa7ed mnhom 2swed 3ashan 7'a2em"
*(Instead of "in the name of God the all merciful" they said*
*The most important place in the church is the altar. They made the plan in the form of a cross and in the intersection they placed the dome. The apostles were 12 and so always in the church there were 12 columns one of them was black to stand for Hayiim).*
Notes written by hand during a lecture by a university student whose age is approximately 20 years majoring in engineering.

6) "ana begad 2edaye2t menek 3la mawdoo3 el T.phone. 3ashan law mesh 3yza tekalmeeny enty 7ora mesh ha7'aleeky t cal me 3'azben 3anek."
*(I was really angry with you over the issue of the telephone. Because if you do not want to call me you are free to do so. I will not make you/force you to call me.)*
A handwritten note exchanged during a lecture by two females who were approximately 20 years old.

7) 3sher siniin raam bardu *(Ten years is still a worthy number)*
A big sign hung in a bilingual educational institution by members of a students' club to celebrate the club's tenth anniversary.

## Hybridization: Usage of Latin script

Using Latin script in all of these handwritten language stretches (despite the fact that some are entirely in colloquial Arabic) is the first and clearest sign of hybridization. It is also one that writers of the above mentioned samples have mentioned they adopted due to their extensive usage of the same form of writing in CMC. In other words, it is a feature transferred from CMC. It is also interesting to note here that Latin script was used for lexical items within religious contexts whether Islamic (like sample 3 and 5) or Christian (sample 5). Such contexts (even in speech where mixing of varieties is more common) were reserved for the standardized variety (MSA), which makes usage of Latin script here a more obvious incursion into new areas.

## Hybridized colloqualization: Mixing English and colloquial Arabic

Besides the usage of Latin script, one of the most important features that mark these samples of handwritten texts is the tendency to freely mix English and colloquial Arabic in the process of expressing meaning. English and Arabic seem to co-exist in the sentence (as compared to code switching where the sentence is basically in language 'A' and then the writer switches to language 'B' for a particular reason before switching back to language 'A'). By co-existence I mean that it is hard to establish whether the samples, as linguistic stretches, belong to one language, thus making the other just a temporary switch. For example, in the first two samples, the writer seems to rely on both Arabic and English equally. In sample one 50% of the message is written in English and the other 50% is in Arabic, in a linear fashion (language 'A' is next to language 'B'). However in the second sample the movement from language 'A' to language 'B' seems to be happening in a more recursive fashion (from 'A' to 'B', then back to 'A' and then 'B' and so on). In the first sample there seems to be two equally important and independent English and Arabic syntactic and semantic units (though lack of punctuation may suggest otherwise). However, in the second sample, for example, the writer starts with Arabic in Latin script (*ana walahy kalmet _____ manaftalkeesh*), then uses an English clause: *but she did not answer me*; this is followed by a new English sentence (though this is not made clear by use of punctuation): *i will cal her tom*, followed by usage of God's name for the assertion: *walhy*, an English sentence to reassure the reader *don't worry*, then the Arabic *insha2allah* (God willing) as Arabs almost always do when speaking of future plans. This semantic, syntactic, and even cultural co-existence of English and Arabic establish the hybrid nature of the written text. In sample six the first language stretch represents an English syntactic unit expressed using mostly Arabic lexical items: *Instead of Bismilah al ra7man 2l ra7him they say 2abana 2alathy fel samawat w besm 2al 2ab wal 2bn wal ro7 2l Kodos*. The second part of the same sample on the other hand is basically Arabic both lexically and syntactically *2aham makan fel kenisa (al mathba7)* → *altar 'al haykal'.3amalo 2l plan bshakl 2l cross we fel intersection 7atto al dome*. This is again an example of the juxtaposition or co-existence of colloquial Arabic and English in a manner that makes it difficult to consider hybridized language used as being basically one, and usage of the other as a form of code switching. *2l 7awareyoon kano 12 wa7ed fa dayman fi fel kenisa 12 3amood wa7ed mnhom 2swed 3ashan 7'a2em*. The most interesting sample however is number three:

> *Rasulak said alnas who make u remember Allah when u see thm r 7'iyar elnas*.

Syntactically the sentence structure of sample three could work as English and Arabic for it seems to be using a syntactic structure that is acceptable in both (noun + verb + noun + relative clause) but with predominantly English lexical items. It is interesting to note that despite its being a mainly religious statement, it includes relatively more English lexical items compared to all other samples. Using English lexical items to create a message about Islam is quite surprising, since one of the main reasons for the call to preserve Arabic is to maintain contact with Islamic texts (the Quran, Prophet's sayings, etc.). It is also interesting to note that in samples 3 and 5 the Arabic used is closer to Modern Standard Arabic than colloquial. This is suggested by lexical items/ expressions like the following: *7'iyar elnas, 2abana 2alathy fel samawat, 2l 7awareyoon*. It is clear that contexts within which such samples are produced (a prophet's saying, a lecture) has affected the Arabic language used (it has not, however, forbidden the writer from using English words or Latin script).

## Features transferred from norms of CMC

Further examination of English used in gathered samples of hybrid language presented above also reveals linguistic features like abbreviations (u, tom), lack of punctuation (leading to run on sentences), erroneous spelling (cal), absence of capitalization (ana, i), and others.

Writing Arabic in Latin script has forced users of this variety to improvise in order to produce sounds that Latin script does not include. Like youth around the world when using CMC, Egyptians have resorted to combinations of numbers and letters to create an approximate phonetic rendering (Merchant, 2001) but in this case to produce handwritten texts. In other words, they have resorted to a tool that was employed strictly in the context of CMC and used it in a new context (namely hand written communication).

## Colloquialization: Usage of colloquial Arabic

Most of the samples displayed above (except samples 3 and 5) reveal a heavy usage of colloquial Arabic in the handwritten texts. This is made clear by the forms of negation used, colloquial expressions such as: *manaftalkeesh,*

*3'azben 3anek*, colloquial pronunciation of words as revealed by phonetic spelling that emphasizes usage of glottal stop or figure '2' instead of ق (for example: *302bal, 2edaye2t*), and dependence on nominal rather than verbal sentences. Moreover two are entirely in colloquial, namely samples 4 and 7. As for sample 4 it is written completely in colloquial Arabic (as marked by the word sa7ini) and the only sign of hybridization it includes is the usage of Latin script. This, in fact, is one of the examples that makes one ask about the reason for using Latin script. It would seem that particular statement could have been easily written in Arabic script. The same is true of sample 7, which is both syntactically, and semantically 100% colloquial but written in Latin script.

## Contexts in which samples presented were used

With regard to context, it would seem that most contexts in which the above exchanges were used are informal ones (notes exchanged during classes, written on school notebooks, personal notes taken during a lecture, written on birthday cards for friends or family members). However, there is one sample which reveals that this language has crossed the border from being an informal language exchanged between friends or adolescents to being one used in situations that require a standardized variety like a sign, hung for the public to read. Although usage of this variety on such signs could have been done deliberately to attract attention, it still represents an incursion into or a move from informal to formal contexts.

As mentioned earlier, contexts in which hybridized colloquial is used reflect that it is a language that users prefer or they feel quite comfortable using when expressing themselves; hence the usage of such language in expressing personal feelings (*"ana begad 2edaye2t menek 3la mawdoo3 el T.phone. 3ashan law mesh 3yza tekalmeeny enty 7ora mesh ha7'aleeky t cal me 3'azben 3anek"*– *I am really angry with about the fact that you do not phone; because if you do not want to call me I will not force you to do so*).

Contexts also suggest that users are in absolute control of this variety since it is used in situations that require speed of production like taking notes during a lecture.

Due to the limited number of samples, the above discussion leaves important questions unanswered. These questions are the following: why did this incursion take place? What are the social contexts in which hybridized colloquial could be used? Is the use of this hybrid language in handwritten communication so widespread that we can say that even more than English (where such written messages are so far basically restricted to CMC), Arabic is displaying the fall of the invisible wall separating the written language from the spoken one and the threat of de-standardizing the standard variety? These questions will be answered in the next section of this paper, wherein a questionnaire was used to gather information related to these questions.

## Who is writing hybridized varieties, why, and what is their level of acceptability in different social contexts?

In order to answer all questions that part one of this paper has highlighted, a study was conducted wherein 34 bilingual subjects from different age groups (15–52) answered a questionnaire. All subjects had been educated in bilingual institutions, secondary, or university. Since some of the subjects were friends of the researcher and/or family members the process of answering the questionnaire took the form of a verbal interview. In other words, the researcher provided subjects with a written form of the questionnaire but read the questions verbally to them and asked them to respond. This gave the researcher the chance to probe further into the reasons why respondents provided a particular answer. This situation occurred with eight of the participants in this study. It has to be mentioned here that age groups were not equally represented in this study, since subjects aged above 30 were smaller in number (only six subjects) compared to the rest of the subjects in other age groups (age group 15–20 had 16 subjects and age group 20–30 included 12 subjects). This made it difficult to reach acceptable results when comparing the different groups. However, results here remain suggestive of trends related to the issue being studied. The questionnaire (see Appendix) encouraged subjects to self-report about the following:

- Language varieties that bilingual Egyptians used most when using email, chat rooms, and instant messaging.
- Varieties used most often by different age groups during CMC.
- Number of hours per week that subjects spend using CMC.
- Frequency of usage of Arabic written words using Latin script in handwritten messages.
- Social contexts in which usage of Arabic written in Latin script is acceptable.
- Reasons for writing Arabic in Latin script.
- Respondents' opinion about social acceptability of writing handwritten texts in Arabic using Latin script.

Respondents were asked to circle answers to questions about the above mentioned issues (see Appendix). Despite the problems related to self-reporting, using this method was the easiest way to gather information about the issues at hand.

It was assumed by the researcher, as a result of the interviews conducted prior to developing the questionnaire and by virtue of a pilot study that handwritten Arabic in Latin script will be mostly related to heavy usage of CMC and SMS messages. It was also expected that it would be used more often by adolescents and youth in informal contexts, and that handwritten Arabic in Latin script is becoming more socially acceptable or even the norm in certain contexts.

Despite the fact that different age groups took part in answering the questionnaire, the limited number of subjects in each age group (especially those above 30) has made it difficult to reach clear results about the effect of age on any of the issues included in the questionnaire. The following section will present results of each item included in the questionnaire and what such results indicate.

## Results of the questionnaire

Results concerning language varieties used when using the net to send email, instant messages, chatting or when sending SMS messages were as follows:

- 68.7% of our subjects pointed out that they used English.
- 56.2% used a mixture of English and Arabic written in Latin script.
- 48% used Arabic words in Latin script.
- 6.25% used Arabic.
- 3.12% used a mixture of Arabic in Arabic script and English in Latin script. It has to be mentioned, however that those used SMS messages only (i.e., they did not use any form of CMC).
- None of our subjects used English words written in Arabic script, or a mixture of English and Arabic written in Arabic script.

It should be mentioned here that subjects were encouraged to mark more than one choice when applicable. Thus, choosing one variety does not indicate that other varieties were excluded. However, frequency of choosing a certain variety was indicative of the variety's level of acceptance as a means of communication within the specified context by the participants.

With this in mind we can say that English is the language that subjects resort to most frequently when communicating on the net or SMS messaging. Results also indicate that a substantial percentage of subjects in this study use a mixture of English and colloquial Arabic. A slightly smaller percentage of these bilingual subjects use colloquial Arabic written in Latin script, and a very small percentage use a mixture of Arabic (written in Arabic script) and English (written in Latin script).

In an attempt to discover the subjects' expectations regarding the language most widely used for CMC and SMS messaging, the researcher presented subjects with the following question: in your opinion what is the language people use most while communicating in cyber space or sending their SMS messages? If there is more than one, please numerate starting with the one you believe people use most. The results of this (question 5) are even clearer in indicating that English, mixtures of Arabic and English in Latin script, and colloquial Arabic in Latin script represent the norm when communicating using the net or when using SMS messaging. Results of this question indicate the following:

- 78% expected that English would be used.
- 69% expected that a mixture of English and Arabic in Latin script would be used.
- 60% expected Arabic in Latin script would be used.
- None of our subjects expected any other languages or language varieties to be used.

1. Reasons presented for the high tendency to use the above mentioned varieties while communicating on the web or when sending SMS messages were grouped together by the researcher putting reasons that sounded similar under the same category. For example, a considerable number pointed out that it was easier to use English or English script (33%). Reasons of difficulty of using Arabic or Arabic script however were varied. These included inability to type in Arabic, difficulty of writing in Arabic, or the fear to "mess up Arabic." About 30% however gave answers that indicated that the English language or Arabic in English script was the norm in this medium of communication or as one subject simply put it "cause mail is received like this" or "everybody writes this way."

2. As for using Arabic in handwritten communication 40.6% of the participants in this study admitted that they "sometimes" use Arabic words in Latin script in handwritten notes or messages. More subjects however indicated that they expected to "sometimes" see others use Arabic in Latin script in hand written messages (56.2%). The reason why the second figure is bigger than the first is that some subjects do not use this variety themselves, but they do receive handwritten communication in Latin script from others. Although none of the subjects participating in this study indicated that they would expect to "always"

receive handwritten messages in Latin script, a considerable number of them indicated that they would expect to "sometimes" receive handwritten communications in that form. This clearly reveals that Arabic in Latin script is no longer limited to CMC or SMS messages.

3. Subjects were also asked to mark one age group that they expect would use hybridized language in hand written messages most heavily; 80% of respondents marked the age group 15–20. The last 20% marked two age groups instead of limiting themselves to one (15–20 and 20–30). It is interesting to note that none of our subjects believed that people above 30 would produce handwritten texts in a mixture of English and Arabic using Latin script. This means that subjects related this variety to younger age groups, especially adolescents. Thus, results here agree with Cook's (2002) views indicating that hybridized varieties are related to youth.

4. In order to find reasons for resorting to these hybridized language varieties in handwritten messages, the questionnaire included a set of reasons that users of such hybridized language provided when interviewed by the researcher as part of a pilot study. Subjects were also encouraged to add new reasons if and when those provided by the researcher were not applicable. These reasons were placed after specimens of handwritten communication included in the questionnaire that fulfil a number of communication purposes (note taking, expressing dismay, writing an apology, birthday greetings, expressing anger or frustration). Samples also represented different levels of formality. Subjects were asked to mark what they believed were the reasons for using such hybridized varieties in the provided handwritten communication. The researcher also added space for subjects to write or add reasons other than the ones provided in the questionnaire. Subjects' opinions were as follows: 62.5% found using hybridized language more expressive, 28.12% considered it cute, 25% marked both cool and easy, while 21.8% marked more practical, and 18.12% marked three things: cool, easy, and more expressive. No subjects added reasons other than the ones provided by the researcher. It was interesting to note that two

subjects, who mentioned that they wouldn't use any of the varieties provided in the specimens, marked cool and practical as reasons why people use them in handwritten messages. A clear majority, therefore considered handwritten hybridized forms of communication as more expressive compared to writing them in Arabic or English. As mentioned earlier none of our subjects considered writing handwritten messages in English using Arabic script or in English/Arabic mixtures a viable option.

The next step was to further probe into the acceptability of hybridized texts provided by the researcher. Thus, subjects were presented with the following question: would you use a different language or language mixture, if you were writing any of the above handwritten messages?

5. Results revealed that 56.25% of the subjects would have used the same variety if they wrote the same set of specimens provided in the questionnaire. This indicates that such specimens are totally acceptable to these subjects. But 37.5% mentioned that they would have resorted to Arabic using Arabic script in at least one of the samples. For example, one subject believed that the second sample (which sounded more apologetic) should have been written in Arabic since it would have been more touching if expressed in that variety (the subject did not make clear whether he meant colloquial or MSA). Three subjects believed that notes written about the churches in Egypt should have been written only in Arabic since they contained religious terms. Finally, 18.75% indicated that they would not have resorted to Arabic in Latin script in any of the samples provided. One of those six indicated that using this variety is difficult for him and his friends. Two believed that Arabic script would be easier and more expressive. Three believed that they would rather write either in English or in Arabic (not a mixture of both). The above results seem to indicate that a majority of subjects find using mixtures of Arabic/English and/or Arabic in Latin script totally acceptable.

9 *Arabic in Latin Script in Egypt: Who Uses It and Why?*

6. The final part of the questionnaire attempted to detect contexts in which it was acceptable to use the various language varieties being discussed, which included hybridized and non-hybridized varieties. Respondents made it clear that they would choose the English language for formal situations, like writing greetings to their employer or teacher or writing a report (78.12%). However in informal situations (for example if they were to exchange birthday greetings with friends or parents, taking personal notes in classes or meetings) 59.37% said they would use a mixture of English and Arabic in Latin script. Greetings written to grandparents (which were intended as semi-formal situations) revealed a limited use of Arabic (3.12%), but a majority indicated they would use English (62.5%). Also, a slightly bigger percentage indicated that they would use Arabic in writing notes of a meeting to be seen by their employer or teacher (6.25%). Thus, results indicate that English, English/Arabic mixtures, and Arabic in Latin script are the varieties used most heavily by subjects in various social contexts. Arabic, however, shows very limited usage. Generally speaking, results here indicate that hybridized handwritten communication is becoming socially acceptable, since it can be used in a wide variety of contexts but mostly informal ones. It was interesting to note however that most subjects indicated that they would use English in formal contexts not Arabic or MSA (for example in taking notes for a meeting that their employer will see, or writing a report to their employer). This could have resulted from the fact that most bilinguals work in global multinational corporations or are learning in bilingual institutions where English is, in fact, the language of any official communications. It would therefore seem that for this group English has replaced Modern Standard Arabic (at least to subjects who answered this questionnaire) as being the variety used in formal situations.

7. Results of the questionnaire do not show a clear relationship between the usage of CMC as well as SMS messaging and the usage of hybrid varieties. In fact, some members who mentioned that they cannot understand Arabic when written in Latin script were heavy users of both forms of communication. This proves the earlier assumption

that – like the English language – this process of hybridization did not originate as a result of the technology used for communication, but is the result of a process of simulating speech made necessary by the instantaneous nature of these modes of communication. Thus, it is hybridized speech used by Egyptian bilinguals mirrored by CMC and SMS messages that originated the hybridized form of written communication that first appeared in CMC and then crossed the threshold to other forms of written communication. Communication technology has provided hybridized language the forum that led to its growing into a relatively standardized variety and established its existence (even beyond cyber space) as a choice native speakers can resort to during communication.

8. Results did not show a clear relationship between a certain age group and usage of hybridized varieties, but it did show that a clear majority of respondents would expect that users of hybridized varieties in handwritten communication would be between the ages of 15–20. In other words, they relate this age group to this variety when used in handwritten texts. This could explain the usage of this variety to advertise a type of products that target adolescents.

## What do the above results indicate about the present status of the Arabic language and its future prospects?

All the above mentioned results suggest that a clear incursion is taking place from English or English/Arabic hybridized varieties into spaces that were previously filled by Arabic (whether Modern Standard Arabic or colloquial) in the case of bilingual language users. Hybridization started in bilinguals' speech, as noted by Hassan (2010), much earlier than written hybridized texts, as a result of the dominant position of English in Egyptian society. In Egypt, like many other societies, the dominant position of English is

9 Arabic in Latin Script in Egypt: Who Uses It and Why?

related to "the role English plays in encoding technological information and permitting access to that information," "access to English was (is) a prerequisite for any individuals or societies expecting to compete in the international marketplace" (Grabe, 1988 cited in Bruthiaux, 2002, p. 130). Then, encouraged by the fall of the unseen wall that separates the spoken language from the written one (making the latter more standardized and less prone to change) in cyber space, written hybridized texts crossed the first threshold from being spoken to written varieties. This crossing that took place on the web was further encouraged by English language dominance in cyber space, which is pointed out by both Cook (2004) and Bruthiaux (2002). English being the "norm" in cyber space has probably made it easier for Egyptian youth to consider using Latin script as a viable option or even the norm in written communication on the web.

The above only relates to how hybridized Arabic has crossed the first threshold from speech to written language used in CMC and SMS messaging. It does not, however, show how this hybridized variety has crossed the second threshold from being limited to CMC to being used in handwritten messages, as demonstrated by samples presented by this study and results of the questionnaire presented to a sample of educated bilingual Egyptians. Respondents to the questionnaire pointed out that their reasons for using this hybridized variety in handwritten messages were that it was: easier, more practical, more expressive, and/or cool. And "cool" is understandable with regards to the previously mentioned dominant position of English in Egyptian society. However, considering hybridized varieties as "easier" or "more practical" could seem quite odd at first, because the effort (and ingenuity) needed to create and relatively standardize a variety like the one being used is enormous. A key in understanding reasons like "easier", "more practical" and/or "more expressive" is what my daughter (a heavy user of this variety herself) has pointed out when she added "we write in the same way we speak." With regards to the diglossic situation in the Arab world, this could mean that this group of language users finds it "easier and more practical" to write using the same language they speak (colloquial Arabic or mixtures of colloquial and English). In other words, the fall of the wall separating the written from the spoken in cyber space has, in fact, fulfilled an already existing need for such young people, which could explain its rapid spread. Another aspect is what one subject wrote as her reason for using Latin script when writing Arabic namely her fear "of messing up the Arabic." This fear is again referred to – though indirectly – in a third comment that states "my Arabic writing is not good." It would seem that what we have here is an expression of the need for communicating without the fear or thought of "language police," as Tagliamonte and Denis (2008) put it. Although this need is not limited to Egyptian bilinguals, the diglossic situation in the Arab world has made the need for "language police" more serious and the changes required to make the spoken fit written communication more drastic. In other words, the diglossic situation gave rise to institutions (whether educational or cultural) whose main goal was to verify that written language does not reflect any of the features of the spoken colloquial variety. It would seem that "language police," as represented by school teachers for example, who penalize all errors or features of informal speech to the point of making users feel incompetent, has made a group of users unable to use the language altogether. If we think in those terms, colloquial Arabic written in Latin script could be regarded as a decision or a means for maintaining usage of Arabic (not deserting it). Hybridized texts allow users to continue expressing themselves in their mother tongue while avoiding or worrying about "language police." In this case using Latin script in handwritten messages acts as "a venue in which teenagers are free to use all these features together" (i.e., features of formal and informal language; Tagliamonte & Denis, 2008, p. 38). "Individuals pick and choose from all the available variants that their linguistic system has to offer and draw from the entire stylistic repertoire of the language that exists at a moment of time" (Tagliamonte & Denis, 2008, p. 38). Due to the above it would seem that this language variety has the potential of spreading quickly, since as Bruthiaux (2002) points out, languages with "weak political and administrative control over form and usage;" as well as the ability to "enjoy the freedom to accommodate unplanned user driven change leading to both structural simplification and a degree of creolization as the language adapts to local conditions in a multiplicity of sociolinguistic settings" (p. 131) have a stronger potential of spreading widely.

Thus, results of this study agree with what Cook (2004) suggests, namely that the incursion of English and English/Arabic hybridized texts need not be attributed to communication technology only, but it could also be related to a cultural situation where foreign television, film, pop music, advertising, videogames, etc. (i.e., growth of global media) have over-run cultural features represented by languages other than English. This has happened in many countries in the Middle East, despite criticism that processes of "linguistic import" and the "cultural import" that goes with it will result in the existence of foreign sets of values that do not relate to indigenous populations and are only of benefit to the "wealthier exporting nations" (Pennycook, 1988; Phillipson & Skutnabb-Kangas, 1999, cited in Bruthiaux, 2000, p. 147). English continues as a dominant language in the Middle East and is taking more and more of the space that used to be dominated by Arabic, especially at the formal level. In Egypt specifically there has been a notable increase of multinational corporations, as well as foreign and national academic institutions where the main language used is English. All of the above has led to excessive borrowing from English. This in turn created what Hassan (2010) regards as a general move within society towards what has become "a way of life," since as Bakhtin (1981 cited in Hassan, 2010) points out these hybridized forms of communication do not only include two languages but in fact "two semantic and axiological belief systems."

Thus, caught between the trends of globalization and users need to escape linguistic policing, MSA usage seems to have been reduced immensely within some groups in Egyptian society. In fact, domains traditionally reserved for MSA (like written or religious texts) have been invaded by hybridized varieties. It was even noted by the researcher that hybridized texts have started to appear on billboards for the general public to read. For example, advertisement billboards for a new product in Cairo has added the colloquial word "hatozbot" (set something right or tune it) written in Latin script next to the name of the product advertised (whose name is made up of two English words written as one and of course written in Latin script only). This is an interesting development since in the past foreign words like "shopping centre" written in Arabic script have drawn a lot of criticism, but this new development has so far gone unnoticed. Moreover, the move is an indication that the number of people capable of reading colloquial Arabic in Latin script is considerable since billboards advertising products are not usually written for a limited slice of the community. This could either mean that the number of bilinguals who are capable of deciphering this variety is large or that people capable of deciphering this variety need not be bilingual. In both cases the appearance of colloquial Arabic words written in Latin script on billboards is a definite sign that more and more people are using or at least capable of comprehending this variety. One explanation of this fact could be that English is currently taught to all children, even those in governmental schools, at the age of six; this has made knowledge of Latin script (not necessarily English language) common knowledge for all educated Egyptians. In other words, most Egyptians, though practically monolingual (i.e., they can not communicate or read fluently in English), could in fact use Latin script or read colloquial Arabic in Latin script. In any case, it is a new threshold that this variety has managed to cross and a new threshold into another space that was previously filled by MSA or even colloquial Arabic.

## Conclusion

It would seem that the pervasiveness of the English language (as indicated by the fact that even research written about such pervasiveness is written in English), and the need to escape the shackles of "linguistic policing" caused by the variation between the spoken and the written in Arabic, the general trend in all languages towards colloquialization, and the new communication technologies that encourage all of the above, have led to undermining the usage of MSA in bilingual communities in Egyptian society. We need to prove that youth continue to use the hybridized varieties in written texts even beyond adolescence. We also need to keep track of whether hybridized varieties continue to invade new language spaces previously filled by other varieties. What this research has shown is that youth have found ways to adapt their language varieties to the ferocious pervasiveness of the English language. That is, youth have chosen to continue to use a variety of Arabic (the one closest to their speech) after adapting it to the requirements of the surrounding globalization. It could be that linguistic features of Arabic will go through changes in the same way that happened (and is still happening) as a result of its usage in mass media. MSA as we know it today may need to incorporate more informal features. However, these changes could be checked by processes of language planning allowing for the more successful incorporation of Arabic into cyber space and other forms of technology. As El Khafaifi (2002) points out, efforts by Arabic language planning agencies need to be reviewed in light of similar but more successful efforts carried out by linguistically and ethnically diverse nations (for example Scandinavian countries) to maintain their languages, and efforts at language preservation performed by much smaller nations like Iceland (Holmarsditter, 2001). But more important is for governments to start adopting measures used for language revitalization that reverse the effect of the electronic media and the net towards language preservation rather than its becoming a tool for global English. It has to be mentioned, however, that successful efforts at revitalizing languages like Hawaiian, Hebrew, Catalan, and Welsh have shown that "some ideological link between what is identified as a language to be revitalized and desirable notions of community and identity, often conceived in ethnic terms in a politics of recognition, is vitally important to the creation of these movements of language activism geared toward language renewal and language shift reversal" (Eisenlohr, 2004, p. 63). This basically means in the case of Arab world, the revival of the Arab national identity, which has been related to the Arabic language for centuries, regardless of how outdated it may seem. There is also a need to increase awareness of the fact that language import comes with a price that Pennycook (1988) as well as Phillipson and Skutnabb-Kangas (1999 cited in Bruthiaux, 2000) have warned against, that of importing cultural principles that conflict with those already existing in the Arab world. The result is creating a hybridized cultural situation that can only benefit "wealthier exporting nations" and one that will lead to even further linguistic import.

Thus, the results of the research done by this paper seem to indicate that Arabic in Latin script is becoming an acceptable medium of written communication in the Egyptian bilingual community, especially in the age group ranging from 15–20. Results of this research did not establish a clear relationship between Arabic written in Latin script and use of communication technology, but discussion has shown that CMC has provided Arabic in Latin script with the forum it needed to become a viable choice for youth during communication. Discussion of results in this research, as well as previous studies done on language use in CMC, reveals that Arabic in Latin script could actually represent a means by which bilingual youth in Egypt could express themselves using the same language mixtures they use while speaking. That is, Egyptian youth have chosen to continue to use a variety of Arabic (the one closest to their speech) after adapting it to the requirements of the surrounding global English.

Finally, discussion of the results also reveal that factors like the pervasiveness of the English language, youth's need to escape the shackles of 'linguistic policing' done by most educational and cultural institutions in an attempt to maintain the wall separating the written from the spoken varieties, the general trend in all languages towards colloquialization, and the new communication technologies that encourage colloquialization, have led to undermining the usage of the standardized variety (MSA) within bilingual communities in Egyptian society as indicated by the increased incursion of Arabic in Latin script on space that was previously filled by MSA.

Does all the above mean, however, that MSA which has enjoyed a privileged situation in Egyptian society is about to relinquish such a position even if only in bilingual communities? Two factors need to be taken into consideration before passing this judgment. The first is that much more research is, in fact, needed to prove this conclusion. We need to prove that Egyptian youth continue to use the hybridized varieties in handwritten texts even beyond adolescence. We also need to keep track of whether hybridized varieties continue to invade new language spaces in the Egyptian society, previously filled by other varieties. The second factor is that these changes could be checked by language planning that would allow for more successful incorporation of Arabic into cyber space and other forms of technology.

Results of this research come as a further indication of the fact that language import comes with a price (Pennycook, 1988; Phillipson & Skutnabb-Kangas, 1999, cited in Bruthiaux, 2000) have warned. This price is that of importing cultural principles that conflict with those already existing in the Arab world. The result is creating a hybridized cultural situation that makes the linguistic situation in importing cultures more complex and confusing.

# References

Baron, N. (2001). Who sets the e-mail style? Prescriptivism, coping strategies and democratizing communication access. *The Information Society 18*, 403–413.

Benczik, V. (2003). Communication as source and motivator of language evolution. *Language Problems and Language Planning, 27*(3), 249–268.

Bruthiaux, P. (2002). Predicting challenges to English as a global language in the 21st century. *Language Problems and Language Planning, 26*(2), 129–157.

Cook, S. (2004). New technologies and language change: Toward an anthropology of linguistic frontiers. *APA, 33*, 103–115.

El Khafaifi, H. (2002). Arabic language planning in the age of globalization. *Language Problems and Language Planning 26*(3), 253–269.

Eisenlohr, P. (2004). Language revitalization and new technologies: Culture of electronic mediation and refiguring of communities. *ARA, 33*, 21–45

Hassan, B. (2010). *Language and identity: Impact of globalization on Arabic.* Paper presented at Georgetown University Roundtable for Linguistics (unpublished).

Holmarsditter, H. (2001). Icelandic: A lesser-used language in the global community. *International Review of Education, 47*(3–4), 379–394.

Merchan, G. 2001. Teenagers in cyberspace: An investigation of language use and language change in internet chatrooms. *Journal of Research in Teaching, 24*(3), 293–306.

Segerstad, Y. (2002). *Use and adaptation of written language to the conditions of Computer-Mediated Communication.* Unpublished doctoral dissertation. Department of Linguistics, Goteborg University, Sweden.

Suleiman, Y. (2003). *The Arabic language and national identity.* Washington, DC: Georgetown University Press.

Tagliamonte. S., & Denis, D. (2008). Linguistic ruin? LOL! Instant messaging and teen language. *American Speech, 83*(1), 3–34.

# Appendix

Age:
Language of Education:
Name of institution you are currently enrolled/working in:
Male/Female:

1) *How often do you write emails, send instant messages, visit chat rooms, and/ or send SMS messages?*

    (once a week – twice a week – more than twice a week – once a day – twice a day – more than twice a day.)

2) *How often do you visit English web-pages?*

    (once a week – twice a week – more than twice a week – once a day – twice a day – more than twice a day.)

3) *How often do you visit Arabic web-pages?*

    (once a week – twice a week – more than twice a week – once a day – twice a day – more than twice a day.)

4) *Please circle the language you use most to write your message or while chatting. If you use more than one of the following choices, please numerate starting by the one you use most.*

    – English language.
    – Arabic language.
    – Arabic words written in English letters.
    – English words written in Arabic letters.
    – A mixture of English and Arabic written in English letters.
    – A mixture of English and Arabic written in Arabic letters.
    – A mixture of English in English letters and Arabic in Arabic letters.

## 9 Arabic in Latin Script in Egypt: Who Uses It and Why?

5) *In your opinion what is the language people use most while communicating in cyber space or sending their SMS messages? If there is more than one, please numerate starting by the one you believe people use most.*

_____
_____

6) *Knowing that people could choose freely to use Arabic or English while communicating in cyber space or sending their SMS messages, why do you think they chose to use the language you have mentioned in the previous question?*

_____
_____

7) *Do you use Arabic words written in English letters or mixtures of English and Arabic in handwritten messages or notes?*

Always     Often     Sometimes     Rarely     Never

8) *Do you expect to see or receive handwritten messages or notes that use Arabic words in English letters or mixtures of English and Arabic written in English letters?*

Always     Often     Sometimes     Rarely     Never

9) *Which age group would tend to use Arabic words in English letters or mixtures of English and Arabic written in English letters most in handwritten messages or notes?*
   - 15–20 years.
   - 20–30 years.
   - above 30 years.

10) *In your opinion why did people write the following using English letters (rather than Arabic letters) in their handwritten messages?*

   – *"Happy birthday 3oba 1000000 sana."*
   (cool – cute – practical – easy – funny – writer does not know Arabic – expressive – fast – other reasons are _____ )

- *"ana walahy kalmet _____ manaftalkeesh but she did not answer me i will cal her tom walhy don't worry insha2allah."*
(cool – cute – practical – easy – funny – writer does not know Arabic – expressive – fast – other reasons are _____ )

- *"Early Christian:*
*Instead of Bismilah al ra7man 2l ra7him they say 2abana 2alathy fel samawat w besm 2al 2ab wal 2bn wal ro7 2l Kodos.2aham makan fel kenisa (al mathba7)*
→ *altar al haykal".*
(cool – cute – practical – easy – funny – writer does not know Arabic – expressive – fast – other reasons are _____ )

- *"ana begad 2edaye2t menek 3la mawdoo3 el T.phone. 3ashan law mesh 3yza tekalmeeny enty 7ora mesh ha7'aleeky t cal me 3'azben 3anek"*
(cool – cute – practical – easy – funny – writer does not know Arabic – expressive – fast – other reasons are _____ )

- *"Rasulak said alnas who make u remember Allah when u see thm are 7'iyar elnas"*
(cool – cute – practical – easy – funny – writer does not know Arabic – expressive – fast – other reasons are _____ )

- *"sa7ini 2saa3a sab3a"* (wake me up at seven).
(cool – cute – practical – easy – funny – writer does not know Arabic – expressive – fast – other reasons are _____ )

*11)* *Would you use a different language or language mixture, if you were writing any of the above handwritten messages?*

_____
_____

*12)* *If yes, which one?*

*13)* *If you are writing a handwritten message in one of the following contexts circle the language you would use.*

   – Birthday greeting to a friend.
   (English language. – Arabic language. – Arabic words written in English letters. – English words written in Arabic letters. – A mixture of English and Arabic written

in English letters. – A mixture of English and Arabic written in Arabic letters. –
A mixture of English in English letters and Arabic in Arabic letters.)

– *Birthday greeting to your boss or teacher/professor.*
(English language. – Arabic language. – Arabic words written in English letters. –
English words written in Arabic letters. – A mixture of English and Arabic written
in English letters. – A mixture of English and Arabic written in Arabic letters. –
A mixture of English in English letters and Arabic in Arabic letters.)

– *Birthday greeting to your grand parents.*
(English language. – Arabic language. – Arabic words written in English letters. –
English words written in Arabic letters. – A mixture of English and Arabic written
in English letters. – A mixture of English and Arabic written in Arabic letters. –
A mixture of English in English letters and Arabic in Arabic letters.)

– *A note to your friend to apologize for being late.*
(English language. – Arabic language. – Arabic words written in English letters. –
English words written in Arabic letters. – A mixture of English and Arabic written
in English letters. – A mixture of English and Arabic written in Arabic letters. –
A mixture of English in English letters and Arabic in Arabic letters.)

– *A note to your teacher/professor/boss to apologize for being late.*
(English language. – Arabic language. – Arabic words written in English letters. –
English words written in Arabic letters. – A mixture of English and Arabic written
in English letters. – A mixture of English and Arabic written in Arabic letters. –
A mixture of English in English letters and Arabic in Arabic letters.)

– *Personal notes of a meeting or a class.*
(English language. – Arabic language. – Arabic words written in English letters. –
English words written in Arabic letters. – A mixture of English and Arabic written
in English letters. – A mixture of English and Arabic written in Arabic letters. –
A mixture of English in English letters and Arabic in Arabic letters.)

– *Notes to your boss/teacher/ professor of what went on in a meeting or a class.*
(English language. – Arabic language. – Arabic words written in English letters. –
English words written in Arabic letters. – A mixture of English and Arabic written
in English letters. – A mixture of English and Arabic written in Arabic letters. –
A mixture of English in English letters and Arabic in Arabic letters.)

*– Note to your departing friend with wishes that God blesses him and his family.*
(English language. – Arabic language. – Arabic words written in English letters. – English words written in Arabic letters. – A mixture of English and Arabic written in English letters. – A mixture of English and Arabic written in Arabic letters. – A mixture of English in English letters and Arabic in Arabic letters.)

*– Note to your departing teacher/professor/boss with a prayer that God grant him health and prosperity.*
(English language. – Arabic language. – Arabic words written in English letters. – English words written in Arabic letters. – A mixture of English and Arabic written in English letters. – A mixture of English and Arabic written in Arabic letters. – A mixture of English in English letters and Arabic in Arabic letters.)

ANISSA DAOUDI

## 10 Computer-mediated Communication: The Emergence of e-Arabic in the Arab World

### ABSTRACT

This paper sheds light on the impact of globalization on Arabic, both Modern Standard Arabic (MSA) and vernaculars. Its aim is to highlight the emergence of a new variety of language, which I call e-Arabic, as a direct result of internet and mobile telephone use. In fact, this new language is spreading very fast at various levels (literal and figurative) and is making its way into literature (in its broadest sense). Selected novels are studied to show evidence of how English is impacting Arabic and what exactly is helping language change. Furthermore, the paper discusses the linguistic aspects related to this phenomenon and attempts to shed light on the relationship between language and politics in the Arab world. Data is collected using corpora made of a 150-million word internet-based corpus, semi-structured interviews, and observation in Arab countries. Publications from blogs and emails are used as evidence to support arguments. Findings reveal that new words and expressions have already made their way into Arabic (both MSA and vernaculars) and that the source of borrowing is increasingly from English. The latter is spreading in the whole Arabic-speaking region, including the North African (francophone) countries.

## Introduction

> *A language achieves genuinely global status when it develops a special role that is recognized in every country. This might seem like stating the obvious, but it is not, for the notion of "special role" has many facets.* — CRYSTAL, 2004, p. 3

The "special role" which Crystal describes is a useful point of departure from which to explore the influence of global English on the world in general and on the Arab region in particular. This "special role" is indeed a multifaceted phenomenon. My research focuses on one of the "special roles" of English through the use of the internet and mobile telephony in the Arab world. In other words, it is about the global proliferation of computer-mediated communication (CMC) in general and in the Arabic-speaking countries in particular. Computer-mediated communication has led to changes in how language is being used, including more inventive, faster and highly idiomatic composition and reading of texts (see Crystal, 2004; Danet & Herring, 2007; Merchant, 2001). This study hypothesizes that there is a new variety of Arabic that is emerging in the Arab world, as a direct result of globalization. It differentiates between what is known in Arabic linguistics as Standard Arabic (SA), which can be Classical Arabic (CA) or Modern Standard Arabic (MSA) though, the distinction between the two is "a western invention" as argued by Bassiouney (2009, p. 10). A similar view is also argued by Ryding (2005, p. 7) that both CA and MSA are referred to as *"al-luga al-fusha"* (lit, the eloquent language; Bassiouney, 2009, p. 10). Furthermore, there is also what Mitchell (1986) calls "Educated Spoken Arabic" (ESA), which claims that vernacular Arabic is never "pure," meaning that it is often mixed with MSA, creating a new variety (ESA). It is the interaction between the written language and the vernaculars (Bassiouney, 2009). Its purpose is to allow educated people of various dialects to communicate in a common language without resorting to one particular dialect or MSA.

## 10 The Emergence of e-Arabic in the Arab World

The new variety that this study reveals evidence for is what I called 'e-Arabic'. The questions that need answering at this stage are the following: what is e-Arabic? How different is it from the above-mentioned varieties? What can be included under the umbrella of e-Arabic? The following section is an attempt to answer these questions and to take the argument further into what the relationship between e-Arabic and global English is. Before answering the above questions, it is important to report that I believe that the language change happening to Arabic (MSA and vernaculars) is a natural phenomenon and that e-Arabic is a direct result of language contact. Aitchison (2001, p. 3) argues that "language, like everything else, joins in this general flux. As the German philosopher-linguist Wilhelm von Humboldt noted in 1836: 'There can never be a moment of true standstill in language, just as little as in the ceaseless flaming thought of men. By nature it is a continuous process of development'". Similarly, Ferdinand de Saussure (cited in Aitchison, 2001, p. 4) comments that "Time changes all things: there is no reason why language should escape this universal law." In this chapter, I also highlight the role of the younger generation in the Arab region as being in the vanguard of the processes of language change, as they confidently exploit the possibilities of digital technology (Merchant, 2001). Finally, I will provide concrete examples (e.g., from literature) with explanations of what and how language change occurs.

## What is e-Arabic?

My working definition is that e-Arabic is a variety of languages used on the internet and mobile telephony. It stems from both MSA and Arabic dialects (various degrees). It is different from ESA (Mitchell, 1986) in that it is not the interaction between the written language and the vernacular that remains a spoken form only, hence its title (Educated Spoken Arabic). In fact, it is writing of the spoken form. It is the informal language used by computer literates. It also borrows and adapts words from various languages (e.g., English and French); it allows code switching[1] and code mixing[2] and uses numbers, abbreviations, acronyms, and emoticons. Additionally, it permits the use of Romanized Arabic (both for dialects and MSA).

Furthermore, e-Arabic is not bound by traditional syntactic, semantic, and lexical rules. One of its characteristics is "language distortion" in order to create "impact," aiming to engage not only with the globalized discourse as such, but also to highlight the specific ways in which the local frames the global. The relationship between e-Arabic and global English will be highlighted in a later section. Prior to that, the next section will elaborate upon the dynamics of power in the Arabic-speaking world.

## Language and power in the Arab world

According to Crystal (2004), English, portrayed as a global language, has often been presented as natural, neutral, free of political, ideological, and economic charges and above all beneficial to the world. Critics, however, have argued that language is never a neutral vehicle for communication; contextual factors are inevitably attached. For example, Robert Phillipson's book (1992) *Linguistic Imperialism* highlights the impact of imposing one language on another, shedding light on the cultural, political, social, and ideological embedded messages. He states that "it is an essential constituent of imperialism as a global phenomenon involving structural relations between rich and poor in a world characterized by inequality and injustice" (1992, p. 339). Imperialism for Phillipson is manifested in the "special"

---

[1] Code switching according to Myers-Scotton (1998) does not apply only to switching between different languages, but also to switching between varieties of the same language. This implies that diglossic switching is a kind of code switching (Bassiouney, 2009, p. 29).

[2] Code mixing, on the other hand, is defined as "the mixing of different varieties within a single utterance or even within a single word" (Mazraani, 1997, pp. 8–9). Myers-Scotton (1997, p. 24) does not distinguish between code switching and code mixing, because in her opinion, the distinction creates unnecessary confusion.

relationship whereby one society can dominate another in various ways, e.g. economically, politically, militarily, and culturally. Galtung (cited in Phillipson, 1992, p. 339) divides the world into two domains: the centre (powerful western countries) and the periphery (developing countries). Language, as the medium of communication between the two domains, plays a vital role in shaping and reinforcing borders between them. It is also the vehicle through which the central elite have imposed themselves on the periphery and this notion of "dominant" and "dominated" is at the core of the concept of linguistic imperialism.

The dynamics of power are evident in the way that the languages of colonizing powers, e.g. English and French, are portrayed and viewed in terms of opposition, for example: superiority versus inferiority, civilization versus backwardness, and progression versus regression (Pennycook, 2004). The result, as far as the Arab region is concerned, is illustrated in the alarming proliferation of the use of English in the Middle East and French in North Africa, to the extent that it has devalued and degraded the use of the native language. The reasons for this are related, in my opinion, to the multifaceted special roles of the dominant languages. The fact that a speaker of English or French in the Arab region is likely to have access to *special* benefits (in Bourdieu's (1992) terms *linguistic capital*) that are not available to Arabic monolinguals makes the need to learn these languages greater. This functionalist approach is only one example of the power dynamics of language use.

The relationship between language users and power was developed by Bourdieu (1992) in his book *Language and Symbolic Power*. The dynamics related to language are not only between users of different languages, but can be applied to speakers of the same language. Bourdieu assumes a fundamental link between actions and interests. In fact, he utilizes the economic concepts of market, competition and capital to develop his analysis of cultural, symbolic, and linguistic power. Bourdieu believes that social behaviours are made up of complex and deep rooted dispositions; often acted out at a pre-conscious level. These dispositions are described as *habitus* and are acquired or inculcated in everyday actions. He proposes that aspects of day-to-day life, including leisure, education, and family life are what he calls fields, which help in formulating our patterns of action, perception, and attitudes (Merchant, 2001, p. 295).

Bourdieu's (1992) concept of *linguistic capital* and its relationship to the construction and maintenance of legitimate language can help us understand aspects related to the distinction between Modern Standard Arabic (MSA) and the various forms of Arabic vernaculars. For example in Arabic, the clear division between MSA, also known as (*fus'ha*) and vernacular (colloquial) Arabic known as (*ammiya*) and their relationship provides a good illustration of the dynamics of power. In other words, while the former (MSA) is associated with the written form, used in formal settings, and is the official language in the Arab world, the latter (vernacular) is linked to the spoken form and is used in everyday speech. As far as language status is concerned, with regards to "high" and "low" language, "low" status is given to colloquial Arabic (*ammiya*) and "high" status is reserved for literary/standard Arabic (*fus'ha*), which would be MSA. The latter derives its "high" status from its association with Islam and the pre-Islamic period (Eid, 2002). This clear division about what language is appropriate for what function, is closely related and linked to the politics of access. By this, I mean that the control over the "order of discourse" (Foucault, 1984 [1971], p. 109) and patterns of authority in terms of inclusion or exclusion are set. That is, when we communicate we not only deal with our immediate addressees, "we orient towards what Bakhtin (1986) called a 'super addressee': complexes of norms and perceived appropriateness criteria ..." (Blommaert, 2010, pp. 38–39). The same concept of "super addressee" is applied to what constitutes "high" and "low" status in colloquial Arabic, e.g., some dialects claim to be closer to MSA and therefore, purer and superior (Middle Eastern versus North African dialects). The latter are viewed as a mixture of Arabic, Berber, and French.

Gramsci's theory (see Ives, 2004) of language politics is an important step towards understanding how language operates and how interconnected it is with politics. His conception of *hegemony* has been influential in understanding how dominant groups exert their power through organization of consent and compliance to their power. His analysis of the national common language in Italy and the way the Italian government tried to impose it is very important in understanding language politics in general. Gramsci attacked the strategy of "standardizing" Italian at the end of the nineteenth century, when Manzoni called for the national adoption of the Florentine dialect and dictated that teachers should consequently be recruited from Tuscany, or as close as possible to Florence. For Gramsci, this meant the imposition of a foreign language on the top and to the detriment of the existing, diverse Italian dialects (Ives, 2006, p. 128). A very similar process occurred in some North African countries, e.g., Algeria during the Arabicization movement of the 1970s. After Algerian independence in 1962, the government initiated the Arabicization of Algerian society. This was largely a reaction to cultural elitism and colonial domination and dates back to the revolutionary period when Arabic served as a unifying factor against French colonial forces. Arabicization is seen as a means of engineering national unity and has been used by the national government to secure national sovereignty. The use of Arabic was imposed in courts, in schools, on street signs, and in workplaces (Benrabah, 2007; Djite, 1992). This Modern Standard Arabic was a foreign language that the population had to master and use without any significant planning and despite the fact that 60% of the population could not read Arabic (Sirles, 1999). Teachers were brought in from various Arab countries (e.g., Egypt, Iraq, Syria) to teach Arabic to Algerians, most of whom only knew Algerian Arabic and French. Parallel to the Arabicization movement, there were calls to substitute English for French as the second national language, thereby rejecting the language of the former colonists (Daoudi, 2007).The two movements failed drastically for many reasons (e.g., political and economic). Nevertheless English is now having a direct and profound impact as a consequence of the internet revolution.

Bourdieu's notion of *habitus* and Gramsci's writings on *hegemony* have been used to explain the role of language in the production and reproduction of power relationships (particularly the inequality of power) in the modern state. For example, in most Arab countries, the elite is comprised of an English or French educated population, it extends to kings and presidents (e.g., King Abdullah of Jordan's education started at St Edmund's School in Surrey, England and continued at Eaglebrook School and Deerfield Academy in the United States). This meant that his Modern Standard Arabic was not up to the required level when he first became king (BBC News, 2 November 2001). This phenomenon not only applies to those who studied abroad, but includes those who went to American and British schools and universities in the Arab region, e.g. the American University of Beirut, Lebanon, and the American University in Cairo, Egypt. Gramsci's concept of *hegemony* has been utilized by scholars (e.g., Ives, 2004, 2005) to investigate the reasons why some words, phrases, or entire languages were adopted by certain populations (e.g., borrowing from English as in the case of calques) whereas in other circumstances such linguistic influences faced greater struggle and various degrees of transformation.

Ives (2004, 2005) suggests that the study of Gramsci's politics of language could allow us to understand the contemporary significance of English as a global language (Ives, 2004). In other words, Gramsci's work explains language as a social phenomenon through which we can understand the linguistic impact on national beliefs and heritage, which can be mobilized to use language as social weapons. The difference between Bourdieu's theory and Gramsci's is that while the former fails to account for resistance and change, the latter incorporates the notion of social struggle into his model of social reproduction. The language I highlight in this chapter, which I refer to as e-Arabic, illustrates how linguistic capital is used as both a subject and an object of struggle. By this I mean that e-Arabic is utilized by digital technology coiners[3] as a way of resistance towards social, economic, and political struggles. In fact, e-Arabic coiners are resorting to this language, that is different from the mainstream (standard) one, in order to be noticed and to be distinguished (Bourdieu's concept of distinction). It can also be exploited by, for example, language policy makers and the elite population as an object of struggle. When purists fight for MSA (language as an object), they do that to remain in power. Bourdieu and Gramsci are helpful in order to explain issues related to the concept of "standard" as opposed to "colloquial" Arabic and the multifaceted manifestations of global English in the Arab region. For example the fact that fluency in English, not Arabic, in the Middle East has come to imply intelligence, sophistication, and even affluence is an alarming situation. In fact, if a person struggles with Arabic, it is not always viewed as a problem. An

---

3   Language coiners are people who are a source of new words or new expressions. In other words, they are those who originate or cause or initiate something. For more information see <http://www.thefreedictionary.com/Coiner>.

example that comes to mind is when the Lebanese Prime Minister Saad Hariri gave his inaugural address to parliament in December 2009; he kept mispronouncing words and whole phrases in Arabic and his excuse was the interference of his Anglophone education (El Bahi, 2010). The following section outlines the research context and the methodology used for this research. It is followed by the results of the collected data and will attempt to shed light on concrete examples of language change and will highlight the influence of English on Arabic (both MSA and vernaculars).

## Research context

The internet and its impact on the daily lives of Arabs has been the focus of researchers in various fields for over a decade. In the Middle East and North Africa, studies have been conducted on "internet empowerment" exploring how the internet is empowering women in rural parts of the Arab world. These are women who are illiterate and do not even have access to essential resources such as water and electricity, i.e. women living in underprivileged backgrounds (Davis, 2005). Similar studies on economic empowerment through the use of information and communication technology (ICT) raise many related issues particularly from anti-globalization groups who protest against the hegemony of the northern hemisphere over the south both in terms of ICT and trade (Mitter, 2005). This "hegemony" has been, and still is, the hottest topic concerning globalization. As far as the language (medium) employed by internet users is concerned, computer-mediated communication (CMC) has been examined by applying contemporary critical social theory to this relatively new communicative medium, in order to study its effects upon individuals and organizations (Zuboff, 1989) and the role of communication on the development of societies as a whole (Lawley, 1992). Habermas' models (1984) of communicative theory have also been applied by critical social theorists to a variety of empirical topics, including understanding the medium of CMC, and the patterns of interaction that have been observed in that medium (Dahlberg, 2001).

However, what has received little, if no, attention is the linguistic side of research, the changes that occur to sounds, letters, words, phrases, and sentences. The coinage of words that emerge as a result of language contact has received very little attention. And yet this is the medium through which a vast proportion of communication takes place.

As far as CMC in Arabic is concerned, research has barely begun and the studies conducted on Arabic so far have focused on the theme of the medium used online (Palfreyman & Khalil, 2007; Warschauer, El Said, & Zohry, 2002, 2007). In other words, they look at whether Arab internet users make use of Arabic scripts, in Modern Standard Arabic, or colloquial Arabic (*ammiya*) and/or, Romanized Arabic. In addition, the phenomenon of online language choice by Arabs has been studied in relation to identity (e.g., Warschauer, et al., 2007). Very little attention has been paid to the linguistic changes that are occurring in the Arabic language (both MSA and colloquial) through Information Technology (IT) in general and CMC in particular. As I will demonstrate below, this new language contains instances of code switching, borrowings, and calques.

The internet has also created a public space in which ideas and ideologies interact with one another and compete for attention, each making their case through the debates that take place on websites, blogs, Facebook, Twitter and many more social networks (e.g., the Islamist versus the secular websites), without any conclusive evidence that the interactions within this public sphere are actually leading to change. The various messages are transmitted through the use of language, which is in itself loaded with power-related connotations that either contribute to the existing culture or to the emergence of new cultural phenomena. Hence, the importance of this study lies in highlighting the role of language in shaping a society as a whole. My research questions focus on: how is the internet helping in language change in general and in the Arabic-speaking region in particular? Furthermore, how is the emergence of this new language (e-Arabic) serving its users? The purpose of this study is to investigate the impact of globalization on Arabic (MSA and vernaculars). It specifically analyses the change that is taking place in Arabic and attempts to explain it sociolinguistically.

## Methodology

For this project, data has been collected using the internet and corpora made up of a 150-million word internet-based corpus[4] which stores information about the frequency of words, collocations, and phrases on the internet as a whole, including the following: Facebook, blogs, chat rooms, Arabic websites, 150 Arabic Wikipedia corpus (containing 150 million words), Arabic legal corpus (of 12 million words), and Arabic computer science corpus (2009). Data was also collected from semi-structured interviews of (20 participants) and observations of Algerian subjects (50 participants), in both Algiers, the capital of Algeria, and Msila (a city in southeast Algeria). The two cities are different in terms of size and population and also in their access to technology. That is, while in the capital (Algiers), the majority might either have access to the internet at home or at the cybercafé, in Msila, the case is different. Access to the internet at home is very limited; the only access is at cybercafés. Participants were of both genders, from varied age groups (my observation was done randomly, I did not select my participants according to a specific age) and from different social and educational backgrounds (my participants were from various social and educational backgrounds. I observed students at universities both in Algiers as well as Msila, in addition to cybercafés, where people of various backgrounds come to use the internet). Furthermore, I used publications from blogs and emails in order to support my argument.

---

4   For more information on Arabic Corpora, see <http://smlc09.leeds.ac.uk/query-ar.html>.

## Findings and discussion

### Information technology related borrowings into Arabic

Results from observations, semi-structured interviews, and internet-based corpora (see methodology) reveal that new CMC or internet-related words have already made their way (in great numbers) into Arabic (both MSA and dialects). In Algerian Arabic for example, while collecting data at cybercafés, by observing and recording the new words used by cybercafé users, I noticed that verbs like نافيڨي (navigi) meaning (*I navigate*), نكوبي (nkobi) i.e., (*copier*) in English (*I copy*) originating from French, were used extensively. These verbs are adapted from the Algerian Arabic internal grammatical rules and formulated by keeping the original word (either in French or in English) and adding the appropriate prefixes and/or suffixes that make the word sound like Arabic. For example, the phrase *I format the disk* in English, is rendered into, أنفورماتي الديسك (anfurmati aldisk) in Algerian Arabic. As far as nouns are concerned, a similar process occurs, for example, the word *cybercafé*, in Algerian is السيبار كافيه (el-siber Kafi). I noticed that this language is used by internet users regardless of their age group or educational background. My focus at that stage was not on how the word has been changed or adapted, but from where it originates. The following specimen (collected from observation and interviews in Algeria) gives examples of verbs and nouns in Algerian Arabic, as well as claques in MSA, which exemplify the adaptations, providing the source language and giving evidence that this phenomenon is widespread. At the verb level: verbs like, سوفڨاردي (sufgardi) "*sauvegarder*", كليكي (kliki) "*cliquer*", ڨرافي (gravi) "*graver*", and كولي (koli) "*coller*" have made their way into Algerian Arabic from French. On the other hand, words like, تشاتي (tchati) "*to chat*" and فورماتي (formati) "*to format*" are from English. As far as nouns are concerned, بوات (bouate) "*boite*", السيت (el-siet) "*site* *and* الكونكسيون (el-coneksiun) "*connection*" originate from French; whereas, nouns such as ايميل (imail) "*email*", سكايب (skaib) "*Skype*" and many more nouns made their way into Arabic from English. The verbs mentioned above can be used in the past, present, or future forms and can also be conjugated according the subject. The same example mentioned above, *I format*, in Algerian dialect

## 10 The Emergence of e-Arabic in the Arab World

is: أنفورماتي (anformati), *he formats* is أيفورماتي (iformati). What is noticeable is the source of the language, as seen above; these words originate either from French or English. As the latter is limited in Algeria, I believe that the English words have made their way into Algerian dialect through French. Here, the borrowing did not occur directly but was mediated through the French language. In fact, words like *email, web, blogs*, etc., are attaining a universal status; meaning that they exist in almost all languages of the world. I extend this argument to suggest these universal elements (features) are part of an e-language, hence, my use of the word e-Arabic. This new language occurs in numerous different forms (written and spoken), literal and figurative, and is used at the word, compound word, collocation, and phrase levels. As far as Modern Standard Arabic is concerned, numerous examples are found. The most conspicuous of these are the calques. Striking examples were found in the internet-based corpus used, for example: hard disk القرص الصلب (al-kurs al salb), secure chat تشات محمي (tchāt mahmi), desktop سطح المكتب (desktop), electronic mail بريد الكتروني (bari:d elektūni), floppy disk قرص مرن (kurs marin) and mother board اللوحة الأم (el-lawha al-u:m). These examples illustrate the various types of borrowed language that are making their way into MSA. One visible instance is the impact of globalization on Arabic literature (the written form) and how e-Arabic is contributing to the emergence of a new literary genre.

## Global English and e-Arabic literature

The publication of personal blogs and emails by Dar al Shourouq in Egypt, called Mudawanat Al Shourouq, has contributed to a large growth in publications and readership of new Arabic literature. The books I have selected for this study are categorized according to their linguistic specificities. By this, I mean that they are classified according to the author's use of e-Arabic. The language used is scrutinized in terms of whether the author uses MSA, dialect, a mixture of both, Arabic words in Romanized Arabic, numbers, and emoticons. For example, *Banat Al Riyadh*, 2005 (*Girls of Riyadh*) by Al Sana, is written in MSA, and various dialects such as Lebanese, Egyptian, and Saudi Arabian. Examples of e-Arabic in the book include words like أكنسل /akansil/ to cancel (a mixture of Arabic and English with adaptation to the Arabic grammar, the verb is used in the present tense) and ايميل/ايميلات (email/emails), showing that some of these words are already being used in singular and plural forms. Another category represents the publications (novels) in the dialect, e.g. عايزة أتجوز *Ayzza Atgawiz*, (2008) in Egyptian dialect. Examples of this category include the use of English in Arabic script as in: please (بليز), souvenir (سوفنير), boyfriend (البوي فرند), and others. There are also cases of writing in English, using Roman script, e.g., "panic attack." A third category is the use of a complex mixture of Arabic and English, which reveals that the cognitive process takes place in English, but the resulting writing is produced in Arabic. Examples can be found in the recently published "novel" اسكندرية/بيروت (2009) *Alexandria/Beirut*, in which the English phrase "I have to write you" is translated literally into a language that is not really Arabic (it is certainly not MSA), such as يجب أن أكتبك (p. 30). In the same novel, the author; Nizar uses English in one of her chapter titles "My heart is alive with the sound of music" (p. 39).

This influence of English within e-Arabic literature is increasingly apparent and is manifested in many ways. In fact, this phenomenon not only affects the language of contemporary youth, but has expanded to the point where it is now used by older generations. For example, the latest publication by Ahlem Mosteghanmi, a prominent Algerian writer who is renowned for her eloquent use of MSA, appears to be orientated towards a wider readership through her use of what I call e-Arabic. The title of her 2009 book is نسيان *Com*, (*Nessyane COM*), a clear mixture of English and Arabic. Booth (2008) observes that this new rapidly emerging genre of literature is increasingly popular among Arabs, particularly women. Arab women have sought refuge in, and been empowered by, this kind of writing, as it gives them a powerful and effective means of disseminating their ideas locally and globally. The phenomenon of internet literature and e-Arabic reflects a new culture emerging in the Arab world, which uses a language that is spontaneous, dynamic, and attractive to the younger generation. The following section will illustrate this phenomenon with further examples.

This new linguistic phenomenon is not constrained by the boundaries of a single language, nor is it entirely defined by the cross-pollination of numerous languages. Rather, its importance is derived to a large extent from the message it conveys. Because language is not a neutral vehicle, the specific themes tackled through e-Arabic are worthy of attention. For example, the novel *Girls of Riyadh* (2005) by Al Sana covers topics including homosexuality, premarital romance, class and sectarian issues, and alcohol consumption in Saudi Arabia. Another striking example is the publication of true stories by and about gay and transgendered authors in Lebanon. These stories use English and Lebanese dialect written in Romanized script, substituting numbers for missing sounds in English. This is illustrated in the title of the book *Bareed Mista3jil (Express Mail)* (2009). The writers claim that they used English because Arabic does not contain any terminology for homosexuals without negative connotations (2009, p. 6). Their reference to MSA and the examples they provide support this contention, as the whole topic is considered taboo. Therefore, the motive for using English not only reflects a desire to engage with the global discourse on these taboos, but also the challenges faced when trying to vocalize these ideas in Arabic. Here, the linguistic capital (Bourdieu) is used not only as a form of empowerment, but also as a means of struggle. This applies to both the examples above (*Girls of Riyadh* and *Bareed Mista3jil*), in which language is both a means and an object of struggle.

Speaking in various linguistic registers within the same conversation is becoming the "spontaneous" way of speaking in the Arab world, particularly among the younger generation. In fact, a new form of language is emerging which is inspired by the global, and contextualized by the local. In other words, this language, which is a product of globalization, is being utilized to debate and negotiate local issues, for example, discussing homosexuality in the Arab region, using English and e-Arabic as a means of "Arabizing" the matter. Therefore, the publications of emails and personal blogs are a manifestation of a new global literary genre and are also reflective of the adaptation of global English to an Arab/ic context or vice versa. This is in line with Kachru's argument about "Asian Englishes" (Kachru, 2005, p. 137, p. 154). The dynamism and evolution of language is one way of adapting to the global cultural context in which we now live and the various languages we interact with on a daily basis; at the same time, it provides a vital means of reconciling one's desire to maintain and preserve one's own cultures. In one of the stories in *Bareed Mista3jil* (2009, pp. 174–177) the author debates her religious belief as a Shiite Muslim from Southern Lebanon and then as a lesbian living in Beirut, wearing the veil. The negotiation and tension between these two identities dominates the narrative, the author's aim being to make readers (Arab Muslims in particular), consider the idea that the global can be localized, and there is not necessarily a contradiction between being a lesbian and a Muslim.

Bourdieu (1992) argues that the relationship between identity and symbolic power is inseparable, and this idea can give us insight into the power of language, and in particular its influence on one's identity in the various networks within which we socialize. Speaking Arabic has often been closely related to Arab identity (Barakat, 1993). This of course, as argued by Barakat, denies the division between MSA and the various dialects, the various languages spoken in the Arab world such as English and French (bilingualism), and the minorities who speak Arabic but, are not Arabs, e.g., Berbers. Therefore, the notion of identity should not be understood as a "fixed" phenomenon but as one which is constantly changing. Notions of "pure Arabic" have had to change as the English language is increasingly being used to define/describe commonplace actions which are part of daily life. For example, the language Arabs employ in writing an email or a text is not the same language their parents or grandparents employed to communicate with each other.

## Conclusion

Few contemporary discussions of language in society take place without reference to globalization, and most research focuses on the relationship between globalization and the spread of global English (Bruthiaux, 2008). Two views dominate this field of study. The first refers to the phenomenon of global English as a colonial and neo-colonial practice that aims to "do politics in linguistics and through linguistics" (Calvet, 1974, p. 10) while the second sees global English as an opportunity for the rest of the world and seeks to encourage the spread of the English language through various institutions such as the British Council and American cultural centers. Yet, discussions of global English are not complete without reference to the local language, in this case Arabic. In addition, one cannot fully describe the linguistic context without considering the economic and political contexts of the Arab region. In most Arab countries, the balance between maintaining a relationship with the "modern" world and the conservative project of cultural identity has never been straightforward (Judy, 1999).

The spread of English in the Arab region, as in many other parts of the world, is linked to its associated benefits, such as social mobility, economic power, and societal power. In other words, English is seen as an instrument of economic progress and social, educational, and occupational success (Tan & Rubdy, 2008). In Bourdieu's (1992) terms, English is viewed as a linguistic capital. It is therefore evaluated as a commodity that commands an exchange value. In addition, the vast expansion of the internet in the last decade has made this particular type of access to information and to the wider world, another objectified cultural capital. In other words, computers (as objects) have provided those who possess them with access to the global and the local alike (Bourdieu, 1992). The use of the internet and global interaction does not come neutrally; it needs a medium through which messages are conveyed. As a direct result, there is evidence that Arabic is changing and a new language is emerging (e-Arabic). This new language is being shaped by (amongst other factors) the influence of the English language on Arabic, both MSA and dialects. The examples I have given suggest that "pure Arabic" no longer exists. In everyday language it is now common to hear words or phrases borrowed from at least one foreign language, particularly English. When McLuhan (1964) coined the expression "the global village" and discussed how the world was shrinking, languages were included. This does not mean that languages are going to disappear and that English is the only one that will remain, but it means that the influence from the "inventors" of technologies are the ones who will remain in power, despite voices claiming that globalization is becoming increasingly decentralized.

An important question to be asked is the following: can Arabic fulfill all the needs of its speakers who are greatly impacted by both global English and the internet? According to Elkhafaifi (2002), even a vibrant language like Arabic is at risk of losing its transnational role to English. The demand for English in the Arab region is increasing and international schools are mushrooming, despite governments' encouragement to use Arabic as the medium of instruction in all public schools. Thus, this hybrid language (e-Arabic) is emerging in the Arab region and the rise of English is a striking example of the changes and challenges facing Arabic (both MSA and vernaculars). What is worth noting is that this phenomenon of language change as a result of contact is a natural phenomenon (Aitchison, 2001). It has occurred in the past and will continue to happen. It is also normal that importing technology comes with its terminology and those who invent have the right to control their inventions. This was the case when Arabs were advanced in science, their language influenced other languages and the evidence is in the number of Arabic words that have made their way into English such as *cheque, sugar, algebra*, and many more. Finally, confirmation from data reveals that change in the Arabic language (both MSA and the various vernaculars) is taking place at various levels. Furthermore, English in the Arab region is spreading very fast as it the lingua franca in the area. Also, the internet revolution speeded the process and accelerated the number of borrowings into Arabic.

# References

Adil, A. (2007, August 3). Girls of Riyadh, by Rajaa Alsanea, trans. Marilyn Booth. Funny and chilling: sex in the Saudi city. Review. *The Independent*. Retrieved January 19, 2011, from <http://www.independent.co.uk/arts-entertainment/books/reviews/girls-of-riyadh-by-rajaa-alsanea-trans-marilyn-booth-460023.html>

Aitchison, J. (2001). *Language change progress or decay?* Cambridge: Cambridge University Press.

Alsanea, R. (2005). *Banaat al Riyadh* (7th edn). London: Al Saqi Publisher.

Barakat, H. (1993). *The Arab world: Society, culture and state*. Berkeley and Los Angeles: University of California Press.
Bassiouney, R. (2009). *Arabic sociolinguistics*. Edinburgh: Edinburgh University Press.
Blommaert, J. (2010). *The sociolinguistics of globalization*. Cambridge: Cambridge University Press.
Booth, M. (2008). Translator v. author: Girls of Riyadh. *Translation Studies, 1*(2), 197–211.
Bourdieu, P. (1982). *Ce que parler veut dire: L'economie des echanges linguistiques*. Paris: Fayard.
Bourdieu, P. (1992). *Language and symbolic power*. Cambridge, MA: Harvard University Press.
Calvet, L.J. (1974). *Linguistique et colonialisme: Petit traite de glottophagie*. Paris: Payot.
Crystal, D. (2004). *A glossary of netspeak and textspeak*. Edinburgh: Edinburgh University Press.
Dahlberg, L. (2001). Computer-Mediated Communication and the public sphere: A critical analysis. *Journal of Computer Mediated Communication, 7*(1). Retrieved January 19, 2011, from <http://jcmc.indiana.edu/vol7/issue1/dahlberg.html>
Danet, B., & Herring, S.C. (2007). *The multilingual internet: Language, culture and communication online*. Oxford: Oxford University Press.
Daoudi, A. (2007). *Idiom decoding and encoding strategies by Arab learners with a particular reference to bilingual dictionaries Arabic-English-Arabic*. Unpublished thesis, Leeds University, UK.
Davis, S.S. (2005). *Empowering women weavers? The internet in rural Morocco*. Retrieved January 19, 2011, from <http://itidjournal.org/itid/article/viewPDFInterstitial/253/123>
Djite, P.G. (1992). The Arabization of Algeria: Linguistic and sociopolitical motivations. *The International Journal of Sociology of Language, 98*(1), 15–28.
Eid, M. (2002). Language is a choice: Variation in Egyptian women's written discourse. In A. Rouchdy (ed.), *Language contact and language conflict in Arabic: Variations on a sociolinguistic theme* (pp. 260–286). London: Routledge Curzon.
El Bahi. (2010). Retrieved January 19, 2011, from <http://angryarab.blogspot.com/2010/04/arabic-and-culture.html>
Elkhafaifi, M. (2002). Arabic language planning in the age of globalization. *Language Problems and Language Planning, 26*, 253–269.
Foucault, M. (1984). The order of discourse. In M. Shapiro (ed.), *Language and Politics*, (pp. 108–138). London: Basil Blackwell.

Ferguson, C.A. (1971[1959]). Diglossia. *Word, 15,* 325–340. Reprinted in P.P. Giglioli (ed.), *Language and social context* (pp. 232–251). Harmondsworth, UK: Penguin.
Gramsci, A. (1971). Selections from the prison notebook. In Q. Hoare & G. Nowell Smith, (eds and trans.). New York: International Publishers.
Ives, P. (2004). *Gramsci's politics of language: Engaging the Bakhtin Circle and the Frankfurt School.* Toronto, Canada: University of Toronto Press.
Ives, P. (2004). *Language and hegemony in Gramsci.* London: Pluto Press.
Ives, P. (2005). Grammar. *Historical Materialism 13*(4), 393–401. Retrieved January 19, 2011, from <http://www.internationalgramscisociety.org/igsn/articles/a09_12.shtml>
Judy, R.A.T. (1999). Some notes on the status of global English in Tunisia. *Boundary 26*(2), 3–29.
Kachru, B. (2005). *Asian Englishes beyond the canon.* Hong Kong: Hong Kong University Press.
Lawley, E.L. (1992). *Discourse and distortion in Computer-Mediated Communication.* Retrieved January 19, 2011, from <http://www.itcs.com/elawley/discourse.html>
McLuhan, M. (1964). *Understanding media: The extensions of man.* Cambridge, MA: Massachusetts Institute of Technology Press.
Mitchell, T.F. (1986). What is educated spoken Arabic? *International Journal of the Sociology of Language, 61,* 7–32.
Mitter, S. (2005). Globalisation and ICT: Employment Opportunities for Women. Retrieved January 19, 2011, from <http://gab.wigsat.org/partIII.pdf>
Mosteghanemi, A. (2009). *Nessayane Com.* Beirut: Dar Al Adab Publisher.
Nettle, D., & Romaine, S. (2000). *Vanishing voices: The extinction of the world's languages.* New York: Oxford University Press.
Palfreyman, D., & Al Khalil, M. (2007). A funky language for teenz to use: Representing Gulf Arabic in instant messaging. In B. Danet & S. Herring (eds), *The multilingual internet: Language, culture and communication online,* (pp. 43–63). Oxford: Oxford University Press.
Pennycook, A. (2003). Beyond hegemony and heterogeny. In C. Mair (ed.), *The politics of English as a world language* (pp. 3–18). Amsterdam: Rodopi.
Phillipson, R. (1992). *Linguistic imperialism.* Oxford: Oxford University Press.
Profile: King Abdullah of Jordan. (2001, November 2). BBC News. Retrieved January 19, 2011, from <http://news.bbc.co.uk/1/hi/world/middle_east/1632651.stm>
Ryding, K.C. (2005). *A reference grammar of Modern Standard Arabic.* Cambridge and New York: Cambridge University Press.

Sirles, C. (1999). Politics and Arabization: The evolution of post independence North Africa. *International Journal of the Sociology of Language, 137*, (1), 115–130.
Tan, P.K.W., & Rudy. R (2008). *Language as commodity*. London: Continuum.
Warschauer, M. (2002). Language.com: The internet and linguistic pluralism. In I. Snyder (ed.), *Silicon literacies: Communication, innovation and education in the electronic age* (pp. 62–74). London: Routledge.
Warschauer, M., El Said, G., & Zohry, A. (2007). Language choice online: Globalization and identity. In B. Danet & S. Herring, *The multilingual internet: Language, culture and communication online*, (pp. 303–318). Oxford: Oxford University Press.
Zuboff, S. (1988). *In the age of the smart machine: The future of work and power*. New York: Basic Books.

JOHN ANDREW MORROW AND BARBARA CASTLETON

## 11 The Impact of Global English on the Arabic Language: The Loss of the Allah Lexicon

ABSTRACT

For over 10 years, we have been researching the Allah Lexicon, a linguistic phenomenon which is unique to the Arabic language. In works like *The Allah Lexicon: Frequency and Usage in Arabic* (Ohio University, 2000) and *Arabic, Islam, and the Allah Lexicon: How Language Shapes our Conception of God* (Edwin Mellen, 2006), we demonstrated that the word "Allah" is the most common content word in the Arabic language. In some of our other works, such as "Arabic and the Allah Lexicon: The Loss of Culture in Second Language Acquisition" (2000), we studied how the spread of English contributes to the loss of Arabic culture. In "The Impact of Globalization on the Arabic Language" (*Intercultural Communication Studies*, 2007) and "Arabic Instruction in France: Pedagogy or Politics?" (*The International Journal of the Humanities*, 2007), we examined political attempts to subvert the religious dimension of the Arabic language. In a more recent study, "In the Name of Allah: Reverence Phrases in Arabic," we examined the loss of the Allah lexicon among Arabic speakers in the English-speaking world. If our previous studies demonstrated a diminished use of Allah expressions among Arabic speakers living in the western world, this current study, which is based on a survey of scholarly literature and a survey of 50 Arabic speakers, suggests that the spread of "global English" in the Arabic-speaking world has also started to erode this unique language feature.

## Introduction

Language is a gift a people offer to themselves and their children. Within its myriad variations, language names all that can be seen and other treasures that cannot; it conjures up diverse names and descriptive expressions for feelings that exist within a part of our brain where language has no place. Even that is a conundrum. The human is compelled to communicate: from birth we listen, watch, sort, and define in order to understand all that surrounds us. It is only through language that those elements that arise in a part of the brain where no language component exists – our emotions, reactions, and feelings – are given voice. The tongue finds refuge for all the minds' thoughts, the hearts' yearnings, and the body's functions within the limitless spectrum of the spoken and written word. African clicks, Asian tones, and the marvellous rolls of tongue, glottis, and nasal cavities, are just a few of the sundry sounds which have come into being in order that humans could share themselves, their world, and their ideas with other people. Language performs like the most talented thespian, taking on a myriad of roles in government, business, relationships, and spiritual devotions.

Just like that brilliant actor on the stage, language develops elements, skills and distinctions that slip quietly into our speech almost without notice. Economic changes, cultural variations, new inventions, and disasters all contribute to these new word forms. Populations across the globe adopt them at varying rates, and adjust existing language to make a place for the newer members of the lexicon. "Internet" and "cyber" are two such words. From northern India, to Morocco, to tiny towns in Mississippi or Michoacán, Mexico, anyone can ask for "internet" and be directed to the nearest tech café or computer sales establishment.

Within the spiritual dimension, the retention of all the tools related to religious devotion requires that they, too, be identified, sustained, and passed on to the younger generations. The Prophet Muhammad, in his role as the revealer of truth, considered all these different levels of spiritual life. Islam itself asks for five prayers per day, special prayers in specific situations, the Hajj, and other doctrinal requirements. In his wisdom, the Messenger of Allah also focused on daily speech by promoting and encouraging a change

## 11 The Loss of the Allah Lexicon

in language across the board. The result was the Allah Lexicon, the duly defined, scientifically-sound name for this semantic field of Allah-centric religious expressions.

Fourteen years ago, when a Peace Corps volunteer taught English at a science and technological university in Morocco, she was met with students uniformly polite and willing but also frustrated by the need to learn yet another language. "We've already learned *darijah*," they would say, "and then classical Arabic, and finally French. All of our university classes are taught in French. Now, you are here to teach us English." And she was, at the behest of the Moroccan government, which had recognized a growing trend that has since erupted into what we call "Global English." Even then, as the internet was beginning to gain ground, but before internet cafes with second-hand computers became as ubiquitous as Moroccan coffee shops, foreign governments recognized that English was the language of science, social science, and technology journals. Innovation, invention, and research appeared first in English publications, later in French, and much later, if at all, in the Arabic language.

Whether one likes it or not, English is the most widely published language in the world. According to the latest available statistics from UNESCO, the UK, the US, Canada, and Australia combined publish an average of 400,000 English language books per year. The Chinese publish approximately 136,226 books per year while the Russians publish 123,336. The Spanish speaking nations of the world release an average of 102,250 works per year. The Germans and the Austrians publish roughly 104,000 books per annum. The Japanese churn out some 45,430 books on a yearly basis. Yet, all the Arab countries combined publish a mere 15,000 books per year, many of which are in French and English.

If the number and type of books published per language per year is an important standard index of education, the English language has overwhelmingly become the language of culture, civilization, and science in the twenty-first century. As important as they may be, languages like Chinese, Russian, Spanish, German, and Japanese lag far behind the English language in influence. Although it is spoken by 200 million people in 28 countries, and is the liturgical language of 1.5 billion Muslims, the Arabic language has long lost the privileged role it once had in the transmission of knowledge when the libraries in Islamic Spain churned out as many as 60,000 Arabic works per year (Morrow, 2008, p. 523). Since so few books are translated into the Arabic language, and even fewer books are translated from Arabic into other languages, monolingual Arabic speakers are very much insulated from information that speakers of culturally dominant languages take for granted. In fact, for these Arabs, the door to anything newly written, whether it is in the area of literature, science, technology, or philosophy, is effectively slammed in their faces. If one peruses the type of books now published in Arabic, they are predominantly related to religion, with relatively few concerned with scientific matters, literature, or international issues. This reality anchors Arabic, in the minds of Arabs as well as the rest of the world, firmly in the purview of religion.

As reluctant as certain regimes may be to relegate Arabic to second place in favour of English, the development of their countries currently depends upon it. For example, English is overwhelmingly the primary language of scholarship in the world; one can scarcely find a graduate program which does not require knowledge of English as a basic requirement. As Roy (2004) has explained in *Globalized Islam*, the English language has also become the de-facto language of political Islam. This state is not simply ironic, it is also one vehemently opposed by clerics who are limited by their single language fluency. As Roy further commented in an interview, Islamic fundamentalists are a perfect paradox. They oppose McDonald's and the spread of the English language, yet they speak English and consume *halal* fast-food. As evidence that global English has become the dominant language of the global jihad, the number of English-language sites sympathetic to al-Qaida has increased to more than 200, while radical Arabic language sites have dropped down to approximately 50 (IMRA, 2009).

At first, students like those in Morocco might have shared qualms about abandoning either their first language, Arabic, or even their second, French, in favour of a third, a language best known at the time for being the tongue of the blind supporters of Israel and those nations that were politically antipathetic to the Middle East in general, and Islam in specific. Yet, as young people's cultural attachment to their first language faded in the face of expedience, perceived benefit, and a wave of mobile phone and computer technology, those voices, at first so vehement, have grown mute.

## 11 The Loss of the Allah Lexicon

The sentiments shared by Moroccan students are also shared by young Arabs throughout the Islamic world. As one young Kuwaiti graduate stated,

> English is linked to openness and developed cultures, while Arabic is associated with strict rules and no freedom. So, of course I would be interested in English rather than Arabic. Arabic equals ... no development, while English gives more chances to reach places other than home. (*Kuwait Times*, 2007)

His sentiments echo those of young men and women of ages and ages past, all of whom left home and language to go in search of work and advancement. "In doing so, they joined, willingly or unwillingly, a larger and broader culture, and their loyalties shifted from their geographically [and culturally] constrained origins to a wider society and idiom" (Tonkin, 2001, p. 6).

## The language of prayer and devotion

All over the world, people express their spiritual and religious beliefs in prayer. In many places, the language of prayer is also the language of everyday life. Other locations may have religious traditions so aged or from a source so distant that the language of prayer may no longer be in standard use. Formerly, Catholic masses in Latin were one example of this, as were Hindu services in Sanskrit. Whichever circumstance prevails, the act of applying an ancient linguistic instrument to direct communication with the deity provides a compelling connection. While writing on this topic for a US newspaper, Stephens (2000) observed that "speaking to God in an ancient tongue puts faith on a higher plane."

Talking on that theme, we will not debate the brilliance of the Arabic language, nor argue the intrinsic cultural elements that may disappear if Arabic becomes, as it seems to be, a language in decline. Our focus will be on a single gem from Arabic's linguistic fount. It is the language feature fostered by the Prophet Muhammad, nourished by a devout people, and one now being allowed to wane in the face of English as the world's lingua franca. Arabic has, at the centre of its religious heart, the Allah Lexicon, a panorama of verbiage that extols the deity, comforts the suffering, warns the incautious, and, in short, communicates the supremacy of Allah in every area of life. These phrases, plus the original transmission of the Quran in Arabic, put this linguistic affectation into a sublime realm.

Arabs have historically considered themselves blessed that their communication with Allah occurs in the language He Himself used to deliver divine revelation to the Prophet Muhammad. This reality has led Arabic to be considered a holy language, one that, as Fishman (1996) articulated, is a "direct and presumably unmediated transmission [from God] or something very close thereto" (p. 11). For Muslim Arabs, unlike the followers of many religions, there is no intermediating language between themselves and their prayers or their culture and God.

As a result of the Allah-centric nature of the Islamic faith, the Arabic language has become saturated with Allah expressions. Some of the most common expressions from the Allah Lexicon include, *Bismillah* [In the name of Allah]; *Alhamdulillah* [Praise be to Allah]; *La ilaha illa Allah* [There is no god but Allah]; *insha' Allah* [If Allah wills it], *Wa Allah* [By Allah!]; *Allah yakhlif* [May Allah replace all you have used]; *Allah yi'awn* [Allah will help him]; *Allah yijib* [Allah will bring]; *Allah yasahhal* [May Allah make it easy]; *Allah yafarraj* [May Allah take the burden]; *Fi amanillah* [Go with Allah]; *shukralillah* [Thanks be to Allah]; *Baraka Allahu fik* [May Allah bless you]; *Allahu Akbar* [Allah is the Greatest]; and *Subhan Allah* [Glory be to Allah], among many others, which vary nationally and regionally.

Thus, in addition to the name, Allah, the Prophet Muhammad himself actively campaigned to incorporate a vast collection of Allah-focused phrases into Arabic, thereby replacing a network of pre-Islamic pagan words and idioms. It must be stated that the Allah Lexicon is not a set of words and phrases used within the framework of formal religious devotions, but rather, they are multi-componential and bridge an array of every day speech acts and situations. Our research has demonstrated that features of this Allah Lexicon are traditionally used by Arabic-speaking Muslims frequently each day to remember their Lord (Castleton, 2006). In 1999, we surveyed native-Arabic speakers about their use of this lexicon and found a level of daily use of select phrases to number in the dozens.

## 11 The Loss of the Allah Lexicon

Many professions and particular groups employ specialized vocabulary. For example, you simply cannot interpret literature without employing literary terminology. The ability to use precise technical terms are a linguistic form of determining whether or not one belongs to a specific segment of society. That is the nature of key words; they are essential to the communication of an idea. So, we believe, are elements of the Allah Lexicon, arising out of divine dictum and tradition. The frequency and near infinite occasions for their use constitute a body of "key words," the lifeblood of any culture or belief system (Wierzbicka, 1997).

These Allah-centric expressions, the heart and soul of millions of Muslims' interactions and communications, are now at risk as the parent tongue faces a powerful competitor. Just as Modern Standard Arabic gave way in many locations to local dialects of Arabic, so have both more recently seen the encroachment of another language altogether, English, which now boasts fluent and semi-fluent speakers of over a billion, making it the Walmart® of the language universe. And, like Walmart®, the language serves, supplies, and provides the basics in an array of situations. The drawbacks of this spreading lingua franca, however, should not be overlooked, nor its impact ignored.

In this chapter, we ask a series of questions in relation to this transition and its impact on the use of the Allah Lexicon: (a) What is happening to Arabic? (b) Are native-Arabic speakers aware of the religious history and intent of Allah Lexicon phrases in their language? (c) Are native-Arabic speakers concerned about the diminishment of the use of these phrases when they begin to communicate more regularly in English? (d) What is lost in terms of religious connection when the words that bolster that connection do not translate into the new language? And (e) What might it mean in terms of long-term religious attachment to children growing up in an English-speaking educational system?

Dorian (1998) posits that languages are "seldom admired to death" (p. 3) as she explores the various reasons for the growing frailty and ultimate death of any language. Admiration would seem to offer a guarantee of constancy, at least among the speakers of the language if not with the broader population of the planet. At the same time, "it's fairly common for a language to become so exclusively associated with low-prestige people and their socially disfavoured identity that its own potential speakers prefer to distance themselves from it and adopt some other language" (Dorian, 1998, p. 3). For our purposes, this issue relates to the question, "What is happening to Arabic?"

## The problem

A language that arose in deserts, conquered lands, inscribed monumental literatures, revealed scientific truths, and the tongue that gave voice and form to the Holy Quran is fading in its use among the very people for whom it was long both a source of religious expression and beloved language. What is now occurring in Arabic-speaking societies and the realms beyond is a linguistic anomaly. Arabic, that near-sacred tool of poets and prophets, is being rendered an also ran in favour of English, a language which neither supports the poetic traditions of Arabic, nor the devotional phrases that have added lustre and spirit to its utterances and Muslim traditions. A Syrian Arabic instructor, working in the Middle East, offers, "There is a decline in learning Arabic in public schools now, especially in grammar and dictation. There is no love to the language and there is nothing interesting in the curriculums for students anymore" (*Kuwait Times*, 2008).

Certainly, this trend, of Arabs opting to use another language, has become more evident since 9/11, when American and western hostility to all things Arab and/or Muslim resulted in thousands of hate crime incidents and a high level of suspicion toward anyone who spoke the language, all swarthy men who cultivated facial hair, or women who wore scarves. Annan (2005) diagnosed this bias and offered that, "in too many circles, disparaging remarks about Muslims are allowed to pass without censure, with the result that prejudice acquires a veneer of acceptability" (p. 4).

So rife is the American bias against those of Middle Eastern, Arab, or visibly Muslim background that many are changing their names to mask an unpopular heritage. Thus, two defining attributes, being or looking Arab or following Islam lead to discriminatory behavior on the part of

## 11 The Loss of the Allah Lexicon

functionaries, the legal system, and the airlines. In our own experience, many native-Arabic speakers stopped using the language in airports, out of fear that someone might believe they were plotting a terrorist act, a wise choice given the experience of Arabic speaking travellers (Williams, 2007). Even written Arabic has become an anathema for some, as with the hubbub that arose when a passenger was barred from boarding because he was wearing a tee shirt with Arabic script. The Transportation Safety Authority (TSA) official who approached the passenger "equated Jarrar's [wearing] an Arabic shirt to an airport with 'wearing a T-shirt at a bank stating, "I am a robber,"' the complaint said" (Hazell, 2007). Reported as recently as February 10, 2010, though the incident occurred in the summer of 2009, an American, Nicholas George, was detained, handcuffed, jailed and subjected to five hours of interrogation because he went through an airport screening post with Arabic–English flashcards in tandem with a politically controversial book. "Among the questions the TSA supervisor asked George, according to the complaint filed in the US District Court for the eastern district of Pennsylvania, were: 'You know who did 9/11?' When he replied, 'Osama bin Laden,' the supervisor allegedly said to him, 'You know what language he spoke?', before she held up the Arabic flashcards and asked if George understood why they were 'suspicious'" (*Agence France Presse*, 2010). In both these and other cases documented over the past nine years, the indictment was not against a threat, an action, or a movement. It was against a language, a language that is increasingly being seen as a detriment by those who were born to speak it. "Flying while Muslim" or "Arab while flying" has suddenly become criminalized.

Languages are said to be, "safe, endangered, or extinct" in addition to "moribund" when a language is no longer taught to the young in a manner that will leave them fluent in all skill areas (Crystal, 2000, p. 20). The stages of language loss are known, and, if looking at the first instance, that is, a diminishing number of speakers based on a decrease in population, we will find Arabic failing to measure up. The populations of traditionally Arabic-speaking countries are thriving. The regions of the Mediterranean, North Africa, northern sub-Saharan Africa, and the Gulf boast a combined Arabic-speaking population of 280 million people (Arab News Network, 2006).

Yet, Arabic in the lands of Arabs is going the way of Latin, at least among the urban and educated. The language is now in those telling initial stages wherein Arabic is losing young tongues to speak it. "Schools aren't teaching Arabic as they are supposed to and most of what's being presented to our children is in English," mourned a vice-committee woman in Bahrain, as she and others attempted to push for a resurgence of Arabic in one of its homelands (*Gulf Daily News*, 2008). Across the Arab world, concerns are being voiced. Arab researchers and intellectuals have warned that the Arabic language is facing numerous challenges and threats, and that only the united efforts of Arab nations can help protect it (*Kuwait Times* 2008). Another article from Bahrain gives further evidence of this reality. The Shura Council of Bahrain, one of the wealthiest Gulf nations, recently legislated that Arabic was the first language of the island nation. Henceforth, all legal documents must be submitted in Arabic, with another language as a secondary option. "In reality Arabic is second to English, which shouldn't be the case," said one representative. "We have nothing against other languages," he explained, "but they should be secondary, with Arabic being the country's main language, whether in official letters or signs" (*Gulf News*, 2010).

The fact that English took precedence over Arabic in an Arab nation calls to the looming nature of the issue. The declining importance of the Arabic language among the Arabs themselves is ironic considering that language has always been the primary art form of Arabic culture. Other areas of the world had art or architecture, but for the Arab world, it was the grandiloquent configuration of words off a facile tongue that drew awe and attention. Hitti (1996) quoted a time-weathered ode to Arabic, when he wrote, "Wisdom has alighted on three things, the brain of the Frank, the hands of the Chinese, and the tongue of the Arabs" (p. 26). By honouring the Arabic language, Muslim Arabs honoured the Word of God. Turning away from the Arabic language and script marks a major cultural shift.

As Fishman (1996) suggested before us, we will look at the insider's view of the Allah Lexicon and these issues first, and offer up the outsider's opinions and findings last (p. xviii). It is not without irony that this work is written and delivered in American English, a linguistic manifestation that owes its entirety to so many other languages and cultural influences

## 11  The Loss of the Allah Lexicon

that it evinces only a small measure of ethnic attachment, except insofar as "English Only" might be concerned. As such, native-speakers of American English have "no first-hand experience with the phenomena under discussion," namely the loss of anything worthy in the face of language erosion (Fishman, p. xviii). The fact that most studies on the subject of Arabic linguistics are published in English, as opposed to Arabic, speaks volumes regarding the declining importance of Arabic as an academic language.

On two separate occasions, the fall of 1999 and the winter of 2009–2010, we surveyed groups of native-Arabic-speakers with regard to their use of the Allah Lexicon and their attitudes about English, Arabic, and their traditional culture. In both situations, for reasons ranging from access to the internet in order to send a response, to an ability to speak English in order to reply to the survey, our respondents were generally of the following demographic: (a) predominantly male; (b) urban dwelling, if living in the Arab world; (c) educated; (d) at least bilingual, but often fluent in three or more languages; (e) professionally employed or soon to graduate; (f) interested in Arabic, English, and their relationship as well as the issues arising out of the diverse cultures involved; (g) predominantly Muslim, though not exclusively; (h) resident in the Arab world, although a few live in Europe or the United States.

Naturally, a somewhat narrow band of participants poses some problems. However, since the results of this study largely mirrored those of the previous study, and since many participants are professionally involved in observing language use, the validity of the results seem all the more sound. With 54 participants in the 1999 study, we proved conclusively that the Allah Lexicon is in daily and moment to moment use among Arabic speakers, even those who, by virtue of a higher level of education, have had more opportunity to travel, engage with people from other cultures, and be influenced by the broader print, film, and internet media (Castleton, 2006). It is not our goal to regurgitate those findings, but rather to explore whether the continued use of the Allah Lexicon has been impacted by the greater scope of the English language.

## The study

Fourteen countries from the Arab world were represented in this study, in which we added data from 10 representative participants from the 1999 survey and 40 responding to the 2009–2010 survey. Our participants ranged from 19 to 62 years of age, with an average of 30 years of age, and came from across the Arab world, including Morocco, Tunisia, Egypt, Sudan, Palestine, and Lebanon, as well as Jordan, Syria, Saudi Arabia, Yemen, Oman, the United Arab Emirates, Kuwait, and Iraq. While most of our respondents resided in the Arab world, several of them were French and American citizens of Arab ancestry. Whether they lived in the Arab world or abroad, all participants unanimously described themselves as native-speakers of Arabic with advanced proficiency in the language.

First, we desired to establish English fluency among the participants. Over 83% of our volunteers described themselves as having advanced proficiency in the English language, 14% had basic proficiency, while 3% had no knowledge of the language. Ninety per cent of participants had studied the language for 7 or more years, 3% had studied it for 5 to 6 years, and 7% had studied it for 3 to 4 years.

Morocco and Jordan produced the most responses for the more current survey. This is not surprising, as both these countries are considered more liberal in their outlook and their national leadership has responded more strongly to any encroachment on the government's power to legislate and define the parameters of society. Morocco and Jordan have both had long-standing ties to the West, and thus to the languages of Europe and the Americas. Perhaps as a result of these circumstances, respondents from those countries are less likely to be concerned about the "motives" for this research and instead, be open to sharing their personal experiences with both Arabic and English. By far, the most markedly concerned prospective respondents were Arab students at the Shi'ite Seminary in Qum, Iran, who, with a sole exception, believed our study might be a Zionist plot to destroy Arabic and Islam. The Arab seminary students in Qum, most of whom are Iraqis and Lebanese, with whom we communicated by email and through our representative in the sacred city, manifested a sort of siege mentality, which made them particularly suspicious of studies being conducted by strangers.

The one question we did not ask any of the participants was "How religious are you?", since that is a question that has tenuous value in terms of this language feature. While we are interested in any erosion in the use of the Allah Lexicon as Arabic collides and gives ground to English, we discovered years ago, though it will not surprise anyone who has lived in an Arabic-speaking country, that the Allah Lexicon is regularly used without regard to religion specifically. Christians in the Arab world use the lexicon, though, as one stated, "Christian Lebanese do not say many of the phrases ... especially the ones such as *La ilaha illa Allah* as they are distinctly Muslim in nature" (Wajdi, 1999). Visitors to the Middle East, Gulf, or the Maghreb, if they stay more than a few days may find themselves, like a willow tree bending to the wind, beginning to pepper their conversation with *insha'Allah* [If it be God's will], *wa Allah* [By God!], or *Alhamdulillah* [Praise be to God] (Langewiesche, 1991). Though created as a body of language to be used for the reasons stated earlier, the Allah Lexicon has become so embedded in the Arabic language that it attracts all speakers.

## Findings

One of the first issues we analysed was the frequency of use of 24 Allah Lexicon phrases. The results of our two surveys on nearly identical populations, as defined above, demonstrate marked similarities in terms of usage. The group from 1999 declared a use of 69% of the 24 different Allah Lexicon phrases in the survey. That is, they professed to use at least 69% of them on a regular basis. A caveat must be offered here, due to the fact that some phrases, such as *insha' Allah*, are used far more frequently than others, such as *La ilaha illa Allah*, which are more situationally specific. Despite 9/11, the negative press from some countries about Islam and Arabs, and the spread of global English, the results from 2010 were remarkably close, at 70% of the phrases in general usage. This demonstrates that, among those who still rely on Arabic as a form of communicative address, the Allah Lexicon is holding its own. Although all forms of the Allah Lexicon are employed, the 10 most commonly used Allah expressions in Arabic include: *Insha' Allah* (100%); *Allah yakhlif* (97%); *Alhamdulillah* (97%); *Bismillah* (93%); *Allah yahfadh* (93%); *Allah yafarraj* (90%); *Sir 'ala Allah* (90%); *Allah yarham al-walidin* (89%), *Allah yikhalak* (79%); and *Afak Allah* (75%).

Although Allah expressions remain an integral part of the Arabic language, our survey clearly showed that the overwhelming majority of these expressions were not transferrable into the English language. More specifically, the phrases can be translated, but the lexical environment where they may be used does not arise. If the use of Allah expressions ranged from 40% to 90% in Arabic, the use of Allah expressions in English dropped to as little as 4% among our participants. While some subjects insisted on inserting calqued Arabic expressions such as "God-willing" and "Thank God" into their English, virtually all Arabic speakers suppressed these sayings when speaking English to non-Muslims. In fact, 82.5% of our respondents insisted that the English language does not provide space and acceptance for Allah expressions. The existence of core cultural concepts that do not translate clearly confirms the scholarly stance of Thorndike, Evans-Pritchard, Williams, Parkin, Moeran, Sapir, and Wierzbicka in opposition to the academic arguments made by Chomsky and Pinker regarding the universality of human thought (Morrow, 2006, p. 8). In addition, nearly 60% of the participants felt uncomfortable integrating *Bismillah*, *insha' Allah*, and *Alhamdulillah* into their English language speech, whether in their Arabic original, or an English equivalent.

Respondents noted, however, that while they generally suppressed Allah expressions when speaking with non-Muslims, they integrated them into their English when speaking to Muslims, which suggests the existence of a double discourse, a standard secular English used with non-Muslims and an Islamic English used with members of their own community. This could be likened to the formalized Japanese speech based on a cultural belief of the sanctity and respect due to elders and those of higher rank. The Japanese language forged these beliefs in an intricate social design that, even today, reinforces this attitude at every level of interaction and

## 11 The Loss of the Allah Lexicon

follows it up with respectful movement, eye contact (or lack of), and so forth. Yet, the Japanese are prepared to forego these linguistic and physical demands when engaged with people from another culture, precisely because those people are from a different culture, and the Japanese want to honour their foreign counterparts' distinct set of beliefs. Nevertheless, religious honorifics are not presented in the Quran as choices, but as requirements, perhaps not quite as elevated as the pillars of Islam, but certainly with an implication of importance.

Still, when we examine the Allah expressions that these Arabs use when speaking English to Muslims, we find that they are not unique Arabic expressions being integrated into English: they are simply parallel expressions which are shared by both languages. According to our statistics, the cognitive suppression of Allah expressions ranges from 57% to 93.5% of those used. The only Allah expressions that Arabs integrate into English, at a rate of 66.5% of the time, are "God willing," "God help you," "God bless you," "May God reward you," and "May God give you good health," all expressions that already exist in English. While these expressions are not nearly as common in English as they are in Arabic, they are standard phrases, and can be integrated without sounding too strange or alien. Idiomatically untranslatable and awkward Allah expressions like "May God fix," "May God have mercy on your parents," "Go with God," "May God heal," "May God remove your burden," "God will bring you what you need," "May God replace," are consequently rarely used in English.

One of the ironies that came to light in this research is that, although most of our respondents repress Allah expressions when they speak English, 80% of them viewed the phrases as essential to their Arab/Muslim persona. This presents something of a paradox. Why is it that what is considered essential in Arabic is so easy to release in English? While we did not ask volunteers for information regarding their degree of religiosity, it can be assumed that the 20% of Arabs who did not view Allah expressions as essential were more secular-minded. Despite the fact that 80% of our respondents regarded the Allah Lexicon as essential to their Arabic-Islamic identity, only 50% of them reported that their children employed these expressions as often as the parents did, suggesting a generational decline in the use of religious expressions. Children will not embed linguistic patterns if they are not encouraged to and/or if they stop hearing the phrases at the same level previous generations may have due to the distractions and immediacy of alternate media. Considering the fact that 85% of the volunteer participants believed that the use of Allah expressions increases God-consciousness, and then find the youth not as attached to these words, seems to indicate the degree of devotion to the Islamic faith, as evidenced by verbal expression, may be in decline among young Arab Muslims. Conversely, only 37.5% of our respondents believed that a reduced use of the Allah Lexicon indicated less religious devotion. Although these responses may seem contradictory, they may be reconciled to a certain extent. It would appear that for many Arabic-speaking Muslims, the use of Allah expressions is a type of *dhikr* or mantra, one which helps bring people closer to God. Merely because one does not invoke God perpetually, however, does not necessarily mean that one is less devoted to Islam. One may still be a pious Muslim. After all, most Muslims do not speak Arabic, and may use few if any examples from the lexicon. Without a doubt, we are focusing on Arabic-speaking Muslims, who, historically, have had the double bond of language and religion.

The attitude of our respondents towards the Arabic language was unanimously positive and optimistic. Over 93% of participants felt that Arabic played a valuable role in their lives. As many expressed, they viewed the Arabic language as central to their identity, be it Arab or Islamic. Approximately 80% of our volunteers were optimistic about the future of the Arabic language, while the other 20% was pessimistic. Even the more encouraged among the respondents admitted that the Arabic language was facing problems. Still, they believed it had a bright future, that it was spreading throughout the world, and that it would live forever. They considered that the increased attention that the Arab culture and Islam were receiving would bode well for Arabic as a viable language of the future. Some especially enthusiastic respondents believed that Arabic was making a come-back worldwide, and would remain the language of not only the Arab world, but of the Muslim world as whole. Others insisted that the future of Arabic was firmly linked to the future of Islam. Many others commented that Arabic would continue to prosper and flourish in the future.

## 11 The Loss of the Allah Lexicon

Pessimistic contributors pointed out that the Arabic language was declining in countries like the UAE, which is subject to strong western influence. They feared that the language was endangered by both the hegemony of other languages and the negative attitude of some of its own speakers. Some believed that Modern Standard Arabic would continue to lose ground at home, while spreading globally for religious and economic reasons; whereas, the colloquial dialects would continue to becoming increasingly contaminated by French and English borrowings. Several volunteers described the Arabic language as "threatened," and "endangered". Others believed that Modern Standard Arabic will go the way of Latin, and become merely a language of limited use relegated to religious and literary realms.

The attitude of our respondents towards the English language was almost entirely positive. For every one, it was merely another means of communication, one that was becoming increasingly important in a globalized world. While many Arabs may be averse to the negative aspects of globalization, they have no problem with the English language per se. In short, nationalistic attempts to outlaw or limit the use of the English language, as have taken place in Quebec, would probably find little support in the Arab world.

Overall, the impact of the English language on Arabic speakers can be clearly gauged by these results. A full 50% of participants indicated that they used English extensively on a daily basis, while another 14% used it sporadically on a daily basis. In fact, respondents living in Arab countries reported that they listened to English-language media nearly as much as they listened to Arabic-language media. For many participants, opting for English as opposed to Arabic was related to issues of content and comprehension. Many turned to English language media in an attempt to obtain a more balanced perspective on world events. For others, following the news in English was far more facile than following it in Modern Standard Arabic, the choice of the Arabic audio media. Such comments are curious since our respondents were almost exclusively university students and professors, all of whom were perfectly proficient in MSA. If even educated speakers of Arabic found it tiring to listen to *al-lughah al-'arabiyyah al-fasihah*, it makes us wonder the degree of difficulty and even despair the uneducated *'amiyyah* or dialect speakers must face when trying to follow the news on television.

Thus, while Arabic remains strongly rooted in much of the Arab world, 65% of our respondents explained that English has taken precedence over Arabic in the realm of commerce, while 47.5% remarked that English has taken precedence over Arabic in their national educational systems. In his study on the spread of global English in Singapore, Viniti (2008) found that English dominated Mandarin, Malay, and Tamil in the public and educational domains, that it competed with them in the domain of family, friends, and the media, and that that the native languages dominated English only in the domain of religion. According to his findings, religion now plays a major role in retaining native languages and acquiring knowledge of sacred languages such as Arabic. One can only wonder if English will become the global language of business and education in the Arab world, relegating colloquial Arabic to the family kitchen and classical Arabic to the mosque.

Rather than resent the spread of English, 100% of respondents believed that English played a valuable role in their lives. This is a remarkable finding considering that 93% of them believed that Arabic also played a valuable role in their lives. It seems that, for at least 7% of respondents, the English language is of more value to them than their mother tongue, due to the fact that they depend on English for their sustenance and career advancement. As numerous volunteers explained, they did not view English as a British or American language: they view it as an international language of communication. Some 37.5% of respondents believed that the spread of English in the Arabic world would lead to an Arabization and Islamization of the English language. This aspiration may appear to be misplaced optimism given the state of international politics. Yet, there is a courageous hope in this response, one that speaks to the belief in the power of one language to influence another. Certainly, English has adopted thousands of words from other languages over the last 1,000 years. While half of Arabic speaking Muslims believed that English could be Islamized, 70% believed that the Arabic language could not be secularized.

The idea that Arabic is a sacred language seems to be deeply ingrained in the Arabic-Islamic mindset. As was demonstrated in "The Omnipresence of Allah in the Arabic Language," Muslim languages like Persian, Turkish, Urdu, and Malaysian have only been superficially Islamized when compared

## 11 The Loss of the Allah Lexicon

to Arabic (Morrow, 2006, pp. 7–70). Attempts by Muslim converts from the West to "Islamize" English have thus far failed. The Allah expressions and Arabic terms they include in their English use are only marginally significant when compared to the whole. The sole exception to this fact seems to be the Aljamiado Spanish of the Moriscos which is so saturated with Arabic Allah expressions and religious terminology that several scholars describe it as "an Islamic variant of Spanish" (Gómez Renau, 2000; Hegyi, 1985; Sánchez Álvarez, 1988).

In our most recent survey, it was equally important to determine the extent to which the Arabic language was being passed down to the next generation, thereby providing a platform for speculating on the many upcoming generations. As we have already noted, 50% of Arabic-speaking parents have observed that their children use fewer Allah expressions than they do. In fact, only 60% of our respondents said their children could speak Arabic, 47% could write Arabic, and 53% could read it. In contrast, 50% of our respondents reported that their children could speak English, and 57% reported that they could read and write it. It would advance our understanding of the younger generation's attachment to Arabic if we knew whether they were being taught in Arabic at school or in English. This last issue is shown to be a proliferating pattern based on the current media evidence we gathered and discussed earlier. The data from our survey indicates that our respondents, all adults, did not themselves belong to the English-educated Arab elite. The vast majority of them had been schooled in Arabic at the elementary, secondary, and university levels. If these parents are already noting a decline in the use of Arabic Allah expressions, and even cases of Arabic attrition among their children, one can only wonder the extent of language loss occurring among the children of the English-educated products of the private schools that are well nigh ubiquitous in some parts of the Arab world. If our results are indicative, Arab parents are presently producing the first fully bilingual generation of Arabic/English speakers. However, with the dominance of English, Arab children may be entirely and exclusively Anglicized in generations to come.

While exposure to English varies greatly throughout the Arab world, there has been an increase in the spread of English-language schools and English-language instruction in North Africa and the Middle East. Despite the French government's paternalistic attitude towards its ex-colonies and its fears about a decline in the use of French, many countries in the Maghreb are now focusing on English as opposed to French. Algeria, in a foresighted move, left the *francophonie*, dropped French as an official language, removed it from the school system, and replaced it with Arabic and English. Although the relationship between Morocco and France has often been sour, Morocco has always had excellent relations with the United States. Like Algeria, Morocco is determined to drop the use of French and replace it with English instruction. However, because it receives "French language support" funds from the French government, it may be a while before the change is fully implemented. Tunisia, like Algeria and Morocco, has moved away from the ambitious Arabization plans of the past, and is, instead, embracing a policy of Anglicization through education. The Arabization plans have been dropped in most Arab countries for a long host of reasons, including, the political failure of Pan-Arabism, the discouragingly deep divide between Arabic dialects and MSA, and the ever increasing need to communicate in English, the current language of political and economic power.

In Egypt, a former British colony, knowledge of English has always been encouraged. In Lebanon, where French was once the language of prestige, English has become the "cool," contemporary, and most modern language for today's youth. In countries like Kuwait and the United Arab Emirates, English has become the unofficial second language. In fact, English is so dominant in Dubai that lawmakers felt obliged to declare Arabic as the official language in the UAE in 2008. As Kitbi, Professor of Political Science at Al-Ain University noted, "To my knowledge, there is no nation that allows an invasion of foreign languages in government institutions the way we did in the UAE. The move [naming Arabic as the official language] will correct the imbalance" (Tristam, 2008, p. 1). Despite this symbolic gesture, English remains the overwhelmingly dominant language in the UAE Although Arabic is the language of public education, English is strongly stressed.

The primary language in most private schools throughout the Arab world is English, a fact that is, year after year, producing new generations of Arabs who, while they speak colloquial Arabic, have little or no comprehension of MSA, and cannot even read or write the language (Gawab,

2010). One generation back, and thence ages and ages past, the ancestors of these young people could all read the Quran, even if they read nothing else. In Islamic Spain, for example, there was scarcely a boy or girl over the age of twelve who could not read or write Arabic (Morrow, 2008). Becoming proficient was considered a duty as well as a privilege. While it is not unusual for language attrition to occur among emigrants, it is highly unusual for a situation like this to develop, where individuals lose a language while still living in the birthplace of that language. Rather than attempt to communicate in Arabic, many young Arabs have succumbed to the easy appeal of the English language.

One manifestation that we have noted personally among children raised in the United States of Arabic-speaking parents is that when the children are very young and Arabic is the language of the home, they come to understand and respond automatically to communications verbalized by their parents or other Arabic-speaking family members. When they are older, however, and have begun attending a preschool or kindergarten, where the spoken language is English, the easy fluency of their first years dissipates somewhat as English, or any other language in its place, comes to be seen as "dominant" and "more useful." It is then that a linguistic tug of war begins. It is not a war in which there will necessarily be one victor. In bilinguals, what will happen is that the speaker will begin "code switching." Code switching is a process in which, while speaking one language, the speaker will insert a word from his or her second language, in effect substituting one language for another (Heredia & Altarriba, 2001 p. 164). Language dominance would then be determined by which language is the language of "flow" and which one is the language of "insertion."

The results we have received from our respondents clearly confirm the growing influence of the English language in the educational system throughout the Arab world. A question about the language of instruction employed at the elementary, secondary, and university levels in their respective home countries provided the picture presented in Table 1.

| Language | Elementary | Secondary | University |
|---|---|---|---|
| Arabic | 34 | 30 | 12 |
| English | 8 | 12 | 21 |
| French | 4 | 3 | 4 |

Table 1

It is evident that, in many Arab countries, elementary, secondary, and university education is bilingual, either Arabic–French or Arabic–English. What is interesting is the exponential increase of English, as opposed to French, usage, from the time many Arabs are children to the time they are university students, and the significant decrease in Arabic language instruction. The use of Arabic declines from one third, while the use of English increases nearly three-fold. As numerous participants pointed out, while Arabic may remain the language of instruction in public schools, English is the language of instruction in private schools. Increasingly, English is a language of privilege in the Arab world, one which may contribute to a more profoundly disparate class system than mere money might allow. Since many specialized fields of study are taught exclusively in English in Arab universities, Arab children who completed their studies in private, English-language schools, find themselves at a distinct advantage over their poorer peers from the public school system. These elite, English-speaking Arab students, may well enter engineering and medical programs, while their economically disadvantaged monolingual peers, end up in economically unprofitable fields, such as Islamic Studies or Arabic literature.

The question of how this situation has arisen remains a conundrum. Although we assumed that the decline in MSA usage was attributed to poor pedagogical approaches, we were surprised to find that 45% of respondents believed the materials and resources used to teach Arabic to Arabs were good. Another 31% found them to be excellent, and 21% considered the books, media, and instruction to be of fair quality. Only 3.5% of respondents viewed the material as pedagogically poor. Coincidentally, 63% of respondents rejected the notion that studying MSA was both boring and difficult. Those who did find it dull blamed the textbooks used to teach it, in addition to great difficulty due to the difference between their colloquial dialects spoken at home and MSA. Still, when asked to compare the method used to teach English and the method used to teach Arabic, 60% of respondents described English as being more appealing. This response may point to the more modern approach used to teach English. It relies more on communicative methods and less repetition than the traditional method used to teach MSA. As far as our participants were concerned in relation to the materials used to teach English in the Arab world, 47.5% viewed them as good while 25% viewed them as excellent. Another 20% opined that the English textbooks were poor and 7.5% found them fair. When asked whether Modern Standard Arabic should be the main language of instruction in the Arabic speaking world, 80% of respondents responded affirmatively, while 20% argued that the language of instruction should be colloquial Arabic. When asked whether English should be the main language of instruction, 95% of participants rejected the idea.

The results from our survey stand in sharp contrast from those presented by al-Abed and Oqlah (1996). Their survey of 1,176 undergraduate students in Saudi Arabia concluded that English does not spread westernization, does not weaken national identity, and does not corrupt religious commitment. If we are to believe their results, most university students in Saudi Arabia believe that learning English is both a religious and national duty. As a result of their findings, the researchers recommended that a rigid English language policy be implemented in the Kingdom. Objectively, given the responses we have received from a wide range of Arabic speakers, it is difficult to believe that Saudis view learning English as a religious obligation versus an economic or cultural advantage. The Prophet taught Muslims to "seek knowledge from the cradle to the grave," yet, not all knowledge leads to wisdom. Thus, to take on a language like English, one that is profoundly secular and brings with it a world of controversial ideas, overt sexuality being the least of them, as a religious obligation, begs intense reflection and understanding. We have pointed out that even those who are briefly in an Arabic speaking country will find themselves, without conscious thought, utilizing the more common Allah phrases. Who, then, can learn English without learning all that comes along with it?

When we embarked on this socio-linguistic mission, we sought to determine whether the spread of global English would lead to the de-Islamization of the Arabic language. As evidence of the decline of Allah expressions observed in previous studies by Ferguson (1983) and Morrow (2006), 52.5% of respondents believe that global English is eroding Arabic–Islamic identity and culture and that globalization spreads secularism. These results seem to suggest that the issue of globalization and its impact on culture remains a contentious, or perhaps little understood, issue. Interestingly, most respondents distinguished between the spread of English, which they did not view as a threat towards their religion, and globalization, about which they had more qualms. While they may disagree on the damage caused by global English, 70% of our respondents assert that the Arabic language was critical to understanding Islam. A loss of Arabic, then, would inevitably weaken the influence of Islam in the world.

It might be that modern life and its myriad adjustments, this time in the form of global English, has resulted in a new schema that cannot always support the specific terms and exchanges comprising this matchless feature of the Arabic language. What then, can take their place where Arab Muslims gather and English is spoken? It may be that, in the way of any relic whose time is past or whose survival is not a priority, the Arabic language will evolve as many of its dialects have, into a language only spoken by a few and written less and less. In that case, what becomes of Arab identity? These are the questions that all Muslims and Arabs who traditionally speak Arabic but may now be moving away from it, need to ask themselves. How will Muslims support, layer, and enhance their devotions through the spoken word, a task Prophet Muhammad saw as so vital? In Arabic, it is said that "the strength of a person is in his intelligence and tongue" (*quwatu al-insani fi 'aqlihi wa lisanihi*). The Allah Lexicon has been an inseparable part of the language and the culture for fifteen centuries.

Perhaps the first step is this one, to assure that as many as possible are made aware of the history of these phrases and the reasons they became such a verbal force in all areas of life. Those who may be releasing this body of connection should be reminded of the frequency and diversity of these phrases and become conscious of what will be sacrificed solely in aid of modernity or sophistication or professional advancement. Perhaps the willing sacrifice of such a linguistic boon should be approached with due caution and some consideration of the societal, cultural, and religious ramifications. Yet, even we cannot propose the optimal response to the possible demise of this feature, and certainly we cannot presume know what it should be for others. Nevertheless, each of us has drawn a line in the sand at one time or another, saying, "This far and no further," with regard to the retention of something we cherish. Perhaps, that moment is now, even as secular society tries to encroach on what we hold dear.

## References

Al-Abed, F., al-Haq, G., & Smadi, O. (Nov 1996). Spread of English and westernization in Saudi Arabia. *World Englishes, 15*(3), 307–317.
Al-Arabi holds seminars on Arabic language. (2008, January 16). *Kuwait Times.* Retrieved January 15, 2010, from <http://www.kuwaittimes.net/read_news. php?newsid= NTg4NTQyNDc=>
Annan, K. (Dec 2004-Feb 2005). Combating Islamophobia depends on unlearning intolerance. *UN Chronicle, 41*(1), 4–5.
Arabic bill is blocked by shura. (2010, January 19). *Gulf Daily News.* Retrieved February 2, 2010, from <http://www.gulf-daily-news. com /NewsDetails. aspx?srch=1&storyid=268797>
Arabic speakers, a dying breed in the Arab world? (2007, December 27). *Kuwait Times.* Retrieved February 10, 2010, from <http://www.kuwaittimes. net/read_news. php?newsid=MzA5NTkzOTI1>
Bermingham, H. (2010, January 26). English: The key to success? *Arab News.* Retrieved February 10, 2010, from <http://www.arabnews.com/?page= 9&section=0&a rticle=131825&d=26&m=1&y=2010>
Castleton, B. (2006). Frequency and function of religiously-based expressions. In J.A. Morrow (ed.), *Arabic, Islam and the Allah Lexicon: How language shapes our concept of God.* (pp. 71–114). Lewiston, NY: Edwin Mellen Press.
Curiel, J. (2005, February 6). Islamic verses. *San Francisco Chronicle,* E1: 6.
Crystal, D. (2000). *Language death.* Cambridge: Cambridge University Press.

Dorian, N. (1998). Western language ideologies and small-language prospects. In L.A. Grenoble & L.J. Whaley (eds), *Endangered languages: Language loss and community response*. Cambridge: Cambridge University Press.

Ferguson, C.A. (1983). God-wishes in Syrian Arabic. *Mediterranean Language Review 1*, 65–83.

Fishman, J.A. (1996). *In praise of the beloved language: A comparative view of positive ethnolinguistic consciousness*. Berlin: Mouton de Gruyter.

Gawab, A. (2010, March 3). Are Arabs saying "yalla, bye" to Arabic? *Elan: The Guide to Global Muslim Culture*. Retrieved March 20, 2010, from <http://www.elanthemag.com/index.php/site/blog-detail/are_arabs_saying_yalla_bye_to_arabic-nid487931896/>

Give Arabic its due. (2008, December 16). *Gulf Daily News*. Retrieved January 15, 2010, from <http://www.gulf-daily-news.com/NewsDetails.aspx?srch=1&storyid=237802>

Gómez Renau, M. (2000). La lengua aljamiada y su literatura: una variante islámica del español.*Castilla 25*, 71–83.

Hazell, D. (2007, August 10). Lawsuit claims US Airline blocked man wearing Arabic t-shirt from boarding. *New York Daily News.com*. Retrieved January 10, 2010, from <http://www.nydailynews.com/news/2007/08/09/2007- 009_lawsuit_claims_jetblue_blocked_passenger.html>

Hegyi, O. (1985). Una variante islámica del español: la literatura aljamiada. *Homenaje a Álvaro Galmés de Fuentes 1*, 647–655.

Heredia, R., & Altarriba, J. (2001). Bilingual language mixing: Why do bilinguals code-switch? *Current Directions in Psychological Science 10*(5), 164–168.

Hitti, P.K. (1996). *The Arabs: A short history*. Washington, DC: Regency Publishing.

Ibrahim, Z. (2009). To use "God" or "Allah"? *Association of Muslim Social Scientists, 26*(4), i–iv.

IMRA. (2009, November 27). Spread of English-language jihadist websites. Retrieved January 10, 2010, from <http://www.imra.org.il/story.php3?id-46562>

Interview with Olivier Roy: author of *Globalized Islam: The Search for a new Ummah*. (n.d.) Columbia University Press. Retrieved January 10, 2010, from <http://cup.columbia.edu/static/Interview-roy-olivier-globalized>

Labov, W. (1963). The social motivation of a sound change. *Word 19*, 273–309.

Langewiesche, W. (November 1991). The world in its extreme. *The Atlantic Monthly*, 43–44.

Morrow, J.A. (2008). The pre and early Islamic period. In G. Watling (ed.), *A cultural history of reading* (pp. 521–540). Westport, CT: Greenwood Press.

Morrow, J.A. (2006). The omnipresence of Allah in the Arabic language. In J.A. Morrow (ed.), *Arabic, Islam and the Allah Lexicon: How language shapes our concept of God* (pp. 7–70). Lewiston, NY: Edwin Mellen Press.

Parry, W. (2002, March 21). Some Arabs in the US are changing their names, citing Sept. 11 bias. *Spartanburg Herald-Journal*, A6. Retrieved January 10, 2010, from <http://news.google.com/newspapers?nid=1876&dat=20020321&id=8EAf AAAAIBAJ&sjid=atAEAAAAIBAJ&pg=6890,2672715>

Ross, O. (2007, October). English is cool in trendy Beirut; pushes aside French as the language of status in Lebanese capital. *Toronto Star, 8,* AA03.

Sánchez Álvarez, M. (1988). Sobre la variante islámica del español del siglo XVI. In M. Viguera Ariza, A. Salvador Plans, and A. Viudas Camarasa (eds), *Actas del I Congreso Internacional de Historia de la Lengua Española* (pp. 1355–1363). Madrid: Arco/Libros.

Shakespeare, W. (1954). *The Tempest.* F. Kermode (ed.). London: Methuen.

Slackman, M. (2008, June 20). With a word, Egyptians leave it all to fate. *The New York Times*, A9.

Stephens, L. (2000, March 16). For some, speaking to God in an ancient tongue puts faith on a higher plane. *Fort Worth Star Telegram.* Retrieved January 10, 2010, from <http://www.lexisnexis.com.proxy.alameda.peralta.edu/us/lnacademic/results/docview/docview.do?docLinkInd=true&risb=21_T9614769 784&format=GNBFI&sort=RELEVANCE&startDocNo=1&resultsUrlKey=29_T9614769787&cisb=22_T9614769786&treeMax=true&treeWidth=0&csi=222065&docNo=1>

Student detained over Arabic flashcards, lawsuit says. (2010, February 10). *Agence France Presse.* Retrieved March 3, 2010, from <http://www. google.com/hostednews/afp/ article/ALeqM5i-JHBrLMJVn_S_ymxLHjmAgrNyZg>

Tonkin, H. (2001). Language learning, globalism, and the role of English. *ADFL Bulletin 3* (2), 5–9.

Tristam, P. (2008, March 9). UAE makes Arabic its official language. *Pierre's Middle East Issues Blog.* Retrieved January 10, 2010, from <http://middleeast. about.com/b/2008/03/09/uae-makes-arabic-its-official-language.htm>

UAE Ministry of Education striving to deepen national identity. (2008, April 16). *Emirate News Agency.*

Use Arabic in university. (2008, December 29). *Kuwait Times.* Retrieved January 10, 2010, from <http://www.kuwaittimes.net/read_news.php?newsid=MTI1NDY5NTM4OA==>

UNESCO. (2006, March). *Book Production: Number of Titles by UDC Classes.* Paris: UNESCO.

Views by region chart. *Arab News Network*. Retrieved January 10, 2010, from <http://www.ann-tv.net/ uk/website/accueil/pdf/VIEWRS_BY_REGION.pdf>

Viniti, V. (2008, August–November). Mother tongues, English, and religion in Singapore. *World Englishes* 27(3/4), 450–464.

Wajdi. (1999, December 6). Personal correspondence with author.

Wierzbicka, A. (1997). *Understanding cultures through their key words*. Oxford: Oxford University Press.

Williams, C. (2007, November 2). Arabic-speaking passengers detained on way home from marine training sue American Airlines. *The Associated Press*. Retrieved January 10, 2010, from <http://www.defence.pk/forums/members-club/8080-arabic-speaking-passengers-sue-american.html>

NADINE SINNO

## 12 Navigating Linguistic Imperialism, Cultural Hybridity, and Language Pedagogy

ABSTRACT

In this chapter, I describe and reflect on my experiences learning Modern Standard Arabic and English as a foreign language while growing up in Beirut, Lebanon in the 1980s and 1990s. Specifically, the chapter sheds light on issues including the challenges, rewards, and punishments associated with learning English and Arabic; the methods that were employed in the teaching of these languages in many private Lebanese schools; and the consequences of these teaching methods on the linguistic acquisition process, identity formation, and the overall sense of selfhood and belonging among Lebanese children and teenagers. Within a postcolonial framework, I investigate some of the assumptions about Arabic that many children of my generation inherited from well-intentioned mentors who advocated mastery of English as a means of escaping the violence and economic instability of war-torn Lebanon, in search of new homelands such as the United States. Additionally, I show how getting a higher education in the United States was truly my ticket to a "better life", a life that now includes studying and teaching Arabic language and literature. The final section asserts that for our children to have a more positive experience studying Arabic, our fairly rigid Lebanese curriculum, as well as our negative attitudes towards Arabic, must be reformed. Only through taking such steps, the chapter concludes, can our children have a better chance at achieving proficiency in Arabic and at genuinely enjoying their native language and culture.

# Introduction

In the first section of the essay, I provide some background information about Lebanon, specifically highlighting the possible geographical and historical factors that have contributed to its linguistic hybridity. I then trace my journey with Arabic and English, two languages I grew up learning and speaking in school and at home in Beirut, Lebanon. My private journey with Arabic and English provides a window into the world in which I and many Lebanese children and teenagers grew up, as we negotiated at least two languages and cultures that were never completely separate due to the cosmopolitan nature of our Beiruti society. I investigate my complicated relationship with these two languages and shed light on issues about language, culture, and identity, including the rewards and punishments associated with learning English and Arabic, the various pedagogical methods that were employed in the teaching of these languages in the 1980s and 1990s in many private/westernized Lebanese schools, the prevailing perceptions regarding the status of English and Arabic, and the repercussions of the predominant teaching methods and perceptions on the linguistic acquisition process, identity formation, and the overall sense of self-worth among myself and others of my generation.

Postcolonial theory provides a ready framework for analysis of my ambivalent relationship with Arabic and English. I investigate some of the internalized assumptions about Arabic (and Arab culture) that were passed on to us, children and teenagers, by well-intentioned parents and teachers who wanted us to excel at English because they predicted it was our ticket to a "better life," one free from the political turmoil and economic instability of the country, especially during the Lebanese Civil War (1975–1990). Additionally, I show how deepening my knowledge of English and getting a higher education in the United States were indeed my ticket to a "better life", a life that ironically now includes studying and teaching Arabic language and literature. I demonstrate how learning English helped me "find my way home." The final section discusses my rediscovery of the beauty, and yes, complexity of the Arabic language and literature – my decolonization process – and provides suggestions for teaching Arabic more creatively.

## Contextualizing "Hybrid Lebanon"

Lebanon is located on the eastern coast of the Mediterranean Sea. It is bordered by Syria to the north and east and Israel/Palestine to the south. Lebanon's geographic location has always been regarded by both insiders and outsiders as unique for being the crossroads of various Mediterranean and Arab civilizations, and as such, it is often considered a bridge between the East and the West. Undoubtedly, the country's locality has been crucial to enriching its religious, political, ethnic, and linguistic diversity. It is a hybrid country in every sense of the word.

Historically, Lebanon was home to multiple civilizations, including the Phoenicians, the Ottomans, and the French, and each one of these ruling entities contributed to the making of modern-day Lebanon in one way or another. Before the eruption of the Lebanese Civil War (1975–1990), the country experienced a period of prosperity and was especially famous for its hospitality and laissez-faire banking system, which led to vibrant tourism and regular cultural and business exchanges with its Arab neighbours as well as Europe and the Americas. In fact, during its *"ayyaam al-khayr,"* or its "good old days," Lebanon was known as the "Switzerland of the East," and Beirut, the capital city, was often referred to as the "Paris of the Middle East." At the end of the war, there were massive local and international efforts to revive the country's economy and rebuild its infrastructure from scratch. These efforts helped revive the tourism sector tremendously, and despite the occasional wars with Israel – such as the summer 2006 war, which wreaked massive human and material losses – the country still attracts thousands of tourists during its calmer periods.

This brief background helps contextualize Lebanon's socio-linguistic "aura." Undoubtedly, Lebanon's rich history and its unique geography have shaped its overall makeup, including its educational system. Educated Lebanese are trained to navigate different languages at the same time. While French was an official language, in addition to Arabic, during and after the French mandate period (1920–1943), English has become more prevalent in the last couple of decades. This may be attributed to the United States' increasing socio-economic power and its global influence in the region. It is safe to say that many public and private schools incorporated the mandatory teaching of English as a second or third language in their curricula during the 1980s and 1990s.

That said, many Lebanese people who do not have a formal education are still fairly comfortable dealing with foreigners and foreign languages. This is also a result of Lebanon's geography, history of migration, as well as its dependence on tourism and the regular influx of foreign visitors. In other words, Lebanese "returnees" or former expatriates, who have lived abroad for some period of time, often come back with at least a basic proficiency in English, French, Spanish, or German. On the other hand, those who never left the country have been interacting with tourists as well as resident foreigners on a regular basis, and are thus used to hearing and using foreign languages, especially English and French. In brief, many Lebanese without a formal education are self-taught with regard to foreign languages. They have learned foreign languages through direct immersion.

The interplay among various languages and cultures is thus part of the fabric of Lebanese society – something that presents both an advantage and a challenge to the creation and reinforcement of a solid national identity and national language, in this case Arabic. Furthermore, it is important to note that such a multi-linguistic and multi-ethnic environment inevitably places some pressures on Lebanese citizens in Lebanon as well as abroad. We are almost "expected" to possess and flaunt our linguistic prowess, more so in the case of those who have had the privilege of pursuing a formal education at a "reputable" institution.

In the following section, I describe my experience growing up in "hybrid Lebanon" and how navigating such a pluralistic society can be simultaneously challenging and rewarding. I also describe the rigorous and, at times, "self-defeating" Lebanese educational system, that, like any other institution in Lebanon, has been influenced by the cross-cultural encounters shaping the country.

# "He who loves you beats you!"
## The trials and tribulations of learning formal Arabic

I was born and raised in Lebanon until the age of 22. As a child, I attended a fairly small private elementary school and later an international high school, where English was the main language of instruction and where formal Arabic (*fus'ha* or Modern Standard Arabic, MSA) and, later, Arabic philosophy, were the only subjects taught in Arabic. In both schools, language proficiency in both Arabic and English was constantly emphasized, but the unspoken message always seemed to be that while we could get away without mastering MSA – a language that was presented by educators as inherently difficult and impossible to master in the first place – our English had to be excellent if we wanted to succeed in those prestigious schools. As for learning Arabic, our native tongue, the journey was never easy for many of us for various reasons. Among them is the fact that spoken and written Arabic are fairly different, so the language we spoke at home did not exactly match the one we learned at school; on the contrary, there were times when our dialect interfered with our formal Arabic, leading us to make mistakes in pronunciation, sentence structure, and grammar and provoking the anger of our purist Arabic language teachers.

In their defence, our dialect, which often included borrowed phrases from English and French, made their job harder as they toiled to teach us proper, formal Arabic, a job that was almost always hampered by what they regarded as other "contaminating" languages and dialects. Moreover, the way we learned Arabic was modelled after the old French system, which relied heavily on the rigorous memorization of an original text and a mimetic reproduction of it when the test came. A good example of such assignments was "auto-dictation," where students would memorize a whole lesson (2–3 pages) and reproduce it in class. We were graded on both our ability to reproduce the text from memory and on our spelling. As children, this process was often nerve-wracking for many of us because of the tremendous amount of pressure it presented. The slightest mistake or slip in memory would mean failing the whole "auto-dictation," because forgetting one word could lead to forgetting a whole section and could automatically result in a failing grade.

Similarly, we often memorized entire poems and plays and recited them in class. This exercise is not inherently bad because students should be exposed to and even learn by heart the poetry of great poets as it makes them better writers and readers. However, it was the way that it was conducted that I find questionable. Arabic teachers, often armed with stern looks and, in some cases, steel rulers that they were not afraid to use, would ask students to stand up one by one and recite to the whole class; and the slightest mispronunciation would lead to a public shaming where the same teachers – who often criticized the interference of English and French with our Arabic learning process and who acknowledged the gap between spoken and formal Arabic – would belittle us for not knowing "our own language." This is not to condemn individual Arabic teachers, or to dismiss them summarily, for I am the first to say there were some who truly did their best to bridge the gap between our multilingual way of life and the expectations they placed upon us. Many of them did not resort to humiliation as a means of punishment. At any rate, it is important to emphasize that even those "stern" teachers were not inherently mean or vicious; rather, it is fair to assume that they had been trained to approach teaching/discipline in the way that they did. Accordingly, if changes are to be implemented, the whole system should be modified and reformed.

Even "creative" assignments were not that creative; when asked to write an essay about a certain topic; we were expected to write something that was based on a "sample" essay that they provided us with ahead of time. Our creative impulses were thus stifled, rather than nurtured or praised. In fact, many times our creative essays resembled one another throughout elementary and middle school. We could also predict the subject of the essay, depending on the time of year; among the most popular topics in elementary and middle school were: "describe your summer break," or "describe your favourite season," and "describe what you saw on TV during the official celebration of Lebanon's Independence." Thus, we learned to memorize and rehash the official rhetoric and clichés associated with each of these essay topics, instead of thinking for ourselves.

Once again, Arabic teachers should not be blamed for this authoritarian system; after all, it was their duty to prepare us for the terrifying government official exams, where such questions were the norm for all subjects, not just Arabic. In fact, I remember a handful of Arabic teachers, as well as other instructors, expressing their desire to include various media-related activities that would enhance our critical thinking and creativity; however, they were understandably apprehensive because of the time such projects would take, when we needed to concentrate our energies on completing the government set curriculum in preparation for the official exams – our ticket to a university education.

It is important to note that traditional Arabic learning materials were seldom attractive. I remember my elementary Arabic textbooks being mediocre and lacklustre, in comparison to their English counterparts. The drawings that accompanied a reading, for instance, reflected an underestimation of children's sense of logic, reality, and aesthetics. Human figures were not proportional, houses and gardens were not visually pleasing, and women were consistently painted in traditional roles and almost always in the kitchen – something which did not reflect the more complex realities that we saw in our own lives. Audio-visual material was scarce as well, partially because the technological revolution had not exploded yet, and partially because such material may have been regarded as a distraction from our rigorous Arabic curriculum.

Add to all this is the fact that the rewards of being proficient in Arabic were never appealing. Rather, they often boiled down to a "lack of punishment," or negative reinforcement. If you could pass Arabic, you were spared a number of unpleasant things, such as chastising, punishment, Arabic summer school, and public shaming. At best, we soon realized that Arabic teachers, unlike their English counter-parts, were in the business of dishing out tough love. "*Mann Ahabbaka Darabaka*!" "He who loves you beats you," one of my elementary Arabic teachers would say with a smile. The implication was that Arabic was a tough language and that only the select few could ever get close to mastering it over a long period of time. Throughout your Arabic journey as a student, however, your "loving" teachers had to "beat" you, literally or metaphorically, so you could get better at it with every day that passed! Perfection, however, was beyond anyone's reach for Arabic, many teachers emphasized, was the language of the Quran, and only God was perfect. Making an A in Arabic was simply unthinkable, and if you did make an A against all odds, you rarely felt thrilled; others resented you because that meant that you were spared the reprimand bestowed on the rest of the class. You were seen as a traitor, escaping the wrath of the Arabic masters! In fact, I remember hiding my quizzes whenever the teacher would give them back because I was often worried about being ostracized by other classmates.

Worse still, I remember becoming an object of suspicion by one of my Arabic teachers himself. As he handed back my first Arabic test for the semester, my teacher promised to monitor me closely for the rest of the year because I got a B+, the highest possible grade he gave. "Sinno," he said, glaring. "I'm not convinced you were able to produce all that text from memory. I'll be watching you to make sure you're not sneaking in any cheat sheets into the test room. *Allah ysa'dik*, may God help you, when I finally catch you!" That day, I felt humiliated. His comment took away from my achievement, and, for years to come, I would distance myself from my own language because being good at it had landed me in the same spot as those who failed it: denigration. I just wanted to do well enough to escape that fate; I wanted to simply "get by" – not to excel – so that I could become invisible to both, frustrated classmates and untrusting Arabic teachers.

## From iron fists to Hershey Kisses and Big Macs: The conquest of English

My elementary school and my high school both prided themselves on hiring native or near-native speakers of English who marketed English as a "hip" and "cool" language, in contrast to its poor rival, Arabic. Our English teachers insisted that students constantly use English in the classroom and provided all sorts of incentives for students who separated themselves from the crowd by excelling in it. While Arabic teachers were trained to show tough love, English teachers seemed to perfect the art of positive reinforcement. I remember an American elementary school teacher who never ran out of Hershey Kisses and colourful stickers, which she would bring back from her trips to the United States and generously distribute among those who won spelling contests or wrote the most "creative" essays.

English also meant access to colourful, interactive textbooks, American movies, and daily compliments from fun, encouraging instructors who wore jeans, put their hair in ponytails (instead of tight buns!) and let you call them by their first names – something unheard of where Arabic was concerned. It was an entirely new culture. Later in high school, American teachers would speak to us about the advantages of getting a higher education in the United States as they emphasized the importance of perfecting our English. They taught us that the sky was the limit for any ambitious student who invested in her education. Not unlike them, our parents seemed to believe that as well. In a country ravished by war, it was natural for people to be constantly looking for alternatives abroad. Accordingly, our parents wanted for us what they may not have been able to achieve for themselves: a safe escape and a dignified standard of living in countries like the United States. Therefore, as far as English was concerned, we had both our teachers and parents cheering us on to conquer the language so we could get student visas and head for greener pastures. And given the position of our country – especially our capital city – as a bridge between East and West, it was not difficult for us to plunge into a world of English language and become bi-lingual, bi-cultural hybrids, because our city itself, as we had religiously memorized from history books, was *"multaqa al-Hadaarat,"* the place where all civilizations meet.

Furthermore, as is the case with many postcolonial nations, many Lebanese, including our parents, idealized English and English-speaking countries, often at the expense of our mother tongue and native culture. In retrospect, I suspect this was a manifestation of "internalized racism" experienced and projected by many Lebanese people. In other words, like many young nation-states, Lebanon has yet to recover from the inferiority complex inherited from colonial times. As a result of being told by foreign occupiers, missionaries, and even modern-day western as well as Arab media that Arabic culture and language are inferior to western cultures and languages, many Lebanese have accepted this so-called "fact" and learned to propagate it among themselves. For example, I remember my father getting upset when he would walk in on us watching Arabic television shows, like Egyptian soap operas or Arabic cartoons. "What the hell are you watching?" he would say. "Your English is never going to get better unless you watch American movies. Plus, whatever you're watching is junk. You should know better." Like many other parents who sent their children to international schools, my parents would urge us to speak more English with each other at home so we could practice, and they would take great pride in hosting dinners for our American teachers and friends, thus exposing us to English every chance they could.

In brief, both our parents and teachers would heap praise and material benefits upon those of us who embraced English and took their linguistic proficiency to another level. While it might have felt odd at first to be told that Arabic was not "good enough," many of we children simply accepted those assumptions precisely because they were handed down to us by adults whom we loved and respected. We learned to separate our every day life, where daily conversation was conducted mainly in the Lebanese dialect, with the occasional French and English expressions, from our "higher" academic pursuits, which relied heavily on English. Arabic may have been our language at home, our "mother-tongue," but English was certainly our language of success. And at times, our language at home, including our recreational movie time, was sacrificed for the sake of nurturing our budding academic personas.

Years later, when I read Ngugi wa Thiong'o in graduate school, it all fell into place, and I found a way to better comprehend and articulate this process of internalized colonialism, which is common among many postcolonial nations. Wa Thiong'o (1994) speaks of linguistic imperialism, often manifested in the benefits heaped upon those children who adopted English at the expense of their native African tongue. According to wa Thiong'o, "... [A]ny achievement in spoken or written English was highly rewarded; prizes, prestige, applause; the ticket to higher realms; English became the measure of intelligence and ability in the arts, the sciences, and all the other branches of learning. English became *the* main determinant of a child's progress up the ladder of formal education" (p. 438). To date, the words of wa Thiong'o remain relevant in Lebanon as well as many other Arab countries. Edward Said (1978) articulates the same sentiment about the perils of western imitation and the adoption of western value systems in his seminal work, *Orientalism*. He writes, "In the Arab world, what we consider good is an imitation of the West and a copy of its priorities – engineering, business, economics ... dedicated by the West's market economy. Such is the effect of 'modernization,' employed and carried out by the intelligentsia. Our ideas of progress, modernization, and culture come from the States too" (p. 325).

The trend of replacing Arabic with English, even in our daily lives, and not only in "formal" educational settings, is becoming even more prominent – and justifiable – with the expansion of diasporic communities. For instance, both my sisters live abroad, one in Saudi Arabia and the other in Canada; and both their children, unfortunately, do not speak Arabic fluently. My sister, who lives in Canada, argues that her son won't speak at home a language that he doesn't speak in the classroom, and my sister in Saudi argues that her son feels "weird" when he speaks with a Lebanese accent with other Arab friends, so they all resort to English as a "neutral" common language. Therefore, in addition to being an Arab child's promise of a better world, as it was during my days growing up in Lebanon, global English is increasingly becoming a quasi common ground to Arabs living in diaspora.

When they come to Lebanon for a visit, my nephews (and other children of their generation who live abroad) rarely speak in Arabic because they are not well-versed in it and feel self-conscious conversing in a dialect that sounds alien to them. After all, language, including dialect, requires practice, and without practice, these children simply cannot improve their Arabic, let alone the Lebanese dialect. It seems to me that the parents' reactions to this phenomenon are quite ambivalent and mixed. For example, my sister "wishes" that her son would use more Arabic and expresses concern that he does not, but she admits to surrendering to the fact that he will never master it because he is not sufficiently exposed to it in his daily life abroad. More interestingly, she complains that it would "take forever" for him to understand her Lebanese Arabic and to accomplish any task if she were to speak to him in Lebanese Arabic only. In other words, it is a vicious circle of lack of usage and lack of proficiency. My sister is by no means an exception. Many of my friends who live abroad share her experiences and attitude. Some even brag about their children's mastery of English, and they do not express the slightest regret about their children's inability to communicate in Arabic, even at the most basic level. They too perceive

English as a universal language, without which success cannot be achieved. Arabic, on the other hand, does not have the same status for them. This reality is so prevalent and normalized at this point in Lebanese society that only a handful of my relatives find it alarming that our own children are incapable of speaking their "mother tongue."

I cannot speak of global English without touching upon the impact of multinational corporations vis-à-vis this globalization process, for that too is another factor in making English more popular and appealing in the eyes of coming-of-age teenagers. As teenagers, we grew to idealize neighbours and well-off friends who flaunted their American-made jeans, games, and gadgets. All things made in America were deemed superior, no questions asked. And with the proliferation of American chains such as Dunkin Donuts, Pizza Hut and McDonald's, things could only get more complicated. In addition to wearing American brands and speaking a hybrid language of Lebanese dialect *and* English, we were now "eating in English". The American dream was in full swing. We were the converted. While these franchises provided us with a "taste" of the American dream, our everyday reality of political turmoil and economic instability made our individual dreams of leaving Lebanon to countries like the United States or England all the more palpable – and legitimate.

Given all these complex factors, it was only normal that we grew to equate English with "cool" and "superior" and Arabic with "inferior", "dull", and even "oppressive". For the most part, we would remain oblivious to the beauty of the Arabic language, literature, and culture because our energies were focused on "getting by" in Arabic class, rather than on appreciating what our language had to offer. Unlike English, Arabic was not presented to us as something that would expedite our entry into some glamorous, bright culture and/or future. On the contrary, it was unfortunately associated with an oppressive educational system, low self-esteem, and a distressing era of our nation-state, including war, chaos, and destruction. For many of us, English translated into our ticket to a better reality.

Recognizing and acknowledging the intricate relationship between language and culture is crucial for understanding why schoolchildren have been receptive to English much more than Arabic in Lebanon. It is also important for educators of the Arabic language to be mindful of that connection when teaching Arabic, whether their students are young impressionable Arab children and teenagers or adult non-native speakers of Arabic. To date, whenever I run into old classmates, they are bewildered at the thought of me becoming an Arabic professor, because learning Arabic was a nightmarish experience that made many of us question our self-worth – it was something "*tinzakar wa ma tin'aad*," that is, "to be mentioned but not repeated." Furthermore, our problematic relationship with Arabic translated into an ambivalent sense of identity and belonging precisely because national language and national identity are intricately connected. I believe our diminished loyalty to Arabic must have inevitably contributed to our sense of disconnection from our "Arabness," let alone our "Lebaneseness." According to wa Thiong'o:

> Language carries culture, and culture carries, particularly through orature and literature, the entire body of values by which we come to perceive ourselves and our place in the world. How people perceive themselves affects how they look at their culture, at their politics and at the social production of wealth, at their entire relationship to nature and to other beings. Language is thus inseparable from ourselves as a community of human beings with a specific form and character, as specific history, a specific relationship to the world. (p. 442)

Perhaps unsurprisingly, the language that my former classmates and I use when we meet is a hybrid language, consisting of Arabic, English, and, sometimes, French. "Code switching," or the smooth shifting from one language to another, is the most comfortable form of communication for us precisely because while we spoke mainly in Lebanese Arabic at home, our education and our "higher thinking" was done in English. Therefore, depending on the topic we are discussing, we will resort to the language that best "fits" that topic and allows us to articulate our thoughts most clearly.

I majored in English literature when I went to college and later earned my MA in English as well. At the American University of Beirut (AUB), I read English and American prose and poetry voraciously, and my encounter with Arabic language and literature would fade as time passed. I was insatiable in my pursuit of all things English or American, and I wrote critical and creative papers on western authors such as Shakespeare, Shelley,

Byron, Woolf, Austen, and Hemingway. English and American authors were constantly on my radar, not their Arabic counterparts. Since I was not "forced" to take Arabic, except for one required course at AUB, I read Arabic literature only sporadically – or even in translation – because I wanted to limit my exposure to a language that had caused me so much grief and from which I felt disconnected and estranged. Later, after coming to the United States and studying postcolonial theory, I would realize that like many other Lebanese youth and adults, I had become a replica of various imperial subjects/objects worldwide. I would realize that my uncritical allegiance to foreign cultures and literature was an epitome of the "triumphs" of the Orientalist project and that our very own institutions were culpable. As Said (1978) notes, "One of the "triumphs" of Orientalism is the fact that it's been accommodated by the intellectual classes within the Orient. The Arab world is a "satellite" of the United States. The universities in the Arab world are modelled after inherited models from the States or another former colonial power" (p. 323). In the following section, I discuss my "decolonization" process in detail and show how reconnecting with Arabic language and culture reshaped my entire academic career as well as my life and sense of personhood and belonging.

## Crossing to the "Other" side: Rediscovering Arabic in America

My dream to pursue a higher education in the United States became a reality when I was accepted into the University of Arkansas's Masters of Fine Arts Program in Literary Translation. In fact, when I first applied to the program, I had very little knowledge about literary translation, let alone the state of Arkansas. But I was so adamant about leaving to the United States that I jumped at the first opportunity that presented itself, through the recommendation of an acquaintance of mine who had gone through the program first. So, I packed my life in two suitcases and headed for the United States.

## 12 Navigating Linguistic Imperialism

Among my first "culture shock" experiences was the way people reacted upon hearing me speak in English. Some people, including my university professors, were floored by what they called my "near-native fluency". Even though they meant to compliment me by commenting on my fluency, I was puzzled because being fluent in English or French was something I had taken for granted all my life. It was almost insulting to me when they would ask if I had ever lived in the United States as a child or if I simply spent too much time watching American movies! I was shocked because in my mind English belonged to me as well, and there was no need to "make a fuss" over this issue. Later I would learn that teaching foreign languages was not a top priority at schools and colleges in the United States and that many Americans did not feel the need to invest in learning another language because the rest of the world was learning English, the universal language *par excellence.*

More importantly, by virtue of my major itself, Literary Translation, and, later, Comparative Literature, I started reading Arabic literature again. Revisiting Arabic literature in a "safe" environment proved to be such an unexpected delight. I read or reread the works of Arab authors such Nizar Qabbani, Mahmoud Darwish, Naguib Mahfouz, Edward al-Kharrat, Ghada Samman, Hanan al-Sheikh, Salwa Bakr, and many others. It was as if I had been in a coma, a dark age, of ignorance and oblivion for all these years. My feelings were so complex and included a range of emotions including shock, ecstasy, and even shame. From that point forward, I would rediscover my heritage of Arabic literature. At the same time, I started tutoring my advisor in Arabic. His knowledge of Arabic was at the beginner's level, but he was passionate and serious about learning it. I started seeing my language through his eyes, as he expressed his appreciation of the intricacies of Arabic grammar, which I now found so logical and appealing as I reacquainted myself with it. The more I tutored him, the more I experienced a "teaching high" each time I illuminated a grammatical concept, demonstrating how interconnected and reasonable Arabic grammar rules often are. Little did I know back then that I was now on my path to discovery – of Arabic language and literature – as well as to recovery from my troubled relationship with my native culture and language. I may have been physically in the state of Arkansas, but, on a much deeper level, I was finally "going home." This is not to say that I glorified and idealized all things Arab, but I was finally being open to exploring and acknowledging the merit of my native language and literature. In other words, the more I was exposed to Arabic literature and language, the more I enjoyed them and became engaged with rediscovering them more fully. At the University of Arkansas, I was shielded from the intimidating interactions with my former Arabic teachers and the "colonial bubble" that was so prevalent and powerful in Lebanon. Ironically, travelling to the United States and becoming part of an academic community helped me rediscover my roots. I saw and approached *home* – including Arabic literature and language – with fresh eyes, and the process was irreversible.

Additionally, as a PhD student, I delved into postcolonial studies and read works by postcolonial theorists such as Frantz Fanon, Aimee Cesaire, Edward Said, Ngugi wa Thiong'o, Chinua Achebe, Ella Shohat, Homi Bhabha, and Chandra Talpade Mohanty. Reading these theorists provided me with a framework within which I started to understand my colonization and, later, decolonization process. I finally realized that I had unconsciously adopted my linguistic and cultural hybridity as a "given," rather than by choice. Today, I know that while I cannot and do not want to reverse my hybrid existence, I owe it to myself to unearth a legitimate pre-colonial past, literally and literarily, and to make that literary and cultural heritage part of my present day consciousness and worldview. As Ella Shohat notes, "The defacto acceptance of hybridity as a product of conquest and post-independence dislocation as well as the recognition of impossibility of going back to an authentic past do not mean that the politico-social movements of various racial-ethnic communities should stop researching and recycling their pre-colonial languages and cultures" (pp. 109–110).

All things considered, I have learned to constantly scrutinize my hybrid existence and to make the best use of it, this "third space," to use Homi Bhabha's term, rather than be a mere receptacle of this hybridity. Every day, I struggle with issues of identity and language, but this struggle makes me a better scholar, professor, aunt. On a personal level, I now find myself encouraging my nephews to learn Arabic, and I try to teach it to them with utmost patience, flexibility, and support because I have serious concerns about some of the traditional methods of my Arabic education. At the same time, in my professional life, I am fully invested in teaching Arabic language and literature to students in the United States. This is my career, my calling. I am now also committed to translating and promoting Arabic literature to make some of that literature more accessible in English at a time when Arabs are most under attack and scrutiny. In my classes, I ask my students to pay attention to how translated works are edited and packaged for western audiences, and I urge them to question their own position in the world as they read these texts. I ask them to investigate the ways through which their preconceived "grids" and "expectations" affect their reading of "Third World" texts, including Arabic. Having gone through the fires of decolonization, I now know what stereotypes and misconceptions need to be deconstructed, without being replaced by other essentialist ones. Nonetheless, my decolonization process remains a work in progress both in my personal and academic life because feelings of ambivalence are rarely, if ever, easily resolved.

## Repackaging Arabic:
## Suggestions for teaching Arabic more positively

While there is nothing wrong with wanting Arab children and/or non-native speakers to study Arabic "seriously" and "properly", we must reform our educational system and pedagogical methods. If we want Arabic to be as competitive as other languages, we need to provide our children with better Arabic resources as well as approach them with a more positive attitude. To begin with, our Arabic textbooks must be revised. Even though I am aware there has been a lot of progress as far as the quality of Arabic textbooks, more can be done in that area. At the most basic level, our textbooks should provide aesthetically pleasing imagery that nurtures our children's interest in the language. The content of our textbooks should also be more in harmony with our increasingly progressive societies. Last summer, I was pleasantly surprised when I stumbled upon Arabic storybooks that dealt with issues such as religious tolerance, climate change, and recycling. I believe that such resources should be incorporated into our formal curricula, rather than being promoted as merely extra-curricular readings or "window dressing". I also noticed that more books in children's literature are casting characters in diversified gender roles, not just traditional ones; women are not constantly depicted as full-time mothers, and little girls do other things besides helping with housework, while little boys are not afraid of baking cookies! These changes are certainly commendable and long overdue. At the higher level, our curriculum could benefit from placing less emphasis on memorization and more on critical thinking and creative endeavours. In other words, projects that require multiple skills, including the use of technology, and that address diverse student learning styles should be promoted. In the end, not all students learn the same way. I know from my own experiences in the classroom, that while some students enjoy structured grammatical charts, others are better at immersing themselves in the language through activities such as role-playing and multi-media presentations. What really matters is showing openness towards our students' different talents and language-acquisition processes.

In other words, *how* we teach and perceive Arabic should be as important as *what* we teach in the classroom. When students realize that we are considering their unique abilities, as we plan our lessons, they become much more receptive. Furthermore, because Arabic is a fairly difficult language that requires a tremendous investment and a serious dedication on the students' part, our modes of reinforcement should be all the more positive and appealing. I know from my own experiences as a child, and later as an instructor of Arabic, that instilling fear and punishment in our students' learning process might backfire and result in low self-esteem, resentment, and an aversion to Arabic.

The notion that "he who loves you beats you", is in need of some rethinking and repackaging. I tell my students that because they have made the choice to learn Arabic, they have willingly committed to meeting higher standards. In other words, while we do need to remind our students that they must dedicate themselves fully to this challenging but very rewarding language, we should simultaneously acknowledge and praise their efforts. We should also find ways to make studying Arabic rewarding and enjoyable.

For instance, unlike my well-meaning Arabic teachers in the past, I have no qualms about giving A's when students deserve it. Nor do I feel guilty for teaching food-related vocabulary in a restaurant setting or showing DVDs of Arabic video clips, as students take notes on recurring chorus words and note down cultural insights. I want my students to hear, smell, and taste Arabic, and I want them to love it. I want them to look back at their learning experiences with fondness, and I want them to spread the word about the accessibility and, yes, the humanity, of Arabs and Arabic.

It is hard to predict with any certainty what the consequences of delaying reforms to our educational system would be. However, I can safely say that continued failure to be more proactive about raising our children's consciousness about the importance of learning and using Arabic, be it in Lebanon or in diasporic communities, will only contribute to a more fragmented and unstable Lebanon precisely because our children's estrangement from Arabic (and the Lebanese dialect) ultimately weakens their sense of belonging and identity. More importantly, with the proliferation of English and American pop culture, products, and media, Arabic may not even "stand a chance" if we do not become proactive about repackaging it to our children in ways that make it more enjoyable and palatable. I had the good fortune of joining a "sobering" graduate program that helped me rediscover my national language and culture, but not every Lebanese will get this opportunity.

Implementing some of the suggestions mentioned above, in addition to others provided by other scholars and activists who are concerned about the status of Arabic, is only a step in an arduous, but much needed, journey. We, Arab scholars and activists, are in dire need of starting a dialogue about the status of Arabic and in taking practical steps, including revising our curricula – and negative attitudes – by ensuring that the experience of studying Arabic is rendered more accessible and rewarding for our children and anyone else interested in pursuing it. In the end, we should work to bring about a revival of Arabic language learning. Rather than being a solitary journey, "going home" can be a collective movement that aims at creating a more learner-friendly and constructive engagement with Arabic language and cultures.

# References

Said, E. (1978). *Orientalism*. New York: Pantheon Books.
Shohat, E. (1992). Notes on the post-colonial. *Social Text, 31/32*, 99–113.
wa Thiong'o, N. (1994). The language of African literature. In P. Williams & L. Chrisman (eds), *Colonial discourse and post-colonial theory: A reader* (pp. 435–455). New York: Columbia University Press.

# Notes on Contributors

HASSAN R. ABDEL-JAWAD (Shuqair) is an Associate Professor of English and Linguistics in the Department of English at Sultan Qaboos University in Oman. He earned his PhD in Linguistics from the University of Pennsylvania. His research and teaching interests include sociolinguistics, discourse analysis, language and politics, and translation. His two most recent publications are "Why Do Minority Languages Persist? The Case of Circassian in Jordan" which appeared in the *International Journal of Bilingual Education and Bilingualism* (2006), and "A Linguistic and Sociopragmatic and Cultural Study of Swearing in Arabic" which appeared in *Language, Culture and Curriculum* (2000). He is currently involved in three research projects. The first project investigates the discourse functions of tayyib, enzein, OK and equivalent discourse markers, the second discusses the patterns of variation in Arabic and their identity functions, and the third project studies the impact of foreign labor on the linguistic situation in the Arabian Gulf countries.

ADEL S. ABU RADWAN is an Assistant Professor of Linguistics in the Department of English at Sultan Qaboos University in Oman. He earned his PhD in applied linguistics from Georgetown University in Washington, DC. His research and teaching interests include applied linguistics, first language acquisition, second language acquisition, psycholinguistics and translation. His two most recent publications "A Cross-sectional Study of Translator Trainees' L2 Reading Comprehension Skills and Strategies", co-authored with Dr Omar Atari, appeared in *The Interpreter and Translator Trainer* (2009), and "Input Processing Instruction and Traditional Output Practice Instruction: Effects on the Acquisition of Arabic Morphology" appeared in *The Asian EFL Journal* (2009). He is currently involved in two research projects. The first is a joint project with Dr Hassan Shuqair, and discusses the patterns of variation in Arabic, and the second investigates patterns of rhetorical transfer in the writing of Arab students.

AHMAD AL-ISSA is an Associate Professor of English and Linguistics in the Department of English at the American University of Sharjah (AUS) in the United Arab Emirates (UAE). He earned his PhD in Rhetoric and Linguistics from Indiana University of Pennsylvania. His areas of research include cross-cultural communication, language, culture and identity, global English, interlanguage, classroom research, teaching effectiveness, and curriculum design. His most recent publications (co-authored) include "The Others: Universals and Cultural Specificities in the Perception of Status and Dominance from Nonverbal Behavior" which appeared in *Consciousness and Cognition* (2010) and "Teachers' Attitudes and Practices toward Providing Feedback on Arab EFL Students' Writing" in C. Gitsaki, editor, *Teaching and Learning in the Arab World* (Peter Lang Publishers, 2011). He is currently involved in two joint research projects; one funded by the British Academy studying e-Arabic, the second funded by the German Volkswagen Foundation, investigating nonverbal communication across cultures. He is currently a visiting professor at Al-Imam Muhammad Ibn Saud Islamic University in Riyadh, Saudi Arabia.

FATIMA BADRY is Professor of English and Linguistics in the Department of English at the American University of Sharjah in the UAE. She earned her PhD in psycholinguistics from the University of California, Berkeley. Her research and teaching interests are multidisciplinary, including first and second language acquisition, language in education policies, globalization and identity construction, and Arabic sociolinguistics. Amongst her recent publications, "Milestones in Arabic Language Development" appeared in *The Encyclopedia of Language and Literacy Development. Canadian Language and Literacy Research Network* (2009) and "Positioning the Self, Identity and Language: Moroccan Women on the Move" appeared in *The Places We Share: Migration, Subjectivity and Global Mobility* (2007). She is currently conducting research on the impact of importing western curricula on UAE higher education outcomes.

ELIZABETH BUCKNER is a PhD candidate in International and Comparative Education at Stanford University, California. She holds a BA in Educational Studies and Sociology/Anthropology from Swarthmore College. She was also a Fulbright grantee to Morocco in 2006–2007 and the recipient of a Critical Language Scholarship to Oman in 2008. Her research and teaching interests include the lived experiences of young people in the Middle East, the effects of globalization on youth, the link between education and employment, and recent higher education reforms in Morocco and Syria. Her recent publications include "Syria's Next Generation: Youth Un/employment, Education, and Exclusion" in *Education, Business, Society: Contemporary Middle Eastern Issues*, and "Language Drama in Morocco: Another Perspective on the Problems and Prospects of Teaching Tamazight" in the *Journal of North African Studies*. She is currently a research assistant on a research project funded by the National Science Foundation, which investigates the potential of mobile innovations to improve educational outcomes and cross-border communication in Israel and Palestine. She is also conducting research on youth responses to Syria's economic transition and their perceptions of educational and economic opportunity.

BARBARA CASTLETON is currently an English Language Development instructor at Wm. C. Overfelt High School in San Jose, California. She earned her MA in Applied Linguistics and TEFL at Ohio University. In addition to teaching ESL in university settings, she was sent to India as a Senior English Language Fellow by the United States Department of State and Georgetown University. Her research has been in the area of the Allah Lexicon, a distinct feature of the Arabic language and in its transfer and use among English speaking Arabs. Along with her colleague, Dr John A. Morrow, she has published "Arabic, Islam, and the Allah Lexicon: How Language Shapes Our Concept of God" (2006) and "The Impact of Globalization on the Arabic Language" in *Intercultural Communication Studies* (2007) and "In the Name of Allah: Reverence Phrases in Arabic" in *Islamic Horizons* magazine (2009).

LAILA S. DAHAN is an instructor in the Department of Writing Studies at the American University of Sharjah in the UAE. Her research interests include global English, language and identity, cross cultural communication, and academic writing. Her most recent publications are "Where have all the readers gone? Improving writing through reading for EFL learners in the Arabian Gulf" in the *Iowa Journal of Cultural Studies* (2010) and *Keep*

*Your Feet Hidden: A Southern Belle on the Shores of Tripoli* (2009). She holds a BSLA degree in languages from Georgetown University, Washington, DC and MAs in political science and TESOL. She is currently writing her PhD dissertation on the topic of language use and identity construction of Arab university students through the University of Exeter, UK.

ANISSA DAOUDI is a Research Fellow at the School of Modern Languages and Cultures, Durham University, UK. She earned her PhD in Linguistics and Psycholinguistics from the University of Leeds. Her research and teaching interests include the impact of globalization on the Arabic language (MSA and vernaculars). It extends to take in the various uses of what she calls 'e-Arabic' on the internet as well as on printed material. Her two most recent publications include "Globalization, Computer-mediated Communications and the Rise of e-Arabic" in the *Middle East Journal of Culture and Communication* (2010) and "Globalization and Phraseology: Case Study on Arabic language" in *Studies in Slavic and General Linguistics* (2010). She is currently involved in two research projects funded by the Centre for the Study of the Arab World (CSAW) and the British Academy. The first research project investigates the use of computer-mediated communication (CMC) in the Arabic-speaking world and its style across cultures, and the second looks at e-Arabic and linguistic online identity.

RAGHDA EL ESSAWI is an Assistant Professor and the director of the MA program in Teaching Arabic as a Foreign Language at the American University in Cairo. She earned her PhD in Methods of Teaching Foreign Languages from Al Azhar University in Cairo, Egypt. Her research and teaching interests include second language pedagogy, second language acquisition, and second language teacher training. Her two most recent publications include "A Framework for Teaching Vocabulary through Printed Media" in *Arabic and the Media: Linguistic Analysis and Applications*, and "Arabic Language Learners' Needs: Pedagogical, Cognitive, Affective, and Social" in *Handbook for Arabic Language Teaching Professionals in the 21st Century*. She is currently involved in a research project funded by ACTFL and the Arabic Flagship programs. This project aims at reviewing the ACTFL proficiency guidelines for the four skills of Arabic as a foreign/second language.

ADEL JENDLI is an Associate Professor in the College of Communication and Media at Zayed University, in the United Arab Emirates. He earned his PhD in American Studies from the University of Kansas. He teaches public speaking, intercultural communication, and research methods. His research interests include bilingualism and cultural identity, communication anxiety, and media and youth culture. His most recent publications include a co-edited book and a book chapter, "Oral Communication Anxiety of University Students in the Arabian Peninsula: Incidence and Solutions" in *Developing Oral Skills in English: Theory, Research and Pedagogy* (2010). He has also co-edited several books for TESOL Arabia Publications.

JOHN ANDREW MORROW is an Associate Research Scholar and Consultant on Middle Eastern Studies in the Centro de Estudios Orientales at the Universidad Nacional de Rosario in Argentina. He earned his PhD in Spanish American Literature from the University of Toronto. His research and teaching interests include Hispanic Studies, Amerindian Studies, and Arabic-Islamic Studies. He is particularly interested in the Arabic influence on Spanish literature, the indigenous influence on Spanish American literature, Arabic sociolinguistics, and Islamic medicine. His two most recent publications include *Amerindian Elements in the Poetry of Ernesto Cardenal: Mythic Foundations of the Colloquial Narrative*, published by the Edwin Mellen Press, and the *Encyclopedia of Islamic Herbal Medicine* published by McFarland. He is currently conducting research on Aljamiado literature funded in part by the Spanish Ministry of Culture.

SILVIA PESSOA is an Assistant Teaching Professor of English and sociolinguistics in the Department of English at Carnegie Mellon University in Qatar. She earned her PhD in Second Language Acquisition from Carnegie Mellon University in Pittsburgh, Pennsylvania. Her research and teaching interests include academic language development, biliteracy, bilingualism, and immigration studies. Her two most recent publications include "Undocumented Uruguayan Immigrants: Biliteracy and Educational Experiences," a 260-page manuscript in the series *The New Americans: Recent Immigration and American Society*, and "Hazawi: Stories from Qatar," an edited volume with a section on migrant laborer narratives in Qatar. She is currently involved in two research projects on literacy and migration in

Qatar. The first project is a four-year longitudinal study of the literacy development of the class of 2013 at Carnegie Mellon University in Qatar. The second project, funded by the Qatar National Research Fund, is an empirical study of the challenges of low-income migrant laborers in Qatar.

MOHANALAKSHMI RAJAKUMAR is a writer, educator, and published author who is based in Qatar. She is the creator of the *Qatar Narratives* series, a locally produced and published anthology project in its fourth volume. Dr Rajakumar is the Reading and Development Director of Bloomsbury Qatar Foundation Publishing. A scholar of literature, she has a PhD from the University of Florida with a focus on gender and postcolonial theory. She has published short stories, academic articles, and travel essays in a variety of journals and literary magazines.

LYNNE RONESI is an Assistant Professor in the Department of Writing Studies at the American University of Sharjah (AUS) in the United Arab Emirates. She earned her PhD in Curriculum and Instruction from the University of Connecticut. Her research and teaching interests include language, culture, identity, and education. Her most recent publication entitled "Multilingual Tutors Supporting Multilingual Peers: A Peer-Tutor Training Course in the Arabian Gulf" appeared in the *Writing Center Journal* (2009) and was nominated for the International Writing Center Association (IWCA) Best Article of 2009 Award. Currently, she is engaged in a research project concerning Writing across the Curriculum (WAC) endeavors and second language writers at AUS.

FATMA FAISAL SAAD SAID is a PhD student in Applied Linguistics in the Department of Applied Linguistics and Communication at Birkbeck College, University of London, UK. Her research interests include bilingualism, multilingualism/plurilingualism, the power of language and how these relate to human sociality and identity. She specializes in the linguistics of the Arabic language, both Classical Arabic and spoken varieties, with special interest in the grammars and the current sociolinguistic use by Arabic speakers. She earned her BA (Arabic and Linguistics) and MA (Linguistics, special pathway Arabic) from the School of Oriental and African Studies, University of London; and another MA (Applied Linguistics) from Birkbeck College, University of London. Her current research focuses on young Arab bilinguals and how they use language to reflect their multiple multifaceted identities. She regularly publishes on her blog (arabizi.wordpress.com) on issues surrounding Arabic language, and is a member of research blogging.

NADINE SINNO is an Assistant Professor of Arabic at the Middle East Institute at Georgia State University in Atlanta. She earned an MFA in Literary Translation and a PhD in Comparative Literature and Cultural Studies from the University of Arkansas. Her research and teaching interests include modern Arabic literature and language, teaching Arabic and English as foreign languages, postcolonial studies, literary translation, contemporary women's writings, and transnational feminism. Her most recent publication is a translation of Nazik Saba Yared's novel *Canceled Memories*, originally written in Arabic. Her work also appeared in *Feminism and War: Confronting US Imperialism*, edited by Robin Riley and Chandra Talpade Mohanty. She is currently involved in co-translating a Lebanese novel by Rashid al-Daif.

SALAH TROUDI is a Senior Teaching Fellow at the Graduate School of Education, University of Exeter. Heearned his PhD from Florida State University in Curriculum Instruction and TESOL. He lectures in critical applied linguistics, curriculum and syllabus design, and research methodologies. His research interests include language policies, critical issues in TESOL, and Arabic as a medium of instruction. He is the director of the Doctor of Education in TESOL in Dubai and a supervisor of a number of doctoral students. His most recent publications include "EFL Teachers Vews of English Language Assessment in Higher education in Kuwait and the UAE" in *TESOL Quarterly* (2009) and "Teachers' Feelings during Curriculum Change in the United Arab Emirates: Opening Pandora's Box" in *Teacher Development* (2010). He is currently involved in a research project on EFL teacher efficiency in the UAE.

# Index

Al Jazeera 195, 201
Allah expressions 312, 320–322
Allah lexicon 307, 309, 311–313, 316–317, 319–321
Amazighe 214–215, 217, 227, 229, 232
America 57, 59, 65–66, 69, 185, 193, 200, 205, 335–337, 343, 346, 348–351
American media 353
American University of Beirut 347
Arab identity 50, 55, 59–60, 65, 67, 71, 73, 75, 76, 85, 87, 91–92, 102–106, 110–111, 122, 193, 195, 300, 330
Arabic
    attitudes towards 219, 224–225, 229–236, 238, 239
    authors 349
    colloquial 323–324, 326, 329
    grammar 349
    language 1, 4, 6, 8, 9, 13, 17–18, 22, 36, 39, 45, 59, 62, 65, 72, 75, 85, 87, 91, 104, 106, 109–110, 125, 137–138, 153–160, 162, 167, 168, 171, 180–187, 193–199, 201–204, 206–207, 212, 230, 238, 244, 255, 263, 272, 277, 279–280, 282–284, 294, 302–303, 307, 312, 316, 319, 320–325, 328, 330–331, 3335–336, 339, 346–349, 351, 353
    sacred language 312, 324
    teachers 339–42, 350, 353
Arabic Language Protection Association (ALPA) 181
Arabness 92, 105, 106, 110

bilingual 85, 89, 94–96, 98, 105, 109, 111–112, 129, 133–134, 137, 139, 145, 155, 160, 167–168, 170, 171, 175, 177–178, 209, 223–224, 247, 252, 254–255, 258, 260, 265–267, 271–278, 303, 317, 325, 327–328, 332
bilingualism 5, 17, 50, 53, 56, 58, 67, 69–70, 73–74, 84, 87, 111, 153–155, 157–159, 161, 167–169, 171, 215, 217, 235–236, 300
blog 179, 182, 285, 294–295, 297, 299

calque 292, 294, 297
Carnegie Mellon University 153, 157, 159, 168, 171
code mixing 288
code switching 201, 207, 254, 261–262, 288, 294, 347
coinage 294
colloquialization 257–259, 263, 276, 278
colonialism 21, 79, 104, 115, 125, 169, 216, 303, 344
colonization 8, 130, 217, 241, 350
communication technology 253, 256–259, 271–272, 275, 277
Computer Mediated Communication (CMC) 253, 256–261, 263, 265, 267, 269, 271–273, 277–278, 285–286, 293–294, 296, 303–304
corpora 285, 295–296
corpus 285, 295, 297
creolization 84, 247
critical thinking 63, 74, 164, 167, 341, 352

cultural diversity 12, 15–16
cultural identity 87, 91, 100–101, 106, 155, 189, 220–201, 235, 245, 241, 301
curriculum 7–8, 23, 29, 36, 38, 55, 62, 72, 75–76, 109, 111, 148, 335, 341, 352
cybercafe 295–296

decolonization 336, 348–351
dialect 10–11, 14, 86, 90, 97, 109, 111, 339, 344–346, 353
diaspora 345–346, 353
diglossia 108, 111, 207, 304
diversity
    linguistic 20, 75, 127
dominance 22, 127, 130, 134, 154, 216, 222, 246, 325, 327, 352, 373
dual language education 23, 28, 38

Education City 154, 156–157, 165, 166, 168, 178
education policy 78, 113, 189, 202, 204
educational system 5, 8, 24, 26–29, 44, 85, 88, 92, 156, 195, 198–199, 216, 245, 313, 324, 327, 337–338, 346, 351, 353
e-language 297
English
    attitudes toward 292–236, 238–239
    growth of 217–219
    lingua franca 1, 15–16, 25–26, 34, 37, 46, 49, 50, 54, 82, 85, 124, 129, 134, 135–136, 138, 145, 149, 154, 302, 311, 313, 345–346
    medium schools 5, 13, 23, 40, 54, 72, 156, 162–163, 165, 169, 174–176
English for Specific Purposes (ESP) 137, 143
expatriates 3, 37, 54, 126–127, 132, 145

Facebook 294–295
foreign language 1, 3, 5, 6, 23–24, 79, 88, 92, 128, 132, 142–148, 215, 217, 222, 224–225, 227–228, 231, 335–339, 241, 246, 249–250, 291, 301, 326, 335, 338, 349

*foos'ha* 8, 10–11
francophone 114, 230
French 6, 8, 9, 78, 125, 213–214, 216–219, 221, 222, 227, 229–236, 239–241, 243–244, 309–310, 318, 323, 326, 328, 337–340, 344, 347, 349

gender 12, 19, 56, 79, 93, 95, 117, 131, 156, 170, 172, 178, 209, 218, 222, 225–226, 246, 252
German 309
globalization 1–5, 12–13, 15, 18, 20, 22, 26, 28, 82–85, 89–92, 103, 106, 108, 110, 153–156, 168, 169, 285–286, 293–294, 297, 299–301, 303, 305, 323, 330, 346
glocalization 84
Gulf, Arabian 17, 21–22, 26, 29, 39, 42, 45, 57, 77–79, 125, 155–156, 158, 160, 170, 179

hegemony 24, 29, 43, 124, 125, 145, 147, 222, 290, 292–293, 304
heterogeneity 83–85, 110
homogeneity 83–85, 110
hybridity 74, 107, 115, 153, 168, 209, 210, 335–336, 350
hybridization 255, 257–259, 261, 264, 272
hybridized colloquialization 258, 261–263
hybrid language 253–256, 262–263, 265, 271, 335–338, 343, 346–347

identity 3, 8, 12–13, 19–22, 51–58, 70, 73, 75, 86, 90, 92, 100–101, 103, 106–108, 110–111, 153–161, 163–170, 181, 191–192, 200, 314, 321–322, 329–330, 335–336, 338, 347, 350, 353
imagined communities 52–53, 68, 73
imperialism 4, 19–21, 124, 144, 149, 154, 171, 172, 288–289, 304, 335, 344
Islam 9–11, 20, 46, 68, 149, 160, 184–185, 189, 308, 310, 314, 318–319, 321–322, 330

# Index

Islamic  6, 8, 22, 44, 57, 61, 63, 71, 92,
  148–149, 157, 161, 164, 206–207,
  210, 216, 261, 263, 290, 310–312,
  320–322, 324–325, 327, 328,
  330–332
Islamic Spain  310
Islamization  324, 330

language
  death  15, 19, 185–187, 194, 331
  ecology  25
  loss  15–16, 153–154, 162, 169, 171
  planning  22, 98, 194–195, 204, 208–
    209, 245–206, 253, 277–279, 303
  policy  15, 24, 29–30, 40, 42, 194–
    195, 197, 200, 204–206, 208, 210,
    245–246, 292, 329
  shift  19, 113, 155, 207, 187, 244, 277
  socialization  191
Lebanese Civil War  336–337
linguistic
  dualism  28–29, 43
  genocide  4–5, 16, 21
  human rights  21, 25
  imperialism  19–21, 25, 35, 78–79,
    124, 149, 171–172, 288–289, 304,
    335–354
  translation  348–349

maintenance
  language  19, 127, 144, 155, 159,
    167–168
memorization  339, 352
Middle East  3, 20, 22, 47, 66, 68, 69, 90,
  114, 116, 149, 183, 210–211, 217,
  275, 289, 292–293, 310, 319, 325,
  333, 337
modernity  33, 78, 92, 101, 103, 105–106,
  112, 114, 124, 153, 158, 181, 201,
  208, 210, 215, 330
modernization  3, 16, 55, 82–83, 90, 108,
  128–131, 144, 153–144, 179, 345

Modern Standard Arabic (MSA),  8–11,
  14, 16, 37, 86, 90, 108, 111, 137, 138,
  285–286, 290–291, 294, 297, 305,
  323, 326–329, 335, 339
multilingual  1, 19, 45, 87–89, 103, 111,
  113–116, 148, 171, 207–209, 236,
  245, 303–305, 340
multilingualism  22, 78, 115, 214, 224, 240
Muslim  9–10, 53, 60, 68, 77, 91, 141, 153–
  154, 160–161, 163–167, 169, 171,
  174–178, 206–208, 210, 216, 300,
  309, 312–317, 319–322, 324–325,
  329–330, 332

National Council of Culture (NCC)  181
national identity  213–216, 219–220, 230,
  238, 244
native language  6–8, 10, 12–13, 16–17, 28,
  123, 136, 139, 141, 143, 145, 147, 154,
  147, 154, 158, 168, 170, 187, 224,
  235–236, 246, 289, 324, 335, 350
native speaker model  26–27

Persian  324
postcolonial  51–54, 73, 77, 148, 336,
  343–344, 348, 350
power  3–4, 14, 16, 20, 22, 24–26, 42, 47,
  51–52, 82, 115, 127, 134, 145, 147,
  157, 169, 180, 202, 206–207, 213–
  214, 217, 219, 221–223, 234–236,
  243–244, 246, 288–292, 294,
  300–301, 303, 305, 337, 348
prestige  3–4, 11, 13–14, 17, 139, 146, 161,
  164, 218–219, 255, 313, 326, 344
private schools  5–6, 28, 31, 32, 33, 35, 40,
  91, 129, 154, 159, 174, 325–326,
  328, 337
proficiency  5, 27, 34, 36, 37, 39, 40, 41,
  44, 49, 50, 53, 55, 71, 72, 94,
  123, 134, 136, 137, 139, 146, 164,
  168, 196, 216, 247, 252, 318, 335,
  338–339, 344–345

Qatar University  154, 156–157, 159, 171, 178
Quran  9–11, 59–60, 160, 180, 184–186, 209, 216, 263, 312, 314, 321, 327, 341

religion  2, 11–12, 23, 33, 53, 71, 87, 143, 157, 160, 161, 165–168, 172, 174, 190, 203, 204, 208, 220, 238, 310, 312, 319, 322, 324, 330, 334
resistance  24, 43, 51, 67, 73, 104, 107, 144, 159, 169, 292
Romanized Arabic  288, 294, 297

Sapir-Whorf hypothesis  186, 191
second language  1, 3, 5–8, 17, 27, 44, 49, 52–53, 73, 76, 78, 79, 106, 128, 132, 137, 141, 146, 147, 155, 161, 204, 206, 217, 221, 254, 307, 326–327
Shiite  196
Sunni  196

tagliamonte  257–258, 274

technology  1, 3, 14, 16, 28, 30, 33, 36, 44, 53, 55, 98, 108–109, 124, 128, 129, 131, 141, 143, 147, 169, 172, 181, 210, 223, 253, 256, 258, 272, 274, 277–278, 287, 292–296, 302, 304, 309–310, 352
Twitter  294

values  7, 12, 20, 53, 73, 74, 76, 78, 81, 100, 102, 106, 125, 130, 143, 143, 145, 154, 155, 157, 158, 160, 162–165, 169–171, 175–178, 189–191, 222, 275, 347

Western  13–14, 18, 44, 50, 53–55, 71, 73–74, 81, 83, 91, 100–104, 108, 110, 118–121, 125, 130, 143, 153–158, 160, 163–167, 169–171, 175, 177–178, 215–216, 221, 223, 241, 245, 286, 289, 307, 314, 323, 329, 332, 343–344, 347, 351

# Acknowledgements

We wish to thank the contributors for their commitment to this project and their willingness to respond to our many requests, suggestions, and deadlines. They have all been instrumental in bringing this volume to completion and we appreciate all their efforts.

We also would like to express our appreciation to our institution, the American University of Sharjah (AUS), for a Faculty Research Grant, which helped support this endeavour. Additionally, we wish to thank our many graduate and undergraduate students over the years at AUS, who contributed in countless ways to the idea for this volume, and for their consistent interest in this topic, which helped us remain focused on bringing this issue to light. I am (Ahmad Al-Issa) indebted to the many students who took the following courses with me: Intercultural Communication, Cultures in Contact, Global English in ELT, and Curriculum Design. I thank them for their interest and excitement, and for the opportunity they gave me to discuss issues related to the theme of this book and for the feedback they have given me on various related issues.

Finally, we extend our heartfelt gratitude and love to our sons, Saif and Omar, for their patience throughout this long process. To them, we dedicate this book.

# CONTEMPORARY STUDIES IN DESCRIPTIVE LINGUISTICS

Edited by

DR GRAEME DAVIS, lecturer in the History of the English Language at the Open University, UK, and

KARL A. BERNHARDT, English Language Consultant with Trinity College London and for the London Chamber of Commerce and Industry International Qualification.

This series provides an outlet for academic monographs which offer a recent and original contribution to linguistics and which are within the descriptive tradition.

While the monographs demonstrate their debt to contemporary linguistic thought, the series does not impose limitations in terms of methodology or genre, and does not support a particular linguistic school. Rather the series welcomes new and innovative research that contributes to furthering the understanding of the description of language.

The topics of the monographs are scholarly and represent the cutting edge for their particular fields, but are also accessible to researchers outside the specific disciplines.

Vol. 1  Mark Garner: Language: An Ecological View.
        260 pages, 2004.
        ISBN 3-03910-054-8 / US-ISBN 0-8204-6295-0

Vol. 2  T. Nyan: Meanings at the Text Level: A Co-Evolutionary Approach.
        194 pages, 2004.
        ISBN 3-03910-250-8 / US-ISBN 0-8204-7179-8

Vol. 3   Breffni O'Rourke and Lorna Carson (eds): Language Learner Autonomy: Policy, Curriculum, Classroom.
439 pages, 2010.
ISBN 978-3-03911-980-6

Vol. 4   Dimitra Koutsantoni: Developing Academic Literacies: Understanding Disciplinary Communities' Culture and Rhetoric.
302 pages, 2007.
ISBN 978-3-03910-575-5

Vol. 5   Emmanuelle Labeau: Beyond the Aspect Hypothesis: Tense-Aspect Development in Advanced L2 French.
259 pages, 2005.
ISBN 3-03910-281-8 / US-ISBN 0-8204-7208-5

Vol. 6   Maria Stambolieva: Building Up Aspect. A Study of Aspect and Related Categories in Bulgarian, with Parallels in English and French.
243 pages, 2008.
ISBN 978-3-03910-558-8

Vol. 7   Stavroula Varella: Language Contact and the Lexicon in the History of Cypriot Greek.
283 pages, 2006.
ISBN 3-03910-526-4 / US-ISBN 0-8204-7531-9

Vol. 8   Alan J. E. Wolf: Subjectivity in a Second Language: Conveying the Expression of Self.
246 pages. 2006.
ISBN 3-03910-518-3 / US-ISBN 0-8204-7524-6

Vol. 9   Bettina Braun: Production and Perception of Thematic Contrast in German.
280 pages, 2005.
ISBN 3-03910-566-3 / US-ISBN 0-8204-7593-9

Vol. 10  Jean-Paul Kouega: A Dictionary of Cameroon English Usage.
202 pages, 2007.
ISBN 978-3-03911-027-8

Vol. 11  Sebastian M. Rasinger: Bengali-English in East London. A Study in Urban Multilingualism.
270 pages, 2007.
ISBN 978-3-03911-036-0

Vol. 12  Emmanuelle Labeau and Florence Myles (eds): The Advanced Learner Variety: The Case of French.
298 pages, 2009.
ISBN 978-3-03911-072-8

Vol. 13  Miyoko Kobayashi: Hitting the Mark: How Can Text Organisation and Response Format Affect Reading Test Performance?
322 pages, 2009.
ISBN 978-3-03911-083-4

Vol. 14  Dingfang Shu and Ken Turner (eds): Contrasting Meaning in Languages of the East and West.
634 pages, 2010.
ISBN 978-3-03911-886-1

Vol. 15  Ana Rojo: Step by Step: A Course in Contrastive Linguistics and Translation.
418 pages, 2009.
ISBN 978-3-03911-133-6

Vol. 16  Jinan Fedhil Al-Hajaj and Graeme Davis (eds): University of Basrah Studies in English.
304 pages, 2008.
ISBN 978-3-03911-325-5

Vol. 17  Paolo Coluzzi: Minority Language Planning and Micronationalism in Italy.
348 pages, 2007.
ISBN 978-3-03911-041-4

Vol. 18  Iwan Wmffre: Breton Orthographies and Dialects: The Twentieth-Century Orthography War in Brittany. Vol 1.
499 pages, 2007.
ISBN 978-3-03911-364-4

Vol. 19  Iwan Wmffre: Breton Orthographies and Dialects: The Twentieth-Century Orthography War in Brittany. Vol 2.
281 pages, 2007.
ISBN 978-3-03911-365-1

Vol. 20  Fanny Forsberg: Le langage préfabriqué: Formes, fonctions et fréquences en français parlé L2 et L1.
293 pages, 2008.
ISBN 978-3-03911-369-9

Vol. 21   Kathy Pitt: Sourcing the Self: Debating the Relations between Language and Consciousness.
220 pages, 2008.
ISBN 978-3-03911-398-9

Vol. 22   Peiling Xing: Chinese Learners and the Lexis Learning Rainbow.
273 pages, 2009.
ISBN 978-3-03911-407-8

Vol. 23   Yufang Qian: Discursive Constructions around Terrorism in the *People's Daily* (China) and *The Sun* (UK) Before and After 9.11: A Corpus-based Contrastive Critical Discourse Analysis.
284 pages, 2010.
ISBN 978-3-0343-0186-2

Vol. 24   Ian Walkinshaw: Learning Politeness: Disagreement in a Second Language.
297 pages, 2009.
ISBN 978-3-03911-527-3

Vol. 25   Forthcoming.

Vol. 26   Shahela Hamid: Language Use and Identity: The Sylheti Bangladeshis in Leeds.
225 pages, 2011.
ISBN 978-3-03911-559-4

Vol. 27-30 Forthcoming.

Vol. 31   Ahmad Al-Issa and Laila S. Dahan (eds): Global English and Arabic: Issues of Language, Culture, and Identity.
379 pages, 2011.
ISBN 978-3-0343-0293-7